The CONFIDENT WRITER

Instructor's Edition

The CONFIDENT WRITER

THIRD EDITION

Instructor's Edition

Carol Kanar

HOUGHTON MIFFLIN COMPANY   Boston   New York

Senior Sponsoring Editor: Mary Jo Southern
Associate Editor: Kellie Cardone
Editorial Associate: Danielle Richardson
Senior Project Editor: Fred Burns
Production/Design Coordinator: Lisa Jelly Smith
Manufacturing Manager: Florence Cadran
Marketing Manager: Annamarie L. Rice

Cover image by Marilyn Simler, Copyright © 2001.

Acknowledgments for reprinted material appear on page 519.

Printed in the U.S.A.

Library of Congress Catalog Card Number: 2001131513

Instructor's Edition ISBN: 0-618-13114-0

Student Text ISBN: 0-618-13113-2

1 2 3 4 5 6 7 8 9–QF–05 04 03 02 01

BRIEF TABLE OF CONTENTS

Note: See also complete Table of Contents on page vii.

CONTENTS

RHETORICAL CONTENTS

(Many selections appear under more than one heading.)

NARRATION

DESCRIPTION

PROCESS

COMPARISON AND CONTRAST

CLASSIFICATION

CAUSE AND EFFECT

DEFINITION

ARGUMENTATION AND PERSUASION

PREFACE

The Confident Writer, Third Edition, focuses on the many choices writers make during the process of developing an idea into a finished essay. By providing students with extensive practice in the writing skills needed to make those choices, *The Confident Writer,* Third Edition, helps beginning writers gain confidence in their ability to meet the writing demands of all their college courses as well as those of life or work situations requiring skill in written communication.

NEW TO THIS EDITION

- New readings and example passages throughout the text
- New critical thinking exercise in every chapter
- Expanded explanations of writing and supporting a central idea or thesis
- More information on types of and selection of examples
- An Internet exercise in every chapter
- More writing topics and questions that focus on an author's meaning and strategy
- More focused connection of reading and writing throughout the text
- A section in Chapter 1 on how to read an essay

SPECIAL FEATURES OF THE TEXT

Combination Process and Skills Approach

The text teaches students the fundamentals of writing within the context of a recursive process and encourages students to try out strategies with the understanding that as they gain skills, they will develop a writing process that works best for them.

Reading/Writing/Thinking Connection

Because reading and writing are so intimately linked to critical thought, *The Confident Writer*, Third Edition, integrates critical reading skills with the writing process. Each chapter begins with an essay that serves both as a model of good writing and as a source of ideas for further reflection and writing. Pre-reading and post-reading activities provide a context for the essay and a format for responding to the writer's ideas. This reading and writing connection underscores another of the book's assumptions: writing is intended for an audience, and confident writers write with their audience in mind.

Collaborative Writing Exercises

To promote the establishment of a writing community within the classroom, every chapter contains a highly structured collaborative exercise that enables students to share ideas and try out writing strategies together.

Abundant Writing Opportunities

The Confident Writer, Third Edition, is a student-oriented, interactive text. Abundant writing exercises and activities are integrated with instructional material throughout each chapter so students have an opportunity to practice skills as they are explained.

Integration of Grammar

The Confident Writer treats grammar skills as inseparable from the writing process and as another series of choices available to the writer for clear and correct communication. Knowing what choices are available gives student writers additional power over language.

ORGANIZATION AND CONTENT

The Confident Writer has a flexible organization that allows instructors to cover the writing process in accordance with their teaching styles and their students' needs. Although the chapters follow a logical sequence that takes students through the writing process, the chapters can also be presented in different sequences.

Unit 1, "The Writing Process," begins with an overview of the essay form and introduces the concept of writing as a recursive process. This unit also introduces the student to prewriting strategies, paragraph skills, writing thesis statements, and supporting a thesis with evidence. Chapters 6 and 7 provide extensive coverage of and practical suggestions for revising and editing. Chapter 8 covers library skills and introduces students to the research process.

Unit 2, "Patterns as Options," introduces the concept of rhetorical patterns, treating them as organizational choices a writer makes to provide the framework that best suits the purpose, audience, and thesis. The emphasis is on choosing a pattern that proceeds logically from the writer's goals. Students learn that any topic might be developed in a variety of ways and that the writer is free to decide which pattern or combination of rhetorical patterns to use. Unit 2 makes a connection between the rhetorical patterns presented as writing options in this text and their widespread use in academic thought and writing.

Unit 3, "More Choices: A Collection of Readings," contains ten timely and culturally diverse essays that promote critical reading and thinking, and that serve as models for writing. Two of these essays are new to this edition. Instructors can use this collection in various ways— for example, as supplementary material or as sources for discussion and writing assignments. Pre-reading and post-reading questions frame each essay.

Unit 4, "The Selective Writer," focuses on grammar as another set of choices for the writer. A chart in the Instructor's Resource Manual shows how to integrate the grammar topics covered in Unit 4 with chapter topics.

CHAPTER FEATURES

Each chapter contains the following features:

Awareness Check   This prereading activity creates a context for reading and encourages students to explore some of their assumptions about the topic covered in the essay that follows. Students can complete the Awareness Check individually or in small groups.

Vocabulary Check   As an aid to comprehension, this feature lists words and definitions from the chapter-opening essay that students may find difficult or unfamiliar. They examine the list as part of their prereading activities to prepare themselves for reading the essay.

Chapter-Opening Essay   The high-interest essay in each chapter exemplifies one or more principles of writing covered in the chapter and serves as a springboard to critical thinking and writing.

The Critical Reader   These questions focus on the essay's thesis or central idea, evidence (supporting details), implications (inferences readers can make), and word choice. The questions help students analyze the essays for structure and strategy, and also serve as a comprehension check. Students can respond to these questions either individually or in small groups.

Topics for Writing   Included in this list of writing suggestions and topics are some that relate specifically to ideas generated from chapter-opening essays; some that are more general, but still related to the chapter's content; and one or more related to the academic disciplines. The topics are arranged according to level of difficulty.

Checklist for Revision   Chapter 6 explains how to revise an essay for content, organization, and style. The checklist, which follows the topics for writing in each chapter, reminds students of areas to focus on as they revise their essays. Each checklist emphasizes the specific skills, strategies, or aspects of the writing process that are covered in the chapter.

The Critical Thinker   This feature requires students to use higher-level thinking skills to analyze the chapter-opening essay for the author's strategy and meaning.

Your Discovery Journal   This feature encourages students to think and write about a poem, quotation, concept, or idea that is a reflection of the chapter's content. The assignment challenges students to think creatively and to consider their thoughts and experiences as sources for writing.

Themed Exercises   Every chapter contains one or more exercises designed for collaborative work and one Internet exercise. These exercises are designated by icons.

ANCILLARY MATERIALS

Software: Expressways, Fourth Edition.   Available on CD-ROM, *Expressways* is an interactive software program that provides a tutorial review of key writing strategies and a broad range of writing activities to guide students through the writing process.

Instructor's Edition   The Instructor's Edition contains the complete student text and Instructor's Resource Manual. This manual includes an overview of the text, a sample syllabus, recommendations for using the special features, teaching suggestions for each chapter, and an answer key. The manual emphasizes the connection between reading and writing, and explains how instructors can help students make the connection. Practical suggestions for how to use the essays and exercises are also included.

ACKNOWLEDGMENTS

Writing a textbook is a monumental task that the writer does not accomplish alone. I am deeply grateful to the Houghton Mifflin family of editors and others for the parts they played in the development and production of *The Confident Writer*, Third Edition, and for their dedication to excellence. I especially thank Mary Jo Southern for her inspiration and unfailing encouragement, and Kellie Cardone for her critical eye, technical expertise, wise counsel, and efficiency. With gratitude I acknowledge once again the many contributions of Fred Burns, and I also thank Pat Cabeza. I thank my family, friends, and colleagues for being supportive and my husband, Stephen P. Kanar, for making all things possible. Finally, I thank my students for being who they are and for the delight they have given me over the years. This book is for them.

The many excellent suggestions I received from the reviewers who read my manuscript helped me develop *The Confident Writer* into its present form. To them I give special thanks:

Kathryn Fowler, David Lipscomb University
Julie Moore, Green River Community College
Michael Weiser, Thomas Nelson Community College
Jo Ellen Winters, Bucks County Community College

—Carol Kanar

Unit

1

The Writing Process

Chapter 1

Understanding the Essay: An Overview

As a college student, you will do many kinds of writing during a typical semester or quarter. Your psychology professor may ask you to write a short essay as part of a unit test. Your environmental science professor may require you to write a research paper. Your professors may also have you write reports or submit well-written answers to questions as part of an assignment. In your composition class, not only will you learn how to write but you will produce a lot of writing in the process. When you leave college, the writing skills and practice you have gained will be a strong career asset that may help you get the job you want or the promotion you seek.

Writing is one of the fundamental ways you express yourself. Writing reveals your knowledge about a topic and your position on various issues related to it. Like many students, you may have found yourself holding back in class even when you knew you had something worthwhile to contribute to the discussion. Or perhaps you lack the confidence to speak up when others are expressing opinions that disagree with yours. Writing may enable you to express thoughts and share knowledge you have been keeping to yourself. Through writing you may discover a new, strong voice. Beginning with this chapter, you will

3

start writing. As you complete each chapter, you will build on the skills you learn in Chapter 1 and add new skills. Gradually you will refine your writing process.

WHAT IS AN ESSAY?

An *essay* is a relatively short, nonfictional piece of writing. Essays serve many purposes: to inform, to persuade, to entertain, or merely to express an idea, a feeling, or an impression. Although writers' styles, points of view, and choices of subject matter differ, their essays all share several important characteristics, some of which are these: A clearly stated topic, a central idea, supporting details, words chosen for their impact and effect, and implications for the reader. The *topic* is what the whole essay is about. The *central idea* is a writer's opinion or viewpoint on the topic. The *supporting details* are the facts, reasons, or examples that a writer provides to explain the central idea. A writer's *word choices* reflect his or her *purpose,* or reason, for writing. The *implications* are the writer's messages or special insights that can help you, the reader, relate what you learn from your reading to your daily life. The essay is a powerful form of communication that you—anyone in fact—can learn to use effectively and confidently.

HOW TO READ AN ESSAY

The more essays you read, the more you will become aware of the different ways that authors express and organize their ideas. To read an essay with understanding, follow these steps: *Before you read,* explore your knowledge and assumptions about the author's topic. You can usually determine an author's topic by reading the title and first paragraph. *During reading,* concentrate on following the author's ideas, and pay attention to his or her choice of words, which may reveal the purpose. *After reading,* think about the ideas and the way they are expressed. Ask yourself questions like these:

- What is the essay about? (topic)

- What is the author's opinion or viewpoint on the topic? (central idea)

- What facts, reasons, examples, or other details explain the central idea? (evidence)

- How are the details arranged? (organization)
- What does the author want me to know, think, or be able to do? (purpose)
- How does the information relate to my life or others' lives? (implications)
- What do specific words and phrases tell me about the author's purpose, meaning, or viewpoint? (word choice)

Then share your thoughts either with a study partner or in a class discussion. Each time you write an essay, try to incorporate in it at least one thing that you have learned about writing from the essays you have read. Several features in every chapter of *The Confident Writer* are designed to help you develop your critical reading and thinking processes so that you can apply them to your writing. These features are *Awareness Check, The Critical Reader, Topics for Writing,* and *The Critical Thinker.*

AWARENESS CHECK

Before reading the following essay, explore your thoughts about what parents should teach their children. Think about the questions below and answer them either on your own or in a group discussion.

1. Do you agree or disagree that parents should teach their beliefs and values to their children? Explain your reasons.

2. What are some of the problems that parents from other cultures face when their children are American-born?

3. Read the title, author information, and first two paragraphs of the essay. Based on this preview, what do you think will follow?

Should My Tribal Past Shape Delia's Future?

Dympna Ugwu-Oju

In this essay from Newsweek, *the author explains her indecisiveness as an Ibo woman who would like to see her daughter carry on the tribe's traditions but who also recognizes her daughter's desire for independence.*

VOCABULARY CHECK

rigors (3)	extreme hardships or difficulties
cater (6)	to give what is wanted or required, especially for pleasure
prospective (6)	future
polygamy (7)	having two or more wives, husbands, or mates at the same time
clitorectomies (7)	surgical removals of the external female genitals as practiced in some cultures
vacillated (9)	fluctuated, showed indecision
avail (11)	advantage, use, help, benefit

Recently, my 18-year-old daughter, Delia, left for Princeton University to start her college career. Friends worried about the distance between Princeton and our home in California. I reminded them that I, too, had attended college far from my home and family. The distance hadn't hurt me; rather, I became stronger because of it.   1

In 1974 I traveled to New York for my college education. My home country, Nigeria, was for all intents and purposes as far away as Mars. Back then, it was virtually impossible to reach my family by phone; we could communicate only through snail post and, in an emergency, via telegraph. It wasn't until six years later, after I had completed both my undergraduate and graduate degrees, that I went home for the first time.   2

I reassure my friends that if I, a tribal African girl, could survive the psychological and cultural rigors of attending college in this country, my American-born-and-bred daughter will conquer Princeton. What does worry me is how much of her family's beliefs will be left in the Delia who emerges four years from now.   3

I'm a member of the Ibo tribe of Nigeria, and although I've lived in the United States most of my adult life, my consciousness remains fixed on the time and place of my upbringing. On the surface, I'm as American as everyone else. My husband, who was also raised in Nigeria, and I are both professionals. We live in the suburbs and go to PTA meetings. In my private life, my Iboness— the customs that rigidly dictate how the men and women of my tribe live their lives—continues to influence the   4

choices I make. I see these American and Ibo aspects of my life as distinct; I separate them perfectly, and there are no blurrings. Except for maybe one: Delia.

When I left Nigeria at 18, 1 had no doubts about who and what I was. I was a woman. I was *only* a woman. 5

All my life my mother told me that a woman takes as much in life as she's given; if she's educated, it's only so that she can better cater to her husband and children. When I was Delia's age, I knew with absolute certainty that I would marry the Ibo man my family approved for me and bear his children. I understood that receiving a good education and being comfortable in both the Western and the traditional worlds would raise the bride price my prospective husband would pay my family. My role was to be a great asset to my husband, no matter what business he was engaged in. 6

I understood all of that clearly; I was, after all, raised within the context of child brides, polygamy, clitorectomies and arranged marriages. But then I married and had my own daughter, and all my certainty, all my resolve to maintain my Ibo beliefs, collapsed in a big heap at my feet. 7

First, my daughter's ties to Ibo womanhood are only as strong as the link—meaning me. Therein lies the problem. I haven't been half the teacher to my daughter that my mother was to me. 8

I've struggled daily with how best to raise my daughter. Every decision involving Delia is a tug of war between Ibo and American traditions. I've vacillated between trying to turn her into the kind of woman her grandmothers would be proud of and letting her be the modern, independent woman she wants to be. Each time Delia scores an academic or athletic victory, I start to applaud her, but my cheers get stuck in my throat as I hear both her grandmothers' voices warning, "She's only a woman." I know in my heart that her achievements will not matter to her relatives; they will judge her by the kind of man she marries, and the children—preferably male—that she bears. 9

At 18, Delia knows very little about the rules that govern the lives of Ibo women. She knows just enough about housekeeping to survive. She will most likely not consider my feelings in choosing her spouse. She is not the selflessly loyal daughter that I was to my mother. 10

I wonder about the implications for people like me, women from traditional cultures raising American-born daughters. Should we limit their opportunities to keep them loyal to our beliefs and our pasts, or should we encourage our daughters to avail themselves of all experiences, even at the risk of rejecting who and what we are? 11

Maybe what I feel is what parents all over the world feel: that I could have done a better job of instilling my beliefs in my child. Now, it's too late. 12

Or perhaps I've always known that Delia is her own person with   13
her own life to lead.

Delia called the other night from Princeton. She's coming home   14
soon, and I'm infected by her excitement. But I wonder: will I know the
young woman who steps off the plane?

THE CRITICAL READER

Central Idea

1. The author is torn between teaching her daughter Ibo ways and American ways. Which sentence in paragraph 9 states this thesis in slightly different words?

Evidence

2. The main idea of paragraph 6 is stated in the last sentence: "My role was to be a great asset to my husband, no matter what business he was engaged in." What are the details in the paragraph that explain exactly what the author believed she had to do to be an asset to her husband?

3. In paragraph 4 the author contrasts her American ways with her Ibo ways. What two examples support the statement: "I'm as American as anyone else"? In what part of her life do her Ibo customs influence her decision making?

4. Paragraphs 9 through 11 explain the issues with which the author has struggled in raising her daughter. What are these issues?

Implications

5. Read paragraph 11 again. What are the implications for people like the author who are trying to raise American children? Should they keep their children loyal to traditional beliefs or give them independence? Can they do both? What is your opinion? What evidence from your own life or the experiences of others can you offer in support of your opinion?

Word Choice

6. In paragraph 9 how do the author's choices of "struggled," "tug of war," and "vacillated" emphasize the difficulty she is having in de-

ciding how to raise her daughter? Do you think these word choices are effective? Why or why not?

HOW AN ESSAY DEVELOPS

The central idea of an essay is often called the *thesis*. A writer *develops*, or supports, a thesis with specific evidence, or information. The way the evidence is organized, or arranged, is the essay's *direction of development*. For example, the most usual direction of development is to start with an introduction that leads up to a thesis; continue by providing evidence to support, explain, or prove the thesis; and end with a concluding paragraph that completes the development and perhaps even suggests some implications for readers.

Of course, there are many ways to develop an essay. Some essays have little or no introduction; others have a lengthy introduction. Some writers put the thesis at the end. As a beginning writer you will probably want to follow the more usual direction of development from introduction and thesis, through support, to conclusion. This direction of development helps you achieve an organization that is easy for both you and your readers to follow. The introduction, thesis, support, and conclusion are all important parts of an essay that have specific purposes, as explained in Figure 1.1.

In Dympna Ugwu-Oju's essay on pages 6–8 for example, the first three paragraphs introduce the topic by providing background information about the author and her daughter, Delia. Paragraphs 4 through 11 make up the body of the essay, and paragraphs 12 through 13 state the conclusion. The author builds up to her thesis in paragraph 9 by first explaining where she is from and what her Ibo customs and beliefs are. These details help readers understand why she is struggling with raising her daughter as explained in paragraphs 9 through 11 following the thesis.

An essay's direction of development is reflected in its three parts: the *introduction*, which usually includes the thesis; the *body*, which contains the supporting evidence; and the *conclusion*, which ends the essay.

EXERCISE 1.1   Write one or two pages on the topic *An accomplishment of mine that makes me proud.* This will be a *discovery draft* that has two purposes: First, the

FIGURE 1.1

An Essay's Direction of Development

Introduction	Build readers' interest in your topic by making clear why you are writing about it (your purpose) and how you became involved with it or why readers should care or know about it (background).
Thesis statement	Make your point about the topic so readers know what to expect; it states the central idea of your essay.
Support	Select evidence in the form of main ideas and specific details to support your thesis and explain it to your readers.
Conclusion	End the essay by provoking a response from readers, either in the form of understanding or of taking action.

draft may help you discover what you know about the topic. Second, you may be able to identify what writing skills you already possess that you can improve. Follow these directions to complete your draft:

1. Write everything you can think of on the topic. You might start by asking yourself some questions: What have I done? Why am I proud of it? When did I do it? What happened?

2. Do not worry about grammar yet. Concentrate on getting your ideas down on paper.

3. When you have finished, read your draft. See if you can trace a direction of development; for example, can you identify parts of the writing that could become the introduction, body, and conclusion of an essay?

4. Try to identify a sentence that seems to state a central idea, what the whole piece of writing is about.

5. Finally, comment on what you did well in this discovery draft and what needs improvement.

YOUR CHOICES AS A WRITER

From start to finish, writing is a process of making choices. Each choice leads to an outcome. If you do not like the outcome, you can make another choice. Suppose you are writing an essay. You start writing about the topic you have chosen and very quickly decide you either do not like that topic or cannot think of anything to write. Now you have another choice: Will you keep writing and hope your ideas will finally lead somewhere, or will you choose a new topic and start over?

Some experts recommend discovery drafts, such as the one you wrote for Exercise 1.1, as a way of exploring a topic until an idea for a thesis emerges. Others suggest exploring by using various other *prewriting* strategies to come up with an outline, or other type of plan, before you actually begin to *draft,* or write, your essay. However you decide to begin, you will eventually have to make five choices:

1. What will be your thesis?

2. Who will be your audience?

3. What will be your purpose?

4. What evidence will support your thesis?

5. How will you organize your evidence?

Remember, too, that one of your privileges as a writer is that *all your choices are open to change.*

What Will Be Your Thesis?

To write an essay, you need more than just a topic to write about. You need to have an idea that you want to share with readers, an idea you find interesting, important, humorous, outrageous, or upsetting. When you have decided what the most important thing is that you want to say about your topic, that will be your central idea, or thesis. The *thesis* of your essay is your opinion, comment, or special knowledge about the topic. For example, a thesis could be a fact, idea, belief, or experience that you think is worth explaining. Dympna Ugwu-Oju's topic is her indecision over what she should teach her daughter. Her central idea is that she is torn between two cultures' values. She believes that other parents struggle with this problem, and she wants to share that belief with you, the reader.

One way to make your central idea clear to readers is to write a *thesis statement,* a sentence that clearly shows what your topic is and what you plan to say about it in the body of your essay. Following are three topics and a sample thesis statement for each. As you can see, the topics are very general. The thesis statements are more specific and tell you exactly what the writers plan to say about their topics.

Topics	**Thesis Statements**
1. A movie I would recommend to a friend	*Titanic* is a movie I would recommend to a friend because it contains two major stars, has interesting costumes and sets, and it combines romance with drama.
2. A relaxing place to visit	Tourists looking for a relaxing place to visit will enjoy a trip to coastal Maine for several reasons.
3. A habit I would like to break	Smoking is a habit I am trying to break because it is expensive, messy, and harmful.

A good thesis limits the topic and controls your selection of evidence. For example, in the first thesis statement the topic of movies is limited to one movie: *Titanic.* The type of evidence you select to support this thesis would include details about the *major stars* who appear in the film, one or more examples each of what makes the *costumes* and *sets* interesting, and an explanation of how the film combines *romance* with *drama.* In the second thesis statement, the topic of relaxing places to visit is limited to *coastal Maine.* The evidence you select to support the thesis might include the *reasons* why you think tourists would enjoy a trip to Maine or perhaps some examples of activities, events, and attractions that provide relaxation. In the third thesis statement the topic of habits is limited to *smoking,* and the evidence you select to support this topic would include examples of how *expensive* smoking is, what is *messy* about it, and how it is *harmful* to you.

Having a thesis that you care about and that clearly states what your essay covers may provide the sense of direction you need to write with confidence. For a more detailed explanation of how to write a thesis statement, see Chapter 4.

EXERCISE **1.2**   Read the discovery draft you wrote for Exercise 1.1. Were you able to identify a sentence that states the central idea? Is it similar to the thesis statements on page 12? If not, try to rewrite it so that it is.

EXERCISE **1.3**   Think about one of the following topics or make up your own topic. For example, discuss a movie that you have seen and what you like or do not like about it. Then experiment with writing thesis statements like the three examples on page 12. When you are finished, select your best thesis statement to share with the class.

> a movie I would recommend to a friend
>
> a good part-time job for college students
>
> a habit I would like to break
>
> (add your own topic to the list)

EXERCISE **1.4**

Find out what online resources are available at your college to help students with writing. For example, go to your college's media center, computer center, library, or writing lab—wherever computer support is provided for students on your campus—and ask what software is available to help students with writing. If you do not own a computer, find out what the requirements are for using your college's computers for your writing projects. If you have never used a word-processing program, now is a good time to learn. Find out what instructional support is available at your college. Share your results of this exercise in a class discussion.

Who Will Be Your Audience?

Writing is a communication process between the writer and an *audience* of readers. When you write a letter to a good friend, you expect a reply. Your letter is probably filled with information that interests both you and your friend. You are aware of your friend's preferences, values, beliefs, and attitudes, and they influence what you write. If you know, for example, that your friend is interested in professional basketball, you might write a letter that contains a description of the exciting game you watched last week. When you sit down to write a letter and you begin to think about all the things you have done lately and what your friend would most like to know, you are involved in an essential part of the writing process: *you are considering your audience's needs and interests.*

Similarly, when you write an essay for your composition class, or for any class, consider your audience. The audience for most college writing is professors and other students. If you write a term paper for your American government class, you know that your professor will be reading it to find out how much you know about the topic and which concepts from the material presented in class you have been able to apply to your analysis of that topic. The professor and members of your composition class are your audience in addition to any imagined group of people to whom you want to communicate your ideas. In considering your audience, keep in mind two things: First, they will expect you to demonstrate your knowledge and writing skill. Second, they will expect you to be interested in your topic and to make an effort to interest them.

To determine who your audience is, ask yourself these questions:

- How old are my readers, and what do I know about their backgrounds and experiences?

- What are my readers' primary roles? Are they students, instructors, employees, consumers?

- How familiar with my topic are my readers? Are they beginners or experts?

- Can I assume that my readers are interested in my topic or do I need to arouse their interest?

- What are my readers' opinions or assumptions about my topic?

- What personal preferences, values, beliefs, or attitudes may affect the way my readers respond to the ideas expressed in my writing?

What Will Be Your Purpose?

Having a *purpose* for writing is also important. Why are you attending college? Are you here to pursue a degree that is the first step toward a career? Do you want to upgrade your skills so you can receive a promotion at work or be in a position to apply for a better job? Or are you taking classes for self-fulfillment, to enrich your life? Whatever your reasons, you probably had many decisions to make about which college to attend and what courses to take. Writing also involves many decisions: what topic to write about, what central idea to develop, what details and examples to choose, and which words will best express your ideas. Your *purpose,* or reason, for writing is what unifies all these decisions and gives you a goal to work toward.

To determine a purpose for writing, ask yourself these questions:

- Why do I want to write about this topic?

- What do I expect readers to be able to understand or do after they read my essay?

Throughout the writing process, *audience* and *purpose* should motivate every choice you make. Chapter 2 contains a more detailed explanation of these two essentials of good writing.

EXERCISE 1.5   Read the following list of writing tasks. Imagine that you had to do all of them, then decide what would be your purpose for doing each one and who would most likely be your audience. Share your results with the rest of the class. The first one is done as an example.

1. a personal letter

   a. purpose: to update my reader on the events in my life

   b. audience: a friend or relative who knows me well

2. an invitation to a party

3. a résumé

4. a letter to the editor of your local newspaper

5. a letter of complaint

6. an essay for a writing class

7. an essay test for one of your courses

EXERCISE 1.6   Review Dympna Ugwu-Oju's essay on pages 6–8. Why do you think she wrote the essay and for whom? Try to determine her purpose and audience.

EXERCISE 1.7   Now reread the discovery draft you wrote for Exercise 1.1. Do you think a purpose comes through in this draft? What *is* your purpose in writing about an accomplishment? What do you want readers to know? What can you assume your readers already know about the type of accomplishment you have chosen as your topic? See what you can add or rewrite to make your purpose clearer.

What Evidence Will Support Your Thesis?

You have probably learned from experience that people who ask you questions want reasons and explanations, and when they do not understand your answers, they want some examples that will enable them to relate your ideas to what they already know. In other words, you need to support your thesis, or central idea, with evidence. *Evidence* includes the facts, reasons, examples, opinions, and any other details that help support your thesis. As the thesis statement examples on page 12 illustrate, the thesis can control your selection of evidence by specifying what your essay covers. For more on how to select evidence, see Chapters 3 and 5. In the following short essay, the thesis statement and concluding sentence are underlined. Evidence is bracketed and explained in the margin:

We always thought my grandmother was a pack rat, but when she died a few years ago and we were going through her belongings, our suspicions were affirmed. Grandma's possessions fell into three categories: the used, the unused, and the useless.   *Thesis*

    Grandma was a great believer in recycling, which is why she saved used items that might one day be useful. For example, we found [old greeting cards] in her cedar chest, still inside their envelopes. These were sorted, stacked, and tied with ribbons for easy retrieval if she needed to look up an address or find a card to use in a craft project. She saved [receipts] in case she needed to return something. If someone needed [a paper bag, a bit of string, some tissue paper, wrapping paper, ribbon, or an empty box,] Grandma could supply the item from her stash on her closet shelves.   *Examples of "used" items*

    Not only did she save the empty boxes that her presents came in, she also saved many of the presents themselves—unused. [Nightgowns] in every color, enough [pantyhose] to last a working woman a year, [blouses] folded neatly with the tags still on them, were stored in drawers and on shelves. It wasn't that Grandma had not liked her gifts but that she hated to put on any new clothes when her old ones still had wear in them. Also,   *Examples of "unused" items*

Grandma was thrifty. Having lived through the Great Depression, she was saving her new clothes for a time when they might not be so easy to come by.

Who knows when a useless item—like a used one—might become useful again? Like all pack rats, Grandma was not taking any chances. As a result, we found among her belongings a drawer full of [pencil stubs too short to grasp, dog-eared playing cards] and a shoebox overflowing with [matchbook covers.] She had also collected most of the family's [broken toys, worn-out kitchen appliances, ropes of frayed extension cords, and unmatched drinking glasses] and stored them in her attic.

Examples of "useless" items

Browsing through Grandma's attic was like visiting a museum of the ghosts of our pasts. The [doll] that each of my sisters had played with on summer visits smiled brokenly from underneath its worn sailor hat. The [wooden train] that I had crashed on the rocks below my grandmother's house sat crookedly on a shelf, most of its wheels long gone. Someone's [wedding dress] suspended from a rafter twirled dizzily in the breeze from the electric fan.

Additional examples of "useless" items in the attic that bring back memories

Whoever said, "Everything old is new again" may have had a point when it comes to songs, clothing styles, or even old holiday gift paper, but the evidence in my grandmother's possessions suggests that some old things are exactly that.

Conclusion makes the point that some things may not be worth keeping

EXERCISE 1.8   Using the thesis statement you selected as the best one from Exercise 1.3, make a list of specific details you could use to support it. For example, if you chose a thesis statement about a part-time job for college students, your list might include some facts about the job, such as hours and pay; some reasons why you think it is a good job; and one or more examples showing how the job has helped you learn a skill or gain experience.

How Will You Organize Your Evidence?

A filmmaker creates a film scene by scene. The scenes added together result in a movie in which the story and characters' lives usually unfold in an orderly way. Have you ever arrived late to a movie so that it took you several minutes to figure out what was going on? Your confusion may have occurred because you missed the opening scenes that introduced characters and established the setting and situation. An orderly presentation of ideas is important in writing too. How well-organized your evidence is determines how understandable it will be to your readers.

Organization in writing means presenting your material in an order that makes sense—that is, a *logical* order. Logic involves clear thinking. Arrange your evidence so that facts, reasons, and examples develop your thesis in an orderly way. For example, suppose you decide to write about the breakup of a relationship. You think about what happened and decide that several events led to the breakup. A logical way to explain what happened would be to tell what occurred first, next, and so on, until the final event that caused the end of the relationship. Chapters 4 and 5 explain how to organize evidence within paragraphs and essays.

Organization also requires analysis of your topic. To *analyze* a topic means to look at it from all sides so that you can better understand it

FIGURE 1.2

Organizational Patterns for Thinking and Writing

PATTERN	PURPOSE	ESSAY TOPICS
Narration	To relate an event or series of events leading to an outcome	An award or special recognition you received
		The paintings of Picasso's blue period (humanities)
Description	To describe or create a vivid mental picture of a person, place, etc.	A person you will never forget
		The view from the pulpit of Chartres Cathedral (humanities)
Process	To explain how to do something or how something can be done	A difficult job or activity and how you learned to do it
		How a bill gets enacted into law (American government)

and draw some conclusions about it. *Analysis* involves several thought patterns with which you may already be familiar. For example, if a friend asks how you like your new apartment, you may say that you like it much better than your old apartment. You may go on to compare your new apartment to your old one, explaining their similarities and differences. In answering your friend's questions, you are using *comparison and contrast,* a common thought pattern that many writers use. Because thought patterns can help you organize your evidence, they are also called *organizational patterns.* Figure 1.2 lists the organizational patterns covered in detail in Chapters 9–15. The figure shows each

FIGURE 1.2 (cont.)

Organizational Patterns for Thinking and Writing

PATTERN	PURPOSE	ESSAY TOPICS
Classification and division	To break down a topic into categories	Types of restaurants in your community
	To divide a topic into parts	The division of labor within a Kibbutz (sociology)
Comparison and contrast	To explain similarities and differences between two things	The car you own now versus the car you would like to own
		How Freud's and Jung's theories of personality differ (psychology)
Cause and effect	To explain the reasons for something, the results of something, or both	The positive or negative effects of an important choice you had to make
		The causes and prevention of AIDS (biology)
Definition	To define a term or even a situation, perhaps because you think many people misunderstand it or because it has a unique meaning to you	Your definition of *a good friend*
		What are *fractals?* (math)

pattern's purpose and two possible essay topics for which each pattern might be suitable. The first topic listed after each pattern is for a personal essay, and the second topic is for an academic essay. Patterns are simply options, or choices, for organizing evidence. Whether you decide to use any or none of the patterns suggested in Unit 2 of this book is one of your many choices as a writer.

Writing involves many other things that you will learn about in the chapters following, but these five—*thesis, audience, purpose, evidence,* and *organization*—are characteristic of all good writing and are a good starting point.

WRITING AN ESSAY: THE PROCESS

Writing an essay is a process that begins with an idea and ends with a completed piece of writing. How you get there will probably take you through three stages, each of which requires you to make choices. As you proceed through the chapters of this book, the writing process will gradually unfold, and you will have ample opportunity to explore and practice. What follows is a quick preview of the process and how it works.

Stage 1: Prewriting

Think of this stage as a *readiness* stage: you are getting ready to write. Your choices include selecting a topic, thinking about the topic, making some notes about it, and perhaps even coming up with a tentative thesis and outline. At this stage you are generating ideas—what you know and do not know about your topic. Sometimes you need a reliable strategy to get the thinking process started. Writing a discovery draft is one strategy. *Clustering* is another prewriting strategy that can help you gather and organize evidence to support a topic. Chapter 2 explains several more ways to think of ideas for writing. Figure 1.3 illustrates an idea cluster for the topic "A Behavior I Wish People Would Change."

The cluster in Figure 1.3 illustrates how one writer thought through her topic. First, she decided that chronic lateness was the behavior she wanted to write about, so she wrote that topic in the middle of her paper and circled it. As she thought some more about the topic, she asked herself: "What are some of the problems chronic lateness causes?" Branching out from the first circle, she wrote "creates a bad impression" inside a new circle. She then thought of three more prob-

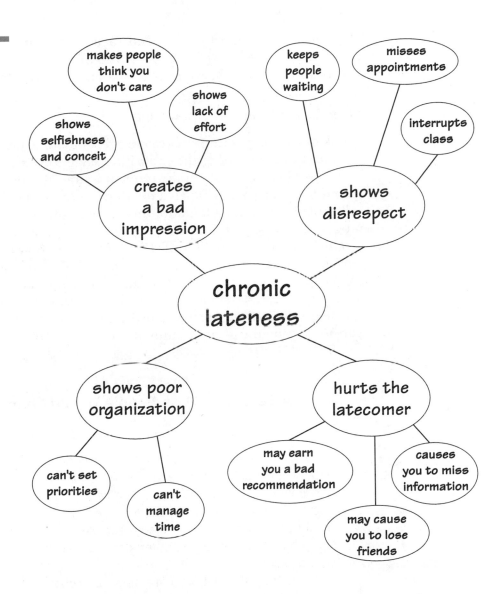

FIGURE 1.3

Idea Cluster for "A Behavior I Wish People Would Change"

lems, which she wrote inside more circles. Now she had four major divisions of an essay. To explain the problems of chronic lateness, she had to come up with some evidence. As she continued to think about her topic, she added new circles to her cluster. For example, one way that chronic lateness hurts the latecomer is that it "may earn you a bad recommendation." When the cluster was complete, the writer had a preliminary pattern of organization to follow. She would discuss chronic lateness in terms of four problems it causes and how these problems affect latecomers and those around them. Clustering not only helps you to organize your evidence, but it also provides a visual representation of your ideas so that you can *see* the organization clearly.

Stage 2: Drafting and Organizing

Think of this stage as an *exploratory* stage: You are experimenting with the ideas you got during the prewriting stage to come up with a *first draft* of your essay. Later you will refine this draft through successive revisions to a *final draft*. A *draft* is a rough piece of writing. Your first draft will probably contain a tentative thesis, some support, and the beginning of an organizational plan. As you write, your choices include whether to stick with the thesis you have chosen, how much and what kind of support you need, and how to organize your ideas logically. These choices are explained in greater detail in Chapters 3–5. Following is a first draft developed from the idea cluster in Figure 1.3. As you can see, this draft is sketchy, and the instructor's comments suggest ways to develop the ideas in future drafts.

First Draft of
"A Behavior I Wish People Would Change"

Introduction needs to establish purpose and background for thesis

Provide evidence to show "what" his attitude is and "how" it shows disrespect

Again, explain "what" the impression is

Chronic lateness is a behavior I wish people would change because it not only hurts others but it also hurts themselves.

Jim has never arrived anywhere on time in his life. He is late for work, late for class, late for dates, late for appointments. Jim's attitude is a good example of how a person's chronic lateness shows disrespect and a lack of consideration.

Without realizing it, Jim is creating a bad impression on his boss and coworkers. However, he may need a recommendation someday, so he should take the job more seriously.

Jim's lateness hurts him in other ways too. To be late to class sends a message to the instructor that a student lacks organization. Also, Jim does not date a woman for very long. She is just not going to keep seeing a guy who does not respect her enough to arrive on time. His friends

Add an example

do not even want to <u>invite him places where time is a</u> <u>factor.</u>

Add an example

    Most people who are chronically late are like Jim. They either do not realize the effect their behavior has on others or the ways lateness can hurt them. If they did, maybe they would make more of an effort to arrive on time.

Can you expand con-clusion? What might result from a change in behavior?

Stage 3: Rewriting

Rewriting involves two steps: *revising* and *editing*. Each time you *revise* a draft, you are rewriting it to make it better. Your choices at this stage include whether to add content, improve organization, or refine your style. Whether to add, take out, or rearrange sentences and paragraphs are other choices you can make. Revision, therefore, is an ongoing process that starts the minute you begin to make changes in your first draft.

    Editing is also part of the rewriting process. When you edit, you read your draft carefully to find and correct errors in grammar, spelling, and punctuation before writing your final draft. You also make an effort to tighten and trim your essay by eliminating unnecessary words and phrases. *Proofreading* is one last editing check before handing in your essay. Proofreading is a close reading to find any previously missed errors and to make sure that your essay is neat and legible. For more detailed information on the rewriting stage of the writing process, see Chapter 6 for *revising* and Chapter 7 for *editing*. Following is a revised and edited draft of "A Behavior I Wish People Would Change."

Revised Draft of "A Behavior I Wish People Would Change"

Being late once in a while is excusable, but the chronically late are late for everything, all the time. They are rude and inconsiderate of others' feelings. What they do not seem to realize is that their lateness creates a bad impression, making them appear disrespectful and disorganized. Chronic lateness is a behavior I wish people would change because it not only hurts others but it also hurts the latecomers.

    Jim has never arrived anywhere on time in his life. He is late for work, late for class, late for dates, late for appointments. As far as he is concerned, no one at work has complained, so why should he knock himself out to get there on time? As for his professors and the students in his classes, "They can start without me." He probably thinks his dates are so grateful to get to go out with him that they are willing to wait for hours for him to show up. As for appointments, well, everyone knows that dentists, doctors, and barbers overschedule. If he arrived on time, they would make him wait! Jim's attitude is a good example of how chronic lateness shows disrespect and a lack of consideration for others.

Without realizing it, Jim is creating a bad impression. His boss and coworkers can assume that Jim's job is not very important to him. For example, they may figure that the job is just something Jim has to do for the money while he is in school, so he does not put any more effort into it than necessary. But he may need a recommendation from these people someday, and he should take this job as seriously as any other.

Jim's lateness hurts him in other ways. Being chronically late to class sends a message to the instructor that Jim is disorganized and unable to manage time effectively. Students who do arrive on time are annoyed when he walks in late, interrupting a lecture by noisily getting into his seat and shuffling papers. Jim does not date a woman for very long. To hear him tell it, he is the one who ends the relationship, but I don't believe it. A woman is just not going to keep seeing someone who does not respect her enough to be on time. Even Jim's friends have begun to quit inviting him places where time is a factor. They do not want to miss the beginning of a concert or a movie because Jim is late.

Most people who are chronically late are like Jim. They either do not realize the effect their behavior has on others or the ways lateness can hurt them. If they did, maybe they would make more of an effort to arrive on time. Perhaps our lives would be improved as well. For example, we could get through a movie without latecomers tripping over us, spilling popcorn in our laps, and whispering loudly to their friends who had arrived on time, "What did I miss?"

The three stages of the writing process overlap and are neither entirely separate nor do they necessarily follow in order. During the prewriting stage, you may do some organizing. During the drafting and organizing stage, you will do some revising and may even go back to prewriting. For example, you may discover that your evidence does not support your thesis. Then you might use a prewriting strategy to explore your subject some more and either rewrite your thesis or collect new evidence. Even some editing may occur during the drafting and organizing stage. When you find an error, you may choose to correct it then instead of waiting until you finish your draft. The overlap of the three stages is called *recursiveness,* a term that means "falling back on it-self." Writing is a recursive process *because* the stages overlap and there is much moving back and forth among them. Figure 1.4 illustrates the recursive nature of the writing process.

There is no one best way to write an essay, but as you prewrite, draft and organize, and rewrite essay after essay, you will develop a process that works for you. What is important is that you state a thesis and support it, that you organize your ideas logically and state them clearly, and that you spend enough time revising and editing so that your essay represents your best achievement.

FIGURE 1.4

Writing Is a Recursive Process

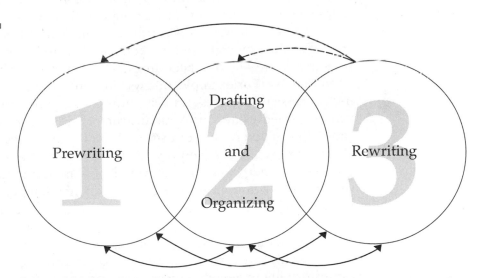

The solid arrow at the top of the diagram illustrates a writing process that moves from the rewriting stage back to the prewriting stage. For example, during the revision process you might decide to further limit your topic or even to change your topic. In that case, you might need to return to the prewriting stage to do some more brainstorming. The broken arrow at the top of the diagram indicates a movement from rewriting back to drafting and organizing. For example, you may decide you need to improve the way you have organized your details in one paragraph, or you may need to add details to another paragraph. The arrows at the bottom of the diagram show that your movement through the three stages of writing can go back and forth as needed. In other words, at any stage in the process you might need to do some brainstorming, editing, or revising.

EXERCISE 1.9   Think about the most recent essay you have written. List the stages you went through to write your essay. Compare your stages with the three stages of the writing process explained on pages 20–25. What conclusions can you draw? Which part of the process is easiest for you? Which part is most difficult? On which part of the process do you need to spend more time?

THINKING CRITICALLY AND CREATIVELY

Critical and creative thinking inform every part of the writing process from prewriting, to drafting and organizing, to rewriting. Broadly defined, **critical thinking** is *the process of constructing and evaluating meaning.* More specifically, critical thinking is *logical, or analytical, reasoning* that helps you make sense of your reading and that helps you make appropriate choices for writing. Critical thinking is also the process of *self-reflection,* whereby you examine your actions and their consequences both to achieve self-understanding and to determine what changes you need to make. For example, one way to think critically about your writing process and progress is to carefully consider the errors marked on your returned essays and your instructor's written comments. These can help you determine your strengths and weaknesses so that you can chart a course for your improvement. Finally, critical thinking is both *conscious and purposeful.* You know that you are doing it and you know why. Good writing and good reading do not happen automatically. Both require your active involvement and your use of proven decision-making strategies. For example, accessing your prior knowledge before you read, taking notes during reading, and deciding what is important after reading are proven strategies for improving comprehension. Brainstorming to generate ideas, selecting and organizing your details, and revising and editing are proven strategies for improving your writing. The key to thinking critically is to think analytically: Determine what you already know. Find out what you need to know. Have a plan for completing the task, and know how to evaluate the outcome.

How does **creative thinking** differ from critical thinking? The tool of the critical thinker is *analysis.* The tool of the creative thinker is *invention.* Analysis is the process of logical reasoning. When you make an outline for your essay's introduction, body, and conclusion or when you choose an appropriate organizational pattern for arranging your details, you are thinking analytically. When you research all sides of an issue you are thinking analytically. However, you are thinking creatively

FIGURE 1.5

Critical and Creative Thinking Strategies

CRITICAL THINKING	CREATIVE THINKING
Determine what you already know.	Become a careful observer.
Find out what you need to know.	Be open-minded rather than close-minded.
Have a plan for completing tasks.	Welcome change.
Know how to evaluate the outcome.	Be willing to take risks.

when you draw your own conclusions and formulate your own opinions based on a consideration of what you have learned from your research. You are also thinking creatively when you read a draft of an essay and seek ways to improve it. The key to thinking creatively is to think inventively: Become a careful observer. For example, look at everything as if you were seeing it for the first time. Be open-minded. For example, question your and others' assumptions, take nothing for granted, and be willing to deviate from popular opinion. Welcome change, and be willing to take risks. For example, try any new writing strategy that your instructor suggests. Choose writing topics that challenge your thinking and your writing skills. Figure 1.5 above summarizes these critical and creative thinking strategies.

EXERCISE 1.10

Write a brief essay in which you introduce yourself to your classmates. Before you begin, think critically about the assignment by answering the following questions:

1. Determine what you already know: Who is your audience? What would they expect you to write in an essay in which you introduce yourself to them?

2. Find out what you need to know: In addition to fulfilling your readers' expectations, what else would be appropriate to include in your essay?

3. Have a plan for completing the task: What will be your thesis? What details will best support your thesis? How will you conclude your essay?

4. Know how to evaluate the outcome: What standard will you use to determine your success? For example, will the essay be graded? Will your classmates be involved in the evaluation process? Based on what you have read in this chapter so far, what do you think are the characteristics of a good essay?

EXERCISE 1.11

This exercise will give you practice in thinking creatively. Do the exercise by collaborating with a group. Successful group interaction depends on each member's full participation. Use the list of roles and responsibilities in Figure 1.6 as a guide for a four-member group. Larger or smaller groups can share the responsibilities as needed. When collaborating, you should first determine the responsibilities for each group member. Next, follow the directions below to complete the exercise.

Read and discuss each person's essay from Exercise 1.10. Your discussion should focus on two things: (1) Based on the facts presented in each essay, what do the members of your group have in common? (2) What is unique about each person in the group? Write a report in which you summarize your group members' similarities and differences. Then introduce your group to the whole class by reading your report.

FIGURE 1.6

Roles and Responsibilies for Group Members

Leader	The leader keeps time, interprets the exercise directions, keeps the discussion on target, and makes sure everyone participates.
Recorder	The recorder acts as secretary, taking notes and compiling the final group report, which consists of the group evaluation and any other writing called for in the exercise.
Researcher	The researcher consults the textbook, the instructor, or other resources as needed to settle matters of confusion or controversy.
Reciter	The reciter reports back to the class, using the recorder's report for reference.

GROUP EVALUATION

What did each person contribute to the group's activity? Was your group's performance successful? Why or why not? What additional questions do you have about thinking creatively?

TOPICS FOR WRITING

1. If you liked the results of your discovery draft for Exercise 1.1, then rewrite it, and try to improve your work using suggestions from this chapter.

2. Choose one of the topics below, or make up your own essay topic. Write another essay in which you apply what you have learned so far about introduction, thesis, support, and conclusion.

> a political or social issue that is important to you
>
> a value or tradition that you would like to pass on to your children
>
> the reasons you are attending college
>
> a person you admire and why
>
> a movie you think people of all ages would enjoy
>
> a book you think everyone should read

Checklist for Revision

As you revise and edit your essay, check for the following:

1. Does your essay introduce the topic?

2. Does your essay contain a sentence that clearly states your central idea? (thesis)

3. Have you supported your thesis with evidence—have you given examples or stated reasons why you think the way you do?

4. Does your essay have a definite conclusion?

5. Are your sentences error-free?

THE CRITICAL THINKER

To examine Dympna Ugwu-Oju's essay in more depth, think about and discuss the following questions. Then choose one of them as a topic for writing:

1. In reference to her Ibo beliefs, the author says in paragraph 5, "I was *only* a woman." Using evidence from the essay, explain what she means by this statement. Then explain how the author's viewpoint of a woman's role either differs from or is similar to your own viewpoint.

2. Using evidence from the essay, first explain what the author's "tribal past" is and then explain to what extent she does or does not answer the question she asks in the title.

3. Read again paragraph 12. Explain why you agree or disagree with the author that parents all over the world may feel that they could have done a better job of instilling their beliefs in their children.

4. Do you think that the author's tribal past should shape Delia's future? Using evidence from the essay and from your own experience, write an essay in which you answer this question. Assume that the author and her daughter are the audience for your essay.

YOUR DISCOVERY JOURNAL

A journal is a place to record ideas, impressions, thoughts, and feelings—anything that may be useful to you as a writer. Here is how one writer, Joseph Reynolds, explains why he writes in a journal. This excerpt is from his essay "I Think (and Therefore Write), in a Journal," which appeared in the *Christian Science Monitor:*

> My journal is a storehouse, a treasury for everything in my daily life: the stories I hear, the people I meet, the quotations I like, and even the subtle signs and symbols I encounter that speak to me indirectly. Unless I capture these things in writing, I lose them.

For your first journal entry, briefly do one of the following:

1. Recount an interesting story you heard.

2. Describe someone you have just met who has made an impression on you.

3. Write down a quotation you like and explain what it means to you.

Chapter 2

Using Prewriting Strategies

*Y*ou are sitting in your favorite study place, ready to write. Whether you are facing a blank sheet of paper or an empty computer screen, you have been staring at it for what seems like hours. If only you could get started. Perhaps you are taking an essay exam. Although you understand the topic and have studied sufficiently, you do not know where to begin. Suppose your supervisor at work has asked you to write a report. You know where to look for information and what format to follow. Now you have only one question in mind, "How do I get started?" Do any of these situations sound familiar? If so, you are not alone. Getting started can be a challenge for any writer, no matter what the writing task is.

All writing begins with an idea, and one idea leads to another. To get the first idea that starts the others flowing, many writers have a favorite prewriting strategy, a method for generating ideas and planning what to write. Writing a discovery draft, as explained in Chapter 1, is one of the many choices available. This chapter explains several other prewriting strategies that can help you get started. Try them all; then choose the one that works best for you and make it part of your writing process.

AWARENESS CHECK

Before reading the following excerpt, explore your thoughts about writing. Think about the questions below, and answer them either on your own or in a group discussion:

1. Is getting started an easy or difficult part of the writing process for you? Why?

2. What helpful tips for getting started have you received from instructors or others?

3. Read the title, headnote, and first two paragraphs of the excerpt. Based on this preview, what do you think will follow?

Start with One Brick
Robert M. Pirsig

The following excerpt is from Robert M. Pirsig's, Zen and the Art of Motorcycle Maintenance. *The book is about a cross-country trip in which a man and his son search for life's meaning. This excerpt is about teaching, writing, and a common problem many student writers share: trying to think of something to say.*

VOCABULARY CHECK

innovating (1)	introducing something new
extensively (1)	in great amount, or over a wide area
disparagement (2)	reduction in esteem
confirmed (4)	supported
drudge (4)	one who does boring, unpleasant work
insight (5)	the capacity to understand the true nature of a situation
trivial (13)	unimportant
mimicking (13)	copying

He'd been innovating extensively. He'd been having trouble with students who had nothing to say. At first, he thought it was laziness but later it became apparent that it wasn't. They just couldn't think of anything to say. 1

One of them, a girl with strong-lensed glasses, wanted to write a five-hundred-word essay about the United States. He was used to the sinking feeling that comes from statements like this, and suggested with disparagement that she narrow it down to just Bozeman. 2

When the paper came due she didn't have it and was quite upset. She had tried and tried but she just couldn't think of anything to say. 3

He had already discussed her with her previous instructors and they'd confirmed his impressions of her. She was very serious, disciplined and hardworking, but extremely dull. Not a spark of creativity in her anywhere. Her eyes, behind the thick-lensed glasses, were the eyes of a drudge. She wasn't bluffing him, she really couldn't think of anything to say, and was upset by her inability to do as she was told. 4

It just stumped him. Now *he* couldn't think of anything to say. A silence occurred, and then a peculiar answer: "Narrow it down to the *main street* of Bozeman." It was a stroke of insight. 5

She nodded dutifully and went out. But just before her next class she came back in *real* distress, tears this time, distress that had obviously been there for a long time. She still couldn't think of anything to say, and couldn't understand why, if she couldn't think of anything about *all* of Bozeman, she should be able to think of something about just one street. 6

He was furious. "You're not *looking!*" he said. A memory came back of his own dismissal from the University for having *too much* to say. For every fact there is an *infinity* of hypotheses. The more you *look* the more you see. She really wasn't looking and yet somehow didn't understand this. 7

He told her angrily, "Narrow it down to the *front* of one building on the main street of Bozeman. The Opera House. Start with the upper left-hand brick." 8

Her eyes, behind the thick-lensed glasses, opened wide. 9

She came in the next class with a puzzled look and handed him a five-thousand-word essay on the front of the Opera House on the main street of Bozeman, Montana. "I sat in the hamburger stand across the street," she said, "and started writing about the first brick, and the second brick, and then by the third brick it all started to come and I couldn't stop. They thought I was crazy, and they kept kidding me, but here it all is. I don't understand it." 10

Neither did he, but on long walks through the streets of town he thought about it and concluded she was evidently stopped with the same kind of blockage that had paralyzed him on his first day of teach- 11 ing. She was blocked because she was trying to repeat, in her writing, things she had already heard, just as on the first day he had tried to repeat things he had already decided to say. She couldn't think of anything to write about Bozeman because she couldn't recall anything she had heard worth repeating. She was strangely unaware that she could look and see freshly for herself, as she wrote, without primary regard for what had been said before. The narrowing down to one brick destroyed the blockage because it was so obvious she *had* to do some original and direct seeing.

He experimented further. In one class he had everyone write all   12
hour about the back of his thumb. Everyone gave him funny looks at the beginning of the hour, but everyone did it, and there wasn't a single complaint about "nothing to say."

In another class he changed the subject from the thumb to a coin,   13
and got a full hour's writing from every student. In other classes it was the same. Some asked, "Do you have to write about both sides?" Once they got into the idea of seeing directly for themselves they also saw there was no limit to the amount they could say. It was a confidence-building assignment too, because what they wrote, even though seemingly trivial, was nevertheless their own thing, not a mimicking of someone else's. . . .

THE CRITICAL READER

Central Idea

1. What is Pirsig's central idea about teachers and writing?

Evidence

2. Pirsig states three examples of writing assignments that made students do original thinking. What are they?

3. How does the teacher in the excerpt compare himself to the girl who can't think of anything to say?

Implications

4. Does the teacher think that any student is capable of thinking originally and creatively? Use evidence from the excerpt to support your answer.

> ## Word Choice
>
> 5. Read the excerpt again, and underline all the adjectives the au-
>   thor uses to describe the girl who had nothing to say. How does
>   the author's choice of words create an impression of what this girl
>   is like? If you wanted to write about someone who was the oppo-
>   site of the girl in Pirsig's essay, what adjectives would you use in-
>   stead of the ones in the excerpt?

THE SELF YOU BRING TO WRITING

Think of yourself and the roles you play. Whether you are someone's
mother, father, son, daughter, sister, brother, friend, husband, wife,
lover, boss, coworker, student, or classmate, you have a background of
experiences associated with that role that affects how you see and relate
to the world. For example, your positive and negative experiences as a
student influence the way you interact with teachers and classmates,
just as the way you were raised as a child has an effect on how you raise
your children. You also have a private self, a part of you that has made
decisions about what is right or wrong, and about what your political,
social, and religious values are. Your *self* is the person you are in all of
your outer roles and in all of your inner values. How much of this self
you reveal as a writer depends upon what seems most appropriate to
the topic you have chosen, and to the audience you are writing for.

Before you begin writing about a topic, you must spend time thinking about it in relation to your experiences and values. Suppose the
topic is an issue such as "Should women in the military be allowed to
engage in combat?" Congress debated this issue in 1992 and rejected a
bill that would have allowed women to fight alongside men in armed
conflict. Members of Congress and citizens who favored the bill believed that women who serve their country in the military should be allowed to participate fully. Supporters of the bill argued that women
who are not allowed to engage in combat are automatically denied pro-
motions to higher ranks that are based on combat experience. They
also pointed to other countries where women have engaged in combat
and have been successful.

Those who did not favor the bill expressed values that focused on a
woman's traditional role as nurturer, one who gives life rather than
takes it. Some also expressed fears that if men and women were to en-

gage in combat together, the men might be more concerned about protecting the women in their ranks than about carrying out their duties as soldiers.

To a large extent, experiences and values shaped the views of people on both sides of the issue. The feelings of voters who had lost sons in combat, for example, may have been very different from those of servicewomen who felt discriminated against. To write about this or any issue you should explore your experiences and values to determine where you stand and why. This process will help you arrive at the point of view from which you will write your essay.

The *self* you reveal in your writing also expresses your unique point of view. If you were writing on the issue of women in combat, would your point of view be that of a man or woman who has served in the military, a father or mother who has daughters to protect, a citizen who believes that equal opportunity should apply to women in the service, or a citizen who thinks women have no place in the infantry? When the teacher in the excerpt on pages 33–35 asks the student to write about just one brick, he forces her to see for herself, instead of repeating what others have said—to use her experience to come up with a unique point of view. He asks her to relate topic to *self*.

EXERCISE 2.1   To see yourself and your experiences in relation to the topics you write about, you have to first know who you are. Though some take the question "Who am I" for granted, many great men and women have spent their lives trying to answer it. Listed below are some categories of experience. Write the categories on a sheet of paper, skipping several lines between them. Then make some notes about yourself under each category. The finished list should give you a picture of yourself and bring into focus what makes you unique.

origins, background, family heritage

special talents or accomplishments

places lived or traveled

work experience

political views

social/moral values

personal likes and dislikes

life/career goals

CHOOSING AND LIMITING TOPICS

The **topic** is the *subject* of your essay. In thinking about the topic, decide what you know about it, what experiences you have had with it, and what you would like to tell readers about it. Anything can become a topic for writing: people, places, objects, ideas, problems, and processes. The best topics are those that are familiar to you and that appeal to your interests.

Mai Chan is a college student who came to the United States from China several years ago. She works as a waitress in her family's restaurant. She hopes to finish college someday, but she has not decided what her major or career will be. Like many students in her writing class, Mai often has difficulty getting started, but she is learning to use her experience as a source for ideas. A recent topic the professor assigned was "a favorite holiday and how you celebrate it." Many of the students wrote about Christmas, Hanukkah, or Thanksgiving. Mai chose to write about Chinese New Year and how it is celebrated in her native country. As she thought about her topic, she jotted down some notes about the traditions surrounding the holiday, the food and activities associated with it, and what the holiday means. The category of personal experience that Mai used to relate self to topic is *origin, background, family heritage.*

As you think about your topic, make sure it is not too broad. A broad topic is one that is general and covers a lot of territory. An important step in your prewriting process should be to *narrow,* or *limit,* your topic to something you can explain fully in a short essay. "Holidays," for example, is too broad. If you tried to write an essay about holidays in general or all the holidays you could think of, you might fill pages without saying much of significance about any one holiday. A good topic is one that has been limited sufficiently to focus on a single central idea that can be developed in an essay. Mai's topic, "a favorite holiday and how you celebrate it," limited her to one holiday and how she celebrates it. To get started, all Mai had to do was decide which holiday to write about, then gather her evidence on how the Chinese celebrate the new year.

Remember that in the excerpt on pages 33–35 the student at first wanted to write a five-hundred-word essay about the United States. The teacher narrowed the topic down to Bozeman, then to the main street of Bozeman, and finally to just the front of one building, starting with the upper left-hand brick. The student's first topic was too broad. Once she had understood how to limit the topic, she was able to write a five-thousand-word essay.

EXERCISE 2.2   Practice limiting topics by thinking about the topics below, then rewriting them so that they focus on a single idea. The first one is done as an example.

1. General topic: friends

   Limited topic: <u>the most important quality of a good friend</u>

2. General topic: family traditions

   Limited topic: _____

3. General topic: games or sports

   Limited topic: _____

4. General topic: ways to save energy

   Limited topic: _____

5. General topic: election campaigns

   Limited topic: _____

6. General topic: travel destinations

   Limited topic: _____

7. Write your own general topic: _____

   Write your own limited topic: _____

EXERCISE 2.3   Using your list from Exercise 2.1, decide which categories of personal experience would help you to think about and generate ideas about the topics you limited in Exercise 2.2. For example, if you wrote about the limited topic "the most important quality of a good friend," you would be drawing upon the categories of social/moral values and personal likes and dislikes.

CHOOSING A PREWRITING STRATEGY

Many writers believe that it helps them to spend some time thinking about their topics and making notes before they begin to write. *Prewriting* is the planning stage of the writing process. During this stage, you think about your topic and make some decisions about what aspect of your topic you will cover, your central idea, your purpose, point of view, and perhaps even how you will organize your essay. You also think about your audience and what you want them to know about your topic. At this stage, your planning is tentative. You are giving yourself directions to follow so that you can get started. As you begin to draft your essay, your plans may change. Prewriting is also useful for rethinking your topic whenever you get stuck during the writing process. You might be in the middle of a rough draft, for example, and decide that what you have written so far isn't working out. Now you could use another prewriting strategy either to generate some more ideas about your topic, or even to help you think about a new topic.

Brainstorming a Topic

Whether you write about a familiar topic or one that you need to research, *brainstorming* is a useful prewriting strategy for thinking about topics and generating ideas that may become the evidence to support a thesis or central idea of your essay. Start with a blank sheet of paper. Write your topic at the top. Think about the topic, and list everything that comes to your mind. Do not worry about whether the ideas are related, and do not try to write complete sentences. Jot down whatever words and phrases come to mind, and do not stop until you have at least twenty items on your list. Later you can decide which ideas to use, which ones to leave out, and how to organize those that are left. Following is a student's brainstorming list for the topic "grades and testing," which he limited to "final exams."

Final exams

cramming

staying up all night

fast food

headaches

notes

old exams

study groups

the need for breaks

music or not?

ways to study

jitters

test anxiety

worrying about grades

fear of failure

comfortable clothes

good-luck charms

best place to sit

what to take to the exam

how to relax

what to study

pressure

After reading over his list, the student decided that his ideas fell into three categories. He then rearranged his ideas into three lists with new headings:

Problems students face during finals	**Preparing for exams**
cramming	notes
staying up all night	old exams
fast food	study groups
headaches	music or not?
test anxiety	what to study
jitters	ways to study
pressure	
worrying about grades	

Taking exams

comfortable clothes

good-luck charms

best place to sit

how to relax

Now the student had a clearer idea of what he wanted to write about. As a topic, "final exams" was still too broad. His lists reminded him of something he had learned from experience, though: that most of the problems students face when studying for and taking exams are the result of poor preparation. The student therefore limited his topic to "avoiding exam-week jitters by being prepared." He still needed to come up with a thesis statement, and he also realized that his lists needed more work. For example, he needed more ideas for "preparing for exams" and "taking exams." Even so, he knew that with the evidence he had collected so far he was off to a good start.

EXERCISE 2.4

Choose a topic that interests you. What would you like to write about? Is there a problem you would like to see solved? Is there a piece of advice you would like to give readers that would make their lives easier or better? After choosing and limiting your topic, write a brainstorming list of twenty or more items. If you like the results, use the list as part of your planning for an essay.

Freewriting

The term *freewriting* means exactly what it says: free, unrestrained writing. It is a process in which you write down whatever comes to mind without pausing to think about spelling or the rules of grammar. The purpose of this type of writing is merely to generate ideas, and to get the writing process going. Some writers and educators disagree about the value of freewriting. Some say that most of what you get when you freewrite is unusable. But others find it a valuable tool to use when they have trouble getting started. For those writers, just the process of writing something—anything—helps them think about their topic.

Those who do find freewriting helpful say that it works best if you take time to limit your topic first. Then your focus is narrowed to writing and thinking about a single idea. To begin, write your limited topic at the top of a blank sheet of paper. Using a timer if possible, write for ten minutes without stopping. Write everything you can think of about your topic. Do not worry about grammar or spelling. When you have finished, read what you have written. Much of it may not be useful, but some of it may contain a few details you can use or an idea that you can develop into a thesis or central idea. If your freewriting did not generate a few useful ideas, then choose another topic and try again, or try another prewriting strategy.

EXERCISE 2.5

Try freewriting on a computer. Choose a topic, limit your topic, and freewrite for about five minutes to generate ideas. First, dim the computer screen so that you are not tempted to look at what you have written until you are finished. Next, begin typing. Write whatever comes to mind about your topic. The dark screen frees you from the need to stop, revise, or edit your ideas. When you are finished, brighten the screen and read what you have written. Delete anything that is not useful, and save anything that you might be able to use in a current or future writing assignment.

Asking the Journalist's Six Questions

When gathering facts for a story, journalists often ask six questions: *Who? What? Where? When? Why?* and *How?* For example, a journalist might ask: *Who* is involved? *What* happened to him or her? *Where* did the event take place? *When* did it happen? *Why* did it happen? *How* did anyone find out about it? To help you remember the questions, think of them as *five W's and an H.* Answering these questions about your topic is another good way to generate ideas in the prewriting stage to come up with evidence you need to support a thesis. Following are several examples that show you how to adapt the journalist's questions to different kinds of topics.

EXAMPLE 1: WRITING ABOUT A PERSON

Who am I writing about? Who is my reader? (audience)

What happened between me and the person? What is my opinion or viewpoint? (topic and central idea)

Where did we meet? Where did the event I describe occur? (evidence)

When did we meet? When did something significant happen in our relationship? When did we break up, and so forth? (evidence)

Why do I like (or dislike) this person? Why am I writing about him or her? (purpose)

How have my feelings changed or remained the same? How has this person affected my life, and so forth? (implications)

EXAMPLE 2: WRITING ABOUT A PLACE

Who was with me in the place? Who is my reader? (audience)

What place am I writing about? What is my opinion or viewpoint? (topic and central idea)

Where is the place? (evidence)

When did I go there? When did the event I describe occur? (evidence)

Why do I like (or dislike) the place? Why am I writing about it? (purpose)

How did I find out about the place? How did it affect me? (implications)

EXAMPLE 3: WRITING ABOUT AN ISSUE

Who influenced me or made me aware of the issue? Who is my reader? (audience)

What is the issue? What is my position, opinion, or viewpoint? (topic and central idea)

Where did I learn about the issue? Where did a certain event related to the issue occur? (evidence)

When did the issue become an issue? When did I become interested in it? (evidence)

Why do I feel the way I do? Why am I writing about the issue? (purpose)

How has the issue or my involvement in it affected me? How does it affect others? (implications)

To think creatively about issues, add one more question to the journalist's list: *"What if?"* This question forces you to think about outcomes and consequences. For example, what if the residents in an inner-city neighborhood decided to take back control of their streets from gangs and drug dealers? How could they do it, and what if they were successful? Suppose that you have earned poor grades on the last two tests in one of your courses. What if you were to change your study habits? What if you were to do nothing? In either case, the outcome might be different. Thinking about outcomes and consequences is another way to generate ideas for writing and find solutions to problems.

Clustering

Clustering as explained briefly in Chapter 1, pages 20–22, is a prewriting strategy that not only helps you generate ideas that you may later use as evidence, but also helps you see the relationship among your ideas. An idea cluster is an illustration or visual representation of how ideas relate. Figure 2.1 is an idea cluster for the limited topic "avoiding exam-week jitters by being prepared," which a student narrowed down from the topic "final exams."

To make an idea cluster, first write your topic, or an abbreviated version of it, in a circle in the middle of a page of clean paper. As you think about your topic, decide how you would break it down into parts that you can discuss one at a time in your essay. These parts, or divisions, may become the main ideas of body paragraphs. As soon as you decide what one main idea will be, draw a line out from the center circle to another circle in which you write the idea. If you can break that idea down into more specific supporting details to use as evidence, draw lines out to additional circles and write the details in those circles. For example, in the following cluster, one of the divisions, or main ideas, is "preparing for exams." As the student thought about the items on the brainstorming list he had made earlier, he decided he could improve on them by reorganizing them and by adding more items. From the "preparing for exams" circle, he drew three more circles: "what to study," "how to study," and "when to study." These were his major details. From the circles containing major details, he could add more circles to contain his more specific minor details. Making the cluster helped the student to discover his thesis: *You can avoid exam-week jitters by eliminating their causes and by knowing how to prepare for and take exams.*

How many circles you add to your idea cluster and how detailed you want to be in writing in them is up to you. The main ideas and details you write down may become the evidence you use to support your thesis, or the cluster may be only a starting point from which you will make more clusters until you have collected enough evidence and done enough organizing to begin drafting your essay. Moreover, you can use clustering in any part of your writing process, not just for prewriting. Sometimes it is necessary to rethink a draft you are

FIGURE 2.1

Idea Cluster for: "Avoiding Exam Week Jitters by Being Prepared"

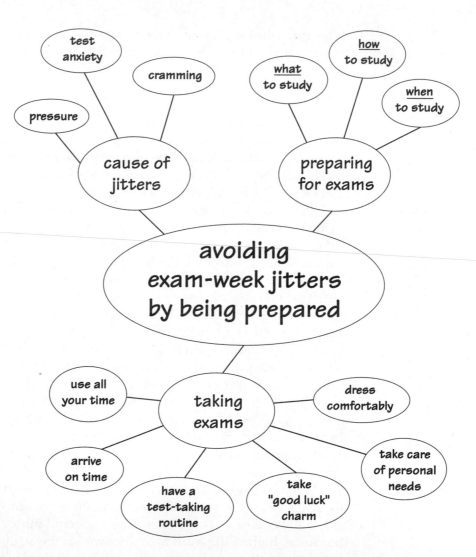

working on. A cluster on which you "outline" what you have written so far may help you see what needs to be added or changed in order to finish your draft.

Using *START* to Plan an Essay

START is an acronym formed from the first letters of *self, topic, audience, reason,* and *tone*—five essentials to consider as you begin to plan your essay during the prewriting stage. Using START *and* one of the other prewriting strategies explained in this chapter not only will help you gather evidence for your essay, but it will also help you focus on your audience's needs. A student who was having difficulty choosing a major decided to visit her college's career center on the recommendation of a friend. She made an appointment for career counseling, took several tests and inventories, and based on the results decided on a major that would help her reach her goals. Because she felt that other students should know about the center and the services it provides, she decided to write an essay about it. Figure 2.2 illustrates how she used START to plan her essay.

The first two of START's essentials, *self* and *topic,* are explained on pages 36–37 and 38–39. During the prewriting stage you should limit your *topic* and think about it in relation to your experiences and values, which make up the *self* you bring to the writing process. The following sections explain *audience, reason,* and *tone* as three more essentials to consider as part of your preliminary planning of an essay.

FIGURE 2.2

Using *START* to Plan an Essay

	QUESTIONS TO ASK	ANSWERS
Self	What self do I want to reveal?	I am a student like many of those who might read my essay.
Topic	How will I limit my topic?	My topic is the career center and the services it offers to students.
Audience	Who is my audience, and what can I assume about my readers?	Other students are my audience, and I can assume that some of them are uncertain about their futures.
Reason	What is my purpose for writing about this topic?	I want to inform students about the center's services and the kind of help it provides.
Tone	What tone do I want? How do I achieve it?	I will choose words that make me sound serious and confident.

The Audience for Your Essay

You can write for one of two possible audiences, a general one or a specific one. Most of the time in college, you will write for your peers—that is, your classmates and your instructor. What assumptions can you make about them? First of all, they are part of your college community, so they share your interests, concerns, and problems as a college student. Since they are also part of the larger community in which you live, they are members of a *general audience.* You can assume that they have shared many of your same experiences and that they may be aware of current events and of the social issues that affect everyone's lives. In addition, people of varying races, cultural backgrounds, nationalities, and ethnic groups are all part of a general audience in the United States today and are also part of your classroom audience. It is important to keep in mind that some of your readers will have had experiences that are very different from yours. You therefore cannot assume that readers will always know what you mean unless you explain it to them.

Sometimes you may write for a *specific audience.* Perhaps you have decided to write about a controversial topic—animal rights, for example—and you imagine that some of the people reading your essay will strongly disagree with you. To write effectively for this audience, determine what their views are so that you can choose your evidence and develop your thesis to answer these views. How to set up an argument and how to write an essay on a controversial topic is explained in Chapter 16, "Arguing Persuasively."

How you write about a topic will differ depending upon who the audience is and what your purpose is. In the following examples, the topic is the same, but the audiences are different. The topic is "competency testing for college students." Notice how *purpose* and *audience* affect the writing.

The first example is a paragraph from a typical news article a journalist might write in response to a new state law requiring college students to take a competency test in math and English. The purpose of the article is to inform readers about the test. The general public is the audience.

EXAMPLE 1:

Soon, all college students in our state will have to take a basic skills test. The test comes at a time when educators across the country are expressing concern about declining SAT scores and about complaints from employers that college graduates lack basic communication skills. The purpose of the test is to ensure that students who want to continue in college are able to demonstrate that they can read, write, and compute at a basic level. Students who fail one part of the test will have an opportunity to retake that part without having to repeat the whole test. Though the test is still in its experimental stages, eventually every student will have to take it in order to be eligible for an Associate of Arts degree and to continue his or her education. Students will have to pay a fee to take the test; however, the price has not yet been determined. . . .

The next two examples are possible letters to the editor of a local newspaper in a community where competency testing has been going on for some time. One writer defends the test, and the other condemns it. Parents of college students are the specific audience for both letters, and the writers' purpose is to persuade them either to support or reject the test.

EXAMPLE 2:

Dear Editor:

When I was in school you either learned, or else. The "or else" came in the form of a rap on your knuckles with the teacher's ruler. No one passed to the next grade who had not learned the lessons. I remember one boy in the sixth grade who was 18 years old. Eventually, he graduated and went on to earn a living and support his family like the rest of us.

I don't advocate a return to those times. I know that all students are entitled to the opportunity to continue their education, not just those who can afford the tuition. However, I think it's a shame that so many kids graduate from college who can't even spell.

After all these years of social promotion and lack of accountability on the part of schools and teachers, I'm glad that my child will have to take the state competency test. Maybe because of this test, he'll work harder in school and his teachers will feel obligated to help him succeed. I hope all parents will get behind the state's efforts to upgrade education and support the testing program.

A Concerned Parent

EXAMPLE 3:

Dear Editor:

My daughter has always been a good student except in math. In high school she made mostly A's and B's. She has done well in her college courses too, but now her graduation is being delayed because she didn't pass the math part of the state competency test. She is spending another semester at the community college to brush up on her math skills so she can pass the test. I'm worried that she may never pass this exam because math is the one subject that has always given her trouble.

What a lot of parents do not realize is that students have to pay for this test, and in my case I am having to pay my daughter's tuition for another semester in college, which I had not planned on and I can ill afford.

Not only does the test cause students needless anxiety, but it is very discouraging to them when they fail. How can one test be a measure of a person's ability, and why should one test determine whether a student gets to continue her education? Furthermore, the test is timed. When students are under that kind of pressure, it is no wonder that they do not do well. I am sure I am not alone when I say that I think the test is unfair. I urge parents to write their legislators opposing the test.

A Concerned Parent

The writers of Examples 1, 2, and 3 know their audiences. Each knows the extent to which his or her audience is informed about the topic; what additional information about the topic the audience needs; why the audience should be interested in or concerned about the topic; and what new information would enlighten the audience.

The writer of Example 1 assumes that some readers may know about the new competency test but that most of them do not. He also assumes that most of them are aware that educators are concerned about college graduates' declining performance. He probably thinks that they do not know what the test covers or that all college students will have to take it. Because many of the members of this writer's audience are parents, they are probably interested in or concerned about competency testing because their children will have to take the test if they expect to graduate from college. As a result of reading the article, parents may be inclined to encourage their children to succeed in those subjects that the test covers. Though some readers of the article undoubtedly may have heard that their state had established competency testing, they may not have realized that failing the test could delay or even prevent graduation. That students would have to pay a fee to take the test may also have struck some readers as new information. This writer states facts without making judgments, and the language is formal and unemotional.

The writers of Examples 2 and 3 are writing at a time when the competency test is an established fact. Therefore, they can assume that parents of college students, or students who want to go to college, are aware of the test, what it covers, its cost, and that it is required. These writers can also assume that although some members of the audience are in favor of the test, some oppose it. Both writers make judgments about the test. They rely on personal examples and opinions more than facts for their support, and their language is informal and emotional.

The writer of Example 2 believes that many parents remember the days when students did learn their lessons. She also believes that, like her, many of her readers take for granted that schools and colleges need reform. The test, she thinks, is an effort to improve education. She probably thinks that readers who do not support the test do not realize that it might have a positive effect on the state's education program. She is writing for an audience of readers whom she believes would support the state's testing program were they to see it as both encouraging students to work harder and requiring teachers to provide more help.

The writer of Example 3, on the other hand, believes that those who favor the test do not realize its drawbacks. This writer cites the cost, the inconvenience, and the discouragement of having to take all or parts of the test more than once to pass it, the time limit, and the added cost of delaying graduation—all as hardships for students. For some members of the audience, this additional information may be of some interest and concern, particularly if they have college-age sons and daughters who have failed the test and encountered similar problems.

Both writers of Examples 2 and 3 hope their readers will take action either in the form of supporting the test or writing their legislators to complain about it. Both either know or have studied their audiences well enough to present facts and opinions that will appeal to their readers' interests.

In considering your audience's needs, ask yourself the questions listed on page 14 in addition to these three general questions:

- What do my readers already know?

- What do I think they need to know?

- What do I know that may surprise my readers and add to their knowledge?

EXERCISE 2.6

Apply what you have learned about purpose and audience by doing this exercise with group members. First, review the list of group roles and responsiblities as explained in Figure 1.6, page 28. Next, read and discuss the following scenario and complete the writing task. Then evaluate your group's performance.

> In your state, all college students must take a competency test in English and mathematics to be eligible for graduation. As members of your college's student government association, you have decided to organize a prep session to help students get ready for the test. You have convinced an instructor to conduct the session and give a practice exam and exercises. You think all students who are planning to take the test should take advantage of the prep session. The session is free, but students do have to sign up in the student government office.

Write an article for your campus newspaper to advertise the prep session. Keep your article brief, two hundred words or fewer, and give it a title. To help you generate ideas for your article, refer to the scenario and discuss the following questions.

1. Who is your audience for the article, and what are their needs?
2. What is your purpose?
3. Who is eligible to attend the prep session?
4. How much will it cost?
5. Who will conduct the session?
6. What will it cover?
7. Where will it be held?
8. When will it be offered?
9. Why should students attend?
10. Where do they sign up?

GROUP EVALUATION

What did each person contribute to the group's activity? Was your group's performance successful? Why or why not? What additional questions do you have about purpose and audience?

Having a Reason to Write

Now that you are in college, you write to answer test questions, to complete exercises and assignments, and perhaps even to fill out application forms for scholarships, financial aid, or part-time jobs. Before you graduate, you will probably write a résumé, or summary of your work and other experience, which you will submit along with job applications. In the workplace you may have to write reports or take the minutes of a meeting. In your personal life you may write letters to friends and relatives, to the editor of your local newspaper, or even to your state representative or senator. In each of these situations, you have a clear *reason,* or *purpose,* for writing.

In each case there is something you want—for example, a good grade, a good job, a promotion, or a favorable response. Your purpose should be just as clear before you begin writing an essay. One way to determine a reason for writing is to ask yourself, "Why am I writing this?" Most of the time your answer will reveal one of two reasons: *to inform* or *to persuade.* To inform means to explain, provide facts, give out information for the purpose of clear understanding. To persuade means to influence another's thinking with the hope of perhaps changing a behavior. Persuading also relies upon explanations, facts, and information for the purpose of influencing rather than for simply increasing knowledge and understanding.

If your purpose is to inform readers, you need to tell them something about your topic that will educate or enlighten them. Perhaps you work as a host or hostess in a popular restaurant. To some people it may look as if you have an easy job. You greet people when they come in, take their names if they do not have a reservation, show them where to wait, and then give their names to a server who seats them when their table is ready. However, there is more to this job than people think. You may decide to write an essay to inform your readers that being a restaurant host or hostess is not as easy as it looks.

If your purpose is to persuade readers, you will want to influence them so that they change their opinions or behavior. Perhaps you are concerned about the environment, and you believe everyone should begin to do what is necessary to help preserve the world for future generations. For example, you want people to recycle cans and newspapers, discontinue their use of aerosol sprays, and boycott products that come in nonrecyclable, nonbiodegradable containers. You may decide to write an essay to persuade readers to take these steps.

Writers often have more than one reason for writing. In the process of *informing* readers that there is more to a job than might appear on the surface, you may find yourself *persuading* them not to consider taking this job unless they first find out what is involved. In order to *persuade* readers to recycle cans and newspapers, you may first have to *inform* them that a problem exists.

EXERCISE 2.7   Read each paragraph below and decide whether the purpose is primarily to *inform* or to *persuade*. Underline words or phrases in each paragraph that help you determine the writer's purpose.

1. From his broad, flat bill to his webbed feet, the furry duck-billed platypus is an odd animal. Awkward on land, he is a graceful swimmer. Shrimp are the platypus's favorite food, but you might wonder how he ever finds them since he swims with his eyes closed. Electric sensors on his bill can detect the tiny electric current given off by the movement of the shrimp's tail. Not only do the receptors in the platypus's bill help him find dinner, but they help him navigate, too. Flowing waters create electric fields through which the platypus glides with ease.

2. The last thing we need in our area is a baseball stadium. We already have two convention centers and one sports arena, which the taxpayers have financed—never mind the fact that whenever we were given the chance, we voted against such a waste of our tax dollars. For one thing, these places are private businesses and should be paid for with private funding. Second, their owners who care about nothing but making a profit have gouged consumers to the point that many of us cannot afford to attend events taking place in buildings that we bought. For example, one ticket to a basketball game can cost as much as $150, parking costs $15, and a soft drink is $5. Third, in every case we were told that the center or arena would pay for itself, bring jobs to the community, and promote development from which everyone would profit. However, the only ones who have made any money at all are the owners. Now our city council and

business leaders want to build a stadium to attract a major-league baseball team. I have one question for them: Are you willing to put up your own money to underwrite this venture? Neither are we.

3. "Canned hunts," that's what they're called, and what they are is an excuse for people who call themselves hunters to shoot exotic, often endangered, animals at as much as $3,500 a pop. Often the animals are drugged or chased out of cages into a fenced-in open area where they are trapped. Some sport that is. The real tragedy is that there is money in this grisly business, a lot of it. Exotic animal "preserves" are springing up in some states; these are the wildlife supermarkets where hunt organizers shop. Canned hunts are currently under investigation, but progress is slow because of weak and ambiguous laws. Legitimate hunters and sportsmen should deplore canned hunts and demand that their legislators become involved in this issue.

4. When it comes to mate selection, do you believe in true love or propinquity? Those who believe in true love believe that love happens only once and that there is just one "right" person for everyone. Those who believe in propinquity believe that anyone can fall in love with any number of people, and that the "right" person maybe the one who is the most available at the time. *Propinquity* means closeness or nearness in a physical sense. Two people sitting next to each other in a movie theater have propinquity. One reason so many people marry the girl or boy next door is propinquity. So when you are looking for a mate, chances are you will select someone from your own neighborhood, someone you went to school with, or someone you met at work. Other factors that play a role in mate selection are physical appearance, race, nationality, age, educational level, socioeconomic status, religion, personality characteristics, and shared interests. In other words, you are probably going to marry someone very much like yourself; most people do.

Selecting the Right Tone

Your tone and choice of words can help readers determine your purpose and respond to the self that your tone reveals. As a writer, you have a voice. You can make the tone of your written voice sound different depending upon your attitude toward your topic and audience and the words you choose to express it. Consider how being in a restaurant where there is an unruly child at the next table may affect people in different ways. A person who is also a parent and has been through the process of teaching young children how to eat in restaurants might sympathize with the parents of the unruly child and therefore not become annoyed at the child's behavior. Someone else might be very annoyed. Perhaps this person came to the restaurant with a date for a quiet, pleasant evening and might think that the parents of the unruly child are inconsiderate. If these two restaurant goers were each to write an essay about the experience, their essays would be quite different. One might write with an amused, sympathetic tone. The other might choose an angry, annoyed tone.

Tone is the attitude you convey through your choice of words. Read paragraphs A and B below. They are written on the same topic, "office thieves," but each has a different tone. In the first paragraph, the writer is amused. In the second, the writer is angry. In each paragraph the words, phrases, or sentences that help convey the tone are underlined.

PARAGRAPH A

Humorous words and phrases that mean stealing

An act that usually causes laughter

Office thieves are like those people who are always trying to <u>bum a cigarette</u>: a little annoying, basically harmless, but not criminals. You would think that an office manager would have something more important to do than to waste time crying over a <u>pilfered</u> paper clip. So what if someone <u>lifts</u> a legal pad, <u>rips off</u> a ream of paper, <u>bags</u> a box of number 2 pencils. Surely the office orders a surplus to cover these losses. Some managers <u>guard the supply cabinet with their lives</u>. Just try to get a ballpoint pen out of them if you have already used your allotted quota for the year. If more managers would realize that one of an employee's perks is free supplies and look the other way, then maybe fewer office thieves would <u>steal a colleague's stapler with one hand while bumming a cigarette with the other</u>.

Humorous exaggeration

Creates a humorous visual image

PARAGRAPH B

Words and phrases that suggest anger

Office thieves <u>make life difficult for the rest of us</u>. While <u>we</u> try to cut costs by making supplies last, the thieves are <u>taking more than their share</u> and <u>costing us more</u>. <u>They</u> are <u>selfish</u>, <u>wasteful</u>, and <u>inconsiderate</u>. To <u>them</u>, taking a

"us" against "them"

"we" and "they"
pronouns
emphasize angry
conflict

Strong term for
office stealing—an
angry exaggeration

box of pencils home for their own use is not stealing. Their attitude is that there are plenty more where those came from. A box of pencils costs about $8.50. A box of manila folders or a ream of paper cost around $25.00. Who do these <u>thugs</u> think pays for the supplies? The cost comes out of the office management budget. If <u>we</u> could cut consumption by eliminating the stealing, <u>we</u> might have more money left to upgrade some of the equipment <u>we all have to use.</u> <u>We</u> ought to punish the <u>culprits</u> by adding up the cost of their <u>larceny</u> and deducting it from their paychecks.

an angry
exaggeration

"us" against
"them"

Although you should consider tone during the prewriting stage, you may not know what tone you want until you write your first, or rough, draft. Read your draft to yourself, or have someone read it to you. Try to recall how you felt and what you were thinking as you wrote it. Were you sad, angry, amused, or did you have a different feeling? Also, how do you want readers to respond as they read your essay? Your purpose, what you expect of the audience, and your attitude toward your topic should influence your choice of an appropriate tone. For more information on tone, see Chapter 6, pages 153–156.

EXERCISE 2.8   Examine five pieces of writing and determine the *tone* of each: the excerpt from *Zen and the Art of Motorcycle Maintenance* on pages 33–35, and the paragraphs in Exercise 2.7. Is the tone of each piece of writing appropriate for its purpose? Why or why not? What could you add or change to make the tone more appropriate?

EXERCISE 2.9   Use the START strategy on an essay in progress. Ask yourself questions to determine whether you have adequately considered the five essentials of self, topic, audience, reason, and tone during your prewriting process.

TOPICS FOR WRITING

1. Look over all the writing you completed for the exercises in this chapter. Which prewriting strategy helped you generate the most

ideas for evidence and made you want to pursue the topic further? Using these notes as a start, finish your essay.

2. Use one of the six prewriting strategies below to plan and write an essay on a topic of your choice or one suggested elsewhere in this chapter.

   1. Discovery draft (Chapter 1, pages 9–10)

   2. Idea cluster (Chapter 1, pages 20–22 and Chapter 2, pages 45–46)

   3. Brainstorming

   4. Freewriting

   5. Asking the journalist's questions

   6. START: self, topic, audience, reason, tone

Checklist for Revision

As you revise and edit your essay, check for the following:

1. Have you limited your topic?

2. Are purpose and audience clear?

3. Does your essay have an introduction?

4. Does your essay have a central idea?

5. Have you developed your central idea with evidence?

6. Does your essay have a conclusion?

7. Are your sentences error-free?

THE CRITICAL THINKER

To examine Pirsig's essay in more depth, think about and discuss the following questions. Then choose one of them as a topic for writing.

1. Review the section "Thinking Critically and Creatively" on pages 26–27. Do the teacher's writing assignments in Pirsig's essay require students to think critically, creatively, or both? Explain your answer.

2. Explain what the author means by this statement from paragraph 7. "The more you look, the more you see."

3. Based on what you have learned from this chapter and from Pirsig's essay, what would be your advice to a student writer who cannot think of anything to say? Make a list of suggestions to help the student get started.

4. In paragraphs 12 and 13, the author says that two writing assignments gave the students something to say. Discuss these assignments and explain why you think they worked. Then try one of the two assignments for yourself: either write about the back of your thumb or write about a coin.

YOUR DISCOVERY JOURNAL

As preparation for your next journal entry, reread the letters on pages 48–50. Think of an issue or a situation going on in your community or on campus that is important to you. Imagine that the editor and readers either of your local newspaper or your college paper are your audience. Then write the letter in your journal.

Chapter 3

Improving Your
Paragraph Skills

A *paragraph* is a part, or division, of an essay that develops a main idea which is relevant to the whole essay. At the same time, the paragraph is complete in itself. Though a paragraph may be as short as one sentence or as long as a page or more, most of the paragraphs you write will usually consist of several sentences that support one main idea. The *main idea* of a paragraph expresses its topic and focus. A *topic sentence,* when present, states the main idea. If there is no topic sentence, the main idea may be implied. To *imply* a main idea means to hint at it or to suggest it without stating it directly. If a paragraph has no topic sentence, you can figure out what the main idea is by asking yourself what single idea the details all seem to support or explain.

Essays and articles you read in magazines, newspapers, and even in the chapters of this book will reveal a variety of writing styles and paragraph lengths and types. Professional writers may not always write paragraphs that have topic sentences. As a beginning writer, however, you should strive for a clearly stated main idea. The topic sentence will guide your writing and your readers' thinking and will help you stay on topic. Later, as you begin to experiment with different ways to organize your essays, having topic sentences in your paragraphs will help you connect paragraphs and relate the ideas expressed within them to the central idea of your whole essay. To help you improve your paragraph skills, this chapter explains three keys to writing good paragraphs: main idea, support, and organization.

AWARENESS CHECK

Before reading the following excerpt, explore your thoughts about intelligence. Think about the questions below, and answer them either on your own or in a group discussion:

1. What does the word *intelligent* mean to you? What examples can you give?

2. Can people be "smart" in some ways and not in others? What examples can you give?

3. Read the title, headnote, and first two paragraphs of the excerpt. Based on this preview, what do you think will follow?

The Different Ways of Being Smart
Sara Gilbert

In this excerpt from Chapter 5 of Sara Gilbert's Using Your Head, The Different Ways of Being Smart, *Gilbert categorizes kinds of intelligence. Her thesis, or central idea, is that there are many kinds of intelligence and that each of us is "smart" in one or more ways. As you read the excerpt, try to discover how each paragraph supports its own main idea, and how all the paragraphs together support Gilbert's central idea.*

VOCABULARY CHECK

unique (2)	one of a kind
spectrum (2)	range
conscientious (9)	thorough
symbols (4, 13)	ideas or objects that represent other things

intently (13)	with deep concentration
persistent (13)	refusing to give up
tycoons (14)	wealthy and powerful businesspersons
merits (14)	earned value

Book smarts, art smarts, body smarts, street smarts, and people smarts: 1
These . . . labels . . . describe the various forms of intelligence and their
use. As you might imagine, psychologists and other researchers into
the nature of intelligence have come up with more formal terms for the
types that they have isolated. One set of labels in common use is: convergent, divergent, assimilating, and accommodating. The converger
and assimilator are like our book-smart person; the diverger, like our
art-smart; and the accommodator, like our street-smart and people-
smart. . . .

Whatever categorization we use, we will find some overlap within   2
any individual. In fact, there are probably as many answers to the question "What are the different ways of being smart?" as there are people
in the universe, because each of us is unique. We can't be typecast; we
each have a wide spectrum of special talents.

Still, you probably know well at least one person whose talents   3
generally fall into each of our categories. Keep those people in mind as
you read through the detailed descriptions of them. . . .

At first it might seem that each of those types must call on very dif-   4
ferent sorts of abilities to be smart in his or her own ways. But in fact,
each of the categories of intelligence on our list must use the same
ingredients . . . learning ability, memory, speed, judgment, problem-
solving skill, good use of language and other symbols, and creativity.
Also, the thought processes that go on inside the heads of people with
those varying kinds of smarts include the same steps: planning, perceiving, imaging, remembering, feeling, and acting.

Intelligence expresses itself in different forms, in part because of   5
the differing physical qualities born and built into each person's body
and brain, and in part because of the values and motivations that each
person has learned.

However, the fact that each kind of smarts makes use of the same   6
steps means that anyone can learn or develop skills in any or all of the
categories. . . . Let's take a closer look at the many ways of being
smart.

A *book-smart* person is one who tends to do well in school, to   7 score high on tests, including intelligence tests. He or she is likely to be well-organized, to go about solving problems in a logical, step-by-step fashion, and to have a highly developed language ability. Another label for a book-smart person is "intellectual," meaning someone who uses the mind more to *know* than to feel or to control, and a book-smart person is especially proud of having knowledge. That knowledge may range from literature through science to math, but it is probable that it is concentrated in one area. Research shows that different knowledge areas occupy different clusters in the brain, so that someone whose connections for complicated calculations are highly developed may have less development in the areas controlling speech and writing.

8 Although as we've said, current research indicates that learning centers may be scattered throughout both hemispheres of the brain, the activities of the "logical" left side are probably most important in the lives of book-smart people. Book-smart people may also be creative: many mathematical or scientific problems could not be solved, for instance, without creative insights, but the primary focus of a book-smart person is the increase of knowledge.

9 *Art-smart* people, on the other hand, rely primarily on creativity. They create music, paintings, sculpture, plays, photographs, or other forms of art often without being able to explain why or how they chose a particular form or design. They are said to be "right-brained" people, because it appears that the control centers for such skills as touch perception and intuition—the formation of ideas without the use of words—lie in the right hemisphere. Artistic people tend to take in knowledge more often by seeing, hearing, and feeling than by conscientious reading and memorizing.

10 An art-smart person may not do too well in school, not because he or she is not bright, but because of an approach to problem solving that does not fit in well with the formats usually used by teachers and tests. A book-smart person might approach a problem on a math test logically, working step-by-step toward the right answer, while an art-smart person may simply "know" the answer without being able to demonstrate the calculations involved. On a social studies exam, the book-smart person will carefully recount all the facts, while the more artistic one may weave stories and fantasies using the facts only as a base. In both cases, it's a good bet that the book-smart student will get the higher grade.

11 People who are serious about becoming artists, of course, may need to absorb a great deal of "book knowledge" in order to develop a solid background for their skills. There are other overlaps, as well: People with great musical ability, for instance, also tend to be skilled at mathematics, perhaps because of brain-cell interactions that are

common to both processes. And in order to make use of any talent, art-smart people must have good body control as well.

The people we're calling *body smart* have a lot of that kind of body control. Most of them start out with bodies that are well put together for some kind of athletics—they may have inherited good muscular development for a sport like football, or loose and limber joints for gymnastic-style athletics. Or they may be people whose hands are naturally well coordinated for performing intricate tasks.   12

But although the physical basis for their talent may come from their genes and from especially sensitive brain centers for motor control, to make use of their "natural" skills they must be able to observe accurately—to figure out how a move is made or an object is constructed—and they must think about how to do it themselves. This thinking involves a complex use of symbols that enables the brain to "tell" another part of itself what to do. In other situations, such as school, a body-smart person is probably best able to learn through some physical technique: In studying for an exam, for instance, he or she will retain information by saying it out loud, acting out the facts, or counting them off with finger taps. Although athletes or the manually talented are often teased as being "dumb" in schoolwork, that is not necessarily an accurate picture. To be good in using physical talents, a person must put in a lot of practice, be able to concentrate intently, and be stubbornly persistent in achieving a goal. And those qualities of will and self-control can also be put to good use in more "intellectual" achievements.   13

Persistence is also an important quality of *street-smart* people. They are the ones who are able to see difficulties as challenges, to turn almost any situation to advantage for themselves. As young people, they are the ones who are able to make the most money doing odd jobs, or who can get free tickets to a concert that others believe is completely sold out. As adults, they are the business tycoons, for instance, or the personalities who shoot to stardom no matter how much or little talent they have. A street-smart student may do well in the school subjects that he or she knows count for the most and will all but ignore the rest. When taking exams, street-smart people are likely to get better grades than their knowledge merits because they can "psych out" the test, and because, when facing a problem or question they can't answer, they are skilled at putting on the paper something that looks good.   14

To be street smart in these ways—to be able to achieve highly individualistic goals and to be able to get around obstacles that totally stump others—a person must draw upon a wide scope of mental powers. It takes excellent problem-solving ability, creative thought, good   15 planning and goal setting, accurate perception, persistent effort, skill with language, quick thinking, and a strong sense of intuition.

Intuition plays a major role in *people smarts* as well. This kind of intelligence allows a person to sense what others are thinking, feeling, wanting, and planning. Although we might tend to put this sort of skill down as basic "instinct," it actually relies on higher activities of the brain. People smarts rely on very accurate and quick perceptions of clues and relationships that escape the notice of many, and they include the ability to analyze the information taken in. A people-smart student can do well in school simply by dealing with individual teachers in the most productive way: Some can be charmed, some respond well to special requests for help, some reward hard work no matter what the results, and so forth. The people-smart student figures out easily what is the best approach to take. People with these talents also achieve well in other activities, of course—they become the leaders in clubs, and organizations, and they are able to win important individuals, like potential employers, over to their side. They would probably be typed as right-brained people, like artists, but their skill with language, both spoken and unspoken, is one that draws heavily on the left side.   16

Have you been able to compare these types with people you know in your class, family, or neighborhood? Of course, no individual is actually a type: People with any one of the kind of smarts that we've described also have some of the others. . . .   17

THE CRITICAL READER

Central Idea

1. According to Gilbert, what are the many ways of being smart?

2. Who do you think is Gilbert's audience? What in the excerpt helps you determine the audience?

Evidence

3. List the examples Gilbert uses to explain each type of "smarts."

4. How do you think this evidence supports Gilbert's central idea that there are many kinds of intelligence and that each of us is "smart" in one or more ways?

Implications

5. An *inference* is an educated guess based on your experience and on the knowledge that is available to you. Based on Gilbert's statement "Anyone can learn or develop skills in any or all of the categories," what inference can you make about a person who says, "I can't learn math"?

6. After reading the excerpt, what inferences can you make about intelligence tests and their ability to determine how "smart" a person is?

Word Choice

7. Instead of using the psychological terms *convergent, divergent, assimilating,* and *accommodating,* Gilbert makes up her own terms for the categories of intelligence she describes. Why do you think she does this? What do her word choices tell you about her audience and purpose?

EXERCISE 3.1

If you enjoyed reading this essay, you may be interested in learning about other theories of human intelligence. Using a search engine such as Yahoo!, Lycos, or HotBot, to name a few, do an online search. These key words and phrases may help: *intelligence, types of intelligence, intelligence theories, Howard Gardner, multiple intelligences.* Gardner's theory, for example, describes seven types of intelligence. Find out what you can about his theory and determine which of Gardner's types of intelligence are similar to Gilbert's categories. Then share your results with the rest of the class. After your discussion, save the information you have gathered because you may be able to use it in a future writing assignment either for your writing class or for another class.

MAIN IDEA: THE FIRST KEY

The main idea of a paragraph is what the whole paragraph is about. A paragraph has just one main idea. Often, the main idea is stated in a *topic sentence.* The topic sentence of a paragraph has two characteristics:

1. *Topic:* The topic sentence tells you who or what the paragraph is about.

2. *Focus:* The topic sentence tells you what the writer thinks about the topic or what aspect of the topic he or she will discuss.

In addition to having a topic and a focus, a good topic sentence is neither too narrow nor too broad. It is broad enough to tell your readers what the whole paragraph is about, but it is narrow enough to focus on a single idea that you can explain. Read the next three examples.

EXAMPLE 1: Everyone recognizes that crime is a problem.

This statement is too broad to be a topic sentence because it lacks a *focus.* You cannot tell what aspect of crime the writer will discuss or why he or she thinks it is a problem.

EXAMPLE 2: My parents' home was burglarized two months ago.

This statement is too narrow to be a topic sentence because it simply states a fact that need not be further explained.

EXAMPLE 3: My subdivision's neighborhood watch program has shown us how to discourage robbers.

This statement is neither too broad nor too narrow. It would make a good topic sentence because the topic, *neighborhood watch program,* has a focus: *how to discourage robbers.*

Suppose you choose *drinking* as your topic. As you brainstorm the topic, you recall spending spring break at the beach along with hundreds of other college students who had flocked there in search of fun and relaxation. Looking back, you begin to think that a number of drinking establishments promoted activities and engaged in advertising tactics designed to appeal to young people. Drawn to these places by their party atmosphere and encouraged to drink more than they should, many students overindulged in alcoholic beverages. For some, spring break ended in tragedy. Although you see nothing wrong with students having a good time, you do see something wrong with adults who exploit them. Your thinking leads you to write this topic sentence:

Advertising tactics that make drinking seem safe, fun, and cheap take advantage of students on spring break.

In this topic sentence, the topic is *advertising tactics that make drinking seem safe, fun, and cheap* and the focus is that they *take advantage of students on spring break.* The sentence is neither too broad nor too narrow because it focuses on a single idea that you can explain with specific examples that describe the advertising tactics. As you begin to make notes, you think of three examples to use.

1. Bars that welcome spring breakers and provide a party atmosphere seem like safe places to have a few drinks.

2. Bars that sponsor wet t-shirt and bikini contests attract students who will order drinks while enjoying these events.

3. Bars that advertise two-for-one specials and free drinks for women attract students seeking lots to drink for little cash.

The topic can be developed more fully by adding details to explain each example. To explain the first example, you could add that inexperienced students who may have avoided drinking in bars in the past might be enticed to join in the fun. To explain the second example, you could point out that students attracted to contests are likely to stay for the outcome and drink more as a result. To explain the third example, you could suggest that two-for-one specials and other "free" offers may have a hidden cost, especially if the bar has a two-drink-minimum policy. A good topic sentence will give your topic the focus it needs to help you think of examples or other types of evidence to support it.

EXERCISE 3.2   Read each of the topic sentences below. Underline the topic and bracket the focus. Be prepared to explain your answer.

1. Fast-food junkies can break the habit by following three simple steps.

2. Those who are against the building of a new city hall can think of better ways to spend the money it will cost.

3. The macaw has a number of features that make it a desirable pet.

4. Cereal commercials are aimed at two main groups: children and nutrition-conscious adults.

5. The annual meeting of the EAA (Experimental Aircraft Association) in Oshkosh, Wisconsin, provides activities that the whole family can enjoy.

EXERCISE 3.3   Choose three topics from the list below, limit the topic, and write a topic sentence for each one. Make sure your sentences have a topic and focus. Make sure each sentence is neither too narrow nor too broad. The first one is done as an example.

1. cellular phones

   a. limited topic: cellular phone etiquette

   b. topic sentence: When using your cell phone in public, several rules of good behavior apply.

2. clothing styles

3. apartment living

4. low-calorie foods

5. athletes' salaries

6. required courses

7. types of music

Though some of the paragraphs you read have topic sentences, in others the main idea is *implied,* which means that there is no topic sentence. Instead, you have to infer, or guess, the main idea by reading the whole paragraph, paying attention to the details, and asking yourself such questions as "What is this whole paragraph about?" and "What one idea do all the details explain?" In the next paragraph, the main idea is implied.

The turquoise water blends into the pale aqua sky at the horizon. From my seat at the table on the private porch outside my resort hotel room I can see that it is going to be a hot, humid day just like the last three. I am beginning to like the luxury of having my breakfast brought to me, coffee poured from a silver teapot, an array of fresh tropical fruit from which to choose. A large blackbird shares my breakfast, pecking at the muffin I have tossed on the floor for his culinary pleasure. What will I do today? Take a swim in the Caribbean sea? Visit a pineapple plantation? Check out the sidewalk market in Montego Bay for bargains? Whatever I do, I will not think of two days from now when I will be back at my desk day-dreaming about these quiet moments, wondering when they will come again.

Though the paragraph has no topic sentence, the last sentence suggests that the writer is on vacation, and the rest of the details describe what a morning at the hotel is like. A topic sentence for the paragraph might be: "Mornings are always the same on my Caribbean island vacation."

EXERCISE 3.4

Apply what you have learned about topic sentences and implied main ideas by doing this exercise with group members. First, review the list of group roles and responsibilities explained in Figure 1.6, page 28. Next, read and discuss the following paragraph. Then discuss and answer the questions. When you are finished, evaluate your group's performance.

> The first thing to go wrong was that all the parking spaces were taken, so I had to park on the grass and hope that I would not get a ticket. When I got to the admissions office, there was already a line clear out the door. By the time it was my turn to register, all of the sections for one of the courses I needed were filled, and I had to go back to my counselor and make out a whole new schedule. Although I did register for all my courses and pay my fees, I missed lunch. The next thing to go wrong was that the bookstore had sold out of one of the textbooks I needed. As I was leaving, I wondered what else could possibly happen. Then I saw a campus cop standing beside my car and writing out a ticket.

1. Who is the "I" in the paragraph, and how can you tell?
2. What is the person doing, and what details tell you so?
3. How does the person feel about what he or she is doing?
4. What is the whole paragraph about? What one situation do all the details explain?
5. What is the implied main idea?
6. Using the information you have gathered from answering questions 1–5, write a sentence that you think expresses the main idea of the paragraph and that has a topic and focus.

GROUP EVALUATION
What did each person contribute to the group's activity? Was your group's performance successful? Why or why not? What additional questions do you have about purpose and audience?

As a beginning writer, you may find topic sentences very helpful. A good topic sentence will control your selection of details because every detail will have to explain or relate in some way to the topic sentence. As you gain experience, you may want to experiment with writing paragraphs that have implied main ideas. You can add variety to the paragraphs within an essay by stating some main ideas and implying others.

SUPPORT: THE SECOND KEY

To support a main idea means to explain or prove it with evidence. Evidence may include *facts, reasons,* and *examples.* When you write a paragraph, you are explaining your opinions about a topic. Facts, reasons, and examples give your opinions support so that your readers will understand why you think the way you do.

Facts

A fact is anything that can be proven right or wrong through research, direct observation, or questioning. Facts include statistics and other numerical data; information gathered through the senses of sight, hearing, smell, taste and touch; and information collected from books, other printed sources, or from the testimony of experts. A fact is also anything we have observed so often that we commonly accept it as true, such as the laws of gravity or the process of photosynthesis. An opinion is more convincing if you support it with facts. Following are three topic sentences that state opinions with facts that support them:

Topic Sentences	Facts
Public officials have done a poor job of solving our city's traffic problems.	The city's main highway is operating at four times its intended capacity. Rush "hour" lasts from 6:45 A.M. to 8:30 A.M. and from 4:45 P.M. to 6:30 P.M. Traffic accidents, according to the highway patrol, have more than doubled in the past five years.
Julia Roberts is a versatile actress.	In *Pretty Woman* she plays a likeable prostitute.

	In *The Pelican Brief* she plays a serious law student.
	In *Notting Hill* she plays a famous actress who falls in love with an ordinary man.
	In *Erin Brockovich,* a movie based on a true story, she plays an outspoken legal assistant who uncovers the illegal dumping of hazardous chemicals.
This winter we lived through a destructive storm.	Heavy snow and ice caused numerous traffic accidents.
	Sixty-mile-an-hour winds damaged houses and property.
	Tides of twelve feet caused flooding in some areas.
	Several towns had to be evacuated.

In the first example, facts about the highway's operating capacity, rush hour times, and accident rate support the main idea. In the second example, facts about the types of characters Roberts has played in four of her movies support the main idea. In the third example, facts about the storm's destructiveness support the main idea. The facts listed in these three examples provide readers with a basis for evaluating the accuracy of the opinions stated in the topic sentences.

EXERCISE 3.5   Choose one of the topic sentences you wrote for Exercise 3.3 and list the facts you could use to support it.

Reasons

Reasons help explain why something happens or why something is the way it is. Words and phrases such as *because, since, the causes are,* and *the purpose is* may help readers identify statements in your writing that contain reasons. Because there may be many different reasons to explain just about everything, you need to carefully consider your reasons for thinking the way you do about your topic. You also need to be aware of the reasons others may have for thinking differently. Following are three topic sentences with reasons that support them:

Topic Sentences	Reasons
Though there are several colleges I could have attended, I chose Valencia Community College.	The campus is only three miles from my house. I can save money by living at home. The tuition is affordable. The atmosphere at Valencia is friendly and personal. The programs and services available are helping me plan my future.
To overcome math failure, you must first understand why so many students fail.	Math anxiety afflicts many students who have a "fear of failure." A fear of success can also affect student performance in math. Equating math grades with self-esteem can lead to negative feelings that direct attention away from the task. Procrastination is the reason many math students get behind and never catch up.
So far, our community has remained safe even though we live near a high-crime area.	One reason is that the city has installed quartz halogen bulbs in the street lights to make it harder for criminals to hide. Police make regular neighborhood patrols. Also, we have a successful neighborhood watch program. Our school board approved a crime-prevention program for grades K–12 that has been in effect for several years.

In the first example, Valencia's affordability, atmosphere, programs, and services are the reasons that explain why the writer chose that college. In the second example, the writer cites math anxiety, fear of success, equating grades with self-esteem, and procrastination as the reasons for math failure. In the third example, the community's lighting, police patrols, neighborhood watch program, and crime-prevention program are the reasons that support the main idea. The reasons listed in these examples help readers understand the logic behind the opinions stated in the topic sentences.

EXERCISE 3.6   Make a list of your reasons for attending the college you have chosen. Then, write a topic sentence for a paragraph on your reasons for attending that college.

Examples

An example is an illustration that clarifies a general statement such as a topic sentence. Examples usually appeal to one or more of the five senses of sight, sound, taste, touch, and smell; and they help create clear and vivid pictures in your readers' minds. Examples are one more kind of evidence you can use to support your main idea and explain your opinions. You can use phrases such as *for example* and *to illustrate* to signal your readers that an example follows. An effective use of examples can create clear and vivid images for readers. Following are three topic sentences with examples that support them:

Topic Sentences	Examples
My car is unreliable.	Sometimes it will not start. The gas gauge gives incorrect readings. The oil light comes on even though I have just added oil. The tires will not stay balanced. This morning the brakes failed. For the last year it has been in the shop at least once a month.
My grandmother's house is a collection of aromas, odors, and fragrances.	The aroma of chocolate chip cookies or a turkey baking in the oven fills the house. The fragrances of roses and

gardenias come in through the windows when there is a breeze. The clean smells of wax, furniture polish, and freshly washed linens pervade the rooms.

On clear, cool days when the wind is in the right direction, the unpleasant odors from a paper mill and a charcoal plant mingle with the fragrances in the house.

My job as a volunteer firefighter is a rewarding experience.

I have earned the respect of my male coworkers by proving that I am willing to work as hard as they do.

I know I am making an important contribution to my community because of the commendations our department has received.

I have felt the gratitude of the people I have helped to safety during a fire.

I have developed new confidence in myself because I am doing a job that in the past women were not supposed to be able to do.

In the first example, the problems the writer is having with the car's gauge, oil light, tires, brakes, and trips to the shop are examples that support the main idea. In the second example, the writer supports the main idea with examples of food aromas, flower fragrances, cleaning smells, and outside odors that fill his grandmother's house. In the third example, the writer provides examples of her job's rewards such as the respect of coworkers and the gratitude of those she has helped. The lists of examples that support each of the topic sentences appeal to readers' senses and feelings and may help them to identify with the situations the writers describe.

EXERCISE 3.7   List at least three specific examples you could use to support each one of the three topic sentences below. Then write your own topic sentence on a topic of your choice and three or more examples to support it.

1. My mornings are usually very hectic.

2. When looking for a part-time job, a person should consider several requirements.

3. My apartment is in a bad state of repair.

4. Add your sentence and examples.

Levels of Development

Whether you support a topic sentence with facts, reasons, examples, or some of each, be specific. You can learn to do this by using a three-level development plan that moves from (1) the general statement (topic sentence) to (2) the primary evidence (major details) to (3) the secondary evidence (minor details). For example:

Topic sentence:	**Level 1** My health club has become more of a social gathering place than a fitness center.
First major detail that supports the general statement:	**Level 2** For one thing, people come here to see and be seen.
Minor detail that supports the first major detail:	**Level 3** The men and women wear skimpy outfits that show off their bodies.
Minor detail that supports the first major detail:	**Level 3** The women wear makeup, and their hair is attractively styled as if they were going on dates.
Minor detail that supports the first major detail:	**Level 3** The men seek to impress the women by trying to outdo each other lifting weights.

Second major detail that supports the general statement:	**Level 2** Also, some people use the health club as a meeting place.
Minor detail that supports the second major detail:	**Level 3** Men and women join because they have heard it is a safe place to meet people.
Minor detail that supports the second major detail:	**Level 3** They can observe each other's behavior and get to know each other before going out.

The major details illustrate two ways in which the health club has become a social gathering place. People come there to see and be seen and to meet each other. The minor details provide specific examples of what people *do* to see and be seen, and *how* they use the club as a meeting place.

EXERCISE 3.8   Read the following paragraph, then complete the outline that follows it. The outline, which is partially filled in for you, illustrates the paragraph's three levels of development from main idea through major details to minor details and to the conclusion, which contains a restatement of the main idea.

Getting a college education has not been easy for me. One thing that makes it difficult is that I am a working mother of two children who are still in school. I have to get up early to make their breakfast and see them off. Also, I try to arrange my schedule to be at home when they arrive. Helping them with their homework is important to me but leaves me less time to do my own studying. My job is another thing that makes it hard for me to get an education. I work as a receptionist in a doctor's office in the mornings from 8:00 until 11:30. If a class I need is scheduled at these times, then I have to postpone taking it until it is offered at a more convenient time. Because of my job, it will probably take me a long time to get my degree. Studying adds to these difficulties. It has been a while since I attended school, and my skills are a little rusty. Though getting a college education is difficult, the struggle is worth it not only for me but for the good example I am setting for my children.

Level 1

Topic sentence: Getting a college education has not been easy for me.

    Level 2

    I. One thing . . . _____

        Level 3

        A. _____

        B. _____

        C. _____

        D. _____

    Level 2

    II. _____

        Level 3

        A. I work as a receptionist from 8:30 A.M. to 11:30 A.M.

        B. I have to postpone taking classes offered at these times.

        C. It will take a long time to get my degree.

    Level 2

    III. Studying adds to these difficulties.

        Level 3

        A. _____

        B. _____

Level 1

Concluding sentence: Though getting a college education is difficult, the struggle is worth it not only for me but for the good example I am setting for my children.

ORGANIZATION: THE THIRD KEY

To write a good paragraph not only do you need a main idea and evidence to support it, but you need to arrange your supporting evidence, or details, in the best way possible to get your meaning across. A well-organized paragraph has unity and coherence.

Unity

Unity means *oneness* or *wholeness*. Animal rights activists are *united* in their efforts to protect animals from being exploited. Environmental activists are *united* by their common goal to save the environment. Members of professional, political, and social organizations are *united* by shared beliefs, values, and goals. The sentences of a paragraph are *united* when they all work together to make and support a main idea, and paragraphs within an essay are *united* when they all work together to support a thesis or central idea. Your paragraphs will have *unity* if you state your main idea clearly and stay on topic. When one or more sentences or details within a paragraph do not support the main idea, then unity is interrupted, and the paragraph strays from its topic. The next two paragraphs each contain a sentence that keeps them from being unified. Find the off-topic sentences before reading the explanation that follows the paragraphs.

PARAGRAPH 1

Although many people many not realize it, living on lakefront property in Florida has some disadvantages. For one thing, keeping the lakefront clear of weeds is a full-time job. Also, the noise from jet skis and power-boats is constant on warm days. Another disadvantage is the trash that boaters and fishers throw in the lake and that washes up on shore. Where there is a lake there is dampness. If your house is made of wood, you will have to fight mildew, wood spiders as big as the palm of your hand, termites, and other insects. However, lake-dwelling residents can enjoy boating, fishing, and swimming during most of the year. Insects are not the only creatures known to plague those living on a lakefront. Water moccasins and alligators often come ashore and are a danger to children and pets. One of the biggest disadvantages to living on a lake is the high cost of owning a home. Lakefront residents pay much more in taxes and upkeep on their properties than do other residents.

PARAGRAPH 2

If you would like to get fit and are thinking about joining a health club or gym, you should also consider the advantages of a membership in a hospital wellness center. Unlike some health clubs or gyms, wellness centers hire only trained staff members who have degrees or other certification in such fields as nutrition and fitness. These people are qualified to assess your level of fitness and design a safe program for you that is based on the results of a blood test, a stress test, and your doctor's recommendation. In fact, you cannot even join a wellness center without your doctor's approval. Some health clubs serve as meeting places for young singles. Another advantage of wellness centers over health clubs and gyms is that they offer services other than fitness training, such as nutritional counseling, stress reduction seminars, and weight-loss classes. At a health club or gym you may be left on your own after your first visit, but at a wellness center, someone monitors your progress and continually updates your program as your fitness level increases. Surprisingly, a wellness center membership may cost you a lot less than a membership in a health club or gym, and that is another advantage.

In the first paragraph, the sentence "However, lake-dwelling residents can enjoy boating, fishing, and swimming during most of the year" is off-topic because the paragraph is about the disadvantages of living on a lakefront, not the advantages. In the second paragraph, the unity is disrupted by the sentence "Some health clubs serve as meeting places for young singles." This paragraph is a comparison of wellness centers and health clubs or gyms on the basis of their fitness advantages, not on their social advantages.

Following this very simple rule will help you achieve unity in your paragraphs: *State your main idea clearly and stay on topic.*

EXERCISE 3.9   Read the following paragraphs and evaluate them for unity. If you find any sentences that are off-topic, cross them out. Be able to explain your results.

1. Count Dracula is a character who continues to appeal to filmgoers. Many actors have played him, each one adding something different to the role. In *Nosferatu,* a silent film of the 1920s, Max Shreck plays Dracula as a supernatural being having a ratlike appearance. Frankenstein is another character who appeals to filmgoers. In 1931, Bela Lugosi portrayed Dracula as an attractive, cultured man whose genteel manner barely concealed his violence. Christopher Lee's performances in the 1950s emphasized Dracula's sex appeal. George Hamilton was the first to make us laugh at Dracula in *Love at First Bite,* a cult favorite. The 1970s gave us an updated version of *Nosferatu* in which Klaus Kinski combines aspects of the Shreck and Lugosi roles. In the 1980s Frank Langella showed us a sensitive Drac-

ula who falls in love with a "liberated" woman. Lon Chaney plays the Wolfman as an ordinary fellow fallen on bad times. *Interview with the Vampire* in the 1990s and *Shadow of the Vampire* in 2001 prove that every decade recreates the old and popular vampire legend.

2. American politics has always been a two-party system, but change seemed possible with the campaign of Ross Perot in the 1992 presidential election. Perot is a Texas billionaire who ran for president as the nominee of the Independent party, a third party that has never aroused much interest or support. During the week of the Democratic National Convention, Perot announced that he would not run. Barbara Jordan and Jesse Jackson, both Clinton supporters, addressed the convention. But Perot rejoined the campaign, debated the other two candidates, then lost the election to Bill Clinton. The successful campaign of an Independent Party candidate proved, however, that the Republicans and Democrats were losing some of their influence over the American voter.

3. Though being a dental hygienist may not be everyone's idea of the perfect job, Kelly would not want to do anything else. For a brief time, she had thought she wanted to be a court reporter. One reason she likes her job is that she can schedule her hours so that she works four days a week and is off in the afternoons. This allows her to be at home when her children arrive from school. Since she does not work on Fridays, she has a three-day weekend. Another reason Kelly likes her job is that the work is challenging and pleasant. For example, cleaning children's teeth is a challenge because Kelly has to find ways to distract the children so that they will let her do what she needs to do without making a fuss. Kelly's work is pleasant because just about everyone likes the way his or her mouth feels after a cleaning, and they compliment Kelly on what a good job she does. But Kelly's best reason of all for liking her job is that she gets to be with her family while she is at work. After all, the dentist Kelly works for is her dad, and her sister is his receptionist.

EXERCISE 3.10   Using the topic sentence and examples you wrote for Exercise 3.7, now write a unified paragraph. To make sure you have enough major and minor details to support your topic sentence, you may have to add more examples to the original list you made.

Coherence

Cohere means *to stick together.* A paragraph has **coherence** when it is so well organized that the evidence seems to flow smoothly and to "stick together." To give your paragraphs coherence, use a pattern, or organizing principle, that is appropriate for your topic. Though there are many ways to organize the details within a paragraph, these three basic patterns are a good beginning: *time order, emphatic order,* and *spatial order.*

Time Order

Another name for time order is *chronological order,* and it is appropriate for any subject that can be explained with details that follow a time sequence. Suppose you are reading a textbook chapter on human reproduction that explains what happens during pregnancy. After making some notes, you decide to write a paragraph in which you summarize what you have read. Since pregnancy occurs over a nine-month period, you arrange your details into three 3-month periods. Your informal outline might look like this:

1. The first three months

    a. Little increase in size.

    b. Embryo becomes a fetus.

2. The next three months

    a. Fetus becomes larger.

    b. Heartbeat and movement occur.

3. The last three months

    a. Fetus continues to grow.

    b. Fetal movements increase.

    c. Body prepares itself for birth.

When using time order, help your readers follow your ideas by beginning some of your sentences with signal words and phrases that serve as *time markers,* such as *first, next, third,* and *finally;* times of day, such as *at 10:30;* or phrases that indicate time of day, such as *this morning.* Time order signals help readers to understand when you have finished explaining one step or stage and have moved on to another. In the following excerpt from N. Scott Momaday's *The Names, A Memoir*, signal words and phrases that serve as time markers are underlined for you.

Navajo Dog

<u>Dusk</u> was falling <u>at five o'clock</u>, <u>when the dancing came to an end</u>, and <u>on the way home</u> alone I bought a Navajo dog. I bargained for a while with the thin, wary man whose dog it was, and we settled on a price of five dollars. It was a yellow, honest-to-goodness, great-hearted dog, and the man gave me a bit of rope with which to pull it home. The dog was not large, but neither was it small. It was one of those unremarkable creatures that one sees in every corner of the world. If there were only thirty-nine dogs in Creation, this one would be the fourth, or the thirteenth, or the twenty-first, the archetype, the common denominator of all its kind. It was full of resistance, and yet it was ready to return in full measure my deep, abiding love. I could see that. It needed only, I reasoned, to make a small adjustment in its style of life, to shift the focus of its vitality from one frame of reference to another, in order to be perfectly at home with me. Even as it was nearly strangled <u>on the way</u>, it wagged its bushy tail happily all the while. <u>That night</u> I tied the dog up in the garage, where there was a warm, clean pallet, wholesome food, and fresh water, and I bolted the door. And <u>the next morning</u> the dog was gone, as in my heart of hearts I knew it would be, I believe. I had read such a future in its eyes. It had gnawed the rope in two and squeezed through a vent in the door, an opening much too small for it, as I had thought. But, sure enough, where there is a will there is a way, and the Navajo dog was possessed of one indomitable will. I was crushed at the time, but strangely reconciled, too, as if I had perceived some truth beyond billboards. The dog had done what it had to do, had behaved exactly as it must, had been true to itself and to the sun and moon. It knew its place in the order of things, and its place was away out there in the tracks of a wagon, going home. In the mind's eye I could see it <u>at that very moment</u>, miles away, plodding in the familiar shadows, its tail drooping a little after the harrowing night, but wagging, in its dog's mind contemplating the wonderful ways of mankind.

The story of the Navajo dog develops in a time sequence from late afternoon, through that night, to the following day.

Emphatic Order

Sometimes it makes sense to arrange details in their order of importance, especially if one of your details is clearly more important than another, if you want to save the best of your suggestions for last, or if you want to emphasize the conclusion. Suppose you have learned from experience that cramming for a test does not work, and you write a paragraph that explains an effective way to study for an exam. You may think that the most important thing students can do to ensure success is to review periodically. You might save this suggestion for last and conclude with tips on how to make periodic review easier. Use *words of emphasis* to signal your readers when another important idea is coming or to show a progression of ideas from least important to most important. Words and phrases such as *equally important, the most important of all, major,* and *minor,* and *of primary concern* are helpful signals for readers and may improve the coherence of your paragraphs. In the following paragraph, words of emphasis are underlined.

> The power of television news to capture the public's attention became apparent in the 1960s. In 1963, the nation was gripped by horror and grief at the assassination of President Kennedy; the event and its aftermath kept the nation riveted to television screens for days. Other major events, though reported in newspapers and magazines as well, were likewise widely and instantaneously experienced on television. Several incidents occurred in 1968 alone: the first expedition to set foot on the moon, the assassination of Senator Robert F. Kennedy, the riots at the Democratic National Convention, and North Vietnam's Tet offensive—television coverage of which brought into American homes bloody images from a war that previously had seemed quite remote.
>
> Each of these events, seen over several days by a huge section of the American public, became part of a shared set of experiences, all seen through the eye of television. Since then, television has become the primary source of news information for a large section of the American public, with newspapers, magazines, and radio assuming supplemental roles. . . .

The excerpt explains how television became the primary, or most important, source of news information because of a progression of several televised major events that began with the assassination of President Kennedy in 1963.

Spatial Order

If you want to describe a place or recreate a scene in which the placement of objects is important, you need to give your readers a sense of being there. Imagine yourself in the place you want them to be. Tell readers what would be in front of them, behind them, on either side of them, directly overhead, and beneath their feet if they were to stand in the same spot as you. When you use spatial order, words or phrases such as *in front, behind, near, north,* or *south* can signal a reader where to "look" in his or her mind's eye. The following excerpt is from the first paragraph of "Home," a chapter in *Lake Wobegon Days* by Garrison Keillor. Spatial details provide a description of Lake Wobegon, a Minnesota town. The order of details creates a view of the town that you would see by looking or walking in the direction the writer suggests. Spatial details and the words that signal their order are underlined.

> The town of Lake Wobegon, Minnesota, lies on the shore against Adams Hill looking east across the blue-green water to the dark woods. From the south, the highway aims for the lake, bends left by the magnificent concrete Grecian grain silos, and eases over a leg of the hill past the SLOW CHILDREN sign, bringing the traveler in on Main Street toward the town's one traffic light, which is almost always green. A few surviving elms shade the street. Along the ragged dirt path between the asphalt and the grass, a child slowly walks to Ralph's Grocery, kicking an asphalt chunk ahead of him. It is a chunk that after four blocks he is now mesmerized by, to which he is completely dedicated. At Bunsen Motors, the sidewalk begins. A breeze off the lake brings a sweet air of mud and rotting wood, a slight fishy smell, and picks up the sweetness of old grease, a sharp whiff of gasoline, fresh tires, spring dust, and, from across the street, the faint essence of tuna hot-dish at the Chatterbox Cafe. . . .

The spatial details in this paragraph help you to visualize the imaginary town of Lake Wobegon. The order of details leads you on a visual trip through the town by following the highway south to Main Street, then along Main Street where your eyes travel down the dirt path beside the street and to the sidewalk. You *see* the town through Ralph's grocery, Bunsen Motors, and the Chatterbox Cafe. Sensory details such as the breeze and smells of mud, rotting wood, fish, grease, gasoline, tires, and spring dust complete the picture. The order of spatial details gives them coherence. They draw you into Keillor's image of Lake

FIGURE 3.1

Choosing Coherence Patterns. The Topic is "My Typical Day at Work."

MAIN IDEA	TYPE OF SUPPORT	COHERENCE PATTERN
My typical work day consists of the things I do before lunch and after lunch.	Use details that explain what the duties are and *when* you do them	Time order
A typical work day for me is filled with several important tasks.	Use details that explain what the tasks are and their order of *importance*	Emphatic order
My typical work day is easy because of the way my office is arranged.	Use details that explain *where* everything is	Spatial order

Wobegon just as the arrangement of colors, shapes, and figures in a painting draws you into the picture.

Coherence comes with practice. You may have to revise a paragraph several times to make the ideas flow smoothly and to make one sentence lead logically to the next. In choosing patterns for your paragraphs, let your guide be the main idea and the type of support you have chosen to explain it. Figure 3.1 above illustrates three choices for main idea, type of support, and coherence pattern for the topic "my typical day at work."

EXERCISE 3.11   Read the following three paragraphs and decide whether the details are organized according to *time order, emphatic order,* or *spatial order.* Underline words or phrases that help you decide. Then write your answer beside each paragraph.

_____ 1. When interviewing for a job it is important to look your best. Wear a conservative outfit; stick to neutral colors, and avoid fashion fads. Let the interviewer run the show. Answer questions clearly and completely; stick to the point and do not ramble. Not only should you dress carefully and follow the interviewer's lead, but you should refrain from doing anything that may be out of place. Do not smoke even if the interviewer offers you a cigarette. Let your actions show that you know the difference between a social situation and a business situation. Most importantly, be yourself. You have heard this many times, and it is still good advice. The interviewer wants to know who you are, not who you *think* you are.

_____ 2. It is easy to get a part-time job at my college. Whether you would like to work as an office assistant or a tutor, it is important to follow these steps: First you have to qualify. Financial aid is not available to everyone. To find out whether you qualify, go to the financial aid office and fill out the form. Next you will be given a list of job openings. Before accepting the first one on the list, you will need to find out what each job pays, whether it conflicts with your schedule, and what the duties are. Once you have selected the right job for you, then you are ready to go to work. The whole process, from application to first day on the job, may take several days. Following the steps in the right order may save you a lot of time.

_____ 3. The "new" theater at the Peabody Arts Center is not new. It is a reconstructed opera house brought over from Europe and assembled piece by piece. Once you get past the modern lobby and walk into the theater itself, it is like stepping into another world. If you are sitting about halfway down the aisle in the center of your row, you can look directly overhead and see an immense crystal chandelier suspended above you. In front of you are rows of red plush-covered seats, then the orchestra pit, then the stage flanked on either side by heavy red velvet curtains. When they are closed, you can see the initials PAC. The intertwined letters measure several feet from bottom to top; and they are embroidered in gold and silver thread. To the left, right, and in back of you are more rows of seats. Follow the rows to the end in each direction; then let your gaze travel up the walls, which are decorated with ornate wallpaper. Carved columns support balcony areas on three levels. No matter where you look, the view is sumptuous, reflecting the elegance of another age.

FIGURE 3.2

Signal Words That Identify a Coherence Pattern

COHERENCE PATTERN	SIGNAL WORDS TO USE
Time order	*first, second, third, etc., before, after, next, then, finally,* times (10:30), dates (year, month, day of the week) *morning, afternoon, evening*
Emphatic order	*important, most important, significant, primary, major, minor, unimportant, insignificant, of major concern*
Spatial order	*in front, behind, near, far, above, below, left, right, north, south, east, west, low, high, up, down, over, under, sideways, close, distant*

As you have seen, signal words at the beginnings of some sentences and elsewhere in your paragraph can help your readers follow the coherence pattern you have chosen. Figure 3.2 summarizes the signal words that indicate time order, emphatic order, and spatial order.

EXERCISE 3.12   Revise the paragraph you wrote for Exercise 3.10 for coherence. Add signal words to help readers follow your order.

To help you write fully developed, well-organized paragraphs, remember these three keys:

Main idea	State your main idea in a topic sentence.
Support	Support your main idea with plenty of specific details.
Organization	Organize your evidence so that the details are unified and coherent.

TOPICS FOR WRITING

Choose one of the topics that follow and write a paragraph. Evaluate your paragraph for the three keys: main idea, support, organization.

1. Using time order, write a paragraph on one of the topics below:

    a. A typical day at college or at work.

    b. An ideal weekend or vacation.

    c. An event that changed history.

    d. Make up your own topic.

2. Using emphatic order, write a paragraph on one of the topics below:

    a. Explain why you voted for a certain candidate. Emphasize your most important reason.

    b. Explain why a certain behavior such as smoking, binge drinking, or overeating is harmful. Emphasize your most important reason.

    c. Explain why a certain behavior such as exercising, improving study skills, or managing time is beneficial. Emphasize your most important reason.

    d. Make up your own topic. Explain your reasons and emphasize the most important one.

3. Using spatial order, write a paragraph on one of the topics below:

    a. Describe your work place.

    b. Describe a city park and what people do there.

    c. Describe the objects on a shelf, desktop, or cabinet.

    d. Make up your own topic.

Checklist for Revision

As you revise and edit your paragraphs, check for the following:

1. Have you made the topic and focus clear in your topic sentence?

2. Have you supported your topic sentence with facts, reasons, or examples?

3. Have you organized your details in a clear and meaningful way?

4. Are your details unified; do they all support the topic sentence?

5. Are your sentences error free?

THE CRITICAL THINKER

To examine Sara Gilbert's essay on pages 61–65 in more depth, think about and discuss the following questions. Then choose one of them as a topic for writing.

1. Which one of Gilbert's categories plays the strongest role in the way you think and learn? Use evidence from the essay to explain your answer.

2. Based on your understanding of Gilbert's categories, explain how a certain public figure such as a well-known athlete, entertainer, or politician displays one or more of Gilbert's categories of intelligence.

3. In paragraph 6, Gilbert says "However, the fact that each kind of smarts makes use of the same steps means that anyone can learn or develop skills in any or all of the categories." Explain what you think this statement means. To what "steps" does Gilbert refer? Give one example of something you have learned how to do that required you to use a type of "smarts" that may not be your strongest category. Then explain what the experience taught you.

4. Do you think that Gilbert's categories describe the full range of intelligence? Do you think the categories are limiting? What other categories of intelligence can you add to Gilbert's types?

YOUR DISCOVERY JOURNAL

Linda Pastan has written several books of poetry, including *The Five Stages of Grief*, from which this poem is taken. Read the poem, then write about it in your next journal entry. Put yourself in Pastan's place, and come up with some things that you do every day that could be graded. What grade would you give yourself in these categories? What would friends or family members grade you on, and what grades would they give you?

Marks

My husband gives me an A
for last night's supper,
an incomplete for my ironing,
a B plus in bed.
My son says I am average,
an average mother, but if
I put my mind to it
I could improve.
My daughter believes
in Pass/Fail and tells me
I pass. Wait 'til they learn
I'm dropping out.

Chapter 4

Stating Your Thesis

Your *thesis* is the central idea of your essay. The *thesis statement* is usually one sentence in the introductory part of your essay that states your central idea. A good thesis statement clearly identifies your topic and sets limits that keep your ideas focused on your central idea. Everything you write, especially each main idea or topic sentence of every paragraph, should relate to your thesis. This chapter explains how to write a thesis statement and also suggests strategies for beginning your essay with an effective introduction that sets the stage for your thesis.

AWARENESS CHECK

Before reading the following essay, explore your thoughts about the questions readers ask authors. Think about the questions below, and answer them either on your own or in a group discussion:

1. If you were given the opportunity to meet and talk with a famous author, what questions would you ask?

2. What questions do you think most people would be likely to ask a famous author?

3. Read the title, headnote, and first two paragraphs of the following essay. Based on this preview, what do you think will follow?

Ever Et Raw Meat?
Stephen King

Stephen King is one of the best-selling authors of all time. His books have sold millions of copies worldwide. He is a favorite among readers who enjoy novels and stories whose themes involve the mysterious, the supernatural, or the horrifying. In this essay, which was published in the New York Times Book Review *in 1987, King discusses his responses to the questions readers ask.*

VOCABULARY CHECK

penal (3)	of or relating to punishment
morbid (4)	a preoccupation with unwholesome things
laconic (7)	terse, using few words
enumerate (10)	list or name one by one
grovel (13)	cringe, behave in a submissive manner
toady (13)	flatter, compliment excessively or insincerely
query (22)	to question
impotent (22)	powerless, helpless
cunningly (22)	cleverly, shrewdly
flagellate (24)	to whip or flog
self-abnegation (24)	self-denial
sidles (27)	moves sideways
obligatory (28)	morally or legally bound
modicum (30)	a small or token amount

It seems to me that, in the minds of readers, writers actually exist to serve two purposes, and the more important may not be the writing of books and stories. The primary function of writers, it seems, is to answer readers' questions. These fall into three categories. The third is the one that fascinates me most, but I'll identify the other two first.

THE ONE-OF-A-KIND QUESTIONS

Each day's mail brings a few of these. Often they reflect the writer's field of interest—history, horror, romance, the American West, outer space, big business. The only thing they have in common is their uniqueness. Novelists are frequently asked where they get their ideas (see category No. 2), but writers must wonder where this relentless curiosity, these really strange questions come from.

There was, for instance, the young woman who wrote to me from a penal institution in Minnesota. She informed me she was a kleptomaniac. She further informed me that I was her favorite writer, and she had stolen every one of my books she could got her hands on. "But after I stole *Different Seasons* from the library and read it, I felt moved to send it back," she wrote. "Do you think this means you wrote this one best?" After due consideration, I decided that reform on the part of the reader has nothing to do with artistic merit. I came close to writing back to find out if she had stolen *Misery* yet but decided I ought to just keep my mouth shut.

From Bill V. in North Carolina: "I see you have a beard. Are you morbid of razors?"

From Carol K. in Hawaii: "Will you soon write of pimples or some other facial blemish?"

From Don G., no address (and a blurry postmark): "Why do you keep up this disgusting mother worship when anyone with any sense knows a MAN has no use to his mother once he is weaned?"

From Raymond R. in Mississippi: "Ever et raw meat?" (It's the laconic ones like this that really get me.)

I have been asked if I beat my children and/or my wife. I have been asked to parties in places I have never been and hope never to go. I was once asked to give away the bride at a wedding, and one young woman sent me an ounce of pot, with the attached question. "This is where I get my inspiration—where do you get yours?" Actually, mine usually comes in envelopes—the kind through which you can view your name and address printed by a computer—that arrive at the end of every month.

My favorite question of this type, from Anchorage, asked simply: "How could you write such a why?" Unsigned. If e.e. cummings were still alive, I'd try to find out if he'd moved to the Big North.

THE OLD STANDARDS

These are the questions writers dream of answering when they are 10
collecting rejection slips, and the ones they tire of quickest once they
start to publish. In other words, they are the questions that come up
without fail in every dull interview the writer has ever given or will ever
give. I'll enumerate a few of them:

Where do you get your ideas? (I get mine in Utica.) 11

How do you get an agent? (Sell your soul to the Devil.) 12

Do you have to know somebody to get published? (Yes; in fact, it 13
helps to grovel, toady, and be willing to perform twisted acts of sexual
depravity at a moment's notice, and in public if necessary.)

How do you start a novel? (I usually start by writing the number 1 14
in the upper right-hand corner of a clean sheet of paper.)

How do you write best sellers? (Same way you get an agent.) 15

How do you sell your book to the movies? (Tell them they don't 16
want it.)

What time of day do you write? (It doesn't matter; if I don't keep 17
busy enough, the time inevitably comes.)

Do you ever run out of ideas? (Does a bear defecate in the woods?) 18

Who is your favorite writer? (Anyone who writes stories I would 19
have written had I thought of them first.)

There are others, but they're pretty boring, so let us march on. 20

THE REAL WEIRDIES

Here I am, bopping down the street, on my morning walk, when 21
some guy pulls over in his pickup truck or just happens to walk by and
says, "Hi, Steve! Writing any good books lately?" I have an answer for
this; I've developed it over the years out of pure necessity. I say, "I'm
taking some time off." I say that even if I'm working like mad, thun-
dering down homestretch on a book. The reason *why* I say this is because no other answer seems to fit. Believe me, I know. In the course
of the trial and error that has finally resulted in "I'm taking some time
off," I have discarded about 500 other answers.

Having an answer for "You writing any good books lately?" is a 22
good thing, but I'd be lying if I said it solves the problem of *what the
question means*. It is this inability on my part to make sense of this odd
query, which reminds me of that Zen riddle—"Why is a mouse when it
runs?"—that leaves me feeling mentally shaken and impotent. You
see, it isn't just *one* question; it is a *bundle* of questions, cunningly
wrapped up in one package. It's like that old favorite, "Are you still
beating your wife?"

If I answer in the affirmative, it means I may have written—how 23 many books? two? four?—(all of them good) in the last—how long? Well, how long is "lately?" It could mean I wrote maybe three good books just last week or maybe two *on this very walk up to Bangor International Airport and back!* On the other hand, if I say no, what does *that* mean? I wrote three or four *bad* books in the last "lately" (surely "lately" can be no longer than a month, six weeks at the outside)?

Or here I am, signing books at the Bett's Bookstore or B. Dalton's in   24
the local consumer factory (nicknamed "the mall"). This is something I do twice a year, and it serves much the same purpose as those little bundles of twigs religious people in the Middle Ages used to braid into whips and flagellate themselves with. During the course of this exercise in madness and self-abnegation, at least a dozen people will approach the little coffee table where I sit behind a barrier of books and ask brightly "Don't you wish you had a rubber stamp?"

I have an answer to this one, too, an answer that has been devel-   25
oped over the years in a trial-and-error method similar to "I'm taking some time off." The answer to the rubber-stamp question is "No, I don't mind."

Never mind if I really do or don't (this time it's my own motivations   26
I want to skip over. You'll notice); the question is, why does such an illogical query occur to so many people? My signature is actually stamped on the covers of several of my books, but people seem just as eager to get those signed as those that aren't so stamped. Would these questioners stand in line for the privilege of watching me slam a rubber stamp down on the title page of *The Shining* or *Pet Sematary*? I don't think they would.

If you still don't sense something peculiar in these questions, this   27
one might help convince you. I'm sitting in the café around the corner from my house, grabbing a little lunch by myself and reading a book (reading at the table is one of the few bad habits acquired in my youth that I have nobly refused giving up) until a customer or maybe even a waitress sidles up and asks, "How come you're not reading one of your own books?"

This hasn't happened just once, or even occasionally; it happens *a*   28
lot. The computer-generated answer to this question usually gains a chuckle, although it is nothing but the pure, logical and apparent truth. "I know how they all come out," I say. End of exchange. Back to lunch, with only a pause to wonder why people assume you want to read what you wrote, rewrote, read again following the obligatory editorial conference and yet again during the process of correcting the mistakes that a good copy editor always prods, screaming from their hiding places (I once heard a crime writer suggest God could have used a copy editor, and while I find the notion slightly blasphemous, I tend to agree).

And then people sometimes ask in that chatty, let's-strike-up-a-   29 conversation way people have, "How long does it take you to write a book?" Perfectly reasonable question—at least until you try to answer it and discover there *is* no answer. This time the computer-generated answer is a total falsehood, but it at least serves the purpose of advancing the conversation to some more discussable topic. "Usually about nine months," I say, "the same length of time it takes to make a baby." This satisfies everyone but me. I know that nine months is just an average, and probably a completely fictional one at that. It ignores *The Running Man* (published under the name Richard Bachman), which was written in four days during a snowy February vacation when I was teaching high school. It also ignores *It* and my latest *The Tommyknockers. It* is over 1,000 pages long and took four years to write. *The Tommyknockers* is 400 pages shorter but took five years to write.

Do I mind these questions? Yes . . . and no. Anyone minds questions that have no real answers and thus expose the fellow being questioned to be not a real doctor but a sort of witch doctor. But no one—at least no one with a modicum of simple human kindness—resents questions from people who honestly want answers. And now and then someone will ask a really interesting question, like, Do you write in the nude? The answer—not generated by computer—is: I don't think I ever have, but if it works, I'm willing to try it.

30

THE CRITICAL READER

Central Idea

1. What is Stephen King's central idea in this essay, and where is it stated?

Evidence

2. King's major details are the three types of questions he gets from readers. What are the three types and their characteristics?

3. What are some of King's examples that help explain each type of question?

Implications

4. What purpose does King's first paragraph serve?

5. According to King, where does he get his inspiration for writing? Read again paragraph 8 and explain what the last sentence means.

Word Choice

6. King's subject is the questions readers ask. What do King's word choices and examples tell you about his attitude toward his subject? For example, does he take readers' questions seriously, or does he make fun of them? Is the essay designed merely to make you laugh, or does it also have a serious message? Explain your answer using specific words and phrases from the essay.

EXERCISE 4.1

Most authors have an Internet website. To find an author on the Web, you can try the following: Type the author's full name, with no spaces between first and last name, into the location box on your web browser, followed by *.com.* If there is a listing for your author, his or her home page will appear on screen. Or you can use a search engine like Excite, Yahoo!, Altavista, and HotBot, to name a few. Remember to use quotation marks when you type in your keyword in the dialog box.

As a follow up to Stephen King's essay, search the Web to find out more about him. You may be able to find an interview, a review of his most current book, or a list of books he has published. Then share your results in a class discussion or written report. The following websites may be helpful:

www.nyt.com/books

www.ebooknet.com

RECOGNIZING THESIS STATEMENTS

The *thesis* of an essay is its *central idea.* The thesis is a writer's opinion, viewpoint, or special insight about a topic. Suppose you choose *cartooning* as the topic of an essay. You choose this topic because cartooning is one of your interests. You like drawing cartoons and you enjoy reading comic books and comic strips. In fact, you have become a collector of comics as a result of your research and experience. In your opinion, cartooning is an art form that, like other art forms, requires technical expertise and that expresses political ideas or social values. Based on this background, you write the following thesis statement:

> Contrary to what many people believe, cartooning is an art form that depends on technical skill, political and social awareness, and a consistently expressed viewpoint.

If this were your thesis statement, the body of your essay should clearly and convincingly support your central idea with evidence that explains what you mean by "technical skill," to what extent "political and social awareness" are involved in cartooning, and why a "consistently expressed viewpoint" is important. In addition, your body paragraphs should be packed with facts and other details that support each part of your thesis. *A thesis statement is usually one sentence that combines a writer's topic (subject) and comment (opinion, viewpoint, or insight).*

Not just any sentence will do as a thesis statement. In fact, there is a big difference between a thesis statement and a simple statement of fact. A simple statement stands on its own, requiring no further explanation. The following statements are all simple statements:

- George W. Bush is the forty-third president of the United States.

- Hillary Clinton is the only First Lady to become a U.S. Senator.

- Best-selling author Stephen King lives in Bangor, Maine.

- Martin Luther King, Jr.'s, birthday is celebrated in January.

As you can see, these statements are merely factual statements that do not call for additional support, explanation, or clarification. However, a thesis statement issues a challenge to readers in the sense that it may give rise to questions, comments, or personal feelings. A thesis statement expresses a writer's topic and comment. For example, in the thesis statement about cartooning, explained earlier in this section, the topic is *cartooning* and the comment is that *it is an art form*. The last part of the sentence tells you that cartooning depends on three things: *technical skill, political and social awareness,* and a *consistent viewpoint.* These terms suggest that the essay will have three major divisions. Following are two more examples. The first one is a simple statement and the second is a thesis statement.

- Algebra is a required course at my college.

- Students can improve their performance in algebra by applying ten strategies for success in math courses.

The first statement contains a topic only. All you can do is agree or disagree with the statement. The second statement contains both a topic and a comment. The topic is *performance in algebra* and the writer's comment is that *students can improve their performance by applying ten strategies.* You can do a lot more with this statement than agree or disagree with it. You can ask yourself what the ten strategies are, how to apply them, and whether they will help you improve your performance in algebra.

In the following examples of thesis statements, the topic and comment are annotated for you.

                                    Topic
Example 1:   Television commercials on Saturday morning

              cartoon shows [encourage the development of bad

              habits in children.]
                    Comment
                                        Comment
Example 2:   [Parents should find a more beneficial activity to oc-

              cupy their children on Saturday mornings than]

              watching cartoons on TV.
                    Topic
                                    Comment
Example 3:   [A television program that reflects today's permissive-

              ness in sexual behavior] is *Sex and the City.*
                                        Topic

EXERCISE 4.2   Read and discuss each sentence below, then circle whether it is a thesis statement (TS) or a simple statement (SS). In the thesis statements you identify, draw a line under the writer's *topic* and bracket the writer's *comment,* as in the examples above. Be prepared to explain your choices.

1. I have been working as a teller at First Union Bank on Center Street for the last fifteen years.   TS   SS

2. As a bank teller I have learned several effective ways to deal with difficult customers.   TS   SS

3. Some women work as volunteer firefighters.   TS   SS

4. I like my job as a firefighter because it is both personally rewarding and socially responsible.   TS   SS

5. Armadillos should not be sold as pets because most people cannot provide the food, climate, and habitat these animals need.
   TS   SS

EXERCISE 4.3

Apply what you have learned about thesis statements by doing this
exercise with group members. First, review the list of group roles and
responsibilities as explained in Figure 1.6, page 28. Next, read and discuss the following simple statements. Decide how you could rewrite
them to make them into thesis statements. What would you have to add
or change? Then write the new statements to share with the rest of the
class. As a final step, evaluate your group's performance.

1. My dog is a golden retriever.

2. Most people get a driver's license when they are in their teens.

3. Many students have trouble concentrating.

4. There was an explosion in the fitness center.

5. I do most of my studying in the library.

GROUP EVALUATION

What did each person contribute to the group's activity? Was your
group's performance successful? Why or why not? What additional
questions do you have about thesis statements?

WRITING THESIS STATEMENTS

Though the thesis statement has two basic parts, *topic* and *comment,* the
comment can be broken down further into *opinion, purpose,* and *parts.*
Suppose you believe that participating in a sport is beneficial in several
ways. You have arrived at this opinion because you play tennis and it has
become an important part of your life. You choose tennis as your topic
because it has given you a great deal of pleasure, but you are having difficulty deciding what comment to make about it. Figure 4.1 lists five
questions to ask that will help you think through your topic and come
up with a comment to make an effective thesis statement. Answering
the questions will help you limit your topic and identify the opinion,
purpose, and parts of your comment.

FIGURE 4.1

Writing a Thesis Statement: Five Questions

QUESTION	ANSWER
1. What is the *general topic*?	Sports.
2. What is my *limited topic*?	The benefits of tennis.
3. What is my *opinion* about the limited topic?	Playing tennis is a sport I enjoy because of its benefits.
4. What is my *purpose* in writing about this topic?	I will tell readers why I enjoy tennis so that they will have a better understanding of the benefits of playing this game.
5. How will I break down my topic into *parts* I can explain in two or more body paragraphs?	I will tell readers what the benefits of playing tennis are for me: social interaction, improved fitness, and challenge of the game.

To write a thesis statement that contains *topic, opinion, purpose,* and *parts* combine your answers to the five questions, and write a complete sentence like the ones below:

   Opinion   **Topic**   **Purpose**

1. I enjoy playing tennis because it gives me the benefits of [social interaction, improved fitness, and a challenging game.]
                                Parts

          Topic   **Purpose**

2. Attending a major league baseball game is better than watching one on TV [because the crowd's excitement is contagious, the view of the field is unlimited, and it provides good entertainment for a date.]
            Purpose and parts are combined

EXERCISE 4.4 Choose any two topics from the list on page 103, or make up your own topics based on what interests you. Answer the five questions in Figure 4.1 to limit each topic and break down your comment into opinion, purpose, and parts. Next, write a thesis statement for each of your two topics. The first one is done as an example.

1. U.S. government
    a. General topic: U.S. government
    b. Limited topic: the three branches of the U.S. government
    c. Opinion: Each branch has a different function and purpose.
    d. Purpose: I want to inform readers about the way our government works.
    e. Parts: I will explain the purpose and function of each branch of government.
    f. Thesis: The executive, legislative, and judicial branches of the U.S. government have different purposes and functions, which are designed to keep any one branch from assuming too much power over the others.
2. college careers
3. current fashions
4. recreational activities
5. fitness programs
6. television shows
7. Careers

Although writers may place the thesis statement anywhere in an essay, you will usually find it near the beginning of a short essay or near the end of an introduction to a longer one, as in Stephen King's essay on pages 93–97. It is important for you as a beginning writer to state your thesis at the beginning of your essay for two reasons. First, your thesis lets your readers know what to expect. Second, just as the topic sentence of a paragraph limits and controls what you write in the rest of the paragraph, the thesis statement limits and controls what you write in the rest of your essay and helps you stay organized and on topic. In fact, topic sentences and thesis statements have several characteristics in common, as illustrated in Figure 4.2.

CHECKING THESIS STATEMENTS FOR COMPLETENESS

If your thesis statement is missing a topic, opinion, purpose, or parts, you may run into one of several common problems. Read the example below:

FIGURE 4.2

Comparison of Topic Sentence and Thesis Statement

TOPIC SENTENCE	THESIS STATEMENT
Limits the topic covered in the paragraph	Limits the topic covered in the essay
States the main idea of the paragraph	States the central idea of the essay
Controls the selection of evidence to support the paragraph's main idea	Controls the selection of evidence to support the essay's thesis
Suggests how the writer has organized the paragraph	Suggests how the writer has organized the essay
Helps the writer maintain unity in the paragraph	Helps the writer maintain unity in the essay

1a. We need to do something to solve the problem of crime in our cities.

This statement might work as an interest grabber in an introductory paragraph, but it is not a suitable thesis statement. Although it expresses a topic (crime in our cities) and an opinion (we need to do something) it lacks the *purpose* and *parts* that would limit the thesis and clarify the writer's central idea. It is not clear *why* the writer chose the topic or *what* the writer wants to tell us about it. Also, "crime in our cities" covers a lot of ground. The writer should limit the topic to something more specific, such as "burglaries in our neighborhood." Below is a revision of example 1a that includes purpose and parts:

Purpose and opinion are combined—we started the program because we want to prevent burglaries.

                              Topic
1b. To prevent <u>burglaries in our neighborhood</u> we have
    started a neighborhood watch program that includes
    <u>a five-point plan</u> for home protection.
          Parts

The sentence in example 2a below is a simple statement of fact, telling you only what the latest polls show. It is not suitable as a thesis statement because it does not indicate what the writer thinks about the decline in alcohol abuse or what it may mean to readers. Statement 2a lacks an opinion, purpose, and parts. Example 2b is a revision that includes the missing parts.

2a. The latest polls show that alcohol abuse among college students is decreasing. (unsuitable)

Purpose and parts are combined—why the polls are misleading and who is affected by alcohol abuse.

Topic

2b. Although the latest polls show that <u>alcohol abuse among college students is decreasing</u>, <u>many students do abuse alcohol and cause problems for themselves and for their communities.</u> (better)   Opinion

The topic in example 3a is study skills. The opinion is that study skills are important, and the writer has broken the topic down into three parts: time management, goal setting, and note taking. But what is the writer's *purpose?* As a thesis statement, this sentence is unsuitable because readers cannot tell what the writer wants them to know or do about study skills. Example 3b provides the missing information.

3a. Time management, goal setting, and note taking are three important study skills. (unsuitable)

Parts

3b. Time management, goal setting, and note taking

Topic are three important study skills college students can   Purpose
develop that may help them improve their grades.
(better)   Opinion

The writer of the sentence in example 4a has expressed two different opinions about two different topics in her thesis, so the statement is confusing. As a result, the purpose is also unclear. A thesis statement should cover only *one* topic. Examples 4b and 4c illustrate two ways to revise the statement.

4a. I disagree with people who want to abolish college sports, and I also think college athletes should have to maintain good grades. (unsuitable)

Purpose and parts are combined: why the disagreement, how the topic breaks down.

          Opinion   **Topic**

4b. I disagree with those who want to abolish <u>college sports</u> because sports are a source of revenue for the college, an extracurricular activity that appeals to most students, and an opportunity for athletic scholarships. (better)

Purpose and parts are combined: why athletes should keep good grades; which parts, requirements and careers, will be explained.

          Topic   **Opinion**

4c. <u>College athletes</u> <u>should have to maintain good grades</u> because they should have to meet the same requirements as all students and because they should prepare themselves for careers outside the field of professional sports. (better)

EXERCISE 4.5   Check the thesis statements below for completeness, then rewrite them to add any missing parts.

1. Teenage alcohol abuse is on the rise.

2. People who run for office may have their private lives exposed in the press.

3. Many students are opting for careers in health care.

4. Even if I had the opportunity, I would not want to be sixteen years old again.

5. To gain the approval of voters, a new president of the United States must keep campaign promises, choose qualified people to serve in the cabinet, and act decisively in times of crisis.

6. Right-to-work laws are in effect in several states.

    In addition to stating the writer's topic and comment, a well-written thesis statement is grammatically correct. For example, a thesis statement should be a *complete* sentence, not a sentence fragment or a run-on sentence. If you tend to write fragments or run-ons, if your memory of these terms is rusty, or if you need help writing grammatically correct sentences, see pages 435–436.

INTRODUCING THE THESIS

Writing a good introduction to your essay is a way of building readers' interest and placing your thesis within a meaningful context. Your essay's introduction, therefore, is also the introduction to your thesis statement. Though you can choose among many strategies for writing effective introductions, the five listed below may be especially helpful to you. Each strategy helps create a context for your thesis.

1. Supply *background information.*

2. Relate an *anecdote.*

3. Begin with a *quotation and explanation.*

4. Use interesting *facts and figures.*

5. Ask a revealing *question.*

Supply Background Information

Supplying background information creates a context for your thesis much like setting the scene for a play. To build background, lead up to your thesis by identifying the situation, events, or issues that are relevant to it. Suppose that a certain intersection in your community is known to be dangerous. Residents take other, less convenient, routes through residential areas to avoid this intersection, Your thesis is that by lowering the speed limit approaching the intersection, lives will be saved and traffic will not be diverted into neighborhoods where school children are present. To build background for your thesis, you tell readers that the intersection is at the bottom of a hill. The posted speed limit leading up to the intersection is fifty-five miles per hour, and most vehicles are traveling much faster when they reach the intersection. Truckers especially have difficulty stopping. Some people who could not stop their vehicles in time have caused accidents resulting in serious injuries and death. By supplying this background information, you place your thesis in the context of a problem that requires a solution.

The following excerpt from "I Married an Accountant" by Joe Queenan introduces a thesis by supplying background information. The thesis is underlined.

At the mature age of 39, a somewhat immature 220-pound friend of mine took up ice hockey. Though he had never before strapped on ice skates and is far from fit, he has spent virtually every Sunday evening for the past two summers barreling up and down the ice in a special hockey league for aging neophytes. He may be strange, but he is not boring.

Another person I know moved to Teheran in the late 1970s, met an Iranian woman, converted to Islam so he could marry her, and had to undergo a circumcision—all of this took place against the backdrop of massive civil unrest in Iran. He too may be strange, but he is not boring.

This is equally true of my wife, who for three years wrote video scripts for a man who had previously directed the Gothic soap opera "Dark Shadows." Though the subject of her continuing-education scripts had few ghoulish elements, she can nevertheless claim to have worked closely with a colleague of Jonathan Frid's, the famous TV vampire. It is an honor she will take to her grave. She, like the aging hockey player and the intrepid voyager to Iran, has led a rich, interesting life and has done exciting, unpredictable things. Like them, she is also an accountant.

Accountants have long been the targets of satirists and have been mercilessly lambasted by everyone from Monty Python to the rock group The Kinks. Personally, I hold no brief for accountants as a unit and would be loath to argue that they are, collectively or individually, electrifying fireballs. Yet nothing in my experience would lead me to the conclusion that accountants are quantifiably less interesting than people in other occupations.

Thus I have often wondered why these attacks on accountants continue at a time when numerous other professions would make equally suitable targets. . . .

Queenan's article takes a humorous look at the prevailing stereotype of accounting as boring. Queenan believes that many other professions would make suitable targets as "most boring job." To introduce his thesis, he provides background information in the form of three examples of accountants he knows who have led interesting lives. The rest of the article contains examples of the professionals Queenan thinks are boring—for example: systems engineers, investment bankers, public relations consultants, and writers. Queenan's opinion is that accountants are no less interesting than anyone else. His implied purpose is to persuade readers through the use of humor that other professions are as boring, or even more so, than accounting. The phrase "numerous other professions" implies the parts of Queenan's thesis to be developed in the essay: examples of boring professions.

Relate an Anecdote

An *anecdote* is a brief story or narration of an event. Used as an introductory strategy, the anecdote can vividly establish a context for your thesis.

In the following excerpt, Gregg Easterbrook uses an anecdote to begin his essay "Escape Valve." The thesis statement is underlined.

> A man and woman I know moved in together recently. It was, as such occasions are, a moment of sentiment and celebration. It was also a limited engagement. Before moving in, they had already set a fixed date when they would break up.
>
> They explained their reasons to one and all. In a year, the woman planned to change jobs and cities; the man did not plan to follow. An eventual split is unfortunate, they said, but also inevitable, so why not plan on it? Yet, far from being a sad twist of fate, my woman friend's scheduled departure, I fear, was a liberating force, making possible whatever short-term romance the couple will enjoy. Without the escape clause of a pre-set termination of their affair, they might never have lived together at all.
>
> This situation is not unique. More and more, people are ordering their lives along a principle I call the "automatic-out." In love, friend ship, work, and the community, people increasingly prefer arrangements that automatically end at some pre-set date. . . .

The anecdote builds a context for Easterbrook's thesis statement by relating an incident that illustrates what he means by an "automatic-out"—a concept that may be new to many readers.

Begin with a Quotation and Explanation

Quotations from books, poems, articles, experts in a certain field, or interviews you have had with people who are involved in some way with your topic can add authority to your opinions. Using quotations shows readers that others have thought about your topic and formed opinions about it. If you begin with one or more quotations, you need to explain what they mean and how they relate to your thesis. The quotation may illustrate your thesis or back it up with an expert's opinion. The following excerpt is from the introduction to "Wagon Train Children," an essay by Elliot West. The thesis statement is underlined.

> The historian Francis Parkman, strolling around Independence, Mo., in 1846, remarked upon the "multitude of healthy children's faces . . .

peeping out from under the covers of the wagons." Two decades later, a traveler wrote of husbands packing up "sunburned women and wild-looking children," along with shovels and flour barrels, in preparation for the journey West. In the gold fields of California in the 1850s, a chronicler met four sisters and sisters-in-law who had just crossed the Great Plains with 36 of their children. "They could," she wrote, "form quite a respectable village."

In the great overland migration that lasted from 1841 until the start of the Civil War, more than a quarter of a million people pushed their way from the Missouri valley to the Pacific coast. Probably at least 35,000 of them were young girls and boys; except during the Gold Rush, at least every fifth person on the trails was a child. Yet in all we read today, these thousands of young emigrants are infrequently seen and almost never heard.

The voices of many of them do survive, though. Some kept diaries along the way that have been preserved; many others wrote down their memories later. These records permit glimpses of a life that children of today might easily dream about—a child's life of adventure and purpose, of uncertainty and danger, albeit sometimes of sheer boredom. . . .

The rest of West's article explains some of the experiences recorded in the diaries and memoirs of pioneer children. His purpose is to reveal a fact that historians have ignored even though there is plenty of evidence to indicate that thousands of children traveled in wagon trains to the West. The quotations that introduce the thesis establish this fact and therefore create a context for West's thesis.

Use Interesting Facts and Figures

Facts and figures such as dates, times, names of people, places, and statistics add interest and realism to your writing, and statistics can act as evidence to support your thesis. Suppose you are disturbed by the commercials on children's television programs that promote sugared cereals. To gather evidence, you count the number of times "sugar" or other words that refer to sweetness are mentioned in several commercials. You find that the number is surprisingly large, and you decide to use it in your introduction to establish a basis for your opinion that there is too much of this kind of advertising aimed at children.

Dates also provide historical context as in the excerpt from "Wagon Train Children." The dates mentioned in the essay's introduction, 1841 and 1846, establish the context of the westward migration of families that occurred during this period of America's history. Names of people and places can interest readers in your topic as illustrated in the following example in which the thesis statement is underlined.

> To the list of professional basketball players such as Magic Johnson, Michael Jordan, and Larry Bird who have become household words, we have added another name: Shaquille O'Neal or "Shaq" for short. It seems like only a few short years ago when Shaq was yet another high school basketball player who had dreams of becoming an NBA player. But unlike the great majority of high school hopefuls, Shaq had the unbeatable talent of which sports fame and fortune are made. Shaq began his career with the Orlando Magic. He now plays for the Los Angeles Lakers. How Shaquille O'Neal was discovered and how he became a nationally known player make an interesting story. . . .

People who follow sports will recognize the names of famous athletes that help provide a context for the thesis. Orlando, Florida, is a place many readers may recognize whether they follow sports or not. Shaquille O'Neal is the topic; the writer's opinion is that Shaq's rise to fame is an interesting story, and the writer plans to discuss how Shaq was discovered and how he became a nationally known player. The writer's purpose is to inform readers about Shaq, another household name in the world of professional basketball.

The following excerpt from "The Trouble With Television," an essay by Robert MacNeil, makes use of statistics to introduce the thesis, which is underlined.

> It is difficult to escape the influence of television. If you fit the statistical averages, by the age of 20 you will have been exposed to at least 20,000 hours of television. You can add 10,000 hours for each decade you have lived after the age of 20. The only things Americans do more than watch television are work and sleep.
>
> Calculate for a moment what could be done with even a part of those hours. Five thousand hours, I am told, are what a typical college undergraduate spends working on a bachelor's degree. In 10,000 hours you could have learned enough to become an astronomer or engineer. You could have learned several languages fluently. If it appealed to you, you could be reading Homer in the original Greek or Dostoyevsky in Russian. If it didn't, you could have walked around the world and written a book about it.
>
> The trouble with television is that it discourages concentration. Almost anything interesting and rewarding in life requires some

constructive, consistently applied effort. The dullest, the least gifted of us can achieve things that seem miraculous to those who never concentrate on anything. But television encourages us to apply no effort. It sells us instant gratification. It diverts us only to divert, to make the time pass without pain . . .

Using facts and figures as an introductory strategy builds a context for MacNeil's thesis statement by establishing the pervasive influence of television. MacNeil's topic is television; his comment is that there is *trouble* with television; he specifies the kind or *part* of trouble he will discuss as *discourages concentration.* Although MacNeil's purpose is not directly stated in his thesis, you can assume that he means to inform readers of the ways television discourages concentration. The rest of the essay explains how television's appeal to the short attention span has affected our language, the way we think, and our tolerance for effort.

Ask a Revealing Question

Beginning an essay with a question works best if the question you ask is new, surprising, or something readers may not have thought to ask. The question must also be a *revealing* one that clarifies what the essay is about. The following excerpt is from a section of the first chapter of *The Practical Entomologist* by Rick Imes. The thesis statement is underlined.

Just what are insects, anyway? Often, any small creature with more than four legs is indiscriminately labeled a "bug," but true bugs represent only one of many different groups of insects. What's more, many of these creepy, crawling critters are not insects at all, but may belong to one of several related but very different groups.

Insects, as it turns out, are characterized by several easily recognized traits that set them apart from any other group of organisms. Like other members of the Phylum Arthropoda (which, literally translated, means "jointed foot"), and unlike mammals, for example, insects possess an external skeleton, or *exoskeleton,* which encases their internal organs, supporting them as our skeleton supports us and protecting them as would a suit of armor on a medieval knight. Unlike other arthropods, their body is divided into three distinct regions—the *head, thorax,* and *abdomen.* Insects are the only animals that have three pairs of jointed legs, no more or less, and these six legs are attached to the thorax, the middle region of the body. . . .

The first chapter of Imes's book is titled "The Basics of Entomology," and in the excerpt above, his thesis, or central idea, is that several traits determine which organisms can be classified as insects. The rest of the excerpt following the thesis describes more of the traits. The question that introduces the thesis is a surprising one because most readers think they know what an insect is. Furthermore, the question is central to the development of Imes's chapter, which sets forth the basics of the study of insects and their behavior.

EXERCISE 4.6   Identify which of the following introductory strategies the writers of the next four passages use. In addition, underline the thesis statement in each passage. Explain the reasons for your choices.

- Supply *background information.*

- Relate an *anecdote.*

- Begin with a *quotation and explanation.*

- Use interesting *facts and figures.*

- Ask a revealing *question.*

1. If you heard in a television commercial that half the dentists surveyed recommended SMILE toothpaste, you might want to try it. But if you were a wise consumer, you would realize that the other half didn't recommend the toothpaste, so maybe "half" isn't such a good number after all. You would also realize that although half of 2,000 is 1,000 and that is a lot of dentists, half of two is just one dentist. In either case, however, 50 percent is still 50 percent, which means that half the dentists surveyed would not recommend SMILE toothpaste. Untrained consumers have a way of hearing only the positive side of the messages in television commercials. You can become a wise consumer by learning to spot the seven common tricks that advertisers use to make you want to buy their products. . . .

2. Is high school football a luxury we cannot afford? A school district in our area is considering abolishing athletic events as a way to cut costs. Uniforms cost money. So do coaches' salaries, equipment, concessions at football games, electricity for running the scoreboard and field lights, transportation to away games, and other related expenditures. The money saved from these could be used to buy science lab equipment, new books for the library, and computers, to name a few of our needs that the school board has been exploring.

High school football is something most community members take for granted, and surely the students will be the losers if they do not have the experience of cheering their teams to victory. Perhaps if we can find other ways to cut costs, then football may be the luxury that we *can* afford. . . .

3. When the late president John F. Kennedy said, "Ask not what your country can do for you but what you can do for your country," he exhorted a nation of young people to get involved in the political process and to take an active role in the fashioning of their government. For the first time in the history of the United States, a president appealed to young people as adults, not children, and they rose in force to meet his challenge, joining the Peace Corps and the ranks of others in service to humankind. Kennedy was their man, and since his death there has been no one like him. If future presidents of the United States want to capture the youth vote, they will have to do several things to gain young people's respect and support. . . .

4. The story of the search for radium is a romantic and stirring one. Behind it is a woman who was passionately curious, daring in her convictions, and determined to work in an age hardly encouraging to professional aspirations among those of her sex. From a dilapidated shed, described by one German chemist at the time as a "cross between a stable and a potato-cellar," came a discovery that would throw light on the structure of the atom, open new doors in medicine, and save lives in future generations.

    Marie Sklodowska came to Paris and the Sorbonne in 1891 as a reticent Polish woman of twenty-four. Taking a solitary room in the Latin Quarter, she began her studies in mathematics and physics. By 1897 she had two university degrees and a fellowship, as well as a husband and a newborn daughter. In the physicist Pierre Curie, Marie had found both an adviser and a lover, someone as serious as she, who shared her interests and became drawn into her quest. . . . (Excerpted from "How Did They Discover Radium?" in *How Did They Do That?* by Caroline Sutton)

Now read the next three paragraphs to see how you can introduce the same thesis three different ways. The thesis statement is underlined in each paragraph.

1. The headline "Dieters Gain Back More Weight Than They Lost on Starvation Diet" introduced a newspaper article that appeared after

several famous people who had lost as much as sixty pounds regained the weight. Now most of them are on another diet. Like many people, they are on a harmful gain-lose-regain cycle brought on by quick-loss diets that disrupt the metabolic process. Most doctors and nutritionists recommend that people lose no more than two pounds per week and that they eat balanced meals. <u>To lose weight sensibly and without risking health, people should limit the number of calories they eat, continue to eat balanced meals, and do some form of aerobic exercise several times a week.</u>

2. Only about 10 percent of the people who lose weight on highly advertised quick-weight-loss programs actually keep it off. The other 90 percent gain back all their weight and then some within about three to six months. Quick-loss programs fool the body into thinking it is starving. Metabolism slows down to adjust to the lowered caloric intake. When the dieter returns to normal eating habits, the metabolic rate stays low, so even fewer calories are burned than before the person went on the diet in the first place. As a result, he or she gains back the weight and has even more trouble losing it in the future. Diets do not work. A change in eating and exercise habits does. <u>To lose weight sensibly and without risking health, people should limit the number of calories they eat, continue to eat balanced meals, and do some form of aerobic exercise several times a week.</u>

3. The summer was just beginning, and Marina wanted to take off the weight she had put on during her first year of college. A year of studying and partying had left her no time to fix and eat proper meals and even less time for exercise. Now she wanted to get in shape for a new bathing suit and weekends at the beach. She saw an ad in a magazine selling a new diet program that promised a loss of up to seven pounds in one week. The before-and-after pictures convinced her that in three weeks she could have the body she wanted. She started on the program, and in a little less than three weeks she had lost the weight. Marina was thrilled at first, but when the pounds started creeping back, she did not know what to do. Her doctor told her that quick-loss programs do not work because they disrupt the metabolic process. Most people who try these programs fail to keep the weight off. Marina learned the hard way that most activities that are worth the effort take time. She still wants to lose weight, but now she will follow her doctor's advice. <u>To lose weight sensibly and</u>

without risking health, people should limit the number of calories they eat, continue to eat balanced meals, and do some form of aerobic exercise several times a week.

    The first paragraph begins with a *quotation and explanation*. The second paragraph begins with a *figure*, and the third paragraph begins with an *anecdote*. All three paragraphs contain essentially the same information, and all introduce the same thesis. The choice of an introductory strategy depends upon your purpose and audience. In the examples above, the first two paragraphs might be more suitable for a general audience than the third one, which is aimed at college students.

    How you begin your essay determines what the rest of your essay will be about. Without a well-thought-out introduction and clear thesis statement, you will have difficulty developing your ideas, and your readers will have difficulty following them. To avoid these problems write a thesis statement that contains a *topic* and a *comment* that is broken down into *opinion, purpose,* and *parts.* In addition, use one of the five strategies explained in this chapter to introduce your thesis statement.

EXERCISE 4.7   Write introductory paragraphs for the two thesis statements you wrote in Exercise 4.4, or make up new thesis statements for this exercise. Use a different strategy in each paragraph to introduce your thesis.

TOPICS FOR WRITING

Choose a topic from the list below and write an essay. Choose a strategy for your introductory paragraph, and state your thesis clearly. Follow the suggestions offered in this chapter for writing, introducing, and correcting your thesis statement. Use facts, reasons, and examples to support your thesis.

1. Write about the qualities you admire in a U.S. president.

2. Write about a sport that has harmful or beneficial effects on those who participate in it.

3. Write about a time you accomplished something you wanted, such as making a team, getting a job, or competing in an event and winning. Explain how achieving success affected you.

4. Write an essay using one of the introductory paragraphs you wrote for Exercise 4.7.

5. Make up your own topic.

Checklist for Revision

As you revise and edit your essay, check for the following:

1. Is your thesis statement complete? Can you identify your topic, opinion, purpose, and parts?

2. Does your introductory paragraph establish a context for your thesis?

3. Have you used one of the five strategies for introducing a thesis explained in this chapter?

4. Do your body paragraphs have topic sentences and enough support?

5. Are your sentences error-free?

THE CRITICAL THINKER

To examine Stephen King's essay in more depth, think about and discuss the following questions. Then choose one of them as a topic for writing.

1. Which paragraphs make up the introduction, body, and conclusion of King's essay? What purpose do the headings serve? How does King's choice of a structure for his essay help readers follow his ideas?

2. Are the questions that readers ask King similar to or different from the kinds of questions fans might ask of any celebrity? Give some examples of questions fans might ask of celebrities in the fields of sports, music, or film.

3. To Stephen King, some readers' questions are interesting, some are annoying, some are amusing, and some are boring. Examine the essay for examples of questions that provoke these emotional responses.

4. Review your answers to the Awareness Check on pages 92–93. What questions would you ask Stephen King if you had the chance? What questions do you think most people would ask him? Into which of King's categories do your questions fall and why?

YOUR DISCOVERY JOURNAL

It may sound strange, but one way to improve your writing is to read. The more reading you do, the more you become aware of the different ways writers use words and structure their ideas. The key to enjoying reading is to choose books and articles that appeal to one of your interests. Scan the newspaper or a magazine for an article on a topic that interests you. Read the article; then write about it in your journal. For example, you could write a brief summary of the article, telling what it is about and why you liked it. Or you could write about one idea expressed in the article, explaining why you agree or disagree with the author.

Chapter 5

Supporting Your Thesis

*T*wo college students are sitting outside the student center when an attractive member of the opposite sex walks by. The students exchange looks that clearly indicate what they are thinking, yet no word passes between them. Seeing the grade on a composition the professor has just returned, the writer says, "Yes!" Though no conversation follows in which the student explains the work that went into the essay and the pleasure that comes from having the effort acknowledged, the other students in the class know how this writer feels and are hoping for similar results on their papers. In both cases, either a word or a look effectively communicates an idea that would probably take several sentences to write about in an essay.

Writing is not like having a conversation. When people read your essay, they may not have you there to explain a thesis that you have not clearly stated or to provide an example needed to support a main idea. In writing, everything needs explaining; words have to do the work of gestures, facial expressions, and tone of voice. As explained in Chapter 4, an essay needs a thesis or central idea. Equally important is how you support your thesis, how clearly and completely you explain what you mean so that your readers can identify with you and follow your ideas.

119

This chapter explains how to support your thesis with specific evidence and how to reinforce your thesis in the conclusion of your essay.

AWARENESS CHECK

Before reading the following essay, explore your thoughts about clothes and shopping. Think about the questions below, and answer them either on your own or in a group discussion:

1. What specific items of clothing did you think you *had* to have when you were a child?

2. If you have children or younger brothers and sisters, would you say that shopping with them is usually a positive or negative experience? Why?

3. Read the title, headnote, and first two paragraphs of the following essay. Based on this preview, what do you think will follow?

Shopping with Children

Phyllis Theroux

Phyllis Theroux writes for popular magazines and newspapers, often about family relationships. This essay is from Night Lights, *a collection of her essays published in 1987.*

VOCABULARY CHECK

immaculate (3)	spotless, clean
adder (3)	a type of snake
extremists (3)	those whose beliefs are outside the norm for their group
heartfelt (8)	deeply or sincerely felt
eccentricities (8)	oddities, unusual behaviors
coerced (9)	forced or threatened

genuflect (11)	to kneel out of respect
retrieved (12)	to get back, regain
inventoried (12)	counted items or made a list of items
inadvertently (15)	unintentionally, not meaning to
sustained (15)	maintained, kept up
commodities (16)	useful items or products
cosmic (17)	universal, far reaching

Once upon a time there were three little children. By and large, dress- 1
ing them was a joyful thing. At a moment's notice, their mother could
turn the boys into baby Rothschilds, the girl into a shipping heiress, or
even a Kennedy. In those early days of motherhood, I used to take a lot
of photographs for the scrapbook. Now I flip through the scrapbook
sometimes to remind myself that "those were the days."

The eldest son was the first to establish his individuality: sleeveless 2
army jackets, kneecap bandannas, and a pierced ear hidden under a
lengthening style. Then the youngest son discovered dirt. He formed a
club, still active, called "The All Dirt Association." To qualify, one had to
roll in the mud.

Fortunately, the little girl grows increasingly more tasteful and im- 3
maculate. She will get up at 5:30 A.M. to make sure she has enough
time to wash and curl her hair so that it bounces properly on her shoulders when she goes off to school, and she screams as if bitten by an
adder if a drop of spaghetti sauce lands on her Izod. The entire house
is thrown into an uproar while she races for the Clorox bottle. This is a
family of extremists, and nobody dresses for the kind of success I had
in mind.

Time will tell what happens to these children. Who can say 4
whether my son the dirt bomb will wind up sewing buttons on a seer-
sucker sports jacket, or my daughter the Southamptonian will discover
the joys of thrift-shop browsing. They are still evolving toward personal
statements that are, at this writing, incomplete.

In the meantime, however, they must be dressed, which means 5
taking them to stores where clothing for their growing bodies can be
purchased. Shopping with children is exactly as awful as shopping with
parents. But if the experience is to be survived there are certain rules all
adults must follow. (If you are a child, you may not read any further.

This is for your parents, who will deal with you very harshly if you read one more word!)

RULE I: Never shop with more than one child at a time. This rule is closely related to another rule—never raise more than one child at a time. If you understand the second rule, there is no need to elaborate upon the first. ₆

RULE II: Dress very nicely yourself. After the age of nine, children do not like to be seen with their mothers in public. You are a blot upon their reputation, a shadow they want to shake. I, myself, always insisted that my mother walk ten paces behind me, take separate elevators and escalators and speak only when spoken to—which brings me to the next rule. ₇

RULE III: Do not make any sudden gestures, loud noises or heartfelt exclamations such as "How adorable you look in that!" or "Twenty-nine ninety-five! Are you kidding? For a shirt?" Children are terribly embarrassed by our eccentricities, and it goes without saying that you must never buy their articles of "intimate apparel" in their presence. Children, until enough sleazy adults teach them that is old-fashioned, are very modest creatures. One time I ran out of the store and took the bus home by myself after my mother asked a salesclerk where the "underpants" counter was. Everyone in the store heard her. I had no choice. ₈

RULE IV: Know your child's limits. If he can be coerced into a department store, coaxed into telling you that he wouldn't mind wearing this shirt or that pair of pants, don't insist that he go the whole distance—i.e., don't force him to try them on. Keep the sales slips; if something doesn't fit when he tries it on at home, return it. If he cannot be made to enter the store at all, say, "Fine. When you run out of clothes, wear your sister's." Children who won't go shopping at all save their parents a lot of time. ₉

RULE V: Know your own limits. Do not be dragged to every sneaker store in the metropolitan area to find the exact shoes your child has in mind. Announce: "We're going to Sears—and Sears only—unless you want to wait for six more weeks, which is the next time I am free." Some children, with nothing but time and a passion to improve their image, will cheerfully go to three stores they know about and six more they don't, without blinking an eye. ₁₀

RULE VI: Keep your hand on your checkbook. This is a very hard rule to follow if you are not strong-minded. Children can accuse you of ruining their lives because you do not genuflect before the entire line of Ocean Pacific sportswear, and girls have a way of filling you with guilt by telling you that every other girl in their confirmation class is going to be wearing Capezio sandals and if you want to make her look funny in front of the bishop she will never forgive you as long as she lives. ₁₁

RULE VII: Keep on top of the laundry. Or, if you can't keep on top ₁₂

of the laundry, remember that the wardrobe your son or daughter wants is probably lying in the bottom of a hamper waiting to be retrieved. When packing a trunk for camp or school, insist that everything the child owns be washed (preferably by him or her), folded and ready to be inventoried before you go to the store to fill in the gaps. Your children will hate you for enforcing this rule, but remember that true love is strong.

RULE VIII: Avoid designer clothes. Shut your eyes to labels. Do not be   13
intimidated by the "fact" that your daughter cannot go to the movies without swinging a Bermuda Bag, or that your son will not be able to concentrate in the library without Topsiders on his feet. Tell your children that the best thing about Gloria Vanderbilt is her bank account, fattened by socially insecure people which, thank God, they are not!

Having laid down the rules, it is important to refresh the adult's   14
memory with "remembrances of things past." I have never met a child who did not remind me of how difficult it is to present a confident face to the world. Clothing is only the top blanket shielding them from the elements, and children need all the protective covering they can get.

As a child, I knew in an inarticulate way that I stood a better chance   15
of surviving a windstorm in a circle of trees. My aim was to be the tree in the middle, identical and interchangeable with every other sapling in the grove. How I dressed had everything to do with feeling socially acceptable and when I inadvertently slipped into an individualism I could not back up with sustained confidence, I would try to think what I could do to regain my place in the grove.

It seemed to me that social success depended on having at least   16
one of three commodities: a fabulous personality, fame, or a yellow Pandora sweater. These were the building blocks upon which one could stand.

A fabulous personality was beyond my power to sustain on a daily   17
basis. Fame, like lightning, seemed to strike other people, none of whom I even knew. But a yellow Pandora sweater could be purchased at Macy's, if only my mother would understand its cosmic importance. Fortunately, she did.

For several days, or as long as it took for the sweater cuffs to lose   18
their elasticity, I faced the world feeling buttoned up, yellow and self-confident—almost as confident as Susan Figel, who had a whole drawerful of Pandora sweaters in different shades to match her moods.

Unfortunately, I remember that yellow Pandora sweater a little too   19
vividly. When I am shopping with my children, empathy continually blows me off course in the aisles. On the one hand, nobody wants her child to look funny in front of the bishop. On the other, it has yet to occur to my children that the bishop in full regalia looks pretty funny himself.

THE CRITICAL READER

Central Idea

1. What is Phyllis Theroux's thesis?

2. What strategy does she use to introduce the thesis?

Evidence

3. What are the major details that support the thesis?

4. Briefly summarize Theroux's rules for shopping with children.

Implications

5. In paragraph 6, Theroux does not provide an example to explain "Never shop with more than one child at a time." She says there is no need to elaborate on this rule. Her assumption is that readers will know what she means. Do you agree? Explain your answer.

6. Explain what Theroux means by this statement: "My aim was to be the tree in the middle, identical and interchangeable with every other sapling in the grove." (paragraph 15)

Word Choice

7. Why do you think Theroux uses the following brand names in her essay? *Izod, Capezio, Bermuda Bag, Topsiders, Gloria Vanderbilt,* and *Pandora?* Would the essay have been just as effective, for example, if she had said *yellow* sweater instead of *Pandora* sweater?

8. The tone of Theroux's essay is informal and conversational. What specific words and phrases give the essay its tone?

9. Read the last sentence of the essay again. Why do you think Theroux chose the word *regalia* instead of *costume* or *dress* to describe the bishop's clothes? Use your dictionary to find support for your answer.

SELECTING SUPPORTING EVIDENCE

When you have chosen a topic and written your thesis, the next step is to select the evidence to support your thesis. How you arrange the evidence determines what the major divisions of your essay will be. One way to begin is to make an informal outline by writing down your thesis statement and breaking it down into several subpoints or main ideas, each of which can be explained in a body paragraph. Read the following two examples of a thesis statement and informal outline.

EXAMPLE 1

A good weight-training program should concentrate on how to build and tone the muscles in four major parts of the body.

1. The muscles of the chest
2. The muscles of the back
3. The muscles of the arms
4. The muscles of the legs

In this outline, the writer shows that the essay will have four major divisions. Each of these divisions will become a main idea or subpoint that supports the thesis statement. The four main ideas will specify which muscles receive weight training.

EXAMPLE 2

Many people who are under a great deal of stress believe that there is nothing they can do about it, but they are wrong.

1. Most stress is self-induced.
2. Most causes of stress can be eliminated or controlled.
3. Time management can lead to reduced stress.
4. Relaxation is the key to stress reduction.

This outline specifies that the writer's essay will have four major divisions to support the thesis. The first division will explain why people who believe they cannot do anything about stress are wrong: because most stress is self-induced. The second major division will explain causes of stress that can be eliminated or controlled. The third and fourth major divisions will explain two ways to reduce stress.

EXERCISE 5.1   Following are three informal outlines. Each begins with a thesis statement followed by two or more subpoints that could become the main ideas of body paragraphs. Read the outlines; then add one more subpoint to each.

1. Malls not only provide a place to shop, but they have become popular entertainment centers as well.

   a. They provide teenagers with a place to hang out.

   b. They provide endless subjects for people watchers.

   c. They provide . . .

2. The behavior of some moviegoers is enough to drive me from the theater to the nearest video store.

   a. Some moviegoers do not make their children behave.

   b. Some moviegoers disturb others by leaving their seats frequently.

   c. Some moviegoers litter the theater.

   d. Some moviegoers . . .

3. Going to the movies is better in some ways than when I was a child, but in other ways it is worse.

   a. Better

      1. There are more theaters to choose from.

      2. There is a wider variety of snacks available.

      3.

   b. Worse

      1. Moviegoers are not as considerate as they used to be.

      2. There are not as many good shows for children.

      3.

EXERCISE 5.2   Following are two thesis statements. For each of them, list two to four main ideas that could be developed into the body paragraphs of an essay.

1. Although there may be many qualities that people look for in a good friend, the quality I admire most in my best friend is a sense of humor.

2. Everyone knows you cannot cure the common cold, but while you are waiting for one to go away, try my method to make yourself comfortable.

ARRANGING SUPPORTING EVIDENCE

Not only should you choose specific details, you should arrange them logically. Logical arrangement of details will help give your essay unity and coherence. The thesis is your central idea. *It is also your controlling idea* in that it determines your essay's development and your selection of details. To support your central idea and prove your thesis, break it down into subpoints, which are the main ideas of your body paragraphs. Then support each subpoint or main idea with specific details. If you follow this logical plan from *thesis* to *topic sentence* to *major* and *minor supporting details*, your essay will be unified and coherent. To review how to support a topic sentence with major and minor details, see Chapter 3, pages 76–78.

Example 1 on page 125 shows a thesis statement and an informal outline of the main ideas suggested by the thesis statement. The formal outline below adds supporting details and gives you a clearer picture of how the writer will support the thesis.

THESIS: A good weight-training program should concentrate on how to build and tone the muscles in four major parts of the body.

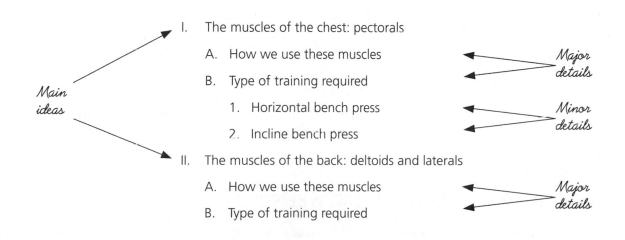

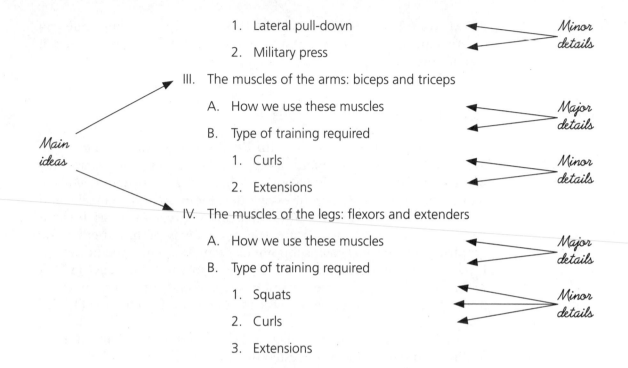

This outline shows that the writer will support the thesis by telling readers which muscles to train, what these muscles help them do, which exercises to do, and how to build and tone each muscle. The details are now more specific, and the outline has helped the writer to arrange them logically so that readers will be able to follow the writer's organizational pattern. Someone else writing on the same topic might choose to arrange the details differently or choose different details. How you support a thesis is up to you, as long as your details are specific and are arranged logically.

EXERCISE 5.3   Choose one of the informal outlines in Exercises 5.1 and 5.2, and add major and minor supporting details so that your outline looks like the expanded one on pages 127–128.

ACHIEVING COHERENCE BETWEEN PARAGRAPHS

Coherence means how well ideas hold together. Just as the sentences of a paragraph must flow smoothly and be logically related, so must the paragraphs of an essay. What ties introductory, body, and concluding paragraphs together are your thesis, your controlling idea, and the transitional words and phrases within and between paragraphs. The following extract from the beginning of "Vocabulary Building," a chapter from Jess Stein's *The Word-a-Day Vocabulary Builder,* illustrates how the author uses a thesis and transitional words and phrases to achieve coherence between paragraphs.

In borrowing so freely, the English language did just what we do as individuals to increase our personal vocabularies. [When we see something strange or experience something new, either we take the name for it that someone else— whether a foreigner or not—is using or, on the basis of some real or fancied resemblance, we take an old word and apply it in a new situation.] This gives it a new meaning and us a new word.

Thesis

Kangaroo is an example. Captain Cook first saw a kangaroo during his exploration of the South Pacific (1768–1771). No European language had a name for this animal, much less an idea of it. It was a very strange and exciting thing. Therefore, it *had* to be talked about at once and that meant it had to have a name. There is a story that when Cook asked a native what the animal was, the native, in his own tongue, said, "I don't understand you." Since that statement sounded something like "kangaroo," Cook mistook it for the creature's name and forthwith called it that.

Repetition of a key word or term

Relates back to: "We take the name . . . that someone else is using"

Though Cook does not tell the story himself, it is a very old story and may very well be true. Nobody has ever found any word in any known Australian native language that describes the beast and sounds like kangaroo. But then, according to the story, that wasn't what the native really said anyway. And the story certainly illustrates a common event in conversation. A asks B a question which B doesn't understand. B gives A an answer which A doesn't understand, but thinks he or she does. Both go along under the impression that they have communicated with each other.

Repetition of a key word or term

At any rate, *kangaroo* is now the animal's name in

English. A word which had never appeared in any European tongue before the latter part of the seventeenth century, and has never been traced to any Australian dialect, is now as fixed in the language as if it could be traced back to Latin. It's accepted as much as *wolf* or *rabbit* or any other name for an animal. . . .

These paragraphs are tied together by one controlling idea: how English borrows from other languages, either by accepting a word that someone else is using or by applying an old word to a new situation. Stein develops the thesis by the extended example of how *kangaroo* became part of the English language: Captain Cook adopted the word he thought he heard an Australian call the animal now known as a kangaroo. Three types of transitions help achieve coherence in Stein's paragraphs:

1. Signal words that establish a relationship between paragraphs

2. Repeating of a word, phrase, or idea in one paragraph that is mentioned in the previous paragraph

3. Repeating of a key word or term throughout the passage

The word *example* in the first sentence of Stein's second paragraph signals that an idea mentioned in the previous paragraph will now be illustrated. In the first sentence of the third paragraph, the phrase "the story" repeats the phrase "there is a story" from the previous paragraph. This transition indicates that the third paragraph will tell readers more about "the story." Throughout the four paragraphs, Stein's repetition of the word *kangaroo* lets readers know that the example continues and keeps their attention focused on the thesis: how English borrows words.

Suppose you had written the first thesis statement in Exercise 5.1:

Malls not only provide a place to shop, but they have become popular entertainment centers as well.

Imagine also that you had begun writing an informal outline using the two subpoints given in the exercise.

1.   They provide teenagers with a place to hang out.

2.   They provide endless subjects for people watchers.

With a little rewriting, you could use these sentences as the topic sentences of your first and second body paragraphs following your introduction. To achieve smooth transitions between paragraphs, you could add a signal word or phrase to your topic sentences, as shown below.

If you visit a shopping mall on any weekend, you will probably see more people milling, or should I say "malling," around than buying. The mall is a place to hang out. For some, it is a place to exercise. For many, the mall is a cheap way to spend an evening. Malls not only provide a place to shop, but they have become popular entertainment centers as well.   *Thesis*

"For example" signals that an example follows to illustrate one way the mall functions as an entertainment center

For example, the mall is a popular hang-out for teenagers. Teenagers looking for an afternoon or evening's entertainment will find it at their local mall. Even if they don't have any money, they can hang out in a video arcade and watch their friends play "World Heroes," or they can roam the aisles of Waldenbooks and see what's new in fiction. If the mall has a food court, they can get an inexpensive meal at a Nature's Table, Chik-fil-a, or Sbarro. They might even take in a movie, check out the new clothes in their favorite stores, or indulge a popular pastime, people watching.   *Circles indicate repetition of key ideas*

"another source" indicates that another example of the mall as entertainment center follows

Endless subjects for the people watcher stroll the mall, providing another source of entertainment. Mall walkers keep up a steady pace in their Nikes and warm-up suits. This group includes men, women, the old, the young— anybody who wants a good aerobic workout in a safe, stimulating, temperature-controlled environment. . . .

To complete the essay, you could add more examples of "subjects" for the people watcher, then one or more paragraphs that explain other ways in which the mall is an entertainment center. Finally, you could conclude your essay using one of the strategies explained later in this chapter.

Each time you revise your essay, you should seek ways to improve the coherence of your paragraphs. For example, in the essay on page 131, you might use "entertainment" or a related concept such as "pastime" or "recreation," as a controlling idea to repeat throughout the essay. You as a writer are free to organize your essay any way you like and select whatever examples, facts, or reasons you think will support your thesis. Of course, not everyone is familiar with large shopping malls characteristic of sprawling suburban areas. Where do city dwellers shop, and where do urban teenagers hang out with their friends? In your neighborhood or community, where do people go for entertainment and what do they do? Let knowledge and experience shape what you write.

Whatever you write, remember to keep your audience in mind. Smooth transitions between paragraphs will give your essay coherence and help your readers keep up with you.

EXERCISE 5.4   Examine Phyllis Theroux's essay on pages 120–123 for the three types of transitions listed below. Find and mark them in the text; then share your results with the rest of the class.

- Signal words that establish a relationship between paragraphs
- Repeating a word, phrase, or idea in one paragraph that is mentioned in the previous paragraph
- Repeating of a key word or term throughout the essay

EXERCISE 5.5   Revise an essay you are working on to improve organization and coherence. To improve organization, try making an outline of what you have written so far. An outline may help to reveal weak spots in your development. For example, you might find that a paragraph consists of one or more general statements with no examples to support them. To improve coherence, read the first sentences of your paragraphs and determine whether transitions are missing, or decide how you can improve on the transitions you have.

EXERCISE 5.6   Do you need more help with unity and coherence? Find out what online resources are available by visiting one of these three sites. Then download an exercise or other information that you find helpful to share with the class.

http:owl.english.purdue.edu

www.bartleby.com/141/index.html

http://leo.stcloudstate.edu

CONCLUDING YOUR ESSAY

A good conclusion brings your essay to a close that satisfies readers and does not leave them hanging. Have you ever turned the page of a book, story, or article only to find you were at the end when you had expected to read more? This might happen to readers if you do not end your essay on a note of finality that makes clear you have said all you intend to say about your topic. Of course you do not want to say to readers, "Now I have concluded my essay." Instead, you need to be less obvious and more creative with your endings. Four of the introductory strategies explained in Chapter 4 also work as good concluding devices:

1. End with an anecdote that reinforces your thesis

2. End with a quotation and an explanation that relates to your thesis

3. Use additional facts and figures to reinforce your central idea

4. Ask one last revealing question that makes readers think about what you have said

The following examples illustrate possible thesis statements and concluding paragraphs of essays for each of these devices:

EXAMPLE 1: END WITH AN ANECDOTE

Thesis: *Superstitions are of three major types: those that come from religious beliefs and practices; those that have a historical basis; and those that have cultural or national origins.*

Concluding paragraph with anecdote underlined:

. . . A friend of mine accompanied me on a shopping trip recently. As we were walking down the street, talking and looking at the window displays, we suddenly had the choice of continuing on our path, which led directly under a ladder or walking out of our way to avoid it.

Without so much as a pause in the conversation, we walked around the ladder. In doing so, we did not stop to think that we were observing an age-old practice to ward off evil. If you should catch yourself falling into an old superstitious habit, just remember that it probably has some religious, historical, or cultural significance.

EXAMPLE 2: END WITH A QUOTATION AND AN EXPLANATION

Thesis: *To successfully prepare for an exam, you need to first understand the material you want to remember; then use one of several common memory aids to help you study.*

Concluding paragraph with quotation and explanation underlined:

. . . Someone once said, "You cannot remember what you do not understand." Preparation alone is not enough, especially when your preparation consists of memorizing without understanding. To make the best use of the tips we have explained, first determine what will be on your test. Next, review your lecture and textbook notes and any other materials until you are sure you understand them. Then apply the memory aids that work best for you.

EXAMPLE 3: USE ADDITIONAL FACTS AND FIGURES

Thesis: *The evidence is conclusive that smoking is a health hazard and that those who smoke should make every effort to kick the habit.*

Concluding paragraph with a fact and a figure underlined:

. . . If you, like some smokers, still believe that the claims of tobacco use causing lung cancer, emphysema, and other diseases are largely exaggerated, talk to your doctor. Better yet, visit a hospital ward for emphysema patients. Although you may not realize it, deaths from tobacco-related illnesses outnumber deaths from drug abuse two to one. In fact, more people die every year from smoking than from automobile accidents.

EXAMPLE 4: ASK ONE LAST REVEALING QUESTION

Thesis: *Selecting a home computer is difficult unless you know exactly what you want your computer to do.*

Concluding paragraph with question underlined:

. . Selecting a computer for home use is no easy task because technology is changing so rapidly that your computer will be outdated almost as soon as you get your programs running. If you do not require "state-of-the-art" equipment, pick a model that will do what you want it to do and will last for several years. Consider all the jobs you normally use a computer for and buy one that does those tasks. <u>Two years from now will you still be happy with your computer, or will you be kicking yourself for the extra money you spent on fancy features you have never used?</u>

You may also want to try these additional concluding strategies:

- Summarize thesis and support.
- Predict the future.
- Challenge your readers.

Summarize Thesis and Support

To summarize your thesis and support in a concluding paragraph restate your thesis in different words, and briefly summarize the main ideas of your body paragraphs. Suppose you had written an essay using the expanded outline on pages 127–128. You could write the following concluding paragraph:

. . . Though there are many weight-training programs to choose from, one that focuses on building and toning the chest, back, arms, and legs will give you the best results. If you join a health club or gym, make sure you get the right type of training for each of these muscle groups.

This short paragraph restates the thesis and summarizes main ideas I–IV on the outline.

Predict the Future

Another way to conclude an essay is to point to some future outcome readers can expect as a result of what you tell them in your essay. For example, you might conclude the essay on a good weight-training program by telling readers what they can expect and how long it will take.

The following paragraph concludes an essay about the presidential election of November 2000 and its outcome. The author believes that the problems associated with this election will lead to election reforms.

> . . . In conclusion, the presidential race of 2000 finally ended in a photo-finish with both candidates carrying 49 percent of the popular vote and with George W. Bush winning by a nose in Florida—enough to give him that state's electoral votes. However, this election dragged on until voters tore up their racing forms, so to speak, and no one was placing any bets on its outcome. Two unprecedented events had voters steaming: Several major networks called the Florida vote for Al Gore before all the ballots were in, and hassles involving confused voters and confusing ballots, recount discrepancies, and lawsuits on both sides prolonged the outcome. As a result we can expect that by election 2004 both the media and the election supervisors in most states will have cleaned up their acts. Like old horses, butterfly ballots and punch-card ballots may be retired and many state legislatures will be re-examining their election laws.

The paragraph begins with a summary of the election's outcome and the problems leading up to it and ends with a prediction about the future of presidential elections in the United States.

Challenge Your Readers

If you are writing persuasively about a topic, one of your purposes might be to get readers to change their behavior or to consider a better way of doing something. For example, suppose you write on the ineffectiveness of smoking and nonsmoking areas in restaurants and you argue that there cannot be a nonsmoking area in a restaurant if there is a smoking area simply because the smoke from one area will drift into the other. You conclude that we need legislation to prohibit smoking *anywhere* in restaurants and other public places in the interest of providing a truly smoke-free environment. Your conclusion might challenge readers who agree with you to write their representatives and demand more nonsmoking legislation.

Following is the conclusion from "Rock Lyrics and Violence Against Women," an essay by Caryl Rivers. Rivers's thesis is that rock music that depicts violence against women sends a subtle message to its listeners that the violence is OK.

. . . I think something needs to be done. I'd like to see people in the industry respond to the problem. I'd love to see some women rock stars speak out against violence against women. I would like to see disc jockeys refuse air play to records and videos that contain such violence. At the very least, I want to see the end of the silence. I want journalists and parents and critics and performing artists to keep this issue alive in the public forum. I don't want people who are concerned about this issue labeled as bluenoses and bookburners and ignored.

And I wish it wasn't always just women who were speaking out. Men have as large a stake in the quality of our civilization as women do in the long run. Violence is a contagion that infects at random. Let's hear something, please, from the men. . . .

Rivers's conclusion challenges readers by asking them to do something about the violence against women that is expressed in some of the lyrics of rock music. Rivers also issues a special challenge to men to speak out.

EXERCISE 5.7

Apply what you have learned about concluding devices by doing this exercise with group members. First, review the list of group roles and responsibilities as explained in Figure 1.6, page 28. Next, complete the four-step activity that follows. Then evaluate your group's performance.

1. Read and discuss the concluding paragraphs of "Should My Tribal Past Shape Delia's Future?" (pages 5–8) and an essay of your choice from Unit 3.

2. Identify the concluding device each author uses.

3. Be able to explain whether or not the conclusion ends the essay on a note of finality and how it helps reinforce the essay's thesis.

4. Explain your group's conclusions in writing to share with the rest of the class.

GROUP EVALUATION

What did each person contribute to the group's activity? Was your group's performance successful? Why or why not? What additional questions do you have about concluding devices?

TOPICS FOR WRITING

1. Choose one of the topics below, or make up your own topic; then plan and write an essay.

   the advantages and disadvantages of shopping with others

   money-saving tips for shoppers

   men or women as consumers

   a favorite item of clothing and what it means to you

   a business that has benefitted (or harmed) your community

   clothes as a form of rebellion or self-expression

2. Imagine you had to buy one gift for each member of your family and you had only twenty-five dollars to spend for all the gifts. Write an essay explaining what you would buy and why.

3. "Dress for success" was a theme of corporate business in the 1980s. Do clothes affect others' perceptions of us? Can the way we dress determine the opportunities that are available to us? Write an essay in which you answer these questions.

Checklist for Revision

As you revise and edit your essay, check for the following:

1. Have you determined the major divisions of your essay?

2. Are the main ideas of your paragraphs clear?

3. Do you have enough evidence to support each main idea?

4. Is your evidence organized logically?

5. Do you have smooth transitions between paragraphs?

6. Have you concluded on a note of finality?

7. Which concluding device have you used, and do you think it is an effective one for your essay?

8. Are your sentences error-free?

THE CRITICAL THINKER

To examine Phyllis Theroux's essay in more depth, think about and discuss the following questions. Then choose one of them as a topic for writing.

1. Why do you think Theroux lists and numbers her rules for shopping with children? Does her list help or hinder readers' ability to follow the ideas? What, if anything, does Theroux's choice of a listing format have to do with her tone in this essay?

2. In paragraph 16 the author says "It seemed to me that social success depended on having at least one of three commodities: a fabulous personality, fame, or a yellow Pandora sweater." On what does "social success" depend today?

3. You have probably heard the old saying "Clothes make the man," although today we would say "Clothes make the person." In either case, what do you think this saying means, and do you agree or disagree with it? Do you see any relation between "clothes make the person" and Phyllis Theroux's comments about shopping with children (pages 120–123)? Write an essay in which you answer these questions, or make up a new saying about clothes, and write an essay explaining it.

4. The difference between what Theroux wants her children to wear and what they prefer to wear might be explained in terms of a generation gap. Do you see evidence of a generation gap today in clothing styles, political views, attitudes toward the environment, or in some other area? Write an essay about the generation gap in one specific area—for example, politics, music, or a personal value, such as honesty or responsibility.

YOUR DISCOVERY JOURNAL

Phyllis Theroux's point of view in this essay is that of a mother who finds shopping with children a frustrating experience. How would her rules be different if she were writing from the point of view of a child who finds shopping with parents a frustrating experience? To experiment with writing from different points of view, imagine that you are a child shopping with a parent. In your journal, write several rules for shopping with parents. Number and explain your rules.

Chapter 6

Revising Your Essays

*T*he first draft you write is rarely, if ever, your best work. Sometimes you do not really know what you think about a topic until you start to write about it, and sometimes what you think you know is not what you end up writing. When you write your first draft, you may try to get down on paper or on the computer screen everything you think you want to say about your topic. Usually, you are writing from an outline or some other prewriting material you have generated. When you rewrite to revise, you compose additional drafts in which you leave out, add to, reorganize, and improve upon the ideas that first came to mind. Your final draft should represent your best work.

Revising takes time. That is why it is important to allow yourself plenty of time to complete writing assignments and not wait to begin writing until the night before they are due. Many experienced writers like to let their ideas *incubate*. They like to write a draft and let it sit for a day or two, then come back to it fresh. When they return to writing, they may have additional ideas or a whole new perspective on their subject. With each draft, your writing has the potential of improving. Athletes, for example, do not learn their sport once and for all, then never practice again; they continually practice and experiment with ways to increase their skill. Tiger Woods, like many professional golfers, has been polishing his skills since he began to play golf as a child. Though he has won many tournaments, he still feels his game needs improving,

141

so he practices every day. The late Anne Sexton, a poet, said her poems were never finished. Once they were published and in print, she could no longer revise them; however, she could still see room for improvement. Writers, like athletes, must practice.

Above all, revising means more than merely correcting surface errors; it means *rewriting* your essay to make structural improvements in content, organization, and style. Proofreading and correcting mistakes are the final steps toward getting your essay ready to hand in. They are part of the *editing* process as explained in Chapter 7. This chapter explains how to revise your essays to improve content, organization, and style.

AWARENESS CHECK

Before reading the following student essay, explore your experiences with storms. Think about the questions below, and answer them either on your own or in a group discussion:

1. Have you ever experienced a tornado or other severe storm? What happened?

2. As a result of your experiences, do you fear storms or take them in stride? Why?

3. Read the title, headnote, and first two paragraphs of the following essay. Based on this preview, what do you think will follow?

A Night to Remember (student essay)
Steve Hackney

Steve Hackney was a student at Valencia Community College in 1994 when he wrote "A Night to Remember" in response to an assignment for his writing class. He revised the essay several times to achieve the results that are displayed in his final draft.

VOCABULARY CHECK

intrigued (1)	interested, curious
foreboding (1)	predicting misfortune

wary (1)	watchful, cautious
patrons (3)	regular customers
eerie (4)	strange and frightening
literal (4)	actual
vain (5)	useless
rendered (7)	made, caused to be

I have always been intrigued by storms. The wind, lightning, and thunder stir my emotions to produce a foreboding curiosity. This feeling draws me near, but at the same time makes me wary of getting too close. My favorite place to watch storms is at the beach. I love to sit out on the balcony of the hotel room at night when a storm passes by. I can sit for hours and watch the blue fingers of lightning dive behind an invisible horizon against the black background of the night. I've often wondered how it would feel to be struck by lightning or what it would be like to experience a hurricane or tornado. Well, I've recently had the opportunity to be involved in some nasty weather. I had the misfortune of driving through the severe storm that ripped through Lake County in March of 1993. After experiencing something like that firsthand, my feelings about storms have definitely changed.   1

To celebrate the beginning of the weekend, my fiancée and I had rented a couple of movies; we had spent most of the evening lying in front of the television. Because we had the VCR on, we were completely uninformed of the bad weather that was approaching.   2

Unaware of the warnings that had been issued by the local weather stations, I started home at about 11:30 P.M. There were no signs of bad weather other than a light drizzle, but that didn't seem to be anything to worry about. It appeared to be an ordinary Friday night, except for one thing: the streets were deserted. The night spots in downtown Mt. Dora usually attract quite a few patrons during the weekend, but not this night. There was no traffic, no pedestrians on the sidewalk, no one anywhere.   3

As I left the eerie streets of Mt. Dora and turned left onto Lakeshore Drive (the road runs along the shoreline of Lake Dora) the weather began to change dramatically. The wind began to blow fiercely, and the rain was getting harder with each passing second. Palm fronds were blowing across the road like leaves. The rain was now coming at me horizontally instead of vertically, blowing from left to right. Within a few minutes, I couldn't see the road directly in front of   4 my car. The force of the rain felt and sounded like a hundred fire hoses aimed directly at the left side of my car. I slowed down to a literal crawl and tried to continue without driving into the lake or a ditch.

After a vain attempt to drive the remaining quarter of a mile to my house, I had to pull over. I couldn't see anything but water. The stretch of road that I was on is particularly close to the shoreline, and apparently the water from the lake was being blown across the road. The reality of what was really happening was beginning to set in, and I started to panic. I knew by the force of the wind that a tornado had to be close by. As I sat beside the road, my car was violently rocked back and forth like a row boat in the middle of the ocean. Horrible images filled my mind. All I could think about was my car flipping over or a tree branch crashing through the window and hitting me in the head. I didn't know what to do other than pray, and I did. I kept saying over and over, "Please, God, don't let me die."   5

A few moments later, I began to think that if there was a tornado in the area, and it was coming my way, I didn't want to be around when it arrived. So, fearing for my life, I forced the car door open and started running. I ran down a side street to the front porch of the first house I came to. I rang the doorbell, but no one answered. I ran to a second house and, again, no answer. Finally, I ran across the street to a house with a light in the window and rang the doorbell. An elderly man answered the door and was kind enough to let me use his telephone. I called my parents to tell them where I was and that I was OK. I stood dripping wet on the man's porch until the rain died down. I then thanked him, ran back to my car, and proceeded to make my way home. When I arrived there, I considered myself lucky to be alive and without injury.   6

Because of the events of that night and how I was rendered helpless by the forces of nature, my feelings about storms have changed. I'm still intrigued by their beauty, but now a different element of thinking comes into my mind: respect for their power and fear of their potential. I still like to watch the storms when I go to the beach, but only if I'm well out of their reach.   7

THE CRITICAL READER

Central Idea

1. What is the essay's thesis? Is it stated or implied?

2. Is the author's purpose to inform you of the dangers of storms, to persuade you to be wary of storms, or to express how he feels about storms? How can you tell?

Evidence

3. Why was the author unaware of the storm's approach?

4. List the details that describe what the storm was like.

5. The author uses time order to organize the essay. What signal words help you follow the chain of events?

Implications

6. The author says his new respect for a storm's power is the result of firsthand experience. Some people would agree that we learn more from direct experience than from the secondhand experience we get from reading or hearing about something. Do you agree or disagree? Why?

Word Choice

7. Explain the author's use of the words *foreboding, wary, invisible,* and *misfortune* in the first paragraph. Why do you think he chose these words? What mood do they create, and how do they help introduce his thesis?

REVISING MEANS REWRITING

It is hard to try to think of everything at once. Most of us do better when we concentrate on one thing at a time. Rather than trying to make your first draft perfect and, therefore, your only draft, think of the first draft as a *discovery draft,* as explained on pages 9–10. In this draft you will *begin* to explore your subject, come up with a preliminary thesis and support, and perhaps discover an organizational pattern that seems right for your topic and purpose. After the first draft, plan on at least three revisions: one for *content,* one for *organization,* and one for *style.*

Rewriting for Content

If you were to ask other students what they find difficult about writing, many of them would answer, "Thinking of something to say." Because you too may find it difficult to think of what to say, your writing may be filled with *generalities,* statements that are too broad to provide readers with a clear vision of what you mean. Specific details not only make your writing clear; they make it interesting, alive. The following example shows a general statement that has been rewritten to make it more specific.

General: A large wave came out of nowhere, causing damage at Daytona Beach.

Specific: At Daytona Beach on July 3, 1992, a towering twelve-foot wall of water crashed to shore, overturning cars and causing injury to beach-goers who were unable to scramble to safety. Scientists could not account for "the mystery wave," though some thought it may have resulted from an earthquake. One survivor, who was driving along the beach at the time the wave hit, later said, "You haven't surfed 'til you've done it in a Jeep."

The general statement becomes more specific by adding *content* in the form of specific details: a date, a description of the wave, examples of the type of damage that occurred, a possible explanation of the wave's cause, and a quotation from someone who was there. The addition of content not only creates a picture of the wave in readers' minds; it gives them a sense of being there.

To rewrite an essay for *content,* read it one paragraph at a time, and underline general words, phrases, or statements that you can make more specific. Make notes in the margin to remind yourself where you need to add content. To gather information, explore your memory, use firsthand observation, interview people, or do some research in the library. For example, if you want to write about Daytona's mystery wave or some other natural disaster, such as a hurricane or flood, you can get all the information you need by going to the library or the Internet and researching newspaper articles that have reported the story.

The following essay has been annotated to show where the writer needs to add content.

Earthquake!

What had you heard that made you want to live there?

Last summer, I visited my cousins in California. I had really looked forward to this trip because I had heard so much about California. In fact, I used to think I wanted to live there someday. Now I am not so sure. On my visit, we had an earthquake. No one was hurt, but the damage it

What month? What city? What are your cousins' names?

caused and the cleaning up we had to do afterward made me realize how disastrous an earthquake can be.

How did it feel? Compare it to something.

We were all sitting around the living room watching television when we felt this little tremor. Then there was another one that lasted longer and got worse. The house began to shake, and things were falling off the shelves. My uncle told us all to either find a doorway and brace ourselves against it or get under a table. When it was all over, the whole house was a mess.

How long? How much worse? Can you describe it?

Replace "things" with specific words.
Add details to explain what each person did.
Describe the damage more.
Add examples— dishes? lamps?

The damage was just unbelievable. Part of the roof had caved in. Just about anything that could break was broken. My aunt lost some of her prized possessions. We were without water and electricity.

Add one or two examples.

How long?

What did you do?

It took us about a week to clean up the mess, fix the roof, and make the house look halfway decent again. When my visit was over, there were still some things left to be done. Even with all this trouble, I still had a good time. In a way, disaster brought us closer.

Add examples.

Give an example.

EXERCISE 6.1   Rewrite the general statements below to add *content* in the form of specific details. To find information, use resources such as your college catalog for Question 1, your experience for Questions 2 and 3, and first-hand observation for Questions 4 and 5. Questions in parentheses indicate which parts of the statements need specific details added.

1. My college provides support services (What kind?) that can be helpful (How?) to students. (Which ones?)

2. Recently (When?), I had a bad car accident. (What was the damage? How did it happen? Who was involved?)

3. My family began to recycle (Recycle what? What is each member doing?) to help save the environment. (How?)

4. A certain television program (Which one?) is harmful for children (How?) because of the bad values it expresses. (What values? How does it express them? What makes them bad?)

5. I would recommend (To whom?) a certain movie (Which one?) for several reasons. (What are the reasons?)

EXERCISE **6.2**   Read your draft of an essay in progress and identify sentences or paragraphs that need rewriting for content. Determine what kind of information you should add. Then rewrite the essay.

Rewriting for Organization

Chapter 1 explains that the direction of development in an essay moves from the *introduction* and *thesis statement,* to the *support* of the thesis with *evidence,* to the essay's *conclusion.* The direction of development is expressed in the essay's three basic parts: *introduction, body,* and *conclusion.* Each part has a specific function.

The introduction builds a context for your thesis either by supplying background information, relating an anecdote, explaining a quotation relevant to the thesis, supplying interesting facts and figures, or asking a revealing question. These introductory devices set the stage for the thesis, which is the central idea of your essay. The introduction also clarifies your purpose for your readers and tells why you have chosen the topic and what you want to tell readers about it. To achieve better organization in the introduction, revise to achieve one of the following goals: make better use of an introductory device; have a more specific or clearly stated thesis that meets the criteria of *topic* and *comment* broken down into *opinion, purpose,* and *parts.*

The body of your essay should contain enough specific details such as facts, reasons, and examples to fully develop your thesis. In addition, the details should be unified and coherent. To achieve better organization in the body of your essay, revise each paragraph so that it has the following:

- a topic sentence that clearly relates to your essay's thesis

- details that do not stray from the topic so that your paragraph has unity

- transitional words and phrases between paragraphs to achieve coherence

- signal words within paragraphs to achieve coherence

The conclusion ends the essay on a note of finality either by summarizing your thesis and support, predicting a future outcome for readers, or challenging readers to change an opinion or to take action. Other concluding devices are an anecdote, quotation and explanation, question that reinforces the thesis, or an additional fact or figure that brings home your central idea. To achieve better organization in the conclusion, revise it for better use of a concluding device or to more clearly reinforce the thesis.

Before you begin the revision process, examine your draft to determine whether it has the three essential parts and whether they fulfill the needed functions. You might either make an outline of your essay to find out what is already there and what needs revision, or you might ask yourself several questions about your essay as suggested in Figure 6.1.

Read the following essay. Then determine what makes it well organized.

FIGURE 6.1

Questions to Ask About Organization

PARTS OF AN ESSAY	QUESTIONS TO ASK YOURSELF
Introduction	Have I used an appropriate *introductory strategy?* Is my *purpose* clearly stated or implied? Do I have a sufficiently *limited topic?* Do I have an effective *thesis statement?* Is my writing directed to a specific *audience?*
Body	Does each paragraph have a *topic sentence* or clearly implied main idea? Do *topic sentences* relate to the thesis? Does my essay have *coherence;* that is, are my ideas arranged in a logical sequence, and do they flow smoothly? Do I have appropriate *transitions* between paragraphs and between ideas within paragraphs? Does my essay have *unity;* that is, do I stay on the topic?
Conclusion	Have I used an appropriate *concluding device?* Does my conclusion end my essay on a *note of finality,* or does it leave readers hanging?

Give Mine to the Birds

Robin Simmons

I realize that worms are a very available food source, that if I dig up rich, damp earth, I can harvest many of these squirming creatures free. Since ground beef goes for about $3.49 a pound, worms would be a considerable savings. I also know that worms are very high in protein and that some cultures consider worms a delicacy. Still, I would never eat worms because they are unappetizing, difficult to prepare, and unpopular with other people.

1

Initially, I would be repelled by the worms' unappetizing characteristics. I am not used to seeing my pork chops writhing on my plate, so wiggling worms would make me queasy. Moreover, I would gag if I stabbed a worm with my fork and it started to squirm wildly. Because they are mucous-coated on the outside, they would slip around in my mouth, sliming my tongue. On the inside, worms are gritty from all the dirt in their digestive tract, so my teeth would grind annoyingly as I chewed. Furthermore, worms are usually bluish-grey and tipped with pink. These colors remind me of chewing gum stuck to the undersides of school desks, a rather distasteful association.

2

Even if I could stomach their unpalatable features, I would not know how to prepare worms. The last time I perused the meat section of Winn-Dixie, there were no cellophane-packaged worms snuggled between the chicken legs and cube steaks. Nor can I buy prepared worms at a deli as I do chicken salad and baked beans. Even if I had a supply of fresh worms, I would not know how to filet the critters because they are so thin and easily punctured. Furthermore, no cookbook has worm recipes. Are worms most tasty scrambled with eggs for breakfast, chopped and sprinkled over ice cream, served as an appetizer on Hi-Ho crackers, or heaped like fried onions on hot sandwiches?

3

The most important reason I would never eat worms is that everyone would think I was crazy. Dad, in anger and disappointment, would disinherit me while Mom would wring her hands and ask over and over, "What did we do wrong?" Next, my friends would no longer accept my dinner invitations or invite me to potluck suppers if they knew I was preparing a worm dish. I would similarly be shunned by my coworkers. Everyone would steer clear of me in the breakroom because no one wants to sit next to a person slurping up worms Alfredo.

4

It is too much trouble learning to stomach the many unappetizing characteristics of worms. I also do not have time to find delicious recipes for cooking these slimy creatures. Nor do I wish to live with the ostracism that eating worms would win me. So until McDonald's creates a McWorm item for its menu, I will leave worms for early birds.

5

EXERCISE 6.3

Apply what you have learned about what makes a well-organized essay by doing this exercise with group members. First, review the list of group roles and responsibilities explained in Figure 1.6, page 28. Next, read and discuss the following questions about "Give Mine to the Birds." Take notes on your discussion, and be prepared to share your results with the rest of the class. Then evaluate your group's performance.

1. Which paragraphs make up the essay's introduction, body, and conclusion?

2. Which of the following introductory devices has Simmons used: *an anecdote, a revealing question,* or *facts and figures?* Is her choice an appropriate one and why?

3. Is her purpose primarily to *entertain, inform,* or *persuade?* How can you tell?

4. Does the introduction include a thesis statement? What is it?

5. Who is Simmons's audience, and how can you tell?

6. Do the body paragraphs have topic sentences? If so, where? How do they relate to the thesis?

7. Find and mark in the essay some transitions Simmons has used both between and within paragraphs.

8. What gives Simmons's essay *coherence* and *unity?*

9. Which concluding device has Simmons used: *Give readers a challenge, restate the thesis, summarize main ideas?* Is her choice appropriate and why?

10. How can you apply what you have learned from Simmons's essay to your own writing?

GROUP EVALUATION

What did each person contribute to the group's activity? Was your group's performance successful? Why or why not? What additional questions do you have about what makes a well-organized essay?

EXERCISE 6.4

Now evaluate one of your own essays for organization, using the same kinds of questions as in Exercise 6.3. Then rewrite your essay to achieve better organization.

Rewriting for Style

The way you express yourself in writing is your writing *style*. Though many factors influence a writer's style, keep in mind these three basic factors as you revise your essays: *diction, tone,* and *sentence variety.*

Diction means *word choice.* Good diction is a matter of selecting words that are appropriate for your audience and purpose and that clearly convey your meaning. In the following passage, the writer's purpose is to convince readers that bats are interesting mammals that we should appreciate for the important ecological role they play. The writer assumes that the audience may include readers who fear bats or who react to them with disgust.

Every evening about sundown bat-lovers, skeptics, and the just plain curious gather at the Congress Street bridge in Austin, Texas, where one of nature's most dramatic events unfolds. The bridge is the home of more than half a million Mexican bats, one of the largest colonies in the United States. As the sun fades and as the lights in high-rise buildings across the river slowly blink on, the bats begin their exodus from under the bridge. For several minutes thousands of the small, furry mammals form what looks like two columns of black smoke originating at opposite ends of the bridge. The bats spiral upward until the two columns merge into one over the middle of the river. Still the bats come, their long black trail spiraling upward over the river until it is too dark to see them.   1

Despite their bad reputation as disease carriers and their association in the public imagination with horrific images of vampirism, bats, like most wild animals, are harmless to humans if left alone. Though there are about a thousand species of bats, they have certain similarities in appearance. Most of them have furry bodies and dog-like faces with bright eyes and sharp teeth. Their wings consist of membranes stretched over bone that look like the halves of an umbrella. Bats are not blind, although most of them use high frequency sounds to communicate, navigate, and find prey. Much to the delight of humans, most bats eat insects. A large colony of bats can consume billions of insects in one season. Scientists say that without bats to control their numbers, insect populations would increase at a rate that would endanger crops and other forms of plant life.   2

So we owe a debt of gratitude to our friend the bat. In fact, many people encourage the formation of small bat colonies in their own backyards by building bat houses: wooden boxes that are partitioned inside and open at the bottom. Bats hang onto the partitions to sleep, hibernate, and nurse their young. At sundown people who have in-   3 stalled bat houses can sit on their porches and watch a mini-version of Austin's nightly drama with the added benefit of a reduction in their backyard mosquito population.

The choice of words in this passage characterizes the bat as a friendly creature in the sense that it performs an essential service for humans: keeping the insect population under control. For example, the word "home" describes the bat's habitat under the bridge. *Home* has pleasant associations for most readers, so it is a better choice than the more scientific *habitat.* The writer could have said that the bat has a rat-like face but instead chose *dog-like,* a descriptive phrase that will seem friendlier to most readers. The repetition of *drama* to describe the colony's flight at sundown characterizes this event as an awe-inspiring natural occurrence and underscores the idea that bats should not be feared.

Tone, as explained in Chapter 2, means *voice*—how you would want your voice to sound if you were reading your essay aloud. Tone also means *mood:* the overall feeling readers get when they read your essay. Diction is a part of tone. Diction is the choice of words, and tone is the overall effect or "sound" of those words. A textbook chapter has a teaching tone that fits its informational purpose. A political speech may have a tone that varies from folksy to outraged to match whatever persuasive purpose the speaker has in mind. Tone, therefore, is linked to purpose. The tone you choose depends upon your purpose in writing and what you expect readers to feel as they read your essay.

A tone can be amusing, angry, objective, serious, or pleading, to mention a few of the many choices available to you as a writer. The tone in the bat essay is informal and conversational. The writer has avoided using scientific or technical terms and has chosen words for their visual effect to appeal to a general audience. For example, *smoke* describes what the mass of bats in flight looks like. The bats' wings are compared in appearance to the *halves of an umbrella.* Though perhaps not a scientifically accurate comparison, it creates a familiar image for readers. In the essay, the sun *fades;* the buildings *across the river* are *high-rise* ones; and the lights *slowly blink on.* These words and phrases create an image of an urban setting in which the natural drama takes place, and they create a *peaceful* mood. Following are a few brief passages and their tones. Words and phrases that establish each tone are underlined.

Passages

Tones

1. In discontinuing its mosquito control program, the county commission has once again displayed <u>poor judgment</u>. With a reported encephalitis outbreak <u>threatening</u> our continued health, we voters should send a message to the <u>so-called guardians of public health</u> who advised the commission to make this <u>unwise</u> budget cut.

Angry (The choice of words encourages readers' mistrust of the commission and its decision.)

2. <u>Still water is a breeding ground</u> for mosquitoes. They lay their eggs in moist environments where water collects in pools. Swamps, <u>for example</u>, are a typical breeding place, as are pools of water that stagnate in drainage ditches and canals.

Objective (Examples and definitions are hallmarks of this tone, as are word choices that are free of emotion and judgment.)

3. Parents, <u>please</u> do not send your children outdoors to play without protection from insect bites and stings. Mosquitoes and flies carry diseases. Yellow jacket stings can be deadly, and many children have allergic reactions to insect bites. I <u>urge</u> you to shop for a safe insect repellent and to use it. I <u>implore</u> you to keep your children's arms, legs, and feet covered during times of the year when biting and stinging insects are most prevalent.

Pleading (The three underlined words indicate a pleading tone, one that begs readers to feel or act in a certain way. A plea is stronger than a simple request.)

4. I doubt that you could live on a <u>steady diet</u> of mosquitoes, though you may enjoy them as an <u>appetizer</u> or <u>delicacy</u>. Covered with chocolate, they are a sweet source of <u>protein</u>. Of course, you may have to eat a <u>glob</u> of them the size of a

Amusing (The tone results from the contrast between seriousness in the underlined food terms, and humor of the slang term <u>glob</u>.)

raisin to taste them, and you may enjoy the experience more if you close
your eyes.

EXERCISE 6.5   Compare the tones of Steve Hackney's essay on pages 142–144 and Robin Simmons's essay on page 150. How are their tones different? How does each writer's tone fit the purpose? What specific words or phrases help you identify the tone in each essay?

Sentence variety can keep your writing from becoming monotonous. If all your sentences are short simple sentences, your writing may sound choppy and unsophisticated. If you *vary* your sentence length and type so that you have a mix of short and long sentences that begin in different ways, your writing will be more interesting, and you will begin to develop a more mature style. Using coordination (pages 446–450) and subordination (pages 450–457) to combine sentences is one way you can begin to add variety to your sentences.

To revise an essay for style, first read through the whole essay and ask yourself whether the tone is what you want and whether it suits your purpose. If it is, read through your essay again, one paragraph at a time, underlining all your descriptive words and phrases. Examine each one of these to see if your word choices, or diction, effectively convey your tone. If they do not, then substitute better choices. A dictionary and thesaurus are helpful guides. If your tone is unclear, think about your whole essay in terms of your purpose and decide which tone you want, then proceed as above, underlining descriptive words and choosing more appropriate ones. Second, one paragraph at a time, analyze your sentences for length and type. If you are using mostly one-sentence length or type, rewrite some of your sentences to achieve variety. See pages 462–469 for four ways to add variety to your sentences. See also Figure 6.2 for a list of tone words and their meanings.

FIGURE 6.2

Tone Words and Definitions

amused	comical, provoking laughter
angry	showing anger or rage
apathetic	indifferent, unconcerned
arrogant	displaying undeserved importance or pride

FIGURE 6.2 (CONT.)

Tone Words and Definitions

bitter	harsh and resentful
cheerful	happy, expressing good will
condescending	displaying a superior attitude
compassionate	showing pity and sorrow for others' suffering
critical	judgmental, evaluating on the basis of worth
cynical	scornful and bitterly mocking
detached	unemotional, uninvolved, impersonal
distressed	upset, worried
earnest	deeply sincere
evasive	vague, intending to be unclear
formal	proper, conventional
indignant	angry with feelings of injustice
intense	profound, showing depth of feeling
ironic	saying one thing but meaning another
mocking	making fun of
objective	considering all sides without judging
outraged	shocked, morally offended
optimistic	positive, looking on the good side
playful	humorous and full of fun
pleading	begging, showing urgency
pompous	displaying an inflated sense of self-worth, egotistical
reverent	respectful
sentimental	overly sensitive or emotional
serious	concerned, responsible
solemn	serious and dignified

EXERCISE 6.6

Revise one of your essays for tone. Underline descriptive words and phrases, and determine whether these are the best choices to convey your attitude toward the topic. For additional help with understanding tone, see Strunk and White's *Elements of Style* at, www.bartleby.com/141/index.html. Use *tone* as your search word.

TOPICS FOR WRITING

1. Write an essay on a topic of your choice. Let your first draft be a discovery draft. Examine it carefully to determine what needs improving. Then revise your essay for *content, organization,* and *style.*

2. Write a new essay on a topic you select from those listed at the end of any previous chapter. Let your first draft be a discovery draft, then revise your essay for *content, organization,* and *style.*

3. Choose a topic from the following list of additional writing suggestions. Write an essay and revise it for *content, organization,* and *style:*

   a public official from your state, city, or county who should or should not be reelected

   a product that is or is not worth the cost

   a TV program that may be beneficial or harmful to viewers

Checklist for Revision

As you revise and edit your essay, check for the following:

1. Is your topic sufficiently limited?

2. Is your purpose clear?

3. Is it clear who your audience is?

4. Do you have a clearly stated thesis?

5. Do you introduce it effectively?

6. Do you have topic sentences or clearly implied main ideas for each paragraph?

7. Are your body paragraphs fully developed with specific facts, reasons, and examples?

8. Have you used good transitions and does your essay have unity and coherence?

9. Do you conclude your essay effectively?

10. Are your sentences error-free?

THE CRITICAL THINKER

To examine Steve Hackney's essay in more depth, think about and discuss the following questions. Then choose one of them as a topic for writing.

1. What introductory and concluding devices does Hackney use in his essay? Are they effective? Why or why not? (To review introductory and concluding devices, see pages 107–113 and 133–137.)

2. In which paragraph does Hackney use time order? In which paragraph does he use spatial order? Are these coherence patterns good choices for organizing the details in these paragraphs? Why or why not? (To review coherence patterns, see pages 82–86.)

3. Using the checklist for revision on pages 157–158, how would you rate Hackney's essay for its overall effectiveness? What areas for improvement do you see in the essay?

4. Steve Hackney's general topic is *an experience that changed my life.* His limited topic is *a night in March 1993 that changed the way I feel about storms.* If you were writing on the general topic, how would you limit it? What experience would you choose, and how has it changed the way you think, feel, or behave?

YOUR DISCOVERY JOURNAL

This chapter's central idea is that revising means rewriting. What does *revising* mean to you? What have you learned from this chapter about revising? In the past, what role has revision played in your writing process, and what role will it play in the future? Answer these questions in your journal.

Chapter 7

Editing Your Essays

*E*diting, like revising, is part of the rewriting process. Editing is the last stage in the process, something you do after you have already revised your essay several times for content, organization, and style. When you *edit,* you read your essay carefully to find and correct any mistakes you have made in grammar, spelling, and punctuation before you write your final draft. You may also find additional changes you want to make in word choice and sentence structure. *Proofreading* is a final editing check. Before you hand in your final copy, *proofread* it for errors you may have overlooked and for neatness and legibility.

Editing your essays is necessary for a few very good and practical reasons. Since the purpose of writing is effective communication, your readers will expect your work to be as neat, legible, and error-free as you can make it. They should not have to struggle with misspelled words and other obstacles to the clear communication of ideas. Most job applications, for example, ask you to explain in writing why you want the job or why you would make a good employee. Surface errors, such as misspelled words and incorrect verb tenses, really stand out on an application. A prospective employer may conclude from them that you would be unable to successfully complete reports and other writing tasks the job may require. Finally, your writing represents you. Like everything else from the way you dress to the way you speak, your writing sends a message. Spend enough time editing so that you can be proud of the message you send.

AWARENESS CHECK

Before reading the following excerpt, explore your thoughts about editing. Think about the questions below, and answer them either on your own or in a group discussion:

1. What kinds of mistakes do you find when you edit your essays? Which ones do you usually overlook?

2. What does the word *clutter* mean to you? What sorts of things could create clutter in an essay?

3. Read the title, headnote, and first two paragraphs of the following excerpt. Based on this preview, what do you think will follow?

Clutter

William Zinsser

William Zinsser has written many books, both fiction and nonfiction. He has also worked as a journalist and a college professor. The following excerpt comes from On Writing Well.

VOCABULARY CHECK

laborious (4)	difficult
pompous (5)	boastful, self-important
ponderous (6)	burdensome
euphemism (6)	flattering term that replaces an unflattering one
tenure (9)	term of office or length of service
arsenal (10)	collection, storehouse

tedious (10)	boring, dull, tiresome
insidious (11)	not obvious
stupefied (11)	bored, made dull
component (12)	part
appended (12)	added on
festooned (13)	draped, adorned, covered with
prune (14)	cut, trim

Fighting clutter is like fighting weeds—the writer is always slightly behind. New varieties sprout overnight, and by noon they are part of American speech. Consider what President Nixon's aide John Dean accomplished in just one day of testimony on television during the Watergate hearings. The next day everyone in America was saying "at this point in time" instead of "now."

Consider all the prepositions that are draped onto verbs that don't need any help. We no longer head committees. We head them up. We don't face problems anymore. We face up to them when we can free up a few minutes. A small detail, you may say—not worth bothering about. It *is* worth bothering about. Writing improves in direct ratio to the number of things we can keep out of it that shouldn't be there. "Up" in "free up" shouldn't be there. Examine every word you put on paper. You'll find a surprising number that don't serve any purpose.

Take the adjective "personal," as in "a personal friend of mine," "his personal feeling" or "her personal physician." It's typical of hundreds of words that can be eliminated. The personal friend has come into the language to distinguish him or her from the business friend, thereby debasing both language and friendship. Someone's feeling *is* that person's personal feeling—that's what "his" means. As for the personal physician, that's the man or woman summoned to the dressing room of a stricken actress so she won't have to be treated by the impersonal physician assigned to the theater. Someday I'd like to see that person identified as "her doctor." Physicians are physicians, friends are friends. The rest is clutter.

Clutter is the laborious phrase that has pushed out the short word that means the same thing. Even before John Dean, people and businesses had stopped saying "now." They were saying "currently" ("all our operators are currently busy"), or "at the present time," or

1

2

3

4

"presently" (which means "soon"). Yet the idea can always be expressed by "now" to mean the immediate moment ("Now I can see him"), or by "today" to mean the historical present ("Today prices are high"), or simply by the verb "to be" ("It is raining"). There's no need to say, "At the present time we are experiencing precipitation."

"Experiencing" is one of the ultimate clutterers. Even your dentist will ask if you are experiencing any pain. If he had his own kid in the chair he would say "Does it hurt?" He would, in short, be himself. By using a more pompous phrase in his professional role he not only sounds more important; he blunts the painful edge of truth. It's the language of the flight attendant demonstrating the oxygen mask that will drop down if the plane should run out of air. "In the unlikely possibility that the aircraft should experience such an eventuality," she begins—a phrase so oxygen-depriving in itself that we are prepared for any disaster.

Clutter is the ponderous euphemism that turns a slum into a depressed socioeconomic area, garbage collectors into waste-disposal personnel and the town dump into the volume reduction unit. I think of Bill Mauldin's cartoon of two hoboes riding a freight car. One of them says, "I started as a simple bum, but now I'm hard-core unemployed." Clutter is political correctness gone amok. I saw an ad for a boys' camp designed to provide "individual attention for the minimally exceptional."

Clutter is the official language used by corporations to hide their mistakes. When the Digital Equipment Corporation eliminated 3,000 jobs its statement didn't mention layoffs; those were "involuntary methodologies." When an Air Force missile crashed, it "impacted with the ground prematurely." When General Motors had a plant shutdown, that was a "volume-related production-schedule adjustment." Companies that go belly-up have "a negative cash-flow position."

Clutter is the language of the Pentagon calling an invasion a "reinforced protective reaction strike" and justifying its vast budgets on the need for "counterforce deterrence." As George Orwell pointed out in "Politics and the English Language," an essay written in 1946 but often cited during the Vietnam and Cambodia years of Presidents Johnson and Nixon, "political speech and writing are largely the defense of the indefensible. . . . Thus political language has to consist largely of euphemism, question-begging and sheer cloudy vagueness." Orwell's warning that clutter is not just a nuisance but a deadly tool has come true in the recent decades of American military adventurism in Southeast Asia and other parts of the world.

Verbal camouflage reached new heights during General Alexander Haig's tenure as President Reagan's secretary of state. Before Haig nobody had thought of saying "at this juncture of maturization" to mean "now." He told the American people that terrorism could be fought with "meaningful sanctionary teeth" and that intermediate nuclear missiles were "at the vortex of cruciality." As for any worries that the public might harbor, his message was "leave it to Al," though what he actually said was: "We must push this to a lower decibel of public fixation. I don't think there's much of a learning curve to be achieved in this area of content."

I could go on quoting examples from various fields—every profession has its growing arsenal of jargon to throw dust in the eyes of the populace. But the list would be tedious. The point of raising it now is to serve notice that clutter is the enemy. Beware, then, of the long word that's no better than the short word: "assistance" (help), "numerous" (many), "facilitate" (ease), "individual" (man or woman), "remainder" (rest), "initial" (first), "implement" (do), "sufficient" (enough), "attempt" (try), "referred to as" (called) and hundreds more. Beware of all the slippery new fad words: paradigm and parameter, prioritize and potentialize. They are all weeds that will smother what you write. Don't dialogue with someone you can talk to. Don't interface with anybody.

Just as insidious are all the word clusters with which we explain how we propose to go about our explaining: "I might add," "It should be pointed out," "It is interesting to note." If you might add, add it. If it should be pointed out, point it out. If it is interesting to note, *make* it interesting; are we not all stupefied by what follows when someone says, "This will interest you"? Don't inflate what needs no inflating: "with the possible exception of" (except), "due to the fact that" (because), "he totally lacked the ability to" (he couldn't), "until such time as" (until), "for the purpose of" (for).

Is there any way to recognize clutter at a glance? Here's a device my students at Yale found helpful. I would put brackets around every component in a piece of writing that wasn't doing useful work. Often just one word got bracketed: the unnecessary preposition appended to a verb ("order up"), or the adverb that carries the same meaning as the verb ("smile happily"), or the adjective that states a known fact ("tall skyscraper"). Often my brackets surrounded the little qualifiers that weaken any sentence they inhabit ("a bit," "sort of"), or phrases like "in a sense," which don't mean anything. Sometimes my brackets surrounded an entire sentence—the one that essentially repeats what the previous sentence said, or that says something readers don't need to know or can figure out for themselves. Most first drafts can be cut by 50 percent without losing any information or losing the author's voice.

My reason for bracketing the students' superfluous words, instead of crossing them out, was to avoid violating their sacred prose. I wanted to leave the sentence intact for them to analyze. I was saying, "I may be wrong, but I think this can be deleted and the meaning won't be affected. But *you* decide. Read the sentence without the

10

11

12

13

bracketed material and see if it works." In the early weeks of the term I handed back papers that were festooned with brackets. Entire paragraphs were bracketed. But soon the students learned to put mental brackets around their own clutter, and by the end of the term their papers were almost clean. Today many of those students are professional writers, and they tell me, "I still see your brackets—they're following me through life."

You can develop the same eye. Look for the clutter in your writing   14 and prune it ruthlessly. Be grateful for everything you can throw away. Reexamine each sentence you put on paper. Is every word doing new work? Can any thought be expressed with more economy? Is anything pompous or pretentious or faddish? Are you hanging on to something useless just because you think it's beautiful?

Simplify, simplify.   15

THE CRITICAL READER

Central Idea

1. *Clutter* is a broad topic. How does Zinsser limit his topic? What does he mean by clutter?

2. In your own words, what is Zinsser's thesis?

3. What is Zinsser's purpose—what does he want writers to be able to do?

Evidence

4. Does Zinsser support his thesis with mainly facts, reasons, or examples?

5. Is Zinsser's essay coherent? What transitional words and phrases do you find?

Implications

6. Zinsser's first paragraph contains a *metaphor,* a figurative comparison that makes a point: "Fighting clutter is like fighting weeds." Zinsser continues the metaphor in that same paragraph when he says that new varieties "sprout" overnight. Where else in the essay does Zinsser compare clutter to weeds, and why do you think he does?

7. Are there occasions when it may be appropriate to use a tired expression in writing? For example, could you use one appropriately in dialogue, in direct quotations, or in certain kinds of business correspondence? Or should you always substitute a fresh expression for a tired one?

Word Choice

8. Jargon is occupational slang. It may be acceptable on the job, but it clutters writing because people outside the occupation do not know what it means. Zinsser's examples of political jargon include "at this point in time" for *now* and "reinforced protective reaction strike" for *invasion*. Business jargon includes terms such as "finalize" for *end* and "empower" for *strengthen*. What other examples of jargon can you think of, and where have you heard them?

ELIMINATING SURFACE ERRORS

Surface errors are the mistakes in grammar, punctuation, and spelling that distract from the content of your essay. Because surface errors stand out, they call attention to themselves, and readers may notice them before they have a chance to consider your thesis and support. If your writing contains surface errors, you need to understand why you make them and what you can do to eliminate them. Surface errors usually result from one or both of the following conditions:

1. Inconsistent application of the rules of Standard English

2. Careless mistakes that, like typographical errors, occur when you are paying more attention to content than to mechanics

To apply the rules of Standard English consistently, brush up on them by reviewing the explanations and exercises on pages 416–517. To find your careless mistakes, proofread.

Editing for Grammar

Become aware of the kinds of errors you most frequently make by carefully examining essays that have been graded and returned to you. Suppose, for example, that your essays often contain pronoun agreement errors. When you proofread, check every pronoun to make sure it agrees in number with the person or thing it refers to. Proofreading essays before you hand them in should help you find typographical errors and other mistakes.

Figure 7.1 lists examples of some common grammatical errors and how to correct them. Read the figure, and find the type of mistake you most often make.

FIGURE 7.1

Correcting Common Grammatical Errors

ERROR	EXAMPLE	CORRECTION
Fragment	When the lights went out.	Connect the fragment to an independent clause: "When the lights went out, we were plunged into darkness."
Comma splice	John felt his way around the room, he was looking for candles and matches.	Replace comma with period or semicolon: "John felt his way around the room; he was looking for candles and matches."
Run-on sentence	We waited for the lights to come back on after an hour we decided to call the power company.	Find the two independent clauses. Separate them with a period or semicolon: "We waited for the lights to come back on. After an hour we decided to call the power company."
Dangling modifier	Sitting in the dark, light came into the room from the full moon outside.	Who was sitting in the dark? After the comma that ends the modifier, insert the subject the modifier describes: "Sitting in the dark, we saw the light that came into the room from the full moon outside."

FIGURE 7.1 (cont.)

Correcting Common Grammatical Errors

ERROR	EXAMPLE	CORRECTION
Pronoun-antecedent agreement	Someone remembered that they had a battery-operated radio.	*Someone* is singular, and it is the antecedent of *they.* Change *they* to either *he* or *she* to agree with *Someone:* "Someone remembered that she had a battery-operated radio."
Pronoun case	John and her went to look for the radio	*Her* is one of the subjects of the sentence. *Her* is an objective-case pronoun. Change *her* to *she,* which is a subjective-case pronoun: "John and she went to look for the radio."
Subject-verb agreement	We heard on the news that people's lights was out all over the county.	Make the verb agree with the subject: "We heard on the news that people's lights were out all over the county."
Inconsistent tense	It was a power blackout, so we listen to the radio and waited for the lights to come back on.	Since the blackout took place in the past, all the verbs should be in the past tense. Make *listen* a past-tense verb: "It was a power blackout, so we listened to the radio and waited for the lights to come back on."
Inconsistent point of view	When the lights came back on, we had gotten so used to being in the dark that you had to adjust your eyes.	*You* is inconsistent because the point of view is first-person plural. Change *you* to *we* and your to our for consistency: "When the lights came back on, we had gotten so used to being in the dark that we had to adjust our eyes."

EXERCISE 7.1   Practice your editing skills on the following paragraph by reading it carefully to find and correct grammatical errors. Share your findings with the rest of the class.

> Recently my husband and me took our children to visit my father who lives on a farm in Pennsylvania. He raises cattle and pigs he grows all his own vegetables. He sell most of them, but he saves enough to have all he wants to eat. He has an apple orchard and he has a pretty good deal going with an Amish settlement near where he lives. He gives them apples for making cider in exchange for all the cider you can drink. We thought it would be good for our children to see what it is like living in the country, and it will not hurt them to participate in the chores. The trip was one of the best we have ever had. Much to our surprise, the children loved helping their grandfather milk cows, feed the pigs, and tend the garden. Our sixteen-year-old sold vegetables from my father's produce stand at the entrance to his property and was thrilled that they let her keep some of the proceeds. Driving home, the visit was one we decided to repeat in the future.

Editing for Punctuation

When you are editing, check for correctly punctuated sentences. When you are drafting, and even when you are writing your final copy, it is easy to leave out commas and end punctuation marks. A quick review of what to look for may help you find and correct punctuation errors. See pages 475–480 for an explanation of how to use commas and pages 470–475 for more punctuation rules.

Editing for Spelling

Spelling errors can interfere with the good ideas you are trying to communicate. If you know you have a spelling problem, you need to use the dictionary when you write. Spelling errors may result from two major problems: not knowing the common rules of spelling and confusing the spelling of words that look or sound alike. See pages 514–517 for an explanation of common spelling rules. See also pages 509–513 for an explanation of the most commonly confused words.

ANALYZING YOUR ERRORS

How much editing you have to do depends upon how many errors you usually make. If your only problem is a misspelled word now and then, one reading may be enough for you to find and correct your spelling errors. If you usually make several errors in grammar, punctuation, and spelling, you may have to do several readings: one for grammar, one for punctuation, one for spelling, and a final reading to see whether you missed anything. Figure 7.2 on page 170 contains an editing checklist that will help you analyze your essays for errors. After you have analyzed several of your essays, you will be able to tell whether the errors you make are random or whether they fall into certain categories. Then you will know what you need to concentrate on when you edit.

EXERCISE 7.2

Using the checklist in Figure 7.2, examine several of your returned essays for errors. What types of errors did you make? What was your most frequent type of error? Search the Web for online exercises that will give you practice correcting your types of errors. Eliminating these errors from your writing will help you communicate your ideas more clearly and effectively. Begin your search by checking the following websites. Then share the results of your search in a brief written report or a class discussion.

http://owl.english.purdue.edu

http://leo.stcloudstate.edu

http://webster.commnet.edu/grammar/index.htm

TRIMMING AND TIGHTENING YOUR ESSAYS

William Zinsser's essay on pages 160–164 explains how our writing can become cluttered with empty words and phrases that interfere with effective communication. *Trimming and tightening* an essay means editing it to eliminate three kinds of clutter:

1. wordiness

2. passive voice

3. tired expressions

FIGURE 7.2

Your Editing Checklist

TYPE OF ERROR:	NUMBER OF ERRORS					
	ESSAY #1	ESSAY #2	ESSAY #3	ESSAY #4	ESSAY #5	ESSAY #6
Fragment						
Comma splice						
Run-on sentence						
Dangling modifier						
Pronoun-antecedent agreement						
Pronoun case						
Subject-verb agreement						
Inconsistent tense						
Inconsistent point of view						
Punctuation						
Spelling						
Other error						
Other error						

As you trim clutter from your essay, tighten it by eliminating wordiness, changing passive voice to active voice, and substituting original ideas for tired phrases.

Wordiness

Wordiness is what results when you say in two or more words what you could say in one carefully chosen word. *Due to* and *due to the fact that* are wordy phrases that mean *because*. Another good replacement for these phrases is *since*. As Zinsser says, *now* is a better word choice than *at this point in time* or *at present*. If you find *until such time as* in your essay, cross it out, and write *until*. You will say the same thing and do it in fewer words. Wordiness is also called *filler* because it pads your writing with needless words and phrases.

EXERCISE 7.3   Trim and tighten the following paragraph to eliminate wordiness. Share your results with the rest of the class.

> Due to the fact that many students work and have families to care for, attending college in today's society can become a juggling act. A student's responsibilities are like a juggler's clubs. There is one club for attending classes, one for doing homework, and another for studying. All three clubs have to be kept in the air. If students drop just one club, for example, if they miss too many classes, they may find themselves withdrawn from a course. There are other clubs in the juggling act of students who have jobs and families. They have to add housework clubs and work-responsibility clubs to their school-responsibility clubs. There is only one way to keep all those clubs in the air, and that is to manage time effectively. Students can do this by making schedules for completion of work, working with employers to arrange convenient hours, and delegating chores to family members. Until such time as they are willing to take these steps, students may find that their juggling acts have flopped.

Passive Voice

Verbs are either *active* or *passive*. If the subject of the sentence performs an action, the verb is in *active voice*.

> The student wrote the essay.

The student writes, so the verb is in active voice. If the subject of the sentence receives the action, the verb is in *passive voice*.

The essay was written by the student.

In this sentence, the subject receives the action, so the verb is in passive voice.

Active voice is usually more effective than passive voice because sentences written in active voice are less wordy and more direct. Passive voice can also be confusing when the performer of the action is not specified. For example:

The essay was left in the instructor's mailbox.

In this sentence, it is not clear who left the essay. To change this sentence into active voice, add a subject:

Toby left the essay in the instructor's mailbox.

Some form of the verb *to be*, such as *is* or *was*, precedes the main verb in a passive-voice sentence. When you edit a sentence by changing the passive voice to active, you get rid of the extra *to be* verbs that precede the main verb and any other words that do not fit the new sentence.

Ryan's hair was cut by Nina.   (passive)
Nina cut Ryan's hair.   (active)

The active-voice sentence leaves out the extra words *was* and *by*.

EXERCISE 7.4   Trim and tighten the following paragraph by finding and changing passive voice to active. Share your results with the rest of the class.

Ben is angry with Cloudy Vale Utilities Company because he feels that he is not getting satisfactory service. His bills keep going up and up, yet the service gets worse and worse. Every day the power goes off for a few seconds. It can happen at any time; for example, one day the power may go off at 3:30 P.M., and the next day it may go off at 6:00

A.M. Although the electricity stays off for only a short time, a lot of trouble is caused by it. Ben's daughter's homework is done on a computer. When the power goes off, everything on the screen is lost, and it has to be rewritten from memory. On weekends, Ben likes to tape the football games on his VCR. If the power goes off during the taping process, it wipes out his programming, and he gets some other show on tape instead of the game. Another problem is that whenever the electricity goes off, all the clocks in the house have to be reset. Ben's family has seven digital clocks: one on the microwave oven, one in each bedroom, one in the utility room, and one each in the family and living rooms. Several letters of complaint have been written, and phone calls have been made to top executives at Cloudy Vale Utilities. Though they listen politely, nothing has been done about Ben's problem. That is why he has concluded that the service is unsatisfactory.

Tired Expressions

A *tired expression,* also called a "cliché," is any word or phrase, old saying, or slang expression that has lost freshness and originality because of overuse. Since normal everyday conversation is filled with tired expressions, you may have to work at keeping them out of your writing. When you edit, eliminate tired expressions and replace them with more interesting and appropriate choices. Figure 7.3 lists some tired expressions to avoid.

EXERCISE 7.5

Apply what you have learned about tired expressions by doing this exercise with group members. First, review the list of group roles and responsibilities explained in Figure 1.6, page 28. Next, complete the following three-step activity, and share your results with the rest of the class. Then evaluate your group's performance.

1. Read and discuss each other's essays in progress.

2. Make a list of any tired expressions you find in the essays.

3. Work together to write a fresh and interesting replacement for each tired expression on your list.

GROUP EVALUATION
What did each person contribute to the group's activity? Was your group's performance successful? Why or why not? What additional questions do you have about tired expressions?

FIGURE 7.3

Tired Expressions to Avoid

in today's society
in this world in which we live
in this fast-pace society
Mother Nature
after all is said and done
last but not least
short but sweet
live and let live
easier said than done
it goes without saying
time and time again
at a loss for words
a blessing in disguise
through thick and thin
day in and day out
What's wrong with this picture?
What part of *no* don't you
　understand?

the whole nine yards
Get a life.
Get over it.
I'm outta here.
your worst nightmare
Are we having fun yet?
You're history.
been there, done that
in your dreams
whatever
a no-brainer
clueless
pretty as a picture
sigh of relief
sick and tired
nine times out of ten
You don't have to be
　a rocket scientist to . . .

PROOFREADING AS A FINAL CHECK

Save proofreading as a last step before handing in your final copy. This is your final editing check to make sure you have not overlooked any surface errors. If you are writing your essay on a word processor, it will be easy to correct your errors and print out a corrected copy. If you have typed or handwritten your essay, you may have to rewrite it, depending on how many changes you have made. If you find only one or two errors, you may be able to white them out neatly with correction fluid and write or type in your corrections. In any case, your final copy should be as neat and error-free as possible. To help make proofreading a productive task, try the suggestions that follow.

Wait a While

Allow yourself enough time to put your final draft aside for a day or two before it is due. When the content is still fresh in your mind, it can distract you from finding mistakes. For example, even though you have misspelled a word, you might read it as correct simply because you are paying more attention to ideas than to the individual words that make them up. If you wait a while to proofread, you will forget some of your content, and it will seem as if you are reading your essay for the first time. Thus, your errors are more likely to stand out.

Pace Yourself

Proofread slowly and carefully. Pace yourself so that you read only one line at a time. Avoid the temptation to look ahead. A wide, twelve-inch ruler is a good pacing device, or you can use a folded sheet of paper. Slowly move it down the page, revealing one line at a time. When you find an error, circle, underline, or highlight it. You may even want to write in the margin what kind of errors you have made, using correction symbols such as *sp* for spelling or *c-s* for comma splice. Develop and use a marking system that works well for you. When you have finished proofreading and marking your essay, go back and make your corrections.

Read Backwards

Even if you wait a while to proofread your essay, you still may become distracted by the content so that you overlook spelling errors. If you know you have a spelling problem, try reading backwards. Start with the last word of the last paragraph and read backwards one paragraph at a time until you work through your whole essay. Reading backwards causes you to read every word, so you are more likely to spot misspellings. Using this method, circle, underline, or highlight misspelled words; then go back and correct them.

Read Aloud

Proofreading aloud can help you find subject-verb agreement errors, pronoun case and agreement errors, and other errors that may result in awkward-sounding sentences. Though you may overlook these errors when reading silently, they may stand out if you hear yourself reading them. If you like to work with a study partner, have him or her read your essay aloud while you read it silently. Proofreading aloud may be especially helpful if your learning style is auditory—that is, if you learn best by listening.

Use Helpful Tools

Have helpful tools available when you are proofreading or doing any writing tasks. A word-processor's spell-check is not only helpful for finding and correcting spelling errors, but it will also give you a word count, which may be useful if your assignment requires you to have a minimum or maximum number of words. A dictionary is necessary for verifying the meaning of a word, and a thesaurus is useful for looking up synonyms when you are trying to avoid repetition or to find better word choices. If you do not have a computer, an electronic spelling checker may be a good investment, especially if you chronically misspell words. This device is about the size of a hand-held calculator. A discount store or your college bookstore may stock some inexpensive models. A word of caution about grammar-checking software: These programs may fail to spot some types of errors and may read some correct sentences or sentence parts as incorrect.

Proofread with a Purpose

If you know from past experience that you usually make certain kinds of errors—for example, spelling, subject-verb agreement, or inconsistent point of view—then proofread once to find your major category of error. Proofread a second time to find general errors other than the one you usually make. By focusing on a certain type of mistake, you are proofreading with a purpose and may be more likely to find and correct your mistakes.

TOPICS FOR WRITING

1. Try out the editing and proofreading suggestions explained in this chapter. Work either on your own or with a partner. Select an essay in progress, or write a new essay, either making up your own topic or using one of the suggestions from any chapter of this book.

2. Write an essay in which you comment on each of the editing and proofreading suggestions and explain what works and does not work for you and why.

Checklist for Revision

As you revise and edit your essays, check for the following:

1. Have you found and corrected grammar errors?

2. Have you found and corrected punctuation errors?

3. Have you found and corrected spelling errors?

4. Have you trimmed and tightened your essay by eliminating wordiness, passive voice, and tired expressions?

5. Are your sentences error-free?

6. Have you spent enough time proofreading your essay?

THE CRITICAL THINKER

To examine William Zinsser's essay in more depth, think about and discuss the following questions. Then choose one of them as a topic for writing.

1. Who is Zinsser's audience, and how can you tell?

2. In his essay, Zinsser explains seven types of clutter. Explain each type, using at least one of Zinsser's examples.

3. Read an article from your local newspaper, an article from your college newspaper, an article from a popular magazine, and a scholarly article from a journal. Your college librarian can help you locate sources. As you read each article, underline any examples of clutter that you find. What conclusion can you draw from the type and frequency of clutter you found in these articles?

4. Review Zinsser's examples of clutter and the tired expressions listed in Figure 7.3. What additional examples of clutter or tired expressions can you recall either from your reading, your writing, or from conversation?

YOUR DISCOVERY JOURNAL

This chapter explains four kinds of clutter to identify and eliminate from your essays: surface errors, wordiness, passive voice, and tired expressions. Based on what you have learned about your writing from doing this chapter's exercises, which kind of clutter gives you the most trouble? What can you do to eliminate it? For your next journal entry, explain what you plan to do to improve your writing.

Chapter 8

Using the Library,
Doing Research

*M*any of your college assignments and many workplace writing tasks require you to seek other people's opinions, knowledge, and experience and to use this evidence in your writing. Where do you get such information? The answer is by doing research. To *research* a topic means to gather information on it from several sources. What do you do with the information once you have found it? As a writer, you have several important choices to make. You must decide what to use, what to discard, how to incorporate it into your paper, and how to credit your sources.

To help you make appropriate choices, this chapter is your introduction to three essentials of research: where to find information, how to use your library, and how to write a research paper.

AWARENESS CHECK

Before reading the following excerpt, explore your thoughts about gathering information for writing. Think about the questions below, and answer them either on your own or in a group discussion:

1. Have you ever written a research paper or done any kind of writing that required you to gather information from outside sources? Were you successful? Was the process easy or difficult, and why?

2. Other than personal experience, what other resources are available to you as a writer?

3. Read the title, author information, and first two paragraphs of the following excerpt. Based on this preview, what do you think will follow?

Where Do You Find Information?

Donald Murray

Donald M. Murray has written many books and numerous articles for the Boston Globe *and other periodicals. Murray is professor emeritus of English at the University of New Hampshire. Following is an excerpt from his book,* The Craft of Revision, *published in 1991.*

VOCABULARY CHECK

mine (1)	to make use of
belt (3)	to hit, punch (slang)
receptive (12)	open to suggestion
hesitation (15)	doubt, uncertainty
dramatic (15)	expressive, forceful
monographs (17)	scholarly writing on a specific subject

One of the reasons I am glad to be a writer is that I am forced to continue to learn. I have to mine my world for the specifics I can use to discover what I have to say. The process of writing is a process of thinking, but if the thinking is to be effective—and if readers are going to read and use it—it must be built from information. And to get that information I have to study my subject.   1

MEMORY

We fear that writing will prove us ignorant. That has often happened in school when we were tested in writing. But, for writers, writing can show us how much we know. Your draft should have revealed your knowledge to you. 2

A writer's memory is an unusual gadget. I don't have a good memory in the TV game-show sense, but when I write about something, information arrives on my page that I have forgotten I knew or that I never knew I knew. My brain has recorded the details of the moment when I saw my first dead soldier in combat generations ago or that wonderful, awful evening when I looked down on my father for the first time and told him that if he hit me again, I'd belt him back. The same thing happens when I write on less personal topics. Ideas, quotations, statistics, references connect on the page. 3

If your draft did not show you how much you knew, you may need to take a step back and discover what you know that you didn't know you knew. 4

BEFORE WRITING

I start collecting information by brainstorming a list, putting down everything I know about the topic I am going to research. Or I fastwrite a "what-I-know" draft to surprise myself. 5

DURING WRITING

While I am writing the draft I encourage the connections I do not expect, or make notes in the draft or on a pad of paper beside my computer of things I suddenly discover in the writing, references to other writing, connections between facts or ideas, new patterns of meaning, sources I have to explore. 6

OBSERVATION

In the academic world observation is often overlooked, yet it can be a productive source of significant information. If you are writing a paper on criminology, visit a police station or a jail; on health care, spend a few hours sitting in a hospital waiting room; on economics, walk through a supermarket or a mall; on literary studies, browse through that part of the library in which your subject is preserved; on government, attend a meeting of the school committee, town or city council. 7

When you observe, make notes. That activity will make you see more carefully as well as preserve what you observe. Note your first 8 impression of a place, a book, a person. Make notes on what is and what is not; what is as you expected and what is not. Look for revealing details: how people interact (does the doctor listen to the patient?); where things are placed (are there forty-seven books about a man writer, two about a woman writer of the same period?); what is happening (are the trees thinner, have fewer leaves and branches because of acid rain?).

Use all your senses: sight, hearing, smell, taste, touch. Take account of how you feel, react. Imagine yourself in the prison cell, as a critic seeing a hundred-year-old work when it was first published, as the patient being examined.   9

INTERVIEW

Live sources should not be overlooked. If you are writing about schools, interview students present and past as well as teachers, administrators, school board members, parents. Read the books and articles about schools, but also go to see the people in the classrooms.   10

Many of the best interviewers are shy. The aggressive, on-the-scene journalist with microphone in the victim's face is *not* the best model for interviewing: "Did you have indigestion after you ate your twins?"   11

Good interviewers are good listeners. Few of us can turn away from a quiet, receptive listener who makes us an authority by asking our opinions. Try not to ask questions that can be answered with a simple "yes" or "no." Not, "Will you vote to make professors sing all their lectures?" but, "Why do you think it is important that professors sing their lectures?"   12

I like to prepare for an interview by listing the questions the reader will ask—and expect to have answered. There are usually five questions—give or take one—that must be answered if the reader is to be satisfied.   13
"Why is tuition being doubled?"
"How will the money be spent?"
"How do you expect it to affect students?"
"Why is it necessary to increase tuition?"
"What are you doing to help students who cannot pay?"

Listen to the questions and follow up on the answers to your questions: "We are raising tuition because the faculty is underpaid." "What evidence do you have that the faculty is underpaid? Can you name faculty members who have left because of pay? What positions are unfilled because the pay is so low?"   14

Note the answers to your questions, but check the ones you have any hesitation about or the ones that are most dramatic and surprising: "We are raising tuition so we can build the first-class ping-pong stadium our students demand." Journalists rarely check back with the per-   15 son they interviewed, but I usually did. The purpose of the interview is not to trick the person being interviewed but to get accurate information to deliver to the reader.

LIBRARY

Libraries are the intellectual closets of humankind where information is stored until we need it. . . . But can we find the information? Not in my closet, I find myself answering. Fortunately, humankind has bred librarians who organize information so that it can be recovered. . . .   16

The starting point for all the resources available to you—books, reference guides, monographs, articles, reports, audio and video tapes—is your librarian. Use the librarian to learn how you can tap into the abundance of information you need to draw on to write—and think—effectively. . . .   17

THE CRITICAL READER

Central Idea

1. Find and underline the thesis statement of the excerpt.

2. Is Donald Murray's audience professional writers, teachers of writing, or student writers? What specific details in the essay help you decide?

Evidence

3. What kinds of evidence are included in the sections following boldfaced headings?

4. How does this evidence support Murray's point?

Implications

5. Murray says that in the academic world, observation as a source of information is often overlooked. Do you agree? Why or why not?

Word Choice

6. In the section under the heading "Before Writing," *fastwrite* is a word coined by the author. What do you think the word *fastwrite* means?

7. How would you describe Murray's tone in this essay: like a journalist reporting the news, like a teacher lecturing to students, or
like a scientist reporting the results of an experiment? If none of
these comparisons fit, make up your own. Find specific words or
phrases that reveal the tone.

USING YOUR LIBRARY

To do effective research, decide what kind of information you are looking for and learn where to find it. Being able to use information retrieval systems and other resources is an essential academic skill that
not only helps you as a writer but also may be useful in the workplace.
Many business transactions and entire careers involve information pro-
cessing. As Donald Murray says, your library is the starting point for all
the resources available to you. Three keys will unlock the mystery of research and help you to find the information you need: *library personnel,
information retrieval systems,* and *your library's resources.*

How information literate are you? To find out, complete the discovery exercise below before reading on.

EXERCISE 8.1   Read each statement, and check the ones that apply to you. After you
finish, read the explanation that follows.

_____ 1. When I go to the library, I usually have a clear idea of what
I am looking for.

_____ 2. The library is a confusing place, and I often have difficulty
finding what I need.

_____ 3. When I have research to do, I make a plan and follow it.

_____ 4. I do not plan my research. I just go to the library and check
out the first book I find that covers my topic.

_____ 5. I usually can determine which sources of information are
likely to cover my topic.

_____ 6. One source seems as good as another to me. I cannot tell
whether a source contains what I want until I start reading.

_____ 7. I am familiar with most of my college library's resources.

_____ 8. I am not as familiar with my library's resources as I need to be.

_____ 9. I can evaluate sources for reliability and usefulness.

_____ 10. I do not know which sources are more reliable or useful than others.

_____ 11. I know what online resources are available in my library, and I know how to use them.

_____ 12. I am inexperienced at doing online research.

If you checked mostly odd-numbered statements, you may already be information literate. If you checked mostly even-numbered statements, you need to develop your information literacy.

Library Personnel

Whether you are researching several sources in the library or trying to find one magazine article, the process of locating that information can be an overwhelming experience. If you are like many students, you may not know where to begin. An important part of a librarian's job is to help you get started.

If you need a general orientation to the library and its resources, ask if there is a guided tour or a videocassette recording that explains what your library provides. Some libraries have a printed guide or handbook available that explains their resources and where you can find them.

You cannot avoid the time it takes to find information in the library, but you can make that time productive and rewarding if you know *how* to find information. Library personnel are waiting to assist you.

Information Retrieval Systems

Suppose you want to write a paper on the possible effects of nutrition on memory, and you wonder whether eating certain foods or lacking vitamins or other nutrients affects your brain's ability to process and retain information. A book on how memory works or an article about the effects of nutrition on memory might contain the information you want. To find a book, use your library's *card catalog*, which is an information retrieval system that organizes books by subject, author, and title. The card catalog may be a physical set of drawers in which you search manually, or it may be an online database—networked with other libraries' holdings—in which you search electronically.

To access a listing for a book from an online card catalog, type responses on a keyboard in answer to questions that come up in the computer screen. First decide which file you want: *subject, author,* or *title.* Once you're in a file, then use search words to find what you need. For example, if you type in "memory," a list of your library's holdings will appear on screen. Print out any listings of books that interest you. The printout will contain call numbers to help you find where the books are shelved.

To access a listing for a book or videocassette recording from a computerized card catalog, type responses on a keyboard in answer to questions that come up on the computer screen. First decide which file you want: subject, title, or author. Once you're in a file, use key words to find what you need. For example, if you type in "memory," a list of your library's holdings on this topic will appear on the screen. If you see a title of a book that interests you, print out the listing, which also has the book's call number. Taking the printout with you, go to the stacks and look for the book.

Your library may have other databases such as computerized indexes to periodicals, newspapers, journals, and other resources. These too may be networked with other listings, and each may require access using a different set of commands. Systems vary from one library to another, so your best bet is to first find out what online resources your library has and what kind of information they contain. Then have a librarian demonstrate each system's use. Online resources are efficient, but they are only one of your library's many resources.

Your Library's Resources

In addition to books, your library contains many other sources of information including *reference works* and *periodicals* (magazines, journals, and newspapers). There probably is a map or drawing posted that shows where you can find these resources. Some of them will be shelved, others may be collected on microfilm or microfiche. *Reference works* include encyclopedias, dictionaries, almanacs, atlases, books of quotations, biographical indexes, indexes to newspapers and periodicals, and government documents. If you want to find Lapland on a map, look in an *atlas,* which is a collection of maps. If you want to know the batting average of a favorite baseball player or the average rainfall in your state, you can find that and other statistics on such subjects as sports, commerce, and politics in an *almanac,* which is published yearly.

If you want to know the site of a geographical area such as a river, volcano, mountain range, or a sea, look in a *gazetteer*. A reference book such as *Bartlett's Familiar Quotations* contains well-known sayings by noteworthy people. You can use this source to find an appropriate quotation to use as the opening of a speech, for example. If you want to find a magazine or journal article on memory, try the *Reader's Guide to Periodical Literature* or the index of a journal that is likely to contain articles of the type you are looking for. For statistics or other information on AIDS in the United States, you might turn to a *government document* on the subject, or your college may have a file on AIDS in its vertical file. The *vertical file* contains large manila envelopes or folders filled with clippings, pictures, pamphlets, and other pieces of information on certain topics. The vertical file is a good place to get an overall feel for a subject you might want to explore in depth, using other resources.

EXERCISE 8.2

Go to the library and find the answers to the following questions. Indicate the resource that contains the information. This exercise will introduce you to some resources you may not have realized are in your library and will serve as a guide to the kind of information they contain.

1. What was the most frequent cause of death among women in 1962? In 1999?

2. Who wrote *The Big Sea,* and when was it published?

3. Who flew the first manned space vehicle?

4. What is the population of Washington, D.C.?

5. What is the definition of *policy wonk?*

6. What college or university did Dr. Martin Luther King, Jr., attend?

7. Who said "I shall return"?

8. An article written by Lynette Clemetson about Oprah Winfrey appeared in the January 5, 2001, edition of *Newsweek.* What is the title of the article?

9. People of what age and sex had the highest number of traffic fatalities in 1997?

10. What teams played at the Superbowl in 1990? Who won?

EXERCISE 8.3

Use the online card catalog to make a list of possible sources for a research topic that interests you. Find the following:

1. a recent book that provides an overview of your topic
2. an article from a magazine on your topic
3. an article from a newspaper on your topic
4. an article from a journal on your topic
5. a passage on your topic from a reference such as *Encarta* at http://www.encarta.com.

Ask a librarian for any help you may need in locating these sources or in choosing appropriate search words.

PLANNING AND WRITING YOUR RESEARCH PAPER

Allow yourself plenty of time to complete a research project. Getting started is much easier if you know what is involved and plan accordingly. Figure 8.1 is an overview of the research and writing process that lists typical steps to follow.

You may not follow all the steps listed in Figure 8.1; for example, you may decide not to try to write a thesis statement until after you have gathered your information and done some thinking about it. Remember that writing is a recursive process, so in this respect, writing a research paper is like writing other kinds of papers. The steps do not necessarily have to be followed in the order listed. During the drafting process you may decide that you need more information and that another trip to the library is necessary. However you adapt the steps to fit your project, schedule your time so that you are not trying to complete the work at the last minute.

Choosing and Narrowing Topics

Though some instructors assign specific research topics, you will often have the opportunity to select your own. When choosing a topic, keep these guidelines in mind:

- **Be realistic.** Select a topic for which resources are readily available, either from your college library or through interlibrary loan.

FIGURE 8.1

Overview of the Research and Writing Process

1. Choose a topic.

2. Narrow topic to an issue (problem or question to be researched).

3. Determine audience and purpose (who will read your paper and why).

4. Write preliminary thesis statement (the central idea of your research paper).

5. Gather and evaluate information.

6. Compile a working bibliography (list of possible sources).

7. Write final thesis statement.

8. Synthesize (put together) information from all your sources using an outline, chart, or other organizer.

9. Draft your paper.

10. Revise your paper and write final copy.

11. Compile a final bibliography (list of sources actually used).

- **Choose a significant topic.** Choose a topic of general interest and concern that allows you to think critically about the facts and opinions you encounter in your research. Avoid trivial, overly technical, or overworked topics such as abortion, capital punishment, and gun control.

- **Choose a topic of personal interest.** Since your research project will take some time, avoid boredom and burnout by selecting a topic that arouses your curiosity or that you think is important.

- **Ask your instructor for ideas.** Your instructor may have some suggestions or helpful hints for narrowing topics. He or she will also be able to tell you the names of major works or authors in your field of interest and steer you in the right direction as you begin your research.

Suppose the human memory has always interested you. "Why do we forget?" and "How can we improve memory?" are questions for which you would like answers. Suppose you do some research into ways to improve memory and stumble upon the idea that listening to music may enhance learning and improve retention. Since you have heard that listening to music interferes with learning and remembering, you begin to wonder what kind of music could enhance learning, and under what conditions it could act as a memory cue. Does listening to music work as a memory aid for only certain kinds of information, or can it improve retention of any material? Now you have a topic to research, a question to answer, and a way to narrow your topic: *Does listening to music help or hinder your memory?* The topic of memory itself is too broad for a research paper. Your narrowed topic deals with only one of the many possible aids to memory.

The prewriting strategies explained in Chapter 2 are useful for narrowing a topic for a research paper. To help you generate ideas, you can brainstorm, freewrite, make a cluster, ask the journalist's questions, or use START. Any one of these strategies may help you to zero in on a narrowed topic suitable for your paper.

EXERCISE 8.4   Following is a list of ten possible research topics. Choose any three and narrow them down to topics you could write about if they were assigned to you.

1. gang violence
2. sports in your city
3. AIDS awareness or education
4. animal communication
5. mandatory drug testing
6. children's TV programs
7. an environmental issue
8. diets
9. the accomplishments of a public figure or celebrity
10. the works of an artist

Limited topic #1 _____

Limited topic #2 _____

Limited topic #3 _____

Determining Audience and Purpose

The *audience* for your paper may be just the instructor, or it may include students. Students and instructors are members of the general public. You can assume that they have some knowledge about your topic, and may have some personal interest or concern as well. To improve your *awareness of your audience,* answer these questions:

> Why is my topic important?
>
> What can I assume readers already know about my topic?
>
> What more do I think readers should know about my topic?
>
> How will their lives or thinking be affected by what I have learned through my research?

The *purpose* for your paper will be either to inform or persuade readers. To determine a purpose, turn your topic, or issue, into a question. If the question can be answered by facts and an explanation, your purpose is to inform. If the question can be answered by your opinion based on a consideration of the evidence you've gathered, then your purpose is to persuade. Consider the following questions:

> *What kinds of music enhance learning and retention of information?*
>
> *Should students listen to music while studying?*

The first question can be answered by facts gathered from research; the purpose, therefore, is to inform. The second question can be answered by stating your opinion based on your understanding of the evidence; the purpose, therefore, is to persuade.

Another way to arrive at a purpose for writing is to consider what effect you want your research to have on your audience. If you expect your readers to be enlightened (to know more about your topic than they did before reading your paper), then your purpose is to inform. If you expect your readers to change their minds or decide to take action after reading your paper, then your purpose is to persuade.

EXERCISE 8.5

For the topics you narrowed in Exercise 8.4, would your purpose be to inform or to persuade? Why?

1. Topic _____

   Purpose _____

   Explanation _____

2. Topic _____

   Purpose _____

   Explanation _____

3. Topic _____

   Purpose _____

   Explanation _____

Writing Your Thesis Statement

The thesis statement of any essay, including a research paper, is its central idea. To arrive at a thesis statement, ask yourself these questions and answer them:

What is my narrowed topic (issue)?	*sex education in middle school*
What question do I have about my topic/issue?	*Why should sex education begin in middle school?*
What is my answer (thesis statement)?	*For sex education to have an impact on teenagers, it must begin in middle school as children near puberty.*

It is common to write a *preliminary,* or working, thesis statement before you begin your research so that you have a clear direction to follow. Knowing the central idea of your paper may guide your research because your primary purpose in writing a research paper is to support the thesis statement. As you learn about your topic, you may revise your thesis statement many times until you arrive at a final thesis statement. On the other hand, you may prefer to wait until you have done some research before you write your first thesis statement.

Suppose that after writing the previous example thesis statement about sex education and researching several sources, you decide that focusing on the age sex education should occur is too narrow. What you really want to write about is what makes an effective sex education program. Therefore, you come up with the following revised thesis statement:

An effective sex education program should include an ethics and values component as well as instruction in birth control methods and safe sex.

A good thesis will control your research paper's development and help you separate relevant from irrelevant information.

EXERCISE 8.6   Using the topics and purposes from Exercise 8.5, now write a thesis statement for each one. Follow the steps outlined below.

Topic #1

1. What is my narrowed topic (issue)?

   _____

2. What question do I have about my topic/issue?

   _____

3. What is my answer to the question (thesis statement)?

   _____

   _____

   _____

Topic #2

1. What is my narrowed topic (issue)?

   _____

2. What question do I have about my topic/issue?

   _____

3. What is my answer to the question (thesis statement)?

   _____

   _____

   _____

Topic #3

1. What is my narrowed topic (issue)?

   _____

2. What question do I have about my topic/issue?

   _____

3. What is my answer to the question (thesis statement)?

   _____

   _____

   _____

Developing Your Research Strategy

No single way to conduct research is best for everyone. However, without a plan to follow you may spend hours searching through sources without finding anything on your topic. To avoid wasting time, develop a research strategy that will help you zero in on the sources most likely to address your topic. If you go to the library with a narrowed topic and perhaps even a preliminary thesis in mind, you have a good chance of finding the information you need. Furthermore, you will have something specific to tell your librarian if you decide to ask for assistance in getting started. A *research strategy* is a plan for finding information that leads you first to general references and then to more specific sources on your topic. The following typical research strategy steps will help you identify key words, know how to document your paper, and evaluate your sources.

1. **Identify key words** that will help you search for information on your topic. Key words and related terms that clearly identify your topic will help you skim through tables of contents in books, headings in periodical indexes, and information stored in electronic databases to find relevant information. If your topic is AIDS, for example, the key words and terms *AIDS, STD* (*sexually transmitted disease*), *venereal disease,* and *immune disorders and deficiencies* may be useful. Your librarian can probably help you compile a list of helpful key words and terms.

2. **Know how to document your paper.** Besides listing all your sources in a bibliography, you must document ideas you take from sources, or you run the risk of plagiarism. *Plagiarism* means taking credit for someone else's ideas; it is a type of stealing. Different academic disciplines have their own *documentation styles,* or preferred ways of indicating the sources from which information is taken. The *MLA style,* developed by the Modern Language Association, is characteristic of research done in the humanities. Those who write in the biological sciences use the *CBE style,* developed by the Council of Biology Editors. If you write a paper for your psychology class, your instructor may want you to use the *APA style,* developed by the American Psychological Association for use in the social sciences.

   Before beginning your research, find out which documentation style your instructor requires. Then, as you are taking notes, be sure to record the information needed for documentation in the style you plan to use. Style manuals are available in your college bookstore, in commercial bookstores, and online.

3. **Evaluate sources** for reliability, objectivity, and usefulness. Primary sources are generally more reliable than secondary sources. *Primary sources* are an author's original work: poems, novels, short stories, essays, autobiographies, diaries, letters, speeches, first-hand reports of research experiments, surveys, and observations. If you use data from any of these sources, you have used primary sources. If you interview an expert or write and conduct your own survey, the data from either are primary sources. *Secondary sources* interpret data from primary sources, analyze experiments and surveys, draw conclusions, and explain events. A news reporter's analysis of a politician's speech is a secondary source. A sports writer's description of a game and conclusion regarding why a team won or lost is a secondary source. A recording of the game or a telecast of the players' and coaches' play analyses are primary sources. Book, film, and play reviews are all secondary sources. How many times have you read a film review (secondary source), then gone to the movie (primary source) and drawn a different conclusion from the reviewer's? A secondary source is only as reliable as its author's quality of research and degree of expertise in the subject.

An objective author reports facts and avoids using unsubstantiated opinions to support claims or draw conclusions. An author who gives even-handed treatment to both sides of an argument and acknowledges opposing views is considered more objective than one who does not. For example, how objective are the views expressed in the publications of the National Rifle Association or the National Organization of Women? Objectivity may be difficult to determine unless you are familiar with an author's qualifications or have extensive background in your subject.

A source is useful only if it is relevant to your topic. Does the research address your subject? Does it provide new data to support your thesis? Furthermore, is it current? Check the publication date of the source before using it. The following checklist for evaluating sources of information may be helpful to you in conducting your research.

- **Is the author an authority?** Check the author's background (degrees held, colleges attended, major field of expertise, works written, accomplishments) in a biographical reference such as one of the *Who's Who* references or the *Dictionary of American Biography.* Ask your librarian which biographical references are in your library's holdings.

- **Is the author a "name" in his or her field?** A recognized expert will be cited in textbooks, reference works, bibliographies, journal articles, and will be well known among other experts in the field. In addition, your librarian will either know or will help you find out how well known an author is.

- **Is the source reliable?** Newspapers and magazines having a wide readership and reputation for accuracy such as the *New York Times* and *Washington Post, Time,* and *Newsweek* are generally reliable. Academic journals are also reliable sources as are books published by large well-known publishers and university presses.

- **Is the source current?** The more recent the copyright date the more likely a source is to contain new research and discoveries. This is especially important in medicine, the sciences, engineering, and computer technology, where research is ongoing and information quickly outdated.

- **Is the source free of bias?** Read carefully to determine whether ideas are supported with hard evidence and logical reasoning. Unsupported opinions and emotional language are not characteristic of authoritative or scholarly research.

Because anyone can publish information on the Internet, be selective about the materials and resources you use. These additional guidelines may help you evaluate the information found on Internet websites.

- **Reputation:** Is the site affiliated, with a well-known and respected group or organization?

- **Scholarship:** Is the information documented? Is proper credit given to its source? Are a variety of sources cited?

- **Links to other sites:** Is the site linked to other reputable sites? Electronic links are like bibliographies. They provide clues to the extent and quality of the author's research.

EXERCISE 8.7   Write a report for the class on a current topic that interests you or choose one from the list in Exercise 8.4. Then go to the library and gather information from three different sources: a newspaper, a magazine, and an additional periodical or government document. Then note any similarities and differences in the way the information is reported. Finally, evaluate your three sources for reliability, objectivity, and usefulness.

TAKING EFFECTIVE NOTES

Three skills essential to taking notes and avoiding plagiarism are *quoting, paraphrasing,* and *summarizing.* These are all ways of indicating that some information is not your own, and all require documentation. Index cards are useful for taking notes. See Figure 8.2 on pages 198–199 for examples of index cards.

Quoting

If you need to *quote,* or state directly, what an author has said, use quotations sparingly and use them only to support your ideas. Do not use a quotation as your thesis statement or topic sentence. Quotations should be integrated within the text of your paper and *framed* by introductory and concluding remarks that explain the quotation's significance, as in the following example from a paper on Edith Wharton's *The Age of Innocence.*

> As the novel opens, the Archers and Wellands are attending the opera. They are only peripherally interested in the music and story; their primary interest is to see who is there and to be seen. The opera is more a social obligation than an entertainment as the narrator suggests in Chapter 1 when commenting on the hasty departure of the spectators after the opera: "It was one of the great livery-stableman's most masterly intuitions to have discovered that Americans want to get away from amusement even more quickly than they want to get to it." This observation hints at one of the novel's minor themes that European art and culture were merely affectations of old New York's upper class, things they knew they should appreciate but did not enjoy, or if they enjoyed them then they did so for the wrong reasons.

Remember to set off direct quotations in quotation marks and to document them according to the style you are using. When your quotation is five lines or longer, single space, indent, and omit quotation marks. See pages 481–484 for an explanation of how to use quotation marks.

Index Cards for Quotation, Paraphrase, Summary, and Bibliography

Quotation

"Those two forces—a powerful surge among American blacks toward freedom, mostly inspired by the *Brown* decision, and a quantum leap in the power of the media—fed each other; each made the other more vital, and the combination created what became known as the Movement. Together, the Movement and the media educated America about civil rights."

Halberstam, David, *The Fifties*. New York: Villard Books, 1993, p. 429.

Paraphrase

The Civil Rights Movement, that began with the outcome of the *Brown* case, was the effect of two events: a growing desire among blacks for freedom and a powerful media that brought their struggle into America's living rooms.

Halberstam, David, *The Fifties*. New York: Villard Books, 1993, p. 429.

FIGURE 8.2 (cont.)

Index Cards for Quotation, Paraphrase, Summary, and Bibliography

Summary

> It took a court decision (*Brown*), a continued struggle on the part of blacks, and the influence of a powerful media to create the Civil Rights Movement.
>
>
>
> Halberstam, David, *The Fifties*. New York: Villard Books, 1993, p. 429.

Bibliography

Call number goes here →

> Halberstam, David
>
> *The Fifties*
>
> New York: Villard Books, 1993

Paraphrasing

Like quotations, paraphrases should be used to support your thinking and should not form the bulk of your evidence. A *paraphrase* is a re-statement in your own words of someone else's words or ideas. A paraphrase restates the entire passage, whether it be a sentence, paragraph, or longer piece of writing, so your paraphrase should be about as long as the original. Paraphrasing from authorities adds weight to your conclusions. To paraphrase accurately, use your own words and sentence structure to restate what the author says. Maintain the intent and emphasis of the original passage, and make sure you copy into your notes all the information you need to correctly document the source, such as page numbers, title of work, and author. The following example shows an original passage, and a paraphrase of it. The passage is about Maria Mitchell (1818–1889) who was the first professional woman astronomer in the United States.

ORIGINAL

Mitchell was a self-taught astronomer, reading mathematics and science while a librarian at the Nantucket (Mass.) Atheneum (1836–56). In 1847, while helping her father, William Mitchell, survey the sky for the U.S. Coast Survey, she discovered a comet, for which she received worldwide attention. In 1848 she became the first woman elected to the American Academy of Arts and Sciences.

In 1865 Mitchell was appointed professor of astronomy at Vassar College. There she gained distinction as a teacher of some of America's leading women scientists, including Christine Ladd-Franklin and Ellen Swallow-Richards. In 1873 her concern with the status of professional women led her to help found the Association for the Advancement of Women.

Mitchell pioneered in the daily photography of sun spots; she was the first to find that they were whirling vertical cavities, rather than clouds, as had been earlier believed. She also studied comets, nebulae, double stars, solar eclipses, and the satellites of Saturn and Jupiter.

From *Encyclopedia Britannica*, Vol. 8, 1992, p. 164.

PARAPHRASE

Maria Mitchell was a librarian in Nantucket from 1836 to 1856. During that time she studied mathematics and science and taught herself astronomy. In 1847, she discovered a comet while working with her father, William Mitchell, on the U.S. Coast Survey. The discovery brought her recognition, and led to several honors and appointments.

In 1848, the American Academy of Arts and Sciences elected her as its first female member. In 1865, Vassar College appointed her as a professor of astronomy. She was a noteworthy professor who taught other women of science; among them were Ellen Swallow-Richards and Christine Ladd-Franklin. In 1873 she was also one of the founders of the Association for the Advancement of Women.

Mitchell was the first to discover through photography that sunspots were cavities, not clouds, and her studies led her to observe a wide range of astronomical phenomena: among them were the satellites of Saturn and Jupiter, solar eclipses, nebulae, double stars, and comets.

Summarizing

A *summary* condenses into a few sentences the central idea of a passage. Therefore, your summary of a passage will be much shorter than the original. The following example is a summary of the passage about Maria Mitchell.

Maria Mitchell, daughter of the astronomer William Mitchell, was a Nantucket librarian who taught herself astronomy. Her discovery of a comet led to world-wide recognition and honors. She became professor of astronomy at Vassar where she taught other women of science. She was the first female member of the Academy of Arts and Sciences and the first to discover the true nature of sun spots. She was a founder of the Association for the Advancement of Women. Her studies led her to observe a wide range of astronomical phenomena.

Whether you quote, paraphrase, or summarize, use a note-taking system that will help you keep track of your sources and compile a bibliography later. Take notes on index cards, because they are much easier to organize than pages. You can lay the cards out on a table and experiment with different ways of putting your information together. If you have more than one card for a source, number the cards. Use a different card for each topic you take notes on from the same source. Identify the source by title, author, and page number at the top of your index card, and indicate what type of note it is, quotation, paraphrase, summary, or your own idea. Use a symbol or a different color ink to distinguish notes that are your own independent ideas from those you get from sources. Once you have decided that you will definitely use a source, make a bibliography card for it. Later, when you compile your bibliography, arrange your cards in alphabetical order and type directly from them. Use Figure 8.2 on pages 198–199 as a guide for writing your note cards.

GATHERING INFORMATION

Now that you have a research strategy, you are ready to begin the search for information. You have many resources available to you; which ones you choose are up to you. You will do most of your research in the library or online, but there are other useful ways to gather information.

Interviewing Experts

An expert can offer an opinion on your topic or provide information either to support or deny what you have already found out. An expert may even suggest ways to approach your topic that you have not considered. Experts include college faculty, business and professional people who know something about your topic, and public officials and employees who act as spokespersons for their various agencies or corporations. To conduct effective interviews, try these tips.

- **Schedule far ahead.** Most people have busy schedules, and you will probably have to make an appointment for your interview. Therefore, if you plan to use interviews as a source of information, get started right away.

- **Prepare a list of questions.** Go to the interview with a clear idea of what you want to find out. If you have thought through the questions you want to ask, you will make better use of the interview time. Phrase your questions so they call for an explanation rather than a yes or no answer.

- **Seek permission to quote the expert.** Also, ask permission if you plan to tape the interview to review later. if your expert does not want to be taped, be prepared to take notes.

- **Evaluate information.** An expert may have a personal bias or special interest that colors his or her views on your topic. It may be useful to interview several people or to weigh the interview information against that gathered from other sources.

- **Express your thanks.** Show your appreciation by thanking the expert and sending a thank-you note.

Making Observations

Suppose you decide to write a paper on criminal justice in your state. The early-release program, whereby criminals who have not served their full sentences are released to make way for new offenders, is a controversial issue. You believe this is an ineffective answer to the problem of crowded prisons and decide to explore the topic further. In addition to any interviews and library research you may do, you decide to spend a few days observing court proceedings to get an idea of the number of prosecutions in a given day and the type of crimes being committed in your city or county.

To *observe* is to watch with a purpose and take notes on what you see. Your observations should be objective or based only on what you see or hear, not on what you think. Thinking about your observations and drawing conclusions come later. During the observation process, your purpose is only to gather facts. This is often difficult, because you may find yourself interpreting the facts in spite of your efforts to be objective. For this reason, you should decide in advance what kind of information you are looking for. Make a checklist of facts you want to find out, or write a series of questions to be answered.

Locating the Best Sources

Plan to spend a minimum of fifteen to twenty hours doing research for a short (5,000–10,000 words) paper. A longer project will take more time. Also, some people work faster than others and some information takes a while to find. Take all of these factors into consideration as you plan your time. You will have to look through many sources, reading some carefully and taking notes and skimming others. Some of the material you want may not be available, and you will have to find alternative sources. All this takes time. Your librarians' assistance is invaluable, and though they will not do the research for you, they will point you in the right direction and teach you how to use any computerized search services your library provides.

A good place to start is with general reference works as explained on pages 186–187, which summarize a tremendous amount of information. From these, move to more specialized references in an academic discipline that relates to your topic. Next, check articles in periodicals that you can find by looking up your topic in a periodical index, such as the *Reader's Guide to Periodical Literature* or the *New York Times Index*—both are general indexes. Even more helpful in locating articles pertaining to your topic are the specialized periodical indexes, such as the *Education Index, Humanities Index,* or *Psychological Abstracts.* Finally, consult books for a more in-depth treatment of your topic. As explained on pages 185–186, most libraries now have a computerized card catalog and other data bases that make conducting an information search easier and more efficient.

EXERCISE 8.8

Apply what you have learned about specialized references by doing this exercise with group members. First, review the list of group roles and responsibilities as explained in Figure 1.6 on page 28. Complete the activity that follows and share your results with the rest of the class. Then evaluate your group's performance.

1. Select an academic discipline from the list below.

business and economics	philosophy and religion
education	political science
fine arts	science and technology
history	social sciences
literature	performing arts (film,
mathematics	television, theater)

2. Go to the library and make a list of up to five specialized references available in your discipline.

3. List the title, author, publisher, and date of each reference and briefly summarize what kind of information it contains.

4. If you have trouble finding the references, ask a librarian for help.

GROUP EVALUATION

What did each person contribute to the group's activity? Was your group's performance successful? Why or why not? What additional questions do you have about specialized references?

PUTTING IT ALL TOGETHER

Your research paper should demonstrate that you understand your information. Rather than being a summary of what you have found, the research should support your thesis by providing the facts to back up your opinion or to answer a question. Writing a research paper is the same as writing any other paper, except that, first, you are using other people's research to support your thesis instead of your own experience; and, second, because your research comes from other sources, you must document your paper.

To write an effective paper, start with an *outline*. Also, you may need to write several drafts to organize and present your ideas effectively. The *first draft* is your first attempt to put your notes together in a coherent way. As you write *additional drafts,* you will refine your organization. You may discover new ways of looking at your topic, leading to additional revisions until you have a *final draft* that is ready to hand in. A research paper develops from the introduction, to the body of the paper, to the summary or conclusion. In the introduction, get your readers' attention by telling them what your topic is, what you're going to say about it, and why it should interest them. In the body of your paper, explain your topic in detail by supporting your thesis statement with evidence you have gathered from your research. In the conclusion, summarize what you have said and leave your readers with a fresh insight in the form of a final thought or challenge.

DOCUMENTING YOUR PAPER

Paraphrasing, summarizing, quoting, or in any way referring to another author's words or ideas requires documentation. To *document* your paper means to cite, or indicate, the source from which you have taken an author's words or ideas. The documentation style you use will depend on the discipline for which you are writing your paper or your instructor's preference. Because the MLA style is the one most widely used, this section contains a brief overview of that style. For a more comprehensive review of the MLA style (or any other style), consult one of the many style manuals available from your college library or bookstore.

You should be familiar with two ways to cite sources: an *in-text citation* and a *Works Cited* list. A Works Cited list goes at the end of your paper and includes all the sources you have used. An in-text citation refers the reader to an author and page number listed in Works Cited. Both types of citations require a special format. For in-text citations, see Figure 8.3. For Works Cited, list all sources, double spaced, on a separate sheet titled "Works Cited." List the sources alphabetically by au-

---

FIGURE 8.3

MLA In-Text Citations

FORMAT

Place the citation at the end of a sentence in which you refer to or quote a source. List the author's last name and the page number in parentheses.

If you mention the author in your sentence, list the page number only.

If your Works Cited list contains two works by the same author, either name the work in your sentence or shorten the title in your citation.

If a source has two or three authors, list their last names in your citation.

If a source has four or more authors, list the first one only followed by *et al.,* which means "and others."

EXAMPLES

According to the author, higher gasoline prices and smaller families helped transform the marketplace of the 1970s (Kahaner 23).

According to Kahaner, higher gasoline prices and smaller families helped transform the marketplace of the 1970s (23).

According to Kahaner in *Competitive Intelligence . . .* (23).

According to Kahaner . . . (*Competitive* 23).

The authors conclude . . . (Reece and Brandt 75).

The authors define . . . (Bernstein *et al.* 215).

thor's last name or by title if no author is given. Figures 8.4 and 8.5 illustrate the formats to use for listing books and articles.

TOPICS FOR WRITING

The best topic for a short research paper is one that interests you. Choose from the list below or make up your own topic. Then follow the suggestions offered in this chapter for researching, planning, and writing your paper.

1. Either use the information gained from Exercise 8.7 or research another career that interests you. Then write about it.

FIGURE 8.4

MLA Works Cited Format for Books

BASIC FORMAT FOR BOOKS

author	title	place of publication

Kahaner, Larry. *Competitive Intelligence* New York:

publisher	date	(Indent second line.)

Simon, 1990.

TIP: Note placement of information and punctuation.

EXCEPTIONS

Two or three authors	Include all names in the order given.
Four or more authors	List first name followed by *et al.*
Two books by same author	For first book list author's name. For next book replace name with three hyphens in front of title.
Book by an editor	List editor's name followed by *ed.*
Edition and publisher	Edition numbers follow the title. Publishers' names are shortened (Simon for Simon & Schuster).

FIGURE 8.5

**MLA Works
Cited Format
for Articles
From
Periodicals**

JOURNAL

     author   **title**   **journal**
Farrell, Thomas J. "Symposium on Basic Writing." *College English*
volume   date   **pages**
    55 (1996): 889–92.

MAGAZINE

      author   **title**   **magazine**   **date**
Morganthau, Tom. "The War Over Weed." *Newsweek* 4 Feb. 1997:
    pages
    20–22.

NEWSPAPER

    author   **title**   **newspaper**
Boyar, Jay. "Who Will Thank the Academy?" *The Orlando Sentinel* 23
      date   **section   pages**
    23 Mar. 1997, sec. F: 1 & 9.

ELECTRONIC SOURCES

                     **date
                     of   medium/   publication
   title/topic   source   source   server**   **information**
"Bell's Theorem" *Encarta* 1994. CD-ROM. Redmond, WA: Microsoft.
    CD-ROM date
    1993

TIP: Note placement of information and punctuation.

2. Gather information on a person you admire. Find out about the person's background, interests, and accomplishments. Then write about the person.

3. Gather information and write about one of the following problems. Suggest a solution in your paper. Remember to narrow your topic.

    drug use among teenagers   alcohol abuse

    athletes and steroid use   cheating in college

FIGURE 8.6

Six Steps for Citing Online Sources

EXAMPLE:

author   story   book
Bodett, Tom "The Dog Fix," *As Far As You Can Go Without a Passport* (9
    date   **url**
    May 2001.) http://tombodett.com/stories.html.

MLA GUIDELINES FOR CITING MATERIAL ACCESSED FROM THE WORLD WIDE WEB

1. Author's full name, last name first

2. "Title of article or story" (for articles or stories in periodicals or anthologies)

3. *Title of publication* (for articles or stories in periodicals, books, or anthologies)

4. Volume, issue, or version number (if given)

5. length (page, paragraph, or section numbers) if given

6. Date of access or URL

Source: Information from Crump and Carbone, *Writing Online,* Updated Second Edition, Houghton Mifflin, 1998, p. 114.

jobs for volunteers	campaign finance reform
racial discrimination on campus	health care reform

Checklist for Revision

As you revise and edit your paper, check for the following:

1. Do you have an effective introduction?

   a. Have you identified your audience?

   b. Have you stated your purpose?

   c. Do you have a thesis statement?

2. Have you supported your thesis sufficiently?

   a. Do your paragraphs have topic sentences and enough support?

   b. Have you used quotations and paraphrases effectively?

   c. Are your paragraphs unified and coherent?

3. Have you concluded your essay effectively?

   a. Have you summarized your research?

   b. Have you left readers with a final thought or challenge?

   c. Have you documented correctly and wherever necessary?

4. Are your sentences error-free?

   a. Have you proofread your essay?

   b. Have you found and corrected any errors in spelling or grammar?

THE CRITICAL THINKER

To examine Donald Murray's essay in more depth, think about and discuss the following questions. Then choose one of them as a topic for writing.

1. Why do you think Murray suggests that the library should be your starting point for finding information?

2. What are Murray's suggestions for making observations, and what are his reasons? Read again Murray's examples of the kinds of topics for which observation is a helpful way to gather information. What other writing topics can you think of for which observation might be helpful?

3. What does the author mean in the following sentences from paragraph 2, and do you agree or disagree? "We fear that writing will prove us ignorant. But for writers, writing can show us how much we know."

4. Of the four sources for finding information that Murray describes, which ones have you used most often and why? Which ones have you not tried or have you found unsuccessful and why?

YOUR DISCOVERY JOURNAL

To make research as enjoyable and challenging as possible, choose topics that are of vital interest to you whenever you have a choice. Take a moment to think about some possible research topics. What idea, discovery, issue, matter of controversy, or social problem is of great importance to you? Is there something you have always wanted to know more about but never had the time to research? List in your journal some possible research topics.

Unit

2

Patterns as Options

Chapter 9

Using Narration

Narration is a pattern of organization that screenwriters, television writers, speech writers, news reporters, fiction writers, and even textbook writers use to relate a series of events. In a biology textbook, for example, you may read a narrative account of what happens to the food you eat as it is digested, processed, and excreted. When you watch a movie or television program, or read a book or a newspaper article, you become involved in the unfolding series of events that make up a story. You, too, use narration as part of your everyday conversation whenever you discuss the details of an event or a situation in which you or others were involved.

Narration is a story-telling pattern. A narrator is one who tells a story. Whether a story is fact or fiction, certain rules apply. These rules are simply readers' expectations. When a story begins, readers expect to know *who* are the people involved, *what* happens to them, *where* the story takes place, *when* it happens, *why* it happens, and *how* everyone is affected. Readers also expect to follow the story, and they may look for clues that signal the sequence of events. Readers usually expect a point to the story, an answer to the question "Why has this happened?" or "What does this mean?"

AWARENESS CHECK

Before reading the following essay, explore your thoughts about conversion experiences, those events in our lives that act as turning points to change us in profound ways. Think about the questions below, and answer them either on your own or in a group discussion:

1. In a religious sense, what does it mean to be "saved" or to be "born again?" How is salvation a conversion experience?

2. In a secular (nonreligious) sense, what other conversion experiences can you describe? What are some of the events that change people's lives?

3. Read the title, author information, and first two paragraphs of the following essay. Based on this preview, what do you think will follow?

Salvation
Langston Hughes

Langston Hughes, one of America's foremost African American authors, has written novels, poetry, short stories, and autobiographical essays. The following essay from Hughes's autobiography, The Big Sea, *tells what happened to him the night he answered a preacher's call to be saved from sin. Hughes died in 1967.*

VOCABULARY CHECK

revival (1)	a meeting for the purpose of awakening religious faith
dire (3)	dreadful, terrible
rounder (6)	an immoral person
wail (7)	a long, loud, high-pitched cry
serenely (7)	calmly
knickerbockered (11)	wearing knee pants

| ecstatic (14) | joyful |
| deceived (15) | misled |

I was saved from sin when I was going on thirteen. But not really saved. 1
It happened like this. There was a big revival at my Auntie Reed's church. Every night for weeks there had been much preaching, singing, praying, and shouting, and some very hardened sinners had been brought to Christ, and the membership of the church had grown by leaps and bounds. Then just before the revival ended, they held a special meeting for children, "to bring the young lambs to the fold." My aunt spoke of it for days ahead. That night I was escorted to the front row and placed on the mourners' bench with all the other young sinners, who had not yet been brought to Jesus.

My aunt told me that when you were saved you saw a light, and 2
something happened to you inside! And Jesus came into your life! And God was with you from then on! She said you could see and hear and feel Jesus in your soul. I believed her. I had heard a great many old people say the same thing and it seemed to me they ought to know. So I sat there calmly in the hot, crowded church, waiting for Jesus to come to me.

The preacher preached a wonderful rhythmical sermon, all moans 3
and shouts and lonely cries and dire pictures of hell, and then he sang a song about the ninety and nine safe in the fold, but one little lamb was left out in the cold. Then he said: "Won't you come to Jesus? Young lambs, won't you come?" And he held out his arms to all of us young sinners there on the mourner's bench. And the little girls cried. And some of them jumped up and went to Jesus right away. But most of us just sat there.

A great many old people came and knelt around us and prayed, old 4
women with jet-black faces and braided hair, old men with work-gnarled hands. And the church sang a song about the lower lights are burning, some poor sinners to be saved. And the whole building rocked with prayer and song.

Still I kept waiting to *see* Jesus. 5

Finally all the young people had gone to the altar and were saved, 6
but one boy and me. He was a rounder's son named Westley. Westley and I were surrounded by sisters and deacons praying. It was very hot in the church, and getting late now. Finally Westley said to me in a whisper: "God damn! I'm tired o' sitting here. Let's get up and be saved." So he got up and was saved.

Then I was left all alone on the mourner's bench. My aunt came and knelt at my knees and cried, while prayers and songs swirled all around me in the little church. The whole congregation prayed for me alone, in a mighty wail of moans and voices. And I kept waiting serenely for Jesus, waiting, waiting—but he didn't come. I wanted to see him, but nothing happened to me. Nothing! I wanted something to happen to me, but nothing happened. 7

I heard the songs and the minister saying: "Why don't you come? My dear child, why don't you come to Jesus? Jesus is waiting for you. He wants you. Why don't you come? Sister Reed, what is this child's name?" 8

"Langston," my aunt sobbed. 9

"Langston, why don't you come? Why don't you come and be saved? Oh Lamb of God! Why don't you come?" 10

Now it really was getting late. I began to be ashamed of myself, holding everything up so long. I began to wonder what God thought about Westley, who certainly hadn't seen Jesus either, but who was now sitting proudly on the platform, swinging his knickerbockered legs and grinning down at me, surrounded by deacons and old women on their knees praying. God had not struck Westley dead for taking his name in vain or for lying in the temple. So I decided that maybe to save further trouble, I'd better lie, too, and say that Jesus had come, and get up and be saved. 11

So I got up. 12

Suddenly, the whole room broke into a sea of shouting, as they saw me rise. Waves of rejoicing swept the place. Women leaped in the air. My aunt threw her arms around me. The minister took me by the hand and led me to the platform. 13

When things quieted down, in a hushed silence, punctuated by a few ecstatic "Amens," all the new young lambs were blessed in the name of God. Then joyous singing filled the room. 14

That night, for the last time in my life but one—for I was a big boy twelve years old—I cried. I cried, in bed alone, and couldn't stop. I buried my head under the quilts, but my aunt heard me. She woke up and told my uncle I was crying because the Holy Ghost had come into my life, and because I had seen Jesus. But I was really crying because I couldn't bear to tell her that I had lied, that I had deceived everybody in the church, that I hadn't seen Jesus, and that now I didn't believe there was a Jesus any more, since he didn't come to help me. 15

THE CRITICAL READER

Central Idea

1. What is the writer's thesis? Can you find one or more sentences that state the central idea? If not, state the thesis, or central idea, in your own words.

Evidence

2. Hughes uses time order to organize the details that explain what happened. Find and mark the transitional words that help you follow the story.

3. Identify the specific details that describe the church, the service, and the congregation. In which paragraphs do you find these details?

Implications

4. At the end of the essay, Hughes says he does not believe in Jesus because he did not *see* him. His aunt had said that he would see Jesus, or did she? What possible differences do you find in the meaning of the word *see* as the boy and his aunt interpret it?

Word Choice

5. What does the dialogue add to the narrative? Would the story have been more effective if the dialogue had been left out? Why or why not?

CHOOSING NARRATION

Choose narration only if your topic would be especially effective if developed as a narrative. For example, a topic such as "my first date" might work very well as a narrative essay. You could describe the date as an event telling who you were with, where you went, how you felt about it, what he or she said or did, how the date ended, and whether you ever saw your date again. To organize your essay, try breaking up the event into time periods. For example, if you are writing about a first date, you could describe your anticipation *before the date,* what you did

during the date, and how you felt *after the date.* To come up with a thesis or central idea for your essay, think of what the date meant to you—for example, what it taught you about yourself, other people, or the dating process.

Although we usually associate narration with novels and short stories, it is also an effective technique for writing essays, articles, and other nonfictional accounts. Writers may choose to use narration whenever they believe that the story-telling method best suits their purpose and thesis. If you decide to use narration as an organizational pattern for an essay, five choices should motivate your planning:

1. Determine the significance of an event.

2. Decide what sequence to follow.

3. Choose a point of view.

4. Select appropriate examples and use descriptive details.

5. Add dialogue for accuracy and variety.

Determine the Significance of an Event

Suppose you are writing about an event such as the birth of a child, winning an award, achieving a victory in a sporting event, or surviving a catastrophe. First decide why this event is important to you or what you learned from the experience. In other words, try to understand the *significance* of the event not only to yourself but to your readers. By analogy, whatever you learn from an experience, your readers should also be able to understand, either by having had similar experiences or by relating to yours. You can help them by having a purpose for writing and by communicating that purpose clearly. In his classic essay "Salvation," Langston Hughes describes the time he got saved. The significance of the event for him is that at the age of twelve he lost his faith because getting saved was not what he expected. The significance of the event to readers is that they, too, may have questioned their faith or lack of it, or they may have had a nonreligious conversion experience that changed their lives. These turning points mark the stages of personal growth that lead to maturity.

EXERCISE 9.1   On a sheet of notebook paper, list three to five important events in your life, leaving several blank lines between them. Think about the events,

and decide what is meaningful or significant about each one. To help yourself determine the significance, ask yourself "What did I learn from the experience?" Following each event on your list, briefly explain its significance. When you have finished, decide which of the events you would like to write about. Then save your notes for a future assignment.

Decide What Sequence to Follow

Events take place within a time frame. Something happens first, then something happens next, then something else may occur, and finally the event is over. If you have a car accident, the highway patrol officer will ask you to explain the series of events that led up to the impact. If you decide to write about your car accident, begin by jotting down, in order, everything you remember about what happened to you. Next, go over your list and decide whether you need to tell *everything* that happened. If some of the events you have listed are not necessary to complete your narration, leave them out. Finally, decide how to organize the events.

Though explaining what happened on a date might follow a before-during-after sequence, you might need to use another sequence to describe a different event. Suppose you write about the last five minutes of an exciting football game. You might begin with a summary of what had led up to those last five minutes and then explain in detail what happened during each remaining minute. Transitional words and phrases are a big help in connecting ideas so that you maintain the sequence without losing coherence and so that your readers can follow your narration. Notice that many of Hughes's sentences in the essay on pages 216–218 begin with a time marker, such as *every night, that night,* or *suddenly.* Figure 9.1 lists some of the transitions you can use to show a passage of time.

In "How Did They Start the Breakfast Cereal Industry?" from Caroline Sutton's *How Did They Do That?* the author describes how the breakfast cereal industry developed. Dates help to mark the passage of time.

> The Reverend Sylvester W. Graham preached that, rather than being 1
> born again, one's life could be salvaged by vegetarianism and bran. Living in New England in the early 19th century, the former Presbyterian preacher was an early champion of the low-fat, low-salt diet, brown bread as opposed to the socially sanctioned white, and fruits and vegetables as against beef or pork. If the Reverend Graham could only see how his flocks have multiplied a century and a half later. As it was,

FIGURE 9.1

22 Transitions for Maintaining a Time Sequence

after	later
at the same time	meanwhile
before	never
beginning	next
during	now
earlier	once
ending	previously
finally	soon
first, second, third, . . .	suddenly
following	when
last	whenever

espousing coarse, unsifted flour, slightly stale bread, and lots of bran, he left his name to a flour and a cracker.

Graham had some notable followers in the 19th century—Thomas Edison, Amelia Bloomer, and Horace Greeley among them. Most critically, though, his influence led Mother Ellen Harmon White of the Adventist Church to found the Western Health Reform Institute at Battle Creek, Michigan, in 1866, where people with stomachaches, too much fat or too little, high blood pressure, and assorted other ailments might find physical and spiritual health. Dr. John Harvey Kellogg, acting as manager, changed the name to Battle Creek Sanitarium and, along with his brother, developed a cereal called Granose, an immediate success. Among the patients at Battle Creek was Charles W. Post. While the absence of meat and lack of stimulants did not cure his ulcer, Post did invent Postum and Grape Nuts, the latter called Elijah's Manna until marketing problems provoked a change of name. The sanitarium must have been a creative place because there, too, Dr. Kellogg invented the corn flake for a suffering patient who broke her false teeth on a chunk of hard egg bread.

2

EXERCISE 9.2   Identify and underline as many transitional words, phrases, and other time markers as you can find in the breakfast cereal passage. Then be able to share with the rest of the class how these transitions help readers follow the sequence of events.

EXERCISE 9.3   Apply what you have learned about relating a sequence of events by doing this exercise with a partner. Then evaluate your performance.

1. Before you meet with your partner, do the following:

   a. Each person should cut out a comic strip from a newspaper.

   b. Read the comic on your own, and determine how each frame relates to the others.

   c. On a sheet of notebook paper, write down the sequence of the frames if you think you might forget.

   d. Cut the strip into separate frames, then mix them up and put them in an envelope to bring to class.

2. When you meet with your partner, do the following:

   a. Exchange comic strips and reassemble them.

   b. When you think you have the frames in the correct sequence, show them to your partner.

   c. Be able to explain why you think the sequence is correct.

GROUP EVALUATION

What did each of you contribute to this activity? Was your performance successful? Why or why not? What additional questions do you have about relating a sequence of events?

EXERCISE 9.4   Choose one of your events from Exercise 9.1. Now think about this event in detail. Chances are the event is made up of several other events or incidents that led up to the outcome. Make a list of these events or incidents. Keep this list as part of your brainstorming activities for a possible essay.

Choose a Point of View

Writers narrate events from a *point of view.* If you describe events in your own life using the pronoun *I*, you are writing from the *first-person point of view.* If your narrative is about what happened to someone else and you use the pronouns *he, she,* or *they,* you are writing from the *third-person point of view.* Sometimes writers speak directly to the reader using the pronoun *you,* which is the *second-person point of view.* The following excerpt from Maxine Hong Kingston's *The Woman Warrior: Memoirs of a Girlhood Among Ghosts* illustrates the first-person point of view:

When I went to kindergarten and had to speak English for the first time, I became silent. A dumbness—a shame—still cracks my voice in two, even when I want to say "hello" casually, or ask an easy question in front of the check-out counter, or ask directions of a bus driver. I stand frozen, or I hold up the line with the complete, grammatical sentence that comes squeaking out at impossible length. "What did you say?" says the cab driver, or "Speak up," so I have to perform again, only weaker the second time. A telephone call makes my throat bleed and takes up that day's courage. It spoils my day with self-disgust when I hear my broken voice come skittering out into the open. It makes people wince to hear it. I'm getting better, though. Recently I asked the postman for special-issue stamps; I've waited since childhood for postmen to give me some of their own accord. I am making progress, a little every day. 1

My silence was thickest—total—during the three years that I covered my school paintings with black paint. I painted layers of black over houses and flowers and suns, and when I drew on the blackboard, I put a layer of chalk on top. I was making a stage curtain, and it was the moment before the curtain parted or rose. The teachers called my parents to school, and I saw they had been saving my pictures, curling and cracking, all alike and black. The teachers pointed to the pictures and looked serious, talked seriously too, but my parents did not understand English. ("The parents and teachers of criminals were executed," said my father.) My parents took the pictures home. I spread them out (so black and full of possibilities) and pretended the curtains were swinging open, flying up, one after another, sunlight underneath, mighty operas. 2

During the first silent year I spoke to no one at school, did not ask before going to the lavatory, and flunked kindergarten. My sister also said nothing for three years, silent in the playground and silent at lunch. There were other quiet Chinese girls not of our family, but most of them got over it sooner than we did. I enjoyed the silence. At first it 3 did not occur to me I was supposed to talk to pass kindergarten. I talked at home and to one or two of the Chinese kids in class. I made motions and even made some jokes. I drank out of a toy saucer when the water spilled out of the cup, and everybody laughed, pointing at me, so I did it some more. I didn't know that Americans don't drink out of saucers. . . .

In the excerpt above, Kingston explains her difficulty in learning English and how she coped with the language barrier by remaining silent. Perhaps becoming a writer was one way for her to overcome the silence of those early years. Through her use of the first-person point of view, Kingston controls the way you, as reader, see her early school years.

The first-person point of view allows you to describe events and people's actions, thoughts, and feelings as *you* see them. A disadvantage for readers, however, is that they have to depend upon your interpretation of events. Suppose you write a first-person account of a car accident. You may describe the events differently from the way someone else would describe them, so readers do not have access to another point of view. When writing from the first-person point of view, use these pronouns: *I, me, my, mine, we* and *ours.*

For an example of the third-person point of view, compare the following excerpt from Carin C. Quinn's "The Jeaning of America—and the World":

This is the story of a sturdy American symbol which has now spread throughout most of the world. The symbol is not the dollar. It is not even Coca-Cola. It is a simple pair of pants called blue jeans, and what the pants symbolize is what Alexis de Tocqueville called "a manly and legitimate passion for equality. . . ." Blue jeans are favored equally by bureaucrats and cowboys; bankers and deadbeats; fashion designers and beer drinkers. They draw no distinctions and recognize no classes; they are merely American. Yet they are sought after almost everywhere in the world—including Russia, where authorities recently broke up a teenaged gang that was selling them on the black market for two hundred dollars a pair. They have been around for a long time, and it seems likely that they will outlive even the necktie.   1

This ubiquitous American symbol was the invention of a Bavarian-born Jew. His name was Levi Strauss.   2

He was born in Bad Ocheim, Germany, in 1829, and during the European political turmoil of 1848 decided to take his chances in New York, to which his two brothers already had emigrated. Upon arrival,   3

Levi soon found that his two brothers had exaggerated their tales of an easy life in the land of the main chance. They were landowners, they had told him; instead, he found them pushing needles, thread, pots, pans, ribbons, yarn, scissors, and buttons to housewives. For two years he was a lowly peddler, hauling some 180 pounds of sundries door-to-door to eke out a marginal living. When a married sister in San Francisco offered to pay his way West in 1850, he jumped at the opportunity, taking with him bolts of canvas he hoped to sell for tenting.

It was the wrong kind of canvas for that purpose, but while talking with a miner down from the mother lode, he learned that pants—sturdy pants that would stand up to the rigors of the diggings—were almost impossible to find. Opportunity beckoned. On the spot, Strauss measured the man's girth and inseam with a piece of string and, for six dollars in gold dust, had [the canvas] tailored into a pair of stiff but rugged pants. The miner was delighted with the result, word got around about "those pants of Levi's," and Strauss was in business. The company has been in business ever since. . . .

4

In the above excerpt, Quinn does not describe her own experience; instead, she reports on a series of events that happened to another person, Levi Strauss. She explains what Strauss and others thought and did, not what she thinks or has done. Notice that Quinn uses third-person pronouns—*he, his,* and *their.* Which point of view you choose for your essay will depend upon whether you describe your own experience or someone else's.

One advantage of writing from the third-person point of view for both you and your readers is that you may look beyond events themselves to the different ways people perceive them. The third-person point of view is characteristic of academic and other types of informational writing. This point of view relies more on information you gain by observing, thinking, and reading, and less on direct experience. Pronouns to use when writing in the third person are: *he, she, they, his, her, their, him, her,* and *them.*

The following excerpt from Tom Bodett's "Mood Piece" illustrates the second-person point of view.

. . . The bad mood scenario goes typically like this.

1

You wake up late, bound out of bed, and jam your foot under the closet door. This dislodges the big toenail from its setting, which hurts worse than if you'd taken the whole leg off at the knee. Recovering through rapid breathing, you throw on some clothes and fire up the

2

coffeepot. While urging the brew cycle to its conclusion you sift through a stack of yesterday's mail and find a piece you'd overlooked, an official envelope from the City. It's one of those "Hold firmly here, grasp and snap" deals that never work. You put your fingers at the indicated points and give it a stiff pull, nearly tearing the entire packet in two. It turns out to have been your personal property tax statement, and the rip went precisely through the amount due, rendering it unreadable.

Your temples start to throb, so you pour a fresh cup of coffee and   3
turn on the radio to try and settle down. A little music usually soothes, but instead of music you're met with a barrage of incomprehensible jazz being forced through a saxophone at a pressure of ninety pounds per square inch. It's about as soothing as listening to an aircraft engine seize up in a small room, so you snap off the radio with a finality that sends the volume knob rolling under the stove. You figure it's time to stop screwing around and go to work. . . .

In the excerpt, Bodett describes how a typical morning begins for a person who is about to develop a bad mood that will last several days. In the essay from which the excerpt is taken, Bodett concludes that bad moods are predictable, they happen to everyone, and the only way to get through them is to maintain a sense of humor.

By using the pronouns *you* and *your,* Bodett is able to address his readers directly, encouraging them to identify with him. As you read the excerpt, you probably thought of your own bad moods, and you may have recalled experiences similar to those Bodett mentions.

An advantage of the second-person point of view is that it puts you and your readers on the same level: They are participants in the discussion rather than outside observers.

Whether you are writing from the first person, second person, or third person point of view, be consistent. Readers will be confused if the point of view shifts unnecessarily or if your essay contains pronoun reference and agreement errors. For an explanation of these types of errors and how to correct them, see pages 485–594.

EXERCISE 9.5   Determine the point of view in "Salvation" on pages 216–218, and in the breakfast cereal excerpt on pages 221–222. Are the points of view similar or different? What do you think motivated each writer's choice of point of view? How would each piece of writing be different if the point of view were different and why?

Select Appropriate Examples and Use Descriptive Details

When using narration, you must do more than list a series of events or list the stages involved in one major event. At times you will need to use examples to support a main idea related to the event, or you may need to add sensory details to create a clear picture of a person or place essential to the point of your narrative. The following excerpt from Daniel Meier's essay "One Man's Kids" is about his work as a teacher. In the following paragraph, he uses examples to support the main idea that being a first-grade teacher is not traditional male work. The main idea is underlined, and the examples are numbered.

> ". . . My work is not traditional male work. **1** It's not a singular pursuit. **2** There is not a large pile of paper to get through or one deal to transact. **3** I don't have one area of expertise or knowledge. **4** I don't have the singular power over language of a lawyer, **5** the physical force of a construction worker, **6** the command over fellow workers of a surgeon, **7** the wheeling and dealing transactions of a businessman. **8** My energy is not spent in **9** pursuing, **10** climbing, **11** achieving, **12** conquering, or **13** cornering some goal or object. . . ."

EXERCISE 9.6   The next paragraph from Meier's essay illustrates another main idea with examples. As in the paragraph above, underline the main idea, and number the examples.

> ". . . At other times, when I'm at a party or a dinner and tell someone that I teach young children, I've found that men and women respond differently. Most men ask about the subjects I teach and the courses I took in my training. Then, unless they bring up an issue such as merit pay, the conversation stops. Most women, on the other hand, begin the conversation on a more immediate and personal level. They say things like "those kids must love having a male teacher" or "that age is just wonderful, you must love it." Then, more often than not, they'll talk about their own kids or ask me specific questions about what I do. We're then off and talking shop. . . ."

Suppose Meier had simply written the main ideas of both paragraphs without adding the examples to explain them. Readers would then have to guess what he meant. As it is, Meier supports his main ideas with examples that enable you to "see" what he means. In the first paragraph, for example, Meier shows you how his work is not like traditional male work by listing all the things he does not do that males in traditional jobs do. In the second paragraph, Meier gives examples of how men and women react when they find out he is a teacher. These examples explain *how* their responses differ.

Descriptive details play an important role in bringing a narrative essay to life. Suppose you are writing an essay about a person. By choosing descriptive details carefully, you can make a point about a person or a place or show the relationship of person and place to the events explained in your essay. In the following paragraph from "Chinese Puzzle," an essay by Grace Ming-Yee Wai, the writer uses descriptive details to make a point about her father and to explain something significant she learned from the incident she describes in the paragraph.

> ". . . My father was a loving and devoted son to my grandparents. He made sure they were happy and comfortable. He wanted them with us so he was assured of their well-being. My grandfather had fallen ill when I was around seven years old. The doctors thought he had cancer. Twenty years ago, that meant certain death. The night the diagnosis was given, I was alone with my parents after the store was closed. Dad was crying. I was frightened because I had never before seen him cry. Taking off his glasses and looking at me with red, teary eyes and unmistakable pain, he asked me, "Do you love your Ye-Ye?" It was difficult to speak to him when he seemed so vulnerable, but with all the courage I could muster and tears welling up in my eyes, I answered, "Yes." Mom was behind Dad comforting him. At seven years of age, I was learning what it is to love your parents, and I was learning even Dads cry. Thankfully, my grandfather's cancer went into remission after treatment. . . .

In this paragraph, Wai explains how she felt—"I was frightened"—and how her father felt—he was "vulnerable" and he was experiencing "unmistakable pain." Sensory details of how Wai *feels* and what she *sees* and *hears* help you put yourself in her place that night her grandfather was diagnosed as having cancer. Seeing her dad cry and her mother comfort him, Wai learns to love her parents even more because for the first time she sees them as human and as sharing her emotions. A more detailed explanation of how to use description follows in Chapter 10.

EXERCISE 9.7   Use the event you listed in Exercise 9.4 and read what you listed as the separate incidents that made up the whole event. Now organize the incidents into a time sequence. Begin by remembering how long the whole event took from start to finish. Brainstorm by listing each incident in order. For example, if the event occurred over a three-hour period, list what happened in the first hour, the second hour, and the final hour. Choose one incident in your sequence that you could explain by using examples. Briefly summarize the examples. Save this exercise as part of your prewriting activities for an essay.

Add Dialogue for Accuracy and Variety

Dialogue adds variety to your writing. When describing actual events, you can give your readers a sense of "being there" by directly quoting what people said. Dialogue makes people come alive. Instead of describing them, you show them in action when you let them speak for themselves. The next time you read a newspaper account of a current event, look for dialogue. Notice that people involved in the event are quoted so that you get the story not just from the reporter's point of view, but from the point of view of those who were there. To sharpen the accuracy of your memory when you are writing about an event, try to remember what the people involved said. Add to your essay only those bits of dialogue that you think will improve readers' understanding of the people and events you describe.

Knowing where and when to use quotation marks is essential to writing good dialogue. Quotation marks are explained on pages 481–484.

EXERCISE 9.8   In Hughes's essay "Salvation" on pages 216–218, put a check beside each paragraph that contains dialogue. Then reread the paragraphs. Choose the paragraph that you think does the best job of using dialogue to create a picture in your mind of the person who is speaking or that helps you draw a conclusion about what the person is like. Then share your results with the rest of the class.

EXERCISE 9.9

Write a narrative essay about a well-known person who is worthy of admiration for his or her achievement in a field such as the arts, sports, science, business, or public service. To find a person to write about or to gather information on a person you have already chosen, go to www.achievement.org to access its *Gallery of Achievers,* which is divided into various *halls of achievement* such as *Hall of the Arts* or *Hall of Science.* For example, Julius Erving, basketball legend, and Tenley Albright, Olympic gold medalist, are listed in the *Hall of Sports.* For each person in the gallery, the site provides a picture, a personal profile, a biography, and an interview. The site also allows you to search for a person by using his or her name as a keyword.

PLANNING YOUR NARRATIVE ESSAY

Any of the prewriting techniques you have used successfully will work for planning a narrative essay. One that works especially well to help you get started is to ask the traditional questions that journalists ask when they investigate a story. These questions may help you sharpen your memory of an event and may remind you to include the basic information your readers need in order to follow the story. Whether you ask these questions about an event that happened to you, an event that happened to someone you know, or an event you have been following in the news, the answers will help you arrive at the essentials of the story:

1. *What* happened?
2. *Who* was there?
3. *When* did it take place?
4. *Where* did it happen?
5. *Why* did it happen, or what caused it?
6. *How* did it happen, or what were the details and circumstances?
7. *What if* it had not happened, or *what if* it had happened differently?

Combining the *why,* the *how,* and the *what if* may lead you to a discovery of the *significance* of the event if that is not already clear to you. Which prewriting strategy you settle on is less important, however, than the thought process you go through in choosing and in using it.

TOPICS FOR WRITING

1. Write an essay about an event that has special significance for you. Following are some suggestions:

   your first date

   a time you received a gift you had been hoping to get

   an event that taught you an important lesson

   an event that had a disappointing outcome

   an accident, illness, or hardship you had to overcome

   an event that cost you a relationship

   an incident that strengthened a relationship

   an event that has been widely publicized in the news

2. Write an essay about an event that happened to someone else. This event could involve someone you know, or it could involve someone you have read about or studied whose character and achievement have impressed you.

Checklist for Revision

As you revise and edit your essay, check for the following:

1. Does your essay have a thesis?

2. Are your body paragraphs developed with sufficient detail?

3. Have you chosen narration because it is an appropriate pattern for your topic?

4. Do you use a time sequence to organize evidence, and do you mark the sequence with transitions that show time?

5. Do you make clear to readers the significance of the event or events described in your narrative?

6. Is the point of view consistent in your essay—do you maintain first-person or third-person pronouns throughout the essay without unnecessary shifts in point of view?

7. Are your sentences varied and error-free?

THE CRITICAL THINKER

To examine Langston Hughes's essay in more depth, think about and discuss the following questions. Then choose one of them as a topic for writing.

1. Hughes's essay begins with two contradictory sentences. What is the author's meaning in these sentences? Use evidence from the essay to explain your answer.

2. Using examples from the essay, contrast Westley's and Hughes's attitudes toward being saved. What conclusion can you draw about the character of the two boys?

3. Disillusionment, a common theme in fiction and in autobiographical writing, is the process by which we become aware that something we believed in or thought to be true is incorrect. For example, children learn that there is no Santa Claus. A person's first love may be disillusioning. Someone we thought was a friend betrays us. Such experiences change us—for better or worse. How is "Salvation" a story of disillusionment?

4. Langston Hughes is also well known for his poetry. Read "Theme for English B." Check your library's holdings for a book that contains this poem or go to *www.poets.org*. This website contains biographical information about Hughes, his picture, and some of his poems, including "Theme for English B." Read the poem, then answer these questions about it in writing: What situation does the poem describe? Who are the people involved, and what do the author's details tell you about them? What specific details or ideas expressed in the poem are especially meaningful to you and why?

YOUR DISCOVERY JOURNAL

What is the best story you have heard lately? Was it something amusing that happened to a friend? Was it a tale of someone's revenge for a wrong that was done? Was it something you read or heard about in the news? Was it the remarkable recovery of someone who was ill? Think carefully about what happened; then briefly summarize the story in your journal.

Chapter 10

Using Description

*T*hink back to your earliest childhood memory. What do you see? How old are you? You probably do not remember learning to walk, but you may recall stories your mother or father told you later about your first early attempts to stand alone. What were these stories like? Does thinking about them create clear pictures in your mind? In Zora Neale Hurston's autobiography, *Dust Tracks on a Road*, Hurston recalls the story her family told about how she learned to walk:

> . . . They tell me that an old sow-hog taught me how to walk. That is, she didn't instruct me in detail, but she convinced me that I really ought to try. 1
>
> It was like this. My mother was going to have collard greens for dinner, so she took the dishpan and went down to the spring to wash the greens. She left me sitting on the floor, and gave me a hunk of cornbread to keep me quiet. Everything was going along all right, until the sow with her litter of pigs in convoy came abreast of the door. She must have smelled the cornbread I was messing with and scattering crumbs about the floor. So, she came right on in, and began to nuzzle around. 2
>
> My mother heard my screams and came running. Her heart must have stood still when she saw the sow in there, because hogs have been known to eat human flesh. 3
>
> But I was not taking this thing sitting down. I had been placed by 4

a chair, and when my mother got inside the door, I had pulled myself up by that chair and was getting around it right smart.

As for the sow, poor misunderstood lady, she had no interest in me except my bread. I lost that in scrambling to my feet and she was eating it. She had much less intention of eating Mama's baby, than Mama had of eating hers.   5

With no more suggestions from the sow or anybody else, it seems that I just took to walking and kept the thing a-going. . . .   6

In this brief passage, you can see the scene clearly: the little child eating cornbread, the sow and her piglets nosing around in the crumbs, and the child scrambling to her feet and hugging the chair for support. Hurston creates a picture in words with her *descriptive details:* words and phrases that appeal to your five senses. You can *see* the cornbread crumbs falling to the floor, recall what cornbread *tastes* and *smells* like, *hear* the child's screams, and experience *tactile* sensations in suggestive words and phrases such as *nuzzle* and *eat human flesh.* Other descriptive details give you a sense of place. These are country people who probably do not have running water because Hurston's mother takes the greens down to the spring to wash them. The setting is the rural South where *collard greens* are a regional dish and "right smart" is a familiar expression that in this context probably means "fast."

Description is the soul of writing and the source of much surprise. Writers surprise us when they suddenly make us see familiar objects in new ways, describe people who seem to come alive on the page, or recreate places and events so that they seem real. Whether an author writes a story, an essay, a textbook passage, or an editorial for the newspaper, descriptive words and phrases are what give life to writing and create interest for the reader. Description is rarely used alone; rather, it is a pattern that almost always combines with other patterns. The foregoing passage from Hurston's autobiography, for example, is a narrative *enhanced by* descriptive words and phrases.

Being able to describe objects, people, and events clearly and accurately is a skill you too can develop. By carefully choosing descriptive details, you can create pictures in your readers' minds, engage their interest, and give them a sense of being there.

Awareness Check

Before reading the following essay, explore your thoughts about family relationships. Think about the questions below, and answer them either on your own or in a group discussion.

1. In your experience, how well do brothers or sisters get along as children, as adults?

2. Do you have a brother or a sister? How would you describe your relationship with your sibling?

3. Read the title, headnote, and first two paragraphs of the following essay. Based on this preview, what do you think will follow?

Brothers

Brett Lott

In this descriptive essay, Brett Lott looks back on his childhood and his relationship with his brother. In the process, he gains insight into his own children's behavior.

Vocabulary Check

shards (5)	bits and pieces
grimaces (9)	facial expressions showing pain or disgust
prophecy (14)	prediction, foretelling
embroidered (18)	added fictitious details to
Chinese junk (18)	flat-bottomed sailing ship
unscathed (56)	unharmed
embarked (57)	began, set out (as on a journey)

This much is fact: 1

    There is a home movie of the two of us, sitting on the edge of the   2
swimming pool at my grandma and grandpa's old apartment building

in Culver City. The movie, taken some time in early 1960, is in color, though the color has faded, leaving my brother Brad and me milk-white and harmless children, me a year and a half old, Brad almost four. Our mother, impossibly young, is in the movie, too. She sits next to me, on the right of the screen. Her hair, for all the fading of the film, is coal black, shoulder length and parted in the middle, curled up on the sides. She has on a bathing suit covered in purple and blue flowers, the color in them nearly gone. Next to me, on the left of the screen, is Brad in his white swimming trunks, our brown hair faded to only the thought of brown hair. I am in the center, my fat arms up, bent at the elbows, fingers curled into fists, my legs kicking away at the water, splashing and splashing. I am smiling, the baby of the family, the center of the world at that very instant, though my mother is pregnant, my little brother Tim some six or seven months off, my little sister Leslie, the last child, still three years distant. The pool water before us is only a thin sky blue, the bushes behind us a dull and lifeless light green. There is no sound.

My mother speaks to me, points at the water, then looks up. She lifts a hand to block the sun, says something to the camera. Her skin is the same white as ours, but her lips are red, a sharp cut of lipstick moving as she speaks. 3

I am still kicking. Brad is looking to his right, off the screen, his feet in the water, too, but moving slowly. His hands are on the edge of the pool, and he leans forward a little, looks down into the water. 4

My mother still speaks to the camera, and I give an extra hard kick, splash up shards of white water. 5

Brad flinches at the water, squints his eyes, while my mother laughs, puts a hand to her face. She looks back to the camera, keeps talking, a hand low to the water to keep more from hitting her. I still kick hard, still send up bits of water, and I am laughing a baby's laugh, mouth open and eyes nearly closed, arms still up, fingers still curled into fists. 6

More water splashes at Brad, who leans over to me, says something. Nothing about me changes: I only kick, laugh. 7

He says something again, his face leans a little closer to mine. Still I kick. 8

This is when he lifts his left hand from the edge of the pool, places it on my right thigh, and pinches hard. It's not a simple pinch, not two fingers on a fraction of skin, but his whole hand; all his fingers grabbing the flesh just above my knee, and squeezing down hard. He grimaces, his eyes on his hand, on my leg. 9

And this is when my expression changes, of course: in an instant I go from a laughing baby to a shocked one, my mouth a perfect O, my body shivering so that my legs kick even harder, even quicker, but just this one last time. They stop, and I cry, my mouth open even more, my eyes all the way closed. My hands are still in fists. 10

Then Brad's hand is away, and my mother turns from speaking to 11
the camera to me. She leans in close, asking, I am certain, what's wrong.

The movie cuts then to my grandma, white skin and silver hair, 12
seated on a patio chair by the pool, above her a green and white
striped umbrella. She has a cigarette in one hand, waves off the camera with the other. Though she died eight years ago, and though she,
too, loses color with each viewing, she is still alive up there, still waves,
annoyed, at my grandpa and his camera, the moment my brother
pinched hell out of me already gone.

This much is fact, too: 13

Thumbtacked to the wall of my office is a photograph of Brad and 14
me, taken by my wife in November 1980, the date printed on the bor-
der. In it we stand together, I a good six inches taller than he, my arm
around his shoulder. The photograph is black and white, as though the
home movie and its sinking colors were a prophecy, pointed to this day
twenty years later: we are at the tidepools at Portuguese Bend, out on
the Palos Verdes Peninsula; in the background are the stone-gray bluffs,
to the left of us the beginnings of the black rocks of the pools, above
us the perfect white of an overcast sky.

Brad has on a white Panama hat, a gray hooded sweatshirt, be- 15
neath it a collarless shirt. His face is smooth-shaven, and he is grinning,
lips together, eyes squinted nearly shut beneath the brim of the hat. It
is a goofy smile, but a real one.

I have on a cardigan with an alpine design around the shoulders, 16
the rest of it white, the shawl collar on it black, though I know it to
have been navy blue. I have on a button-down Oxford shirt, sideburns
almost to my earlobes. I have a mustache, a pair of glasses too large for
my face, and I am smiling, my mouth open to reveal my big teeth. It
isn't my goofy smile, but a real one, too.

These are the facts of my brother: the four-year-old pinching me, the 17
twenty-four-year-old leaning into me, grinning.

But between the facts of these two images lie twenty years of the 18
play of memory, the dark and bright pictures my mind has retained,
embroidered upon, made into things they are, and things they are not.
There are twenty years of things that happened between my brother
and me, from the fist-fight we had in high school over who got the
honeybun for breakfast, to his phone call to me from a tattoo parlor in
Hong Kong, where he'd just gotten a Chinese junk stitched beneath
the skin of his right shoulder blade; from his showing me one summer
day how to do a death drop from the jungle gym at Elizabeth Dicker-
son Elementary, to his watching while his best friend and our next-door
neighbor, Lynn Tinton, beat me up on the driveway of our home, a

fight over whether I'd fouled Lynn at basketball. I remember—memory, no true picture, certainly, but only what I have made the truth by holding tight to it, playing it back in my head at will and in the direction I wish it to go—I remember lying on my back, Lynn's knees pinning my shoulders to the driveway while he hit my chest, and looking up at Brad, the basketball there at his hip, him watching.

I have two children now. Both boys, born two and a half years apart.   19

I showed the older one, Zeb—he is almost eight—the photograph, asked him who those two people were.   20

He held it in his hands a long while. We were in the kitchen. The bus comes at seven-twenty each morning, and I have to have lunches made, breakfasts set out, all before that bus comes, and before Melanie takes off for work, Jacob in tow, to be dropped off at the Montessori school on her way to her office.   21

I waited, and waited, finally turned from him to get going on his lunch.   22

"It's you," he said. "You have a lot of hair," he said.   23

"Who's the other guy?" I said.   24

I looked at him, saw the concentration on his face, the way he brought the photograph close, my son's eyes taking in his uncle as best he could.   25

He said, "I don't know."   26

"That's your Uncle Brad," I said. "Your mom took that picture ten years ago, long before you were ever born."   27

He still looked at the picture. He said, "He has a beard now."   28

I turned from him, finished with the peanut butter, now spread jelly on the other piece of bread. This is the only kind of sandwich he will eat at school.   29

He said from behind me, "Only three years before I was born. That's not a long time."   30

I stopped, turned to him. He touched the picture with a finger.   31

He said, "Three years isn't a long time, Dad."   32

But I was thinking of my question: *Who's the other guy?* and of the truth of his answer: *I don't know.*   33

Zeb and Jake fight.   34

They are only seven and a half and five, and already Zeb has kicked out one of Jake's bottom teeth. Melanie and I were upstairs wrapping Christmas presents in my office, a room kept locked the entire month of December because of the gifts piled up in there.   35

We heard Jake's wailing, dropped the bucket of Legos and the red and green Ho! Ho! Ho! paper, ran for the hall and down the stairs.   36

There in the kitchen stood my two sons, Jacob. with his eyes wet, whimpering now, a hand to his bottom lip. 37

I made it first, yelled, "What happened?" 38

"I didn't do it," Zeb said, backing away from me, there with my hand to Jacob's jaw. Melanie stroked Jacob's hair, whispered, "What's wrong?" 39

Jacob opened his mouth then, showed us the thick wash of blood between his bottom lip and his tongue, a single tooth, horribly white, swimming up from it. 40

"We were playing Karate Kid," Zeb said, and now he was crying. "I didn't do it," he said, and backed away even farther. 41

One late afternoon a month or so ago, Melanie came home with the groceries, backed the van into the driveway to make it easier to unload all those plastic bags. When we'd finished, we let the boys play outside, glad for them to be out of the kitchen while we sorted through the bags heaped on the counter, put everything away. 42

Melanie's last words to the two of them, as she leaned out the front door into the near-dark: "Don't play in the van!" 43

Not ten minutes later Jacob came into the house, slammed shut the front door like he always does. He walked into the kitchen, his hands behind him. He said, "Zeb's locked in the van." His face takes on the cast of the guilty when he knows he's done something wrong: his mouth was pursed, his eyebrows up, his eyes looking right into mine. He doesn't know enough yet to look away. "He told me to come get you." 44

He turned, headed for the door, and I followed him out onto the porch where, before I could even see the van in the dark, I heard Zeb screaming. 45

I went to the van, tried one of the doors. It was locked, and Zeb was still screaming. 46

"Get the keys!" he was saying. "Get the keys!" 47

I pressed my face to the glass of the back window, saw Zeb inside jumping up and down. "My hand's caught," he cried. 48

I ran into the house, got the keys from the hook beneath the cupboard, only enough time for me to say to Melanie, "Zeb's hand's closed in the back door," and turned, ran back out. 49

I made it to the van, unlocked the big back door, pushed it up as quick as I could, Melanie already beside me. 50

Zeb stood holding the hand that'd been closed in the door. Melanie and I both took his hand, gently examined the skin, wiggled fingers, and in the dull glow of the dome light we saw that nothing'd been broken, no skin torn. The black foam lining the door had cushioned his fingers, so that they'd only been smashed a little, but a little enough to scare him, and to make blue bruises there the next day. 51

But beneath the dome light there'd been the sound of his weep- 52
ing, then the choked words, "Jacob pulled the door down on me."

From the darkness just past the line of light from inside the van 53
came my second son's voice: "I didn't do it."

I have no memory of the pinch Brad gave me at the edge of an apart- 54
ment complex pool, no memory of my mother's black hair—now it's a
sort of brown—nor even any memory of the pool itself. There is only
that bit of film.

But I can remember putting my arm around his shoulder, leaning 55
into him, the awkward and alien comfort of that touch. In the photograph we are both smiling, me a newlywed with a full head of hair, he
only a month or so back from working a drilling platform in the Gulf of
Mexico. He'd missed my wedding six months before, stranded on the
rig, he'd told us, because of a storm.

What I believe is this: that pinch was entry into our childhood: my 56
arm around him, our smiling, the proof of us two surfacing, alive but
not unscathed.

And here are my own two boys, already embarked. 57

THE CRITICAL READER

Central Idea

1. In this essay, the central idea is implied, not stated. What do you
   think is the central idea? For example, the author's topic is *brothers*.
   What does the author say about the relationship between brothers
   in general?

Evidence

2. How do the details in paragraph 2 set the scene for the home
   movie described in paragraphs 1–12? How does paragraph 2 serve
   as an introduction to the essay?

3. Paragraphs 13–18 describe a photograph. What are the similarities
   and differences between the photograph and the home movie?
   What "facts" about his brother—as revealed in the movie and
   photo—seem to stand out most for the author?

4. What details in paragraph 18 describe memories of the author's that are not recorded in either the photograph or the home movie? What do these details tell you about the brothers' relationship?

Implications

5. The essay is divided into several sections. Where does each section begin and end? Briefly explain what happens or what is described in each section. What seems to be the advantage, or purpose, of organizing the essay this way?

6. How would you describe the author's feelings toward his brother? Have they changed over time? Support your answer with quotations from the essay.

Word Choice

7. Compare the author's choices of color words in paragraph 2 with those in paragraphs 14–16. Apart from the fact that the movie is in color and the photo is in black and white, how does the author's use of color words affect your understanding of the different images, feelings, or messages conveyed in these paragraphs?

CHOOSING DESCRIPTIVE DETAILS

Describing comes naturally to people. Description is a familiar means of self-expression you use whenever you want to tell a friend about a movie you have seen, a book you have read, a person you care about, or a place you have been. When you visit the doctor, he or she asks you to describe your symptoms. A prospective employer will ask you to describe your previous work experience. In all these exchanges, the people you are talking with can ask questions to clarify anything they may not understand. The readers of your essays, however, have only your words to go on. Therefore your descriptions should be clear enough to prevent any misunderstanding. You can improve your ability to choose descriptive details by doing the following:

1. Make careful observations.

2. Describe with a purpose.

3. Find a controlling idea.

Make Careful Observations

Your five senses are your source of descriptive details. Everything you *see, hear, smell, taste,* and *touch* makes an impression on you. To describe your impressions so that they come alive for readers, observe carefully. Then choose details that will appeal to your readers' five senses. For example, suppose you are writing about what it is like to ride on a subway. Go there. Take a ride, and make notes. What do you see, hear, and smell? Record your impressions as accurately as you can. When you write about the subway, recreate your actual experience on paper, choosing words and details that convey the impression you want your readers to have.

To describe something from memory, picture it in your mind. Then observe that image just as if you had the real object in front of you. Take notes on what you see in your mind's eye. Images you recall from memory may not be as vivid and clear as your direct observations, but you can begin to sharpen your recollections by paying close attention to your surroundings.

EXERCISE 10.1   Without looking at the students sitting on either side of you, list, as accurately as you can from memory, what one of them is wearing. When you have finished writing, test the accuracy of your observations by looking at the student's clothes and comparing what you see what with you have written. Share your results with class members.

EXERCISE 10.2   Apply what you have learned about making observations by doing this exercise with group members. First, review the list of group roles and responsibilities explained in Figure 1.6, page 28. Next, examine Brett Lott's essay on pages 237–242 for details that appeal to your five senses of *sight, sound, smell, taste,* and *touch.* Make a chart like the one in Figure 10.1 for listing the sensory details that create the clearest images for you. Before recording a detail on the chart, make sure you have discussed it and that everyone in your group agrees. Share your chart with the rest of the class. Then evaluate your group's performance.

GROUP EVALUATION
What did each person contribute to the group's activity? Was your group's performance successful? Why or why not? What additional questions do you have about making observations?

FIGURE 10.1

Sensory Details

SIGHT	SOUND	SMELL	TASTE	TOUCH

Describe with a Purpose

Generally you have one or two purposes for describing anything:

1. *Objective purpose:* to report information without bias or emotion.

2. *Subjective purpose:* to explain by expressing your feelings and impressions.

Use the *objective purpose* when you want to describe a topic in an unemotional way without making a judgment about it. For example, perhaps you have done some research on mate selection in the United States, and you find out that couples who have successful marriages have several characteristics in common. You might decide to write an essay informing readers what researchers have said these characteristics are. When writers describe objectively, they report only what they see, hear, smell, taste, and touch. They neither project their feelings onto the people and objects they describe nor interpret events and behaviors.

Use the *subjective purpose* when you want to describe your feelings or impressions. For example, suppose you have recently emerged from a bad relationship, and you realize now that the person you had been involved with was not the person you thought he or she was when you first met. You might decide to write an essay in which you describe the events that made you change your feelings about this person. When writers describe subjectively, they project their feelings onto what they experience through their senses, and they interpret events and behaviors in light of their own beliefs and values.

Your daily newspaper contains examples of both *objective purpose* and *subjective purpose* writing. Many front-page articles have an *objective purpose:* to keep you informed of current events. The editorials and letters to the editor usually have a *subjective purpose:* to describe writers' feelings about subjects of national or local interest and to arouse your feelings about these subjects (perhaps even to change your opinion).

EXERCISE **10.3**   Following are three short excerpts. Decide whether the purpose in each one is *objective* or *subjective*. Be able to support your answer with evidence from each passage.

1. . . . At the end of our two-block alley was a small sandlot play-   1
ground with swings and slides well-shined down the middle with use. The play area was bordered by wood-slat benches where old-country people sat cracking roasted watermelon seeds with their golden teeth and scattering the husks to an impatient gathering of gurgling pigeons. The best playground, however, was the dark alley itself. It was crammed with daily mysteries and adventures. My brothers and I would peer into the medicinal herb shop, watching old Li dole out onto a stiff sheet of white paper the right amount of insect shells, saffron-colored seeds, and pungent leaves for his ailing customers. It was said that he once cured a woman dying of an ancestral curse that had eluded the best of American doctors. Next to the pharmacy was a printer who specialized in gold-embossed wedding invitations and festive red banners. . . .

from *The Joy Luck Club,* by Amy Tan

2. Carnivorous plants are those that get nourishment by trapping and   1
digesting insects. Specially modified flowers or leaves may produce an odor or have a color that is attractive to insects. In some species a sticky coating on the petals holds the insect in place while the flower closes around it, trapping it inside the flower. The plant's juices contain a digestive acid.

　　Carnivorous plants grow in many parts of the world and come   2
in many varieties. One jungle species has a flower that is almost

three feet in diameter. Two carnivorous plants that grow in bogs in the northeastern part of the United States are the *pitcher plant* and the *sundew.* These plants are easy to recognize.

The pitcher plant looks exactly like a small pitcher that has a narrow neck widening to a larger base. Mature plants can be 3 to 5 inches tall. The "pitcher" is dark rusty red with darker vertical striations. It has a base of dark green leaves. 3

The sundew has a flower that looks much like a daisy with shorter, fatter petals. In the mature plant, the flower rises from a clump of dark greenish-brown leaves on a stem about 10 to 12 inches tall. The stem curves down at the top so that the flower hangs down. 4

3. In the West, in the blue mountains, there are creeks of grey water. They angle out of the canyon, come across the brown scratched earth to the edge of the desert and run into nothing. When these creeks are running they make a terrific noise. 1

No one to my knowledge has ever counted the number, but I think there are more than twenty; it is difficult to be precise. For example, some of the creeks have been given names that, over the years, have had to be given up because a creek has run three or four times and then the channel has been abandoned. 2

You can easily find the old beds, where the dust has been washed out to reveal a level of rock rubble—cinnabar laced with mercury, fool's gold, clear quartz powder, and fire opal—but it is another thing to find one of the creeks, even when they are full. I have had some success by going at night and listening for the noise. . . . 3

from *Desert Notes, Reflections in the Eye of a Raven,*
by Barry Lopez

EXERCISE 10.4   Examine Brett Lott's essay on pages 237–242. As a whole, does the essay serve an objective or subjective purpose? Which paragraphs seem to serve an objective purpose? Which ones seem to serve a subjective purpose? How does Lott's choice of details reinforce the purpose(s)?

Find a Controlling Idea

A *controlling idea* is an overall impression a person, place, or object conveys. The controlling idea is part of your thesis, and it *controls* the details you select to support it. In the following short passage, a witness describes a suspect. The controlling idea of the description is the dullness, or ordinariness, of the suspect, and the descriptive details support this idea. The controlling idea is circled, and the supporting details are underlined.

> You ask me to describe the man I saw fleeing from the building. Very well, then, he was a (dull) man. From his medium-length mousy brown hair to his brown shoes, he was an ordinary-looking fellow, a middle-aged man. He wore trousers neither grey nor brown but some shade in between. His shirt may have been white, or beige, or possibly a light yellow. It could have been a polo shirt with one of those little knit collars; then again it might have been a short-sleeved polyester sport shirt or a long-sleeved oxford cloth number. Was there a belt? There may have been a belt. Did he have any distinguishing marks or characteristics? None that I saw. He was clean-shaven, and he was of medium height; I do remember that. No, wait a minute; I think he had a beard. And now I seem to recall that the shirt was definitely the white polo, but I could be wrong.
>
> There was a crowd of people at the end of the block waiting for the light to change. I think the suspect merged with the crowd, and, after that, I lost track of him. Would it help if you showed me some pictures? I do not think so. He could be anyone, or no one.

To find a controlling idea begin by observing the person, place, or object you have chosen as your topic. Then make a brainstorming list. As you read over your list, try to think of one word or phrase that summarizes the overall impression the items on your list convey. For example, suppose you live in a dorm, and you have decided to write a short essay about your roommate, Ray. Your list might look like this:

saves money

takes shortcuts

buys used textbooks

saves time

makes instant coffee with tap water

reverses sheets to "clean" side

lets hair grow

skates to class

sprays deodorant on shirts

finds cheap or free entertainment

cools sodas on window sill in cold weather

trades paperbacks and tapes

blacks out light from windows

blocks out light from under door with black towel

stuffs cotton in ears

uses electric fan to muffle noise

brings food from home

brings toothpaste and other necessities from home

Reading over your list, you choose *resourceful* as a controlling idea and write the following preliminary thesis statement: *My roommate Ray is the most resourceful person I know.* Using this as your working thesis, you look at your brainstorming list again and decide that most of the items can be grouped under two major categories of resourcefulness as listed below:

Saves Time

takes shortcuts

makes instant coffee with tap water

skates to class

reverses sheets to "clean" side

sprays deodorant on shirts

Saves Money

buys used textbooks

lets hair grow

finds cheap or free entertainment

trades paperbacks and CDs

brings food from home

brings toothpaste and other necessities from home

However, you have five items left over from your original list that do not seem to fit into your two categories. Asking questions about these items may help you find a third category for them. For example, why does Ray cool sodas on the window sill? Dorm rooms do not have refrigerators. Why does he black out light from windows and under the door? Perhaps he wants the room to look dark to discourage friends from interrupting his studying. Stuffing cotton in his ears and using a fan to muffle noise may be necessary to achieve quiet. What the items all seem to have in common is that they reflect some of the stresses of dorm life. Now you have a third category, *relieves dorm frustrations,* and an idea for revising your thesis statement: *My roommate, Ray, is a resourceful person who knows how to save time and money and how to relieve the frustrations of dorm life.*

Using your thesis, categories, and lists of items, you can now write an outline for your descriptive essay. By adding details and improving the organization, your final outline might look like this one:

I. Ray is resourceful in saving time.

   A. He knows all the campus shortcuts.

   B. He makes instant coffee with tap water.

   C. He skates to class.

   D. He hates to waste time doing laundry.

      1. He reverses sheets to the "clean" side.

      2. He sprays deodorant on his shirts to keep from washing them.

II. Ray is resourceful in saving money.

   A. He buys used textbooks.

   B. He trades paperbacks and CDs instead of buying them.

   C. He lets his hair grow to save money on haircuts.

   D. He brings food from home.

  1. He raids the refrigerator and pantry.

  2. His mom makes cookies for him.

  E. He brings toothpaste and other necessities from home.

  F. He finds cheap or free entertainment.

III. Ray is resourceful in relieving dorm frustrations.

  A. Having no refrigerator is a frustration.

  1. He keeps an ice chest in our room.

  2. He cools sodas on the window sill in winter.

  B. Friends and noise can also be frustrating.

  1. To discourage unwanted visitors, Ray blocks the light from our windows with black paper.

  2. He uses a black towel to block the light that shines out under our door, creating the impression that we are not at home.

  3. He uses an electric fan to muffle noise from the hall, and stuffs cotton in his ears when studying.

Description is useful in any essay, no matter with what other patterns you may choose to combine it. For example, in Langston Hughes's "Salvation" on pages 216–218, and Brett Lott's "Brothers" on pages 237–242, both authors make use of narration *and* description. A controlling idea will help you select appropriate descriptive details. To find a controlling idea, use the strategies of observation and brainstorming. To organize your details effectively during the planning stages of your writing process, try the strategies of listing and grouping related ideas and outlining. Choose descriptive words that appeal to your readers' five senses and that reinforce your controlling idea.

EXERCISE 10.5   Examine Brett Lott's essay on pages 237–242. What overall impression, or controlling idea, do his details convey? Try to think of one word or phrase that expresses the controlling idea.

EXERCISE 10.6   To practice finding a controlling idea, take time to closely observe your classroom or some other place on campus. Make a brainstorming list of at least twenty items of description. Try to include items that appeal to all five senses. Read over your list and come up with a word or phrase that conveys your overall impression of the place.

EXERCISE 10.7

This exercise will help you understand the difference between the objective and subjective purposes of description. Remember that an objective description is free from judgment or personal opinion. When you describe something objectively, you relate only what anyone might observe directly, as in this example: *The sky is cloudy*. This sentence describes what any observer can see. When you describe something subjectively, you relate the feelings or thoughts that it provokes in you, as in this example: *The sky is gloomy*. This sentence describes a personal judgment or feeling about the sky's appearance.

Select a photograph from your own collection or go to www.photovault.com and choose a photograph that appeals to you. Examine the photograph carefully, take notes on its content, and write a paragraph about it. Include both objective and subjective details in your description. For example, describe exactly what you, or anyone, might see in the photo. In addition, describe your unique impressions of the photo's content. What situation or event is captured in the photo? What seem to be the relationships among any people that are depicted? What memories of yours does the photo arouse? What mood or feelings does it provoke?

TOPICS FOR WRITING

Choose one of the topics below for writing a descriptive essay. Spend some time observing your topic, choosing a purpose for writing, and finding a controlling idea.

1. Describe someone you know well, such as a brother, sister, friend, spouse, or roommate. Try to discover something about this person that you had not noticed before.

2. Describe people who are engaged in some leisure-time activity—for example, people playing a sport or people at a popular nightspot. Try to draw some conclusions about them or about the activity.

3. Describe a place that you take for granted, such as a supermarket, drugstore, gas station, or doctor's office. Try to discover something new about it, and try to make your reader see it in a new way.

4. Describe a person at work or engaged in some other kind of task—for example, a supermarket cashier, construction worker, secretary, or childcare worker. Try to draw some conclusions about the work this person does and whether you would enjoy doing it.

5. Describe something that has a special significance for you—for example, a favorite place on campus, a place you like to visit, a favorite room in your house or apartment, your grandmother's or some other relative's house, or a favorite possession. Try to make the reader understand why you feel the way you do.

6. Use description to write about something you have learned in one of your courses that is of special interest to you. For example, you could describe the work or style of an artist you like, or you could describe a species of plant or animal life you have learned about in a science course.

Checklist for Revision

1. Does your description have a purpose, and have you made that purpose clear?

2. Does your thesis statement provide a controlling idea for your essay?

3. Do your body paragraphs contain sufficient descriptive details to create word pictures in your readers' minds?

4. Are your sentences varied and error-free?

THE CRITICAL THINKER

To examine Brett Lott's essay in more depth, think about and discuss the following questions. Then choose one of them as a topic for writing.

1. Brett Lott's descriptions of the home movie and the photograph contain both objective and subjective details. He describes what any observer might see, but he also describes what only he knows.

Select a paragraph describing the movie or a paragraph describing the photo. Which details are subjective, which ones are objective, and what makes them so?

2. What is the significance of Zeb and Jake's fighting as explained in paragraphs 34–53? What relationship do you see between the boys' fights and the fights between the author and his brother?

3. Read again paragraphs 56 and 57. In these paragraphs, the author suggests that he and his brother—perhaps all of us—are on a journey on which his two children have now embarked. What is the journey? What does the author mean when he says that he and his brother are "alive but unscathed"? What is his implied hope for the future of his boys?

4. Throughout the essay, the author contrasts the facts about his brother with his feelings about his brother to reveal the complexity of their relationship. Write about a relationship between you and a sibling or you and a close friend. What facts and feelings will you select for your description? Do your facts and feelings reveal a relationship that is complex or simple? Are your memories about this relationship mostly pleasant, mostly unpleasant, or somewhere in between?

Your Discovery Journal

Think of several words or phrases that describe you, your personality, or the way you like to do things. For example, are you a workaholic? Are you a "doormat" for your friends? Do you see yourself as an independent or well-organized person? Decide on the word or phrase that best describes you. Then think of as many descriptive details as you can that show what you are like. Write them in your journal.

Chapter 11

Explaining a Process

*I*f you are a mother or father, you probably have had to assemble a toy for your child. If you work in an office, perhaps you have had to change a printer's ink cartridge, add paper to a copy machine, or fax a document to another office. At home when preparing meals you probably follow directions on food packages or cook from recipes. Perhaps you have had to give someone directions to reach a certain destination. When you entered college, you learned how to register for classes; before you graduate, you will have to apply for your degree. Applying for degrees, registering for classes, giving directions to a place, cooking meals, faxing documents, and putting together a child's toy are all processes. For each of these processes there is an expected outcome, a goal to reach, a reason for performing each process, and steps to follow.

Some of today's most popular and best-selling books are the "how-to" manuals that explain every kind of process from how to cook low-fat meals to how to remodel a kitchen. Even the courses you take explain processes. In algebra, you learn how to solve equations. In biology, you learn how organisms carry out the process of living and reproducing. In a composition class, you learn how to write an essay.

Process is a pattern of thought and organization whereby the writer explains steps or stages that lead to an outcome. In a process such as a recipe, the *sequence* of steps is essential. If you do not follow the steps of a recipe in order, the soufflé will fall, or the blueberry pie filling will be

255

runny. In other processes, such as how to manage time, the sequence of steps may not matter. For example, there are many ways to manage time effectively. When explaining how to manage time you can offer alternative ways and leave it to the reader, through a process of trial and error, to find the best solution.

Awareness Check

Before reading the following essay, explore your thoughts about either tackling or avoiding jobs. Think about the questions below, and answer them either on your own or in a group discussion:

1. When confronted with a difficult task, do you start right away or do you procrastinate?

2. What do you think most people do when confronted with a difficult task?

3. Read the title, headnote, and first two paragraphs of the following essay. Based on this preview, what do you think will follow?

How to Put Off Doing a Job
Andy Rooney

Andy Rooney is a commentator whose observations on American life end each segment of the popular TV show "60 Minutes." Rooney also writes a syndicated newspaper column and has published several books. He is a lighthearted social critic who delights viewers and readers with his common-sense approach to everyday life.

Vocabulary Check

grim (1)	gloomy
adhesive (3)	sticky
interim (8)	period of time between one event and another
philosophize (9)	to consider from a moral point of view

February is one of the most difficult times of the year to put off doing   1
some of the things you've been meaning to do. There's no vacation
coming up, there are no long weekends scheduled in the immediate future; it's just this long, grim February. Don't tell me it's a short month.
February is the longest by a week.

Because I have so many jobs that I don't like to do, I've been re-   2
viewing the notebook I keep with notes in it for how to put off doing a
job. Let's see now, what could I use today?

Go to the store to get something. This is one of my most depend-   3
able putter-offers. If I start a job and find I need some simple tool or a
piece of hardware, I stop right there. I put on some better clothes, get
in the car and drive to the store. If that store doesn't have what I'm
looking for, I go to another. Often I'm attracted to some item that has
nothing whatsoever to do with the job I was about to start and I buy
that instead. For instance, if I go to the hardware store to buy a new
snow shovel so I can clean out the driveway, but then I see a can of adhesive spray that will keep rugs in place on the floor, I'm apt to buy the
adhesive spray. That ends the idea I had to shovel out the driveway.

Tidy up the work area before starting a job. This has been useful to   4
me over the years as a way of not getting started. Things are such a
mess in my workshop, on my desk, in the kitchen and in the trunk of
the car that I decide I've got to go through some of the junk before
starting to work.

Make those phone calls. There's no sense trying to do a job if you   5
have other things on your mind, so get them out of the way first. This
is a very effective way of not getting down to work. Call friends you've
been meaning to call, or the distant relative you've been out of touch
with. Even if someone is in California, Texas or Chicago and you're in
Florida, call. Paying for a long-distance call is still easier and less unpleasant than actually getting down to work.

Study the problem. It's foolish to jump right into a job before   6
you've thought it through. You might be doing the wrong thing. There
might be an easier way to accomplish what you want to do, so think it
over carefully from every angle. Perhaps someone has written a how-to
book about the job you have in front of you. Buy the book and then sit
down and read it. Ask friends who have had the same job for advice
about the best way to do it.

Once you've studied the problem from every angle, don't make a   7
quick decision. Sleep on it.

Take a coffee break. Although the term "coffee break" assumes   8
that you are drinking coffee in an interim period between stretches of
solid work, this is not necessarily so. Don't be bound by old ideas about
when it's proper to take a coffee break. If taking it before you get

started is going to help keep you from doing the work, by all means take your coffee break first.

As a last resort before going to work, think this thing over. Is this really what you want to do with your life? Philosophize. Nothing is better for putting off doing something than philosophizing. Are you a machine, trapped in the same dull, day-after-day routine that everyone else is in? Or are you a person who makes up his or her own mind about things? Are you going to do these jobs because that's what's expected of you, or are you going to break the mold and live the way you feel like living?   9

Try these as ways for not getting started.   10

THE CRITICAL READER

Central Idea

1. In your own words, what is Andy Rooney's thesis?

2. What assumptions does Rooney make about his audience?

Evidence

3. What is the process Rooney describes?

4. How many steps are there, and what are the steps?

5. Do the steps have to be followed in order? Why or why not?

Implications

6. Many people have written about how to get started; Rooney writes about how *not* to get started. Why do you think he chose this topic?

Word Choice

7. Andy Rooney is known for his informal, conversational style. Find specific words or phrases in the essay that help Rooney achieve his characteristic tone.

PROCESS WITH A PURPOSE

Processes are of two kinds: *directional* or *informational*. A *directional process* explains how to do something. For example, recipes are directional processes; so are explanations of how to study for a test, the best way to wash a load of laundry, how to survive traveling with small children, and how to buy a house. In other words, after reading the explanation, you should be able to follow the steps to accomplish the task on your own. *Informational processes,* on the other hand, explain how things work or how something gets done. For example, how potato chips are made is an informational process; so are explanations of how your state legislature passes laws and how a fetus develops in the womb. The outcome of these processes is not that you will be able to do them on your own, but that you will improve your knowledge and understanding of the steps involved.

Both kinds of processes are closely connected to your purpose for writing. When writing about a process, one of the first things to consider is why you want to write about it. Do you want to teach your readers how to do something? Or do you want to broaden their understanding of how something works or how something is made or accomplished? The chart in Figure 11.1 may help you visualize the connection between process and purpose.

FIGURE 11.1

The Connection Between Process and Purpose

TYPE OF PROCESS	PURPOSE	OUTCOME FOR READERS
Directional	To give directions that explain how to do something	Readers will be able to follow your steps and complete the process on their own.
Informational	To provide information that explains how something works, gets made, or is accomplished	Readers will be able to understand the steps or stages in the process so that their knowledge of it is broadened.

Exercise 11.1

Apply what you have learned so far about directional and informational processes by doing this exercise with group members. First, review the list of group roles and responsibilities explained in Figure 1.6, page 28. Next, read and discuss the following list of common processes. Determine which processes are directional and which are informational. Be able to support your answers when you share your results with the rest of the class. Then evaluate your group's performance.

> how to build a fence
>
> how to document a research paper
>
> the life cycle of a gypsy moth
>
> the making of a politician's image
>
> how to give CPR (cardiopulmonary resuscitation)
>
> ways businesses have reduced energy consumption
>
> how a newspaper is printed
>
> a method for reducing boredom
>
> how to prepare for the GRE (Graduate Record Examination)
>
> how Congress spends your taxes
>
> how to figure your income tax

Group Evaluation

What did each person contribute to the group's activity? Was your group's performance successful? Why or why not? What additional questions do you have about directional and informational processes?

PROCESS IN CONTEXT

Your decision to write about a process should follow directly from your experience and your audience's needs. Write about processes that you are familiar with through reading and observation or that you have actually done and think are worthwhile. Suppose you believe that everyone should know how to do CPR (cardiopulmonary resuscitation). Maybe you think this way because you took a course in CPR and, by performing this simple maneuver, were able to prevent someone from choking to death. To establish a context for your process you could begin your essay by briefly explaining what happened. From there, you could move to an explanation of the steps involved in performing CPR.

Whatever process you choose to explain, provide a *context* for that process by making clear to your readers why it is important to you and should be important to them as well. For example, tell your readers how you learned about the process, why you do it, or where you have seen it done. You can build readers' interest in *any* process by placing it in context and having a purpose for writing. Consider the following short essay by Laura Tomashek, a Florida college student.

Samples from the Nut Jar

As a college student in search of a quick-energy snack, I devised my own: a low-cost rendition of the ever-popular trail mix. 1

I found that if I could mix my own concoction of nuts, raisins, sunflower seeds and candy-coated chocolates (many of these) in bulk, it would be far less expensive than the store-brand varieties. 2

As I mentioned, I am a college student; therefore, I am on a budget. 3

In creating my mixture, I noticed significance in each of the ingredients and how they pertain to life. 4

The recipe begins with mixed nuts. The large Brazil nuts represent the big projects that we undertake and tend to save for last (ever notice how these seem to remain at the bottom of the serving dish?). 5

The flavorful cashews are the smooth moments that we enjoy in life when everything is going right. 6

The peanuts are plentiful, reminding us of the common, everyday things that we take for granted. 7

Wonderful pecans are the treasured nuts that we search to the bottom of the jar for, just as we search for special things in life. 8

Be careful to look out for the nuts that are bitter or "not quite right"; every mix tends to have a few of these. These nuts call to mind the bitterness and sorrow we face occasionally. 9

Next, add raisins—a cup or so. These sweet, juicy morsels are symbolic of the goodness and sweetness in life. Raisins are good for you— reminding us of Mom and childhood. 10

Even though the raisins are good for us, the chocolate is what we really crave. Add plenty of candy-coated chocolates to the mixture. Milk chocolate brings decadent moments of pure indulgence. These morsels represent the greatest pleasures in life. I like a lot of chocolate in my mix! 11

Last, add the sunflower seeds. Seemingly small and insignificant, 12 these nuts add the substance to the mix: the protein for energy and growth. The mixture should include sunflower seeds without the shell. These nuts are symbolic of those tall, yellow flowers that grow in the summer sun. Sunflowers rise tall and mighty with brilliant blooms and make us smile. Well-tended lives, like sunflowers, grow strong.

After thoroughly mixing the ingredients, place them into recycled   13
jars of every size. The jars keep the snacks fresh and readily available

To partake of a sample of the nut jar, simply pour a small amount   14
into your hand, and always remember to share it with others. A good snack is just like life—no fun to have alone.

The treats are pre-mixed; so like life, take it as it comes.   15

Life is like a sample from the nut jar: moments of tender sweetness   16
mixed with the crunchy, salty bits of daily life, topped with bright-colored moments of pure pleasure.

Enjoy!   17

Tomashek's first four paragraphs establish her purpose and context. She knows how to make a quick-energy, low-cost snack, and her purpose is to pass that knowledge on to her readers. To establish a context for her purpose and process, Tomashek tells readers that she is a college student on a budget and that her snack's ingredients have a special significance. Her steps, which are explained in the body of her essay, tell readers how to make, store, and eat the snack. The concluding paragraphs suggest that the essay is more than a list of steps in a snack-making process: It is also a recipe for enjoying life.

EXERCISE 11.2   Answer the following questions about Tomashek's essay.

1. Is the process the author describes directional or informational, and how do you know?

2. If you were going to make the snack she describes, what ingredients would you need?

3. How do you make the mixture? What do you add first, next, and last?

4. Who is Tomashek's audience, and how do you know?

5. What are Tomashek's thesis and controlling idea?

To write creatively about any process, place the process in context. Have some larger purpose for writing your essay. For example, reveal to your readers something they may not know about the process or about its meaning or importance.

EXERCISE **11.3**   Think about a recipe that reveals some aspect of your culture, family heritage, or region. Imagine you are going to write an essay about your recipe and its significance to your readers' lives. Answer the questions below to determine your purpose for writing. Share your results with the rest of the class.

1. Why do you like this particular food or drink prepared in this way?

2. What pleasant experiences or special events are associated in your mind with this food or drink?

3. Is this recipe a regional or ethnic dish?

4. What is there about this food or drink that might surprise your readers or that might relate to their lives?

EXERCISE **11.4**   Think of everything you have done over the past few days—at home, at work, or on campus—that involved the completion of a process. Make a list of these processes. Circle the one that you think might be most interesting to readers. Decide whether it is a directional or informational process and what your purpose for writing about it would be. Share your results with the rest of the class.

IDENTIFYING, ORGANIZING, AND EXPLAINING STEPS

Identifying, organizing, and explaining the steps of your process are not difficult tasks if you keep your audience in mind. If your purpose is to give directions, your steps must be clear enough so that readers can follow them to accomplish the task. If readers must have special tools or equipment to complete the process you describe, be sure to tell them exactly what they need. If your purpose is to give information, your steps or stages must be clear enough for readers to understand how the process works. If an understanding of the process requires the knowledge of special terms, be sure to define them the first time you mention them. For example, if you are writing about CPR, you have to assume that some readers may be unfamiliar with this process. One of your first tasks is to define CPR by telling what it is and what the letters mean.

Identifying the Steps

If you have decided to write about a process, first brainstorm your topic to determine the steps involved. Narrow your list to three to five major steps. Following is a list of steps for the topic "how to set up a home office":

1. Decide how you will use the office.

2. Choose a place for the office.

3. Select the furniture you will need.

4. Arrange your equipment and supplies.

Next, expand your list of major steps with supporting details. These will help you make the process clear to readers. Following is an expanded list of steps for the topic "how to set up a home office":

1. Decide how you will use the office:

   for study

   for job-related work

   for managing the household, paying bills, and so forth

2. Choose a place for the office:

   a spare bedroom

   an area of another room, such as the utility room, bedroom, or kitchen

   a portable office, such as a cart or table on wheels

   a closet that can be converted to an office space

3. Select the furniture you will need:

   desk or table

   chair

   lamp or light fixture

   bookcase

   file cabinet or file boxes

4. Arrange your equipment and supplies:

   heavy equipment:

> computer and printer
>
> typewriter
>
> fax machine
>
> telephone

supplies:

> paper, pens, pencils, paper clips, and so forth
>
> books and reference materials

Expanding your major steps with supporting details helps you identify any additional evidence needed to explain each step clearly and at the same time provides you with an outline to follow. Your list helps keep your mind focused on the process so that when you are writing your rough draft, you will not leave anything out. Remember that any list or outline you begin with is not final. You may need to modify it as you think of new or better ideas.

EXERCISE 11.5 Write about a process that interests you or choose one from the list on pages 268–269. List the major steps in your process, and then expand them with supporting details. Use the example on pages 264–265 as a guide.

Organizing and Explaining the Steps

Sequence is an appropriate coherence pattern to use with process. Even if the steps in a process do not have to be followed in order, your readers should be able to follow the development of your process from one step or stage to another. Transitional words and phrases can help you achieve coherence as you organize your steps into paragraphs. See Figure 11.2 for a list of some of the transitions that signal sequence.

After you have listed your steps and expanded them with details, read them over carefully to determine whether they are organized logically. If not, revise them to improve the sequence. Next, choose an appropriate transition to introduce each of your major steps. During your drafting process, combine each major step with its supporting details into a paragraph.

Following is a list of the major steps, with appropriate transitions underlined, for the process "how to set up a home office":

FIGURE 11.2

Transitions That Signal Sequence

again	furthermore
also	last
and	later
before	meanwhile
begin by	moreover
begin with	next
besides	still
during	then
finally	too
first, second, etc.	when
following	while

1. <u>The first step</u> in setting up your home office is to decide how you will use your office.

2. <u>The next step</u> is to choose a place for the office that will be best suited to its use.

3. When you have found the right place for your home office, you are ready for <u>the third step</u>, which is to select the furniture you will need.

4. <u>The final step</u> is to arrange your equipment and supplies in your new home office.

Each of the steps above has been expanded into a topic sentence. Suppose you were writing an essay on the topic "how to set up a home office." You could use the topic sentences from the list above to begin each of your body paragraphs. For your details, you could expand the details from the outline on pages 264–265 into complete sentences, adding more details and examples where needed. Keep in mind that there are other transitions you could use and many ways to introduce major steps.

If you compare Laura Tomashek's essay on pages 261–262 with Andy Rooney's essay on pages 256–258, you will see that each of these authors uses the process pattern differently. First of all, their purposes differ. Rooney's purpose is to amuse and entertain readers by pointing out that most of us try to avoid difficult or unpleasant tasks. Tomashek's purpose is to inform readers about her recipe for a low-cost snack, but she also wants to share with readers her insights about life. The essays are structured differently as well. Rooney's entire essay is devoted to explaining the steps of his process. Tomashek's essay combines several patterns: *process, division,* and *comparison.* She explains how to make her snack mixture (process), describes the ingredients that make up the mixture (division), and makes a comparison between each ingredient and a quality of life that it represents (comparison). *Division* is explained in Chapter 12 and *comparison* is explained in Chapter 13. As you can see, process is a useful pattern for writers either by itself or combined with other patterns.

EXERCISE **11.6**   Using your list from Exercise 11.5, add appropriate transitions to each of your major steps, and expand them into topic sentences.

EXERCISE **11.7**   Choose two of the body paragraphs from Andy Rooney's essay on pages 256–258 and outline them to clearly show which are the major steps and which are the details that support them. Share your results with the rest of the class.

EXERCISE **11.8**   Working with a partner, review Tomashek's essay on pages 261–262. Then either underline or list on paper the transitions that help you follow her steps for making the snack mixture. Share your results with the rest of the class.

WRITING YOUR THESIS STATEMENT

Your thesis statement should clearly indicate what process you are explaining and how you will develop it. For example, your thesis might specify the exact number of steps the reader will need to follow to complete the process. If the process occurs through several stages that have names, your thesis could briefly list the names of the stages. Following are two thesis statements; the first one numbers steps, and the second one names stages:

1. To avoid the cost of having the oil changed in your car, follow my *five steps* for a quick, clean, and inexpensive oil change that you can do yourself.

2. Understanding thc three stages of the memory process—*reception, retention,* and *recollection*—can help students make efficient use of their study time.

Each of these thesis statements also makes clear what the writer's purpose is. In the first one, the writer intends to tell readers how they can save money by doing their own oil changes. In the second statement, the writer wants to help students understand how their memory works so they can study efficiently. The next example is a possible thesis statement for the topic "how to set up a home office":

> If having a convenient work space has always been a dream of yours, the four essentials of creating a home office can help you realize your dream.

This thesis statement makes clear that the writer will tell readers how to create a home office by following four essential steps.

EXERCISE 11.9

For tips on how to improve your paragraph skills and use of transitions, visit the following websites, using *paragraph* and *transitions* as search words. Download an exercise or other useful information to share with the class. Go to Purdue University's website at http://owl.english.purdue.edu or Strunk and White's *Elements of Style* at www.bartleby.com/141/index.html.

TOPICS FOR WRITING

1. Write an essay using the topics you brainstormed for the exercises in this chapter, or make up your own topic.

2. Choose a topic from the following list, and write an essay whose purpose is *to give directions.*

   how to write a résumé

   how to get along with coworkers

   how to break a habit

   how to care for an aging parent

how to adjust to college or a new job

how to improve grades

3. Choose a topic from the following list, and write an essay whose purpose is *to provide information.*

how you and your family celebrate birthdays

how something is made or manufactured

how the people of a certain country celebrate a wedding

how students are selected to play on one of your college's athletic teams

how you made an important decision or solved a problem

how a company provides a product or performs a service

4. Identify and write about a process taught in one of your courses. For example, in a personal finance course you study such processes as how to manage credit or how to budget your monthly income. Write about a process that interests you or that you think is important.

Checklist for Revision

As you revise and edit your essay, check for the following:

1. Did you choose as a topic a process that you have experienced?

2. Does your thesis statement make your process and purpose clear to readers?

3. Have you established an appropriate context for explaining your process?

4. Are the major steps of the process clear?

5. Have you included enough details to explain major steps clearly?

6. Do your topic sentences begin with transitions as needed to help readers follow your steps?

7. Are your sentences varied and error-free?

THE CRITICAL THINKER

To examine Andy Rooney's essay in more depth, think about and discuss the following questions. Then choose one of them as a topic for writing.

1. How does Andy Rooney's thesis statement relate to his purpose for writing?

2. What is Rooney's tone? Find specific words and phrases that help you determine his tone,

3. Do Rooney's steps for putting off a job sound familiar? Did you see yourself in any of his examples? Which of Rooney's steps have you taken, or have you seen someone else take, to avoid doing a difficult or unpleasant task?

4. Rooney's essay explains how to put off doing a job. Suppose his topic had been *how to put off writing an essay?* How many of his steps would still apply? Which ones? Explain your answer.

YOUR DISCOVERY JOURNAL

Andy Rooney's essay is about how to *avoid* doing a job instead of how to get a job done. What makes Rooney's essay humorous is his unexpected approach to his topic. Taking Andy Rooney's approach, write in your journal about how *not* to do something. For example, you could explain "how not to act on a date," "how not to get invited back to dinner," or "how not to get a job." Be creative: Think of something most people have to do but would prefer not to do. Then write about how to avoid doing it.

Chapter 12

Using Classification or Division

*S*uppose you and some friends decide to rent a movie. As you discuss the possibilities, you discover that one of you hates horror movies, another is tired of action/adventure films, but all of you like romantic comedies. You go to the video store, head for the comedy section, and select one that everyone likes. Then you spend a pleasant evening watching the film.

The reason it is easy to find what you want in a video store is that the videos are arranged according to type, such as *action/adventure, comedy, horror, western,* and *drama*. Similarly, whenever you shop for anything in any store with which you are familiar, you probably know exactly where to look. For example, in a grocery store you would expect to find yogurt with dairy products and napkins with paper products. *Classification* is the system that makes it possible to sort these objects into convenient categories.

Have you ever taken anything apart or tried to put something together such as a child's toy, a piece of furniture, a motor, or a small appliance? If so, then you know that each part plays an important role in the smooth operation or functioning of the whole. All things are made up of parts. *Division* is the system that names the parts and explains how they are connected.

To help you see the difference between classification and division, think of flowers. A flower can be *classified* as one of several types: a rose or an orchid, for example. A flower can also be *divided* into several parts: The stem and petals are the two with which you are probably most familiar.

Classification and division systems not only help us create order in our lives, they also help writers organize details in meaningful ways. For example, writers choose classification when they want to sort and group items into convenient categories for discussion. Writers choose division when they want to analyze a whole object, system, or idea by looking at its parts.

This chapter explains how you can use classification and division to organize your ideas.

AWARENESS CHECK

Before reading the following essay, explore your thoughts about dish-washing and other household chores. Think about the questions below, and answer them either on your own or in a group discussion:

1. How are the chores divided in your home? Who does what?

2. Which chore do you dislike the most? Which chore do you think most people would name as their least favorite?

3. Read the title, headnote, and first two paragraphs of the following essay. Based on this preview, what do you think will follow?

Dish Demeanor
Tom Bodett

Tom Bodett has been a commentator on National Public Radio's "All Things Considered." He lives in Alaska where he hosts a weekly radio program, "The End of the Road Review." Bodett is the author of three essay collections, among them Small Comforts, *from which this essay is taken.*

VOCABULARY CHECK

controversies (1)	arguments
Melmac (1)	a brand of tableware
surpassed (1)	exceeded, beyond the limits of
methodically (2)	carefully, one step at a time
precariously (2)	dangerously
contention (2)	argument, controversy
teeter (3)	place unsteadily or unsurely
rivaling (3)	equal to or almost equal to
municipal (3)	local or state government
dismantle (3)	take apart
quintessential (3)	the purest or most typical example
zeal (4)	enthusiasm, excessive devotion
virtually (6)	almost, nearly
neurotic (6)	overly anxious
convulsions (6)	uncontrolled fits such as a fit of anger
invariably (6)	constantly, without change
confrontations (7)	clashes of opinion
unprecedented (8)	having no previous example
fragility (8)	quality of being easily damaged or broken
juxtaposed (8)	placed side by side
demise (9)	end

1 Household controversies range from church of choice to the color of the new family car. But nothing on the long list of excuses for domestic disturbance can produce so much fuss as the proper way to wash a dish. Dish-washing techniques are as many and varied as the floral designs on Melmac plates and are surpassed only by bathroom habits in their inflexibility. You can tell a person by his dish-washing style, but as I say, you can't tell him very much.

Dish washers can be broken into two basic categories. There are   2
Wash-and-Driers, who methodically wash a few, dry a few, wash a few,
dry a few, put some away, start over, and when they're done, they're
done. All the rest are *Wash-and-Drippers.* They wash the whole pile,
then stack the dishes precariously in a rubber drainer until the next
morning. Wash-and-Driers show a basic insecurity in not being able to
leave things go. They're the same folks who can spot a dustball under
the sofa from across the room and won't relax until it's swept up.
Wash-and-Driers normally work in teams, which can promote marital
harmony, but which can also lead to whole new points of contention
by allowing two solid opinions near the same small sink. Whereas one
partner might want to do the silverware first to get it out of the way,
the other will surely prefer to let it soak to make the job a little easier.
There is a point of agreement, however, among all dish washers, and
it's that everyone hates to do silverware.

Wash-and-Drippers are the free spirits of the kitchen, and can be   3
divided into two subgroups: *right-brained stackers* and *left-brained
stackers.* Right-brained stackers will randomly clean cup, plate, or serving spoon without regard to shape or size and creatively teeter them on
one another until a dish-sculpture rivaling anything in the modern arts
takes form at sinkside. This is all well and good, but it requires a mu-
nicipal bomb squad to dismantle the stack without breaking anything
or waking up the baby. Right-brained stackers of the Wash-and-Dripper
persuasion reveal a basic love of expression and are the poets and
painters of the twin sink. Picasso was a notorious dish stacker, and his
Crystal Goblet on Salad Tongs in Blue Bowl stands to this day as the
quintessential right-brained dish stack.

Left-brained Wash-and-Drippers would build a good bridge or a   4
level house if given the opportunity. They choose their next dirty dish
with care, basing their selections on size, weight, and shape with no regard to order of appearance. Lefties wash cast-iron skillets and large ce-
ramic bowls well ahead of the bone china, so as the stack grows the
weight bears on the hardier pieces. No left-brained stacker would ever
hang a bowl on a wineglass stem or leave the blades of sharp knives
pointing up. They might, however, in their zeal for orderliness, stack
dishes so close together that even a day later wet plates can be found
tightly layered at the bottom of the drainer. This drives right-brained
stackers absolutely bonkers, because being dedicated Wash-and-
Drippers, they wouldn't put a towel to a dish at gunpoint.

If an argument isn't had over *how* the dishes are to be washed, one   5
will surely come over *when*. Many married and most all single dish
owners are famous procrastinators when it comes to this chore, and
some have been known to put it off until there is not an adequate cup

or plate left in the house. Once the last empty peanut-butter jar has been drunk from, one of two things takes place. The first is to set aside a rainy weekend to scrape, sort, sanitize, and stack the mountain of tableware. The second and more common practice is to sublet or sell the house.

On the flip side of these casual washers are the folks who virtually clean as they go. We've all been witness to the host who rinses out your coffee cup between servings and has it washed, dried, and hung on a hook before the last swallow reaches your belly. These people, when left to their own devices, would choose to eat their meals over the garbage disposal rather than soil a plate or stain a fork. They scour their sinks with neurotic regularity, and finding a noodle dangling from the bottom of a drain-stopper is likely to send them into convulsions. Invariably alone at the end, most *Clean-as-They-Goers* marry but lose their spouses, sometimes to mental institutions, but mostly to well-adjusted slobs.

I believe my wife was quite fortunate in finding herself a well-adjusted slob the first time around. As we are both of the Wash-and-Dripper right-brained stacker persuasion, we have very few cleanup confrontations. In fact, what we have is a healthy competition. We take turns marveling at the sinkside sculptures each devises with his or her stacking skill. We're a pretty even match on this point, and had assumed this playful rivalry would go on forever. Unfortunately we've run into a problem.

Feeling exceptionally inspired one recent evening, I took it upon myself to use our wedding glasses as the foundation for a dish stack of unprecedented ambition. We had several guests for dinner and managed to use every piece of decent tableware in the house, so I was able to arrange them one on top of the other with a ten-pound iron soup kettle at the summit. It's a marvel of balance and fragility with a certain air of grace juxtaposed by the presence of the soup pot.

Picasso himself might have awarded me a spirited slap in the pants with a damp dish rag at the sight of it. The problem is that we're afraid to touch the thing. Those wineglasses, the very symbol of our unity, are holding up every dish in the kitchen. Neither one of us is willing to risk their demise by dismantling my creation. It's going on a week now, and might go on forever. Who knows how long it'll stay standing, but in the meantime, it gives us something to talk about while we scrape the paper plates.

THE CRITICAL READER

Central Idea

1. Is Bodett's thesis stated or implied? If stated, in what paragraph do you find the thesis?

Evidence

2. In the first part of the essay, Bodett classifies people into two categories based on *how* they wash dishes. What are the categories?

3. Which category does Bodett say are the "free spirits of the kitchen?"

4. Bodett divides one of his categories into two subgroups. What is the category and what are the subgroups?

5. Later in the essay, Bodett classifies people into two more categories based on *when* they wash dishes. What are the categories?

Implications

6. Bodett says "Nothing on the long list of excuses for domestic disturbance can produce so much fuss as the proper way to wash a dish." Do you agree or disagree? What other household task can result in an argument?

Word Choice

7. In the essay's title, *demeanor* means the way a person acts or behaves. How do Bodett's thesis and categories reflect the title?

WHAT IS CLASSIFICATION?

Classification is a sorting system that groups items according to what they have in common—their *shared characteristics*. For example, you could classify college students by age, race, sex, or national origin. You could also classify them as state residents or out-of-state residents; commuters or dormitory dwellers; and part-time or full-time attendees. Other categories might be the degree or job certification they are seeking, their major field of interest, the organizations they belong to, and their grade point averages. You could even classify students according to social habits and study habits. For example, some students belong to fraternities or sororities, some are independents, and some form social groups based on shared interests. Some students do nothing but study, some rarely study at all, and others strike a balance between studying and socializing. You can probably think of several other categories that include you and the other students you know.

EXERCISE **12.1** Each list of items belongs to a different category. Read the list and decide what the items have in common. Use your dictionary to look up any unfamiliar words. Cross out any items that do not belong. Then in the blank space above each list, write the name of a category that correctly classifies the items. The first one is done as an example.

1. _Mythical creatures_

    leprechaun

    werewolf

    ~~witch~~

    vampire

    demon

2. _____

    cookies

    bread

    cake

    pudding

    pie

3. _____

    dinner fork

    spatula

    knife

    spoon

    salad fork

4. _____

    sneakers

    boots

    sandals

    slippers

    socks

5. _____

    mosquito

    hornet

    yellow jacket

    ladybug

    bee

6. _____

    violin

    cello

    trumpet

    harp

    viola

7. _____   9. _____

    monopoly   tiger

    badminton   hyena

    checkers   leopard

    chess   lion

    Parchesi   cheetah

8. _____   10. _____

    orchid   Jimmy Carter

    daffodil   George W. Bush

    fern   Al Gore

    rose   Bill Clinton

    lily   Ronald Reagan

EXERCISE 12.2   List three to five items that can be included in each category below. Share your results with the rest of the class.

1. Team sports
2. Types of fish that are good for eating
3. Office equipment
4. Unusual pets
5. Games for children

The Purpose of Classification

Choosing classification, as with chooing any organizational pattern, depends on your purpose for writing. Tom Bodett's purpose is to make us laugh at our dish-washing habits and the arguments they can provoke among family members. Although he could have analyzed his topic in a number of ways, he classifies dish washers by how and when they wash dishes. Suppose you want to write a serious essay about dish washing based on a public television broadcast you saw recently that described the unseen germs living in our kitchens, and you want to offer tips for controlling them. Both your purpose and categories would be different from Bodett's.

Two different students writing about the topic "types of university professors" might come up with entirely different categories based upon their purpose for writing. One student might write an informative article for the college newspaper to explain to freshmen what their professors' titles mean. This student's categories would be "assistant professor," "associate professor," and "professor." Another student might write an equally informative but humorous essay about types of professors based on their teaching styles. This student's categories might be "the dictator," "the calculator," "the communicator."

Both students' writing purposes are influenced by their audiences. The student writing about professors' titles assumes that his audience, college freshmen, may be confused by the titles, so he provides information to clear up the confusion. The student writing about types of professors assumes that many of her readers are experienced students who have encountered professors like the ones she writes about and who will therefore appreciate her humor.

Exercise 12.3   Select a topic that interests you from the list in Exercise 12.2 or make up your own topic. As in the following example, state a purpose or reason for writing about the topic.

Topic: ways to exercise

Purpose: to explain some inexpensive ways to exercise

Tom Bodett may not have set out to write a classification essay. He may have chosen his topic first and the pattern second because it seemed a convenient way to organize his ideas and fulfill his purpose. He may have thought many readers would share his amusement at the ways people wash dishes. Thus *purpose* and *audience* may have determined Bodett's choice of pattern.

Suppose you attend a country festival and craft show and one of the entertainers is a spoon player. You have never seen a pair of spoons used as a musical instrument, and this gives you an idea for a humorous essay about uses of silverware other than as eating utensils. You define as your audience the general public, who you assume believes forks and knives are good only for negotiating the food on their plates. You decide that your topic will be "the little-known uses of silverware," and you come up with these three categories: *musical instruments, unusual jewelry,* and *wind chimes and other crafts.* Your purpose is to inform your audience of these uses.

The Process of Classification

If you choose classification as your organizational pattern, then begin with two or more things and sort them into *categories* of similar *types* or *kinds* of items. The following example classifies some of the items for sale in a college bookstore according to their type.

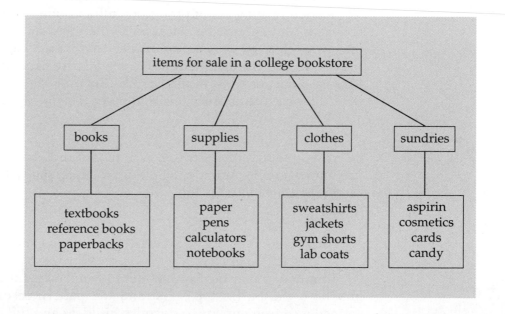

Classification is a useful pattern for explaining a complex subject. For example, in the essay on pages 61–65, Sara Gilbert uses classification to explain several types of intelligence. In the essay on pages 93–97, Stephen King uses classification to explain the kinds of questions readers ask. Textbooks also contain examples of classification. In a psychology text, you may read about Abraham Maslow's categories of human needs. Linnea's classification of animal and plant species is a common topic covered in biology textbooks.

Whether you choose classification as an organizational pattern for an essay depends on your topic, purpose, and audience. If you do choose classification, name your categories and make sure that each one is different from the others. Sort items into your categories based on their shared characteristics.

EXERCISE **12.4**

Apply what you have learned about classification by doing this exercise with group members. First, review the list of group roles and responsibilities as explained in Figure 1.6, page 28. Next, discuss the topics below. Then select one topic and determine a purpose for writing about it. Classify your topic into three or more categories. When you are finished, share your results with the rest of the class. Then evaluate your group's performance.

> ways to spend leisure time
>
> ways to improve fitness
>
> pressures college students face
>
> kinds of magazines
>
> types of music
>
> types of students on your campus

GROUP EVALUATION

What did each person contribute to the group's activity? Was your group's performance successful? Why or why not? What additional questions do you have about classification?

WHAT IS DIVISION?

Like classification, *division* is a useful pattern for explaining a complex subject. But unlike classification, which sorts many items into different categories, *division* deals with one item and the relationship among its parts. For example, a chemist uses division to analyze a solution such as a soft drink or a liquid detergent to determine what ingredients it contains. A movie critic's evaluation of a film relies on division. The critic analyzes the film's components such as the actors' performances, the script, the camera work, and special effects. The film's overall effectiveness and appeal to viewers depend upon how well these components work together. Suppose you want to write an essay on job success. What qualities do employers expect? Punctuality, personal responsibility, interpersonal effectiveness, and ability to communicate are a few of the qualities that make a good employee. As you can see, the solution and its ingredients, the film and its components, the employee and his or her qualities—all are connected by a part-to-whole relationship, which is the basis of division.

Writers often use division and classification together. For example, you can classify undergraduate degree programs by four types: associate of arts, associate of science, bachelor of arts, and bachelor of science. You can then divide each degree program into its components of required courses and electives. You can write about friends by first classifying them as acquaintances, fair-weather friends, or close friends. Next, you can then identify a friend of yours as one of these three types, for example, a close friend. Then you can use division to analyze each personal quality that makes this person a close friend.

As with classification, whether you choose division as an organizational pattern for an essay depends on your topic, purpose, and audience. If you do choose division, state your topic clearly, analyze each of its parts, and explain how they function for the good of the whole.

EXERCISE 12.5   Beside each topic, write C if it suggests classification. Write D if it suggests division.

_____ 1. the qualities that make a good wife or husband

_____ 2. the characteristics of a good news reporter

_____ 3. types of automobile drivers

_____ 4. the stages of grief

_____ 5. careers in the field of sports

_____ 6. the components of an automobile engine

_____ 7. social mistakes you do not want to make

_____ 8. a typical day in your life

_____ 9. the parts of a computer

_____ 10. kinds of bicycles and their uses

The Purpose of Division

Laura Tomashek's essay on pages 261–262 uses division to explain the ingredients of her snack mix. The ingredients are the individual parts that make up the whole mixture. To understand the purpose of division, think about a car's sound system. Most sound systems include a radio, tape deck, and compact disk player. To operate the sound system you must understand each of its parts and their functions. In your car's manual, you may find a diagram of the sound system with each part identified by name and function. Your textbooks provide other examples. In a biology text, you may find a chapter on the human digestive system. Your understanding of how the whole system works depends upon your knowledge of its parts and their functions. The purpose of division is to analyze each part of a complex whole so that the function or significance of the whole is clear to readers.

In the following paragraph, the author's purpose is to inform readers about the parts of a golf club:

> A golf club consists of several parts, each one of which has a specific function. The grip is the part of the club that a golfer grasps in his or her hands to take a swing. The shaft extends from the grip to the club head. The shaft can be flexible or stiff, and it can be made from a variety of materials, depending on the golfer's needs. For example, flexible shafts are for golfers who do not swing fast but who want more distance. Stiff shafts are for those who have a fast swing but who want more control. Tiger Woods uses clubs with extra stiff shafts. The club head has several parts, the most important of which are the hosel and the face. The hosel is a tubular part of the club head into which the shaft is inserted. The face of the club head is the part that meets the ball during the golf swing. The face sits at different angles for different clubs. The angle of the face determines the height and the spin of the golf ball when it is hit. By understanding the parts of a golf club and their functions, golfers can improve their selection of clubs and control the way they hit the ball.

In this paragraph, a golf club is divided into parts and their functions are explained. The significance of this analysis is that all golf clubs consist of the same basic parts, but not all clubs are alike. By knowing how each part of a club functions, golfers can make better use of their clubs and can choose clubs that are appropriate to the way they play the game.

EXERCISE 12.6   Select a topic from the ones you identified as division topics in Exercise 12.5, or make up your own topic. As in the following example, state a purpose or reason for writing about your topic.

> Topic: the components of a successful party

> Purpose: to help readers plan and put together a successful party

The Process of Division

To plan your essay, using the process of division as your organizational pattern, begin by breaking down your subject into its components or parts. Suppose you have visited a museum of natural history, and you think that readers would like to know what the museum contains that might interest them. A good way to describe the museum as a whole is to divide it into parts, or sections, and explain what each one contains. For example, suppose the museum is a four-story building. You could write about what a visitor would find on each floor. You could plan your essay by making a diagram like the one below:

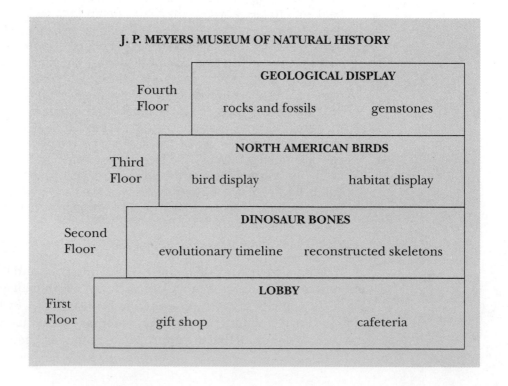

J. P. MEYERS MUSEUM OF NATURAL HISTORY

Fourth Floor — **GEOLOGICAL DISPLAY** — rocks and fossils / gemstones

Third Floor — **NORTH AMERICAN BIRDS** — bird display / habitat display

Second Floor — **DINOSAUR BONES** — evolutionary timeline / reconstructed skeletons

First Floor — **LOBBY** — gift shop / cafeteria

You could also use an informal outline to plan your essay as in the following example:

Thesis: Each floor of the J. P. Meyers Museum of Natural History contains something of interest to visitors.

First Floor: lobby

    gift shop

    cafeteria

Second Floor: dinosaur bones

    evolutionary timeline

    reconstructed skeletons

Third Floor: North American birds

    Bird display

    Habitat display

Fourth Floor: geological display

    rocks and fossils

    gemstones

Whether you use a diagram or an outline for planning, remember that the purpose of division is to explain how parts are related to a whole. For example, knowing the parts of a golf club helps golfers choose the right club for the right purpose. Knowing the parts of a museum helps visitors find the displays that interest them.

EXERCISE 12.7

Many authors have web pages on the Internet. To find an author on the Web, you can try the following: type the author's full name, with no spaces between first and last name, into the location bar on your web browser, followed by *.com.* If there is a listing for your author, his or home page will appear on screen. Or you can use a search engine like Excite, Yahoo!, Altavista, and HotBot, to name a few. Remember to use quotation marks when you type in your keyword in the dialog box.

To find out more about Tom Bodett, go to tombodett.com. At his site you can access his picture and a brief biography, a list of his books and videos, and a selection of his stories. The site is continually updated, so you may find something new each time you visit.

Read "Wait Divisions" on the website. Determine the author's thesis and pattern. Share your findings in a class discussion.

STATING YOUR THESIS

The thesis statement for your essay should make clear what your topic is and how you plan to *classify* or *divide* it. The thesis may also indicate your purpose. In any case, your introductory paragraph should clearly state or imply purpose, audience, and controlling idea if the thesis does not. Following is a possible thesis statement for an essay on folk art that is organized by classification.

> Silverware crafts, aluminum-can crafts, and glassware crafts make amusing gifts and conversation pieces for collectors.

The thesis specifies three categories of crafts: silverware crafts, aluminum-can crafts, and glassware crafts. Now read the following introductory paragraph.

> If you are like me, you probably think knives, forks, and spoons are useful only for negotiating the food from your plate to your mouth. Unless you are convinced of the need to recycle disposable items, you probably throw empty cans, bottles, and jars into the trash. Folk art has far more interesting uses for these items than the ones for which they were intended. Silverware crafts, aluminum-can crafts, and glassware crafts make amusing gifts and conversation pieces for collectors.

The writer's purpose is to inform readers of three unusual crafts that make use of unlikely objects. She assumes that her audience consists of people like her who would normally throw these items away or send them to the recycling bin.

Following are two thesis statements for two different essays that are organized by division.

1. A well-written paragraph has three parts: the topic sentence, the support sentences, and the concluding sentence.
2. Two important components of any successful college orientation program are self-management techniques and academic skills development.

In the first sentence, the topic is *a well-written paragraph,* and the purpose is to inform readers about the parts that make up such a paragraph. In the second sentence, the topic is *college orientation program* and the purpose is to inform readers about two of its components. Both sentences suggest a part-to-whole relationship. For example, each sentence in a paragraph determines how the paragraph functions as a whole. The components of self-management and academic skills determine the success of a college orientation program as a whole.

EXERCISE 12.8   In the next three excerpts, identify the following: topic, purpose, and pattern (classification or division).

1. Although a computer is a complicated piece of machinery, it has three basic parts: *input device, processor,* and *output device.* The input device consists of a keyboard, mouse, or modem. Input devices allow you to enter, access, and send information. The processor is the part of the computer that you cannot see. Inside the computer is the hard disk, an electronic memory and storage system. The words you type on the keyboard are processed through the system and converted into a special electronic language that can be saved and stored. The output device consists of a screen and printer. The screen allows you to see the information that you have either entered or accessed. Whatever you enter shows up on the screen. Similarly, when you want to get information out of the computer, you call up the file on screen. To get a copy of your file on paper, you then use the printer.

2. Oppressed people deal with their oppression in three characteristic ways. One way is acquiescence: the oppressed resign themselves to their doom. They tacitly adjust themselves to oppression, and thereby become conditioned to it. In every movement toward freedom some of the oppressed prefer to remain oppressed. Almost 2800 years ago Moses set out to lead the children of Israel from the slavery of Egypt to the freedom of the promised land. He soon discovered that slaves do not always welcome their deliverers. They become accustomed to being slaves. They would rather bear those ills they have, as Shakespeare pointed out, than flee to others that they know not of. They prefer the "fleshpots of Egypt" to the ordeals of emancipation. . . .
   A second way that oppressed people sometimes deal with oppression is to resort to physical violence and corroding hatred. Violence often brings about momentary results. Nations have frequently won their independence in battle. But in spite of temporary

victories, violence never brings permanent peace. It solves no social problem; it merely creates new and more complicated ones. . . .

The third way open to oppressed people in their quest for freedom is the way of nonviolent resistance. Like the synthesis in Hegelian philosophy, the principle of nonviolent resistance seeks to reconcile the truths of two opposites—the acquiescence and violence—while avoiding the extremes and immoralities of both. . . .

It seems to me that this is the method that must guide the actions of the Negro in the present crisis in race relations. . . .

from "The Ways of Meeting Oppression"
by Martin Luther King, Jr.

3.   We all listen to music according to our separate capacities. But, for the sake of analysis, the whole listening process may become clearer if we break it up into its component parts, so to speak. In a certain sense we all listen to music on three separate planes. For lack of a better terminology, one might name these: (1) the sensuous plane, (2) the expressive plane, (3) the sheerly musical plane. The only advantage to be gained from mechanically splitting up the listening process into these hypothetical planes is the clearer view to be had of the way in which we listen. . . .

from "What to Listen for in Music"
by Aaron Copeland

SUPPORTING YOUR THESIS

Suppose your topic is "the functions of memory" and your purpose is to describe the functions and explain how they work. You begin by naming the functions: *sensory memory, short-term memory,* and *long-term memory.* The evidence you select to accomplish your purpose consists of *how long* each function lasts, *what kind of information* each function is responsible for, and *what role* each function plays in the memory process as a whole. Notice that in this example, the parts and evidence are clearly differentiated.

Generally speaking, whether classification or division is your pattern of choice, the parts or categories you identify should be distinct from one another. Moreover, you should avoid any repetition or overlapping of supporting details. Suppose you are writing about inexpensive ways to exercise. Your categories are mall walking, neighborhood walking, and living room aerobics. As you brainstorm for evidence, you

FIGURE 12.1

Transitions that Signal Classification and Division Relationships

types	categories	parts
kinds	groups	components
divided	broken into	one type, another type . . .

realize that your two walking categories overlap. Except for place, the details you use to explain these categories will be the same. To solve this problem, you create another category and name it "power walking." Then you add one more category: community games. You now have three distinct categories, and the details you use to explain them are less likely to overlap.

Remember that effective transitions can help readers follow your ideas. For example, how do you know that Tom Bodett plans to classify dish washers? At the beginning of paragraph 2 he says that dish washers fall into two basic categories. In this paragraph, *categories* signals classification. From this point on, you know what to read for: the names of the categories, the members of each, and their shared characteristics. Figure 12.1 lists signal words and transitions you can use to achieve effective organization and coherence.

TOPICS FOR WRITING

Write an essay on one of the topics below, or make up your own topic. Have a purpose for your essay, and decide whether you will use classification or division as your organizational pattern.

ways to spend money

cassette tapes or CDs in your collection

the students at your college

the people you work with

your relatives

professional athletes

types of teachers

the neighborhoods in your town or city

Checklist for Revision

As you revise and edit your essay, check for the following:

1. Do you have a purpose for writing?

2. Have you suggested in your introduction or elsewhere who your audience is?

3. Does your thesis clearly state the categories of your classification or the parts of your division?

4. Do you have sufficient evidence to explain parts or categories?

5. Is there any overlapping or repetition of evidence?

6. Are your sentences varied and error-free?

THE CRITICAL THINKER

To examine Tom Bodett's essay in more depth, think about and discuss the following questions. Then choose one of them as a topic for writing.

1. Tom Bodett classifies dish washers according to their dish-washing style, but he also explains the process each type of dish washer uses. In which paragraphs are these processes explained? What are the steps of the different processes, and is the order of the steps important?

2. Bodett's categories are based on people who do dishes by hand. However, many people have dish-washing machines. What differences do you see in the ways people prepare the dishes for washing and load them in the machine? What categories can you think of to describe these dish-washing styles?

3. Who is Bodett's audience and what are his assumptions about his audience? Use evidence from the essay to support your answer.

4. Bodett says that household controversies range from church of choice to the color of the new family car. What "household contro-

versy" over something other than chores have you had either with family members or roommates? How did you resolve the argument?

YOUR DISCOVERY JOURNAL

Stereotyping is a form of classification. Stereotypes are the result of prejudice and have a negative effect on those who are victims of the stereotypes. Have you ever been the victim of a negative classification? Have you ever been guilty of stereotyping a person only to find out later that the person was really very different from what you had expected? Write a brief journal entry about either experience.

Chapter 13

Comparing and Contrasting

*W**hen you compare and contrast any two subjects, you examine the ways in which they are similar and different.* Also you have a reason to compare and contrast. Suppose you are an office manager and you have decided to order a new copy machine. You have narrowed your choices to two different models. Which one will you buy? Each machine's cost, its record of dependability, and its service contract are only three of the many comparisons you might make. After considering each product's advantages and disadvantages, you choose the one that offers more of what you want in a copy machine. Comparing and contrasting are so much a part of daily living that you may not realize how often you use them. Whether choosing a job, selecting courses, or deciding which friends to invite to a party, you probably make comparisons. When describing a friend, family member, or mate, you may compare or contrast his or her qualities with your own or someone else's.

Like narration, description, and other organizational patterns explained in this book, comparison and contrast is another choice for you to consider when you are deciding how to analyze a topic and organize your support of a central idea or thesis. This pattern works best for comparing *two* items, and you can use it for writing compositions, for re-

292

sponding to questions on essay tests and for other writing tasks as well. In a humanities course, you might write an essay comparing works of literature, styles of painting, or types of architecture. In a political science class, you might discuss the differences between democracy and totalitarianism.

AWARENESS CHECK

Before reading the following essay, explore your thoughts about movies and the values they reflect. Think about the questions below, and answer them either on your own or in a group discussion:

1. Have you seen either *Gone With the Wind* or *Titanic?* What is your impression of either or both films?

2. What is the best romantic movie you have ever seen, and what do you like about it?

3. Read the title, headnote, and first two paragraphs of the following essay. Based on this preview, what do you think will follow?

Would Scarlett Accept "First, Save Yourself"?

Steven D. Stark

In this essay, Steven D. Stark compares Titanic, *a popular film of the 1990s, to* Gone With the Wind, *a classic film. The author is a commentator for National Public Radio. The essay appeared in* The Orlando Sentinel *on April 6, 1998.*

VOCABULARY CHECK

saga (1)	a long heroic story
panorama (2)	an unbroken view of a wide area
idealizes (3)	holds to a standard of perfection
resonance (3)	depth of meaning

consummated (4)	a union completed through the first sexual intercourse
paradigm (5)	an example that serves as a pattern or model
vanity (6)	excessive pride in one's appearance or accomplishments
pettiness (6)	triviality, narrow mindedness, unimportance
regionalism (8)	feelings, beliefs, or concerns tied to a geographical region
pyrotechnics (10)	fireworks display, a brilliant display
artifacts (11)	objects made by humans
denigrate (12)	to defame, to attack the reputation of
tenor (12)	general sense or purpose
ostensibly (12)	apparently

With a record-tying 11 Academy Awards and box-office receipts still 1
pouring in, it's clear that *Titanic* is the blockbuster film epic of our age.
As such, the film it recalls the most is a similar saga, *Gone With the Wind,* made almost six decades ago.

There are many similarities. Both *Titanic* and *Gone With the Wind* 2
center on the survival of privileged, rebellious heroines (played by British actresses), caught in a tragic love triangle. Each is set against the sweeping panorama of a well-known American historical event that occurred about 78 to 85 years before it was made. Each movie is quite long by conventional standards and had made headlines by the time of its release for an extravagant budget. That included special effects: What the burning of Atlanta was to 1939 film audiences, the sinking of the Titanic is to ours.

Yet, for all their similarities, what's striking are the differences be- 3
tween the two films in dealing with comparable themes. Take, for example, the way each film idealizes romance. The whole premise of *Gone With the Wind* is that the most meaningful relationships are those that can survive a lifetime of hardships, which in *Gone With the Wind* include a cataclysmic war, the loss of one's wealth and even the loss of a child—circumstances that had great resonance for Depression-era audiences.

In contrast, the ideal romance in *Titanic* is a three-night stand on a   4
boat cruise, which is finally consummated in the back of a car. One can
almost see the follow-up ad: A few nights aboard ship changed Rose's
love life. Now let Carnival Cruise Lines change yours, too!

The view of men and women in each film is far different, too. In   5
one sense, Rhett Butler and Jack Dawson are similar: Both are financial
con artists of a sort who display courage when the chips are down. Yet,
one look at Clark Gable, then at Leonardo DiCaprio, reveals that the
paradigm male today is something of a child, almost a full-generation
younger than his '30s counterpart. Rhett teaches Scarlett about commerce; Jack teaches Rose how to spit. In the culture of the '90s, the
"ideal" man is a perpetual child or young adolescent: Jerry Seinfeld, Don
Imus, David Letterman.

It's no coincidence, then, that the lead woman in each film is also   6
different. For all her vanity and personal pettiness, Scarlett is a grown-
up who runs a business, fights for her land and endures an unhappy
marriage to keep her extended family financially afloat—themes, again,
that struck a chord with Depression-era moviegoers.

By the '90s, of course, such sacritices would strike an audience as   7
absurd. Today's heroine earns her spurs by becoming the anti-Scarlett:
Rose rejects the unhappy marriage that would keep her family credit-
worthy so she can pursue personal self-fulfillment through a relationship with a man she met a few days before. Whatever one thinks of the
choice, it is a revealing quality for a culture to immortalize in a heroine.
Damn the family—full speed ahead!

The historical occurrences that drive the two films are also far dif-   8
ferent. The Civil War was the great event that forged this nation, and
almost any treatment of that conflict is bound to acknowledge, at least
on some level, the defining American issues of regionalism and race.

In contrast, although the Titanic legend has retained a strong hold   9
on the American imagination, it is of trivial historical consequence. What
it is, instead, is the first great tabloid tragedy of the modern commu-
nications media age, precursor to everything from the sinking of the
Andrea Doria, to the rescue of Baby Jessica, to the current coverage of
El Nino. In many respects, James Cameron's *Titanic* is inseparable from
disaster coverage in the tabloids and throughout television: the graphic
portrayal of death and destruction, the emphasis on small, human-
interest—stories and the identification with "the little guy." All that's
missing: Geraldo.

Finally, *Gone With the Wind* was based on the most popular book   10
of its era. Although producer David O. Selznick ordered many scenes
changed or cut from Margaret Mitchell's 1,000-page-plus novel, the
film industry then was new enough that it still looked to books and
plays as a dramatic model. The result is a film that, at least by contem-

porary standards, remains quite theatrical and literary. Despite the visual pyrotechnics, what viewers tend to recall is the complexity of the plot and characters, the outstanding performances and key lines such as "Frankly, my dear, I don't give a damn." The art is such that the technical details fade: One leaves the theater wondering what Scarlett or Rhett will do next.

In contrast, *Titanic* offers no memorable lines, no Oscar-winning   11
performances and not much in the way of plot or character. What it features instead is what popular movies of today often give audiences: spectacular technical effects, a simple soap-opera-like plot and a musical soundtrack that features at least one song that can be played endlessly on MTV. Like so many other movies and cultural artifacts of this decade, the artfulness of *Titanic* is ultimately a self-conscious celebration of the person who created it: One leaves the theater wondering what Cameron will do next.

This isn't to denigrate the director or his *Titanic,* a surprise hit. It's   12
only to suggest that, like *Gone With the Wind,* this movie benefits from mirroring the tenor of its times. Both works are ostensibly about U.S. history. But, in the end, the reason both struck a chord is that each was essentially about the era that embraced it.

THE CRITICAL READER

Central Idea

1. What is the author's thesis, and where is it stated?

Evidence

2. What are at least two ways in which *Titanic* and *Gone With the Wind* are similar?

3. What are at least two ways in which the films are different?

4. According to the author, what are the different views of men and women expressed in the two films?

Implications

5. Does the author's tone or selection of details suggest that he favors one film over the other? Explain your answer using details from the essay.

Word Choice

6. In paragraph 9, the author calls *Titanic* a "tabloid tragedy." Based on the details in paragraph 9, do you think "tabloid tragedy" is or is not an appropriate choice of a term?

UNDERSTANDING THE PATTERN

When you *compare* two subjects, you examine their similarities, the characteristics that make them alike. When you *contrast* two subjects, you examine their differences, the characteristics that set them apart. Since it is difficult to do one without the other, you usually examine both the similarities and the differences between subjects when you are comparing them. In fact, the word *compare* often implies *contrast* as well. Comparison and contrast as a pattern of organization, then, is one you will use when you select as your topic two subjects whose similarities and differences you want to examine. The following four steps will help you plan and write your essay:

1. Choose subjects that have something in common.

2. Compare and contrast with a purpose.

3. Write a thesis that sets up the pattern.

4. Analyze your topic in one of two ways.

Choose Subjects That Have Something in Common

The best subjects to compare and contrast are related in some way or have enough in common to give you a good reason to compare and contrast them. For example, Steven D. Stark's general topic is films. *Titanic* and *Gone With the Wind* are the two subjects of his comparison. Both belong to the same class of films: historical romance sagas. Both have enough similarities and differences to make Stark's analysis interesting. On the other hand, a movie and a hockey game would not make good subjects for comparing and contrasting because they do not have enough in common. They do not belong to the same category, or class, of things. Suppose the topic is "two TV shows." You could approach this topic in many ways. For example, you might compare two sitcoms, two news shows, two soap operas, or you might decide to limit the topic of

TV shows in a different way. For example, you could compare two TV moms, two TV dads, or two TV families. You might even compare two different TV roles a favorite actor of yours has played. Remember that the topic is only a starting point. How you limit your topic is up to you, as long as the subjects of your comparison are of the same class.

EXERCISE 13.1   Read the list of topics below. Decide how you might limit each topic. Make sure that the subjects of your comparison are of the same class. Share your results with classmates. The first one is done as an example.

two athletes: Venus and Serena Williams

two magazines

two machines

two courses

two stores

two games

two subjects of your choice

Compare and Contrast with a Purpose

Suppose the topic you have chosen is *two jobs I have had*. Why do you want to compare two different jobs? What do you want to say about them? Was one easier or more challenging than the other? Did you like one more than the other? Perhaps you just want to explain the similarities and differences between the two jobs without making a judgment about either of them. Suppose you decide that you will compare two jobs you had at two different fast-food restaurants. Though the restaurants were the same type, perhaps there was a great difference in how they were managed. Generally speaking, there are two major purposes for comparing and contrasting subjects:

1. To identify and explain the similarities and/or differences that clearly distinguish between one subject and another of its class

2. To identify and explain the similarities and/or differences between two subjects to show that one has advantages over the other or to make some other judgment about them

If you want to explain all the ways in which your jobs at two fast-food restaurants were different or similar, you have selected the first purpose. If you want to explain why you liked one job better than the other, you have selected the second purpose. First, decide how your subjects are related: their basis for comparison. Then determine your purpose for writing about them. Figure 13.1 lists five topics, the relationship between the subjects to be compared, and two different purposes for the comparison.

FIGURE 13.1

Comparing and Contrasting Subjects

SUBJECTS	RELATIONSHIP	PURPOSE #1	PURPOSE #2
Two microwave ovens	Appliances of the same type	To explain their similarities and differences	To explain why you would rather own one than the other
Two apartment complexes	Two places to live	To show how they differ and explain what each offers	To explain advantages of one over the other as a place to live
Two candidates running for office	Different parties, same issues	To compare each person's position on the issues	To show which candidate would do a better job
Two jobs	Both fast-food restaurants	To compare and contrast both restaurants' characteristics	To explain why one is a better workplace
Two basketball players	Same team, different styles of play	To explain differences between the players' styles	To show how each contributes to the team's success

EXERCISE 13.2   Following is a list of essay topics that suggest the first purpose of comparing and contrasting: *to clearly identify and distinguish between two subjects*. Rewrite each topic so that it implies the second purpose and adds a *judgment* about the subjects. The first one is done as an example. Share your results with the rest of the class.

1. To explain how two TV sitcoms appeal to different audiences: To explain why one TV sitcom is more popular than another

2. To describe two neighborhoods

3. To explain the differences between two comedians

4. To discuss two different places to live

5. To explain your performance in two different courses you took last semester

6. To distinguish between two automobiles made by the same manufacturer.

Let Your Thesis Statement Set Up the Pattern

Your thesis statement should make clear to your readers *why* you are writing about the two subjects you have chosen (purpose) and *how* you plan to compare and contrast them (parts). Imagine that for your psychology class, you must write an essay exam in which you compare Sigmund Freud's and Carl Jung's theories of personality. The audience for your essay is your psychology professor, and your purpose is to demonstrate your understanding of the two theories. You decide to write a purpose 1 comparison, since all you want to do is identify and distinguish between the theories, not make any judgments about them. Your opinion is that the theories differ in two important ways. The parts of your thesis are your two points of comparison: how the two men define the components of personality and how the personality develops. To write your thesis statement do three things.

1. State your topic and purpose:

   to compare the personality theories of Freud and Jung and to show that they differ in two major ways

2. State the terms of comparison:

components of personality

development of personality

3. Combine topic, purpose, and terms of comparison into one complete sentence that is free of grammatical errors:

Sigmund Freud and Carl Jung, two influential theorists, describe personality differently in terms of its components and its development.

Stark's thesis, stated in the first sentence of paragraph 3 of his essay on pages 293–296, tells you that his topic is *two films* and his purpose is to explain how the films deal with comparable themes. The words *similarities* and *differences* tell you that he plans to compare the two films. The essay's following paragraphs each explain one or more of the films' similarities or differences.

There are other effective ways to write a thesis statement, but combining topic, purpose, and points of comparison into one sentence is a reliable method. Also, this type of thesis statement sets up the essay for you. You know what to discuss first and second. You can conclude your essay by making some implications for the reader. For example, picking up on the word *influential* in the thesis statement above, you might briefly explain one or two ways in which Freud's and Jung's theories have influenced the development of modern psychology. Now try the following exercise.

EXERCISE 13.3   Select a topic from the list in Exercise 13.1, or make up your own topic. Write a thesis statement that sets up the pattern for your comparison. Follow the three steps below for writing your thesis statement.

1. State your topic and purpose.

2. State the terms of comparison.

3. Combine topic, purpose, and terms of comparison into one complete sentence that is free of grammatical errors.

Analyze Your Topic in One of Two Ways

A thesis statement that includes your topic, suggests your purpose, and briefly states the points of comparison will help you determine what evidence to use to support your thesis. The next step is to organize the evidence so that your essay develops logically and flows smoothly.

When you compare two items, there are two ways you can organize the evidence. You can say all you want to about first one subject, then the other. This is called a *subject-by-subject* comparison, and it works best if you are doing a brief comparison of two subjects. You can also organize your essay by points of comparison. Under each point, you discuss first one subject, then the other. This is called a *point-by-point* comparison, and it works best if you have a great deal to say about both your subjects.

To do either kind of comparison, you must first decide what your points of comparison are. Whatever you say about one subject, you should also say about the other. For example, if a point of difference between you and your sister is the kind of leisure-time activities you prefer, then you should explain which activities you enjoy and which activities your sister prefers. The following example will help you see the difference between a *subject-by-subject* comparison and a *point-by-point* comparison.

Suppose you decide to write an essay comparing yourself to your older sister. You want to write this essay because people have always assumed that you and your sister are alike. However, people's expectations of you seem to be based on your sister's personality and the choices she has made. You want to set the record straight. Your thesis comes easily: "My relatives expected me to pursue a nursing career like Alice did, but if they really knew how different my sister and I are, they would not be surprised that I chose differently." You have decided that your points of comparison will be *personality traits, study habits, personal preferences,* and *goals,* but you are not sure how to organize your essay.

If you organize your details *subject by subject,* you will discuss your differences and Alice's differences separately. It does not matter whose personality traits, study habits, personal preferences, and goals you discuss first. In the process of planning, drafting, and revising your essay, you may decide which order seems to work best. Figure 13.2, pages 303–304, shows an example of a subject-by-subject outline.

If you organize the same details *point by point,* you will discuss how you and Alice differ in each of the traits, habits, preferences, and goals you have chosen. Your outline might look like the one in Figure 13.3, pages 305–306.

You could use either one of these outlines to write an effective comparison-and-contrast essay. Whether you prefer to discuss your subjects one at a time or point by point is your choice as a writer. Be willing to experiment with both methods of organizing an essay. In the process you may decide that one of them works better for you.

FIGURE 13.2

A Subject-by-Subject Outline

I. Subject: Self

   A. Personality traits

      1. Introverted, self-motivated

      2. Artistic

      3. Need to do things my way

   B. Study habits

      1. Procrastinator

      2. Avoid difficult tasks

      3. Choose courses according to preference

   C. Personal preferences

      1. Want to be my own boss

      2. Enjoy drawing, painting, various crafts, visiting galleries and museums

      3. Like change, hate routine

   D. Goals

      1. Career goal: to work at a job I like that has potential for making a lot of money (interior design)

      2. Life goals: to have privacy, create beautiful surroundings, have leisure time to travel

II. Subject: Alice

   A. Personality traits

      1. Extroverted, other-motivated

      2. Analytical

      3. Needs directions, rules

   B. Study habits

      1. Never procrastinates

      2. Finds difficult tasks challenging

      3. Chooses courses according to need

FIGURE 13.2 (cont.)

A Subject-by-Subject Outline

C. Personal preferences

1. Would prefer to work for someone

2. Enjoys the outdoors, physical activity, sports

3. Hates change, prefers routine

D. Goals

1. Career goal: to work at a job that lets her help people and that she feels is important (nursing)

2. Life goals: to fulfill her lifelong ambition of becoming a nurse, to be respected in her field, to have a comfortable and secure life

EXERCISE 13.4

Apply what you have learned about the two ways to analyze your topic by doing this exercise with group members. First, review the list of group roles and responsibilities as explained in Figure 1.6, page 28. Next, complete the activity that follows and share your results with the rest of the class. Then evaluate your group's performance.

1. Review and discuss Steven D. Stark's essay on pages 293–296.

2. Decide whether he has used a point-by-point or subject-by-subject analysis.

3. Briefly outline Stark's essay. Use the outline in Figure 13.2 or Figure 13.3 as your guide.

4. Be able to explain what changes Stark would have had to make if he had analyzed his topic in the opposite way.

GROUP EVALUATION

What did each person contribute to the group's activity? Was your group's performance successful? Why or why not? What additional questions do you have about the two ways to analyze your topic?

EXERCISE 13.5

Write an essay in which you compare two films of the same type, for example, two romantic comedies, two war movies, two gangster films. To gather evidence for your essay, view both films. Your college may have a

FIGURE 13.3

A Point-by-Point Outline

I. Personality traits

    A. Sociability

        1. Alice is extroverted, other-motivated.

        2. I am introverted, self-motivated.

    B. Creativity

        1. Alice is analytical.

        2. I am creative.

    C. Independence

        1. Alice needs directions, rules.

        2. I need to do things my way.

II. Study habits

    A. Procrastination

        1. Alice never procrastinates.

        2. I do procrastinate.

    B. Facing difficult tasks

        1. Alice finds difficult tasks challenging.

        2. I avoid difficult tasks.

    C. Course selection

        1. Alice chooses courses according to need.

        2. I choose courses according to preference.

III. Personal preferences

    A. Jobs

        1. Alice would prefer to work for someone.

        2. I want to be my own boss.

    B. Activities

        1. Alice enjoys the outdoors, physical activity, sports.

        2. I enjoy drawing, painting, various crafts, visiting galleries and museums.

   C. Change

     1. Alice hates change, likes routine.

     2. I like change, hate routine.

IV. Goals

   A. Career

     1. Alice wants to work at a job that lets her help people and that she feels is important (nursing).

     2. I want to work at a job I like that has a potential for making a lot of money (interior design).

   B. Life

     1. Alice wants to fulfill her lifelong ambition of becoming a nurse, to be respected in her field, and to have a comfortable and secure life.

     2. I want to have privacy, create beautiful surroundings, and have leisure time to travel.

video film library, or you can rent the films from a video store. In addition, read a critical review about each film. Pauline Kael and Andrew Sarris are two well-known film critics. Search the following websites for reviews of films that interest you: http://hollywood.com and http://allmovie.com

ORGANIZING YOUR ESSAY: QUESTIONS TO ASK

Asking yourself the following questions may help you think through the four steps involved in planning your essay. Keep in mind that as you plan your essay, you may need to skip a step and return to it later, or you may need to repeat some steps throughout your writing process.

1. *Choose subjects that have something in common.*

     What are my subjects?

     What is their relationship?

2. *Compare and contrast with a purpose.*

>   Is my purpose to identify and explain what distinguishes one subject from another, or is my purpose to make a judgment about my subjects?

3. *Write a thesis statement that sets up the pattern.*

>   What is my central idea or thesis?

>   Does my thesis clarify my topic (subjects to be compared), purpose, and points of comparison?

4. *Analyze your topic in one of two ways.*

>   Will a point-by-point or subject-by-subject comparison fulfill my purpose?

TOPICS FOR WRITING

1. Choose one of the following topics, or choose your own topic, and write an essay that is organized by comparison and contrast.

two books	you and a friend or relative
two items of clothing	two environmental policies
two public officials	two places you have lived
two comedians	two musicians or music groups

2. Write a serious or humorous essay in which you compare and contrast two groups of people. Choose from the topics below or make up your own essay topic.

bosses versus employees	children versus parents
teachers versus students	Republicans versus Democrats
husbands versus wives	lawbreakers versus law abiders

3. Comparison and contrast is a useful pattern for academic writing. For example, you could use information learned in a humanities course as the evidence for writing an essay in which you compare two styles of architecture, two styles of painting, or two philosopher's definitions of art or education. Using the information you have learned in one of your courses, write an essay in which you compare and contrast two subjects of your choice.

Checklist for Revision

As you revise and edit your essay, check for the following:

1. Did you choose a topic that lets you compare two subjects of the same type or class?

2. Is it clear that your purpose is either to distinguish between your two subjects or to make a judgment about them?

3. Does your thesis set up the pattern?

4. Have you followed a subject-by-subject or point-by-point analysis?

5. Do you have enough evidence to compare and contrast your subjects?

6. Are your sentences varied and error-free?

THE CRITICAL THINKER

To examine Steven D. Stark's essay in more depth, think about and discuss the following questions. Then choose one of them as a topic for writing.

1. Do you think Steven D. Stark's purpose is to distinguish one film from the other, or is his purpose to show that one film is better than the other? Explain your answer using evidence from the essay.

2. How does the author help readers to follow his analysis of the films' similarities and differences? What transitional words and phrases does he use, and where do they occur?

3. In relation to the essay as a whole, what do you think the title means and why?

4. Stark says that both *Titanic* and *Gone With the Wind* mirror the attitudes and values of their times. What recent movie have you seen that reflects one or more of today's values about family, love, friendship, or work, for example? Explain what these values are and how the film reflects them.

Your Discovery Journal

Compare the person you are now to the person you would like to become. What are some of your personality traits? What activities do you enjoy doing? What new activities would you like to try, or what skills would you like to learn? What are your goals? What do you want out of life? Compare the characteristics you now possess with those you hope to have in the future. What do you want to change, and what do you want to remain the same?

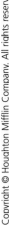

Chapter 14

Explaining Causes and Effects

*A*t least once each day you probably ask the question *why?* Why is your friend angry? Why did you not get a raise in pay? Why did you not make a higher score on your algebra test? Sometimes people ask why you voted for a certain candidate, why you liked a concert, or why you feel the way you do about a person. When you ask people *why,* you are asking them to explain their *reasons* for feeling, thinking, believing, or acting the way they do. Suppose you have not done your assignment. Your professor might ask you *why.* The *reason* you give might be that you did not understand the directions. Whatever the reason, you explain to the professor the *causes* that prevented you from doing the assignment. When people ask you *why,* they want *reasons.* When you give *reasons,* you are explaining *causes.*

Causes lead to *effects.* An *effect* is a *result* of some action. For example, suppose you have a leaky roof. You examine the roof and see that some shingles have come loose. Now you know *why* your roof leaks; the shingles are loose. The loose shingles are the *cause,* and the leaky roof is the *effect.* Some cause-and-effect relationships, like the loose shingles that cause the roof to leak, are easy to determine. If you live in a part of the country where there are frequent thunderstorms, you probably have observed the cloud formations, the changes in temperature, and the sudden winds that signal the approach of a storm. Pilots who fly private planes become adept at watching the weather and determining when they should take off and which route they should follow. If you wake up on a Saturday wanting to go to the beach, but you look outside and see that the sky is covered with dark clouds and it is drizzling, you probably change your plans. You know that the effect of such weather will be a bad day at the beach. In each situation you make *inferences,* or educated guesses, about what might happen based on past observations of causes and effects.

Because so many of life's events seem linked by simple cause-and-effect relationships, you might be tempted to think that everything works that way. In fact, there are many questions whose answers we can only guess. You can find out, for example, what causes hail or fog, but the causes of poverty, homelessness, drug addiction, teen suicide, and crime are not so easy to determine. Though people may have strong opinions about the causes, they still remain only opinions. Have you ever stopped to think about why you love someone, why you belong to a certain political party, why you follow a certain religion, why you have selected your major or career? Have you really thought about the effects of your behavior on others with respect to these matters? If you have, then you have examined some of the *reasons* and *results,* the *causes* and *effects* that operate in your life.

Your courses provide many exciting opportunities to observe causes and effects in action. In an algebra course, you learn what results when you change the value of x in an equation. In a science class, you learn that if you drop a golf ball into a beaker of water, it sinks. But if you add salt to the water, the ball floats. Why? Because salt makes water more buoyant—which is also why you may find it easier to float in the ocean than in a swimming pool. In a psychology class, you learn several theories that explain human behavior. Social scientists make inferences based upon behavioral theories about the ways people might react in a given situation. No matter what course you take, a big part of what you learn is a habit of thinking that involves examining various causes and their effects.

AWARENESS CHECK

Before reading the following essay, explore your thoughts about drinking and alcohol abuse. Think about the questions below, and answer them either on your own or in a group discussion.

1. Is alcohol abuse a problem on your campus or among the college students you know? Explain the extent of the problem.

2. What are some causes and effects of alcohol abuse?

3. Read the title, headnote, and first two paragraphs of the following article. Based on this preview, what do you think will follow?

Students Are Dying: Colleges Can Do More
Rob Waldron

According to Rob Waldron in this essay from Newsweek, *drunk driving is an old problem that continues to plague America's college campuses. Waldron, a San Francisco writer, believes we can find a solution.*

VOCABULARY CHECK	
recounted (2)	narrated, told
toga (4)	a loose-fitting outer garment worn by male citizens of ancient Greece, a costume worn at fraternity "toga" parties
reluctant (6)	hesitant, unwilling
liable (6)	legally obligated or responsible
infirmary (7)	a place where the sick or injured receive care
eulogies (10)	speeches given as a tribute, especially for one who has died

Unfortunately, I am an expert on drinking and driving. As a high-school freshman in Wayland, Mass., I suffered through the death of a classmate on my hockey team who was killed in an alcohol-related crash. Two years later I attended the funeral of another classmate who died while driving under the influence. Twelve months after that a wrestling teammate returning to Wayland from a college break totaled his car in a drunk-driving accident, partially paralyzing himself and causing permanent brain damage. His father, a town firefighter responding to a 911 call, was the one to find him on the roadside near death.

1

After all that, I thought I knew the worst about drunk driving. I was wrong. Three years ago my brother, Ryan, a Middlebury College senior, drove 70–100 miles an hour on a rainy rural road into a tree, ending his life. His blood-alcohol level was nearly three times the legal limit. Witnesses later recounted that he was swerving and speeding on a nearby road.

It was one of the worst accidents that officers at the crash site had ever seen. The two policemen assigned to wipe Ryan's blood and tissue off the car's broken windshield found it impossible even to talk to us about the details of what they found. According to the police report, before officers could transport Ryan to the funeral home, they had to remove a small branch that pierced his permanently flattened lips.

Ryan was last seen drinking on campus at a fraternity house that was serving vodka punch. He left the party intending to drive to his off-campus apartment three miles away to pick up a toga for yet another event. He never made it home. After his death, we found out that Ryan had developed a drinking problem while away at college. But even though he drank to excess at nearly every social function, usually three to four times a week, many of his friends never realized he was on his way to becoming an alcoholic.

It turns out that one of the staff members in the student-activities office where Ryan often came to register his fraternity's parties had suspected that he had a drinking problem. And Ryan isn't the only Middlebury student to be involved in a dangerous alcohol-related incident: in the year before his death one of Ryan's fellow students nearly died in a binge-drinking incident, saved only because the hospital pumped her stomach as she lay unconscious. Her blood-alcohol level was .425 percent.

What should we do about the Ryans of the world? I know that my brother was ultimately responsible for his own death, but in my view, college administrators can work harder to keep kids like Ryan from getting behind the wheel. But many schools have been reluctant to address the problem. Why? Perhaps because taking responsibility for drinking and driving will make trustees and college presidents legally liable for college students' drunk-driving behavior. If administrators accepted this responsibility, they might ask themselves the following questions: Should we expel students who receive a D.U.I.? Has the president of our university met with the mayor to create a unified policy toward drunk driving within our town? Have we contacted organizations like M.A.D.D. and S.A.D.D. to help us implement alcohol-and-driving-education programs?

On campuses like Middlebury's, where many students own cars, administrators can use more aggressive methods to combat drinking and driving. Yet after Ryan's death his university ignored my family's request to fund a Middlebury town officer to patrol the main entry into campus for out-of-control drivers on weekend evenings. This, despite the fact that the Middlebury College director of health services informed me and my family that approximately 15 percent of the school's freshmen were so intoxicated at some point during the last year that a classmate had to bring them to the infirmary.

Why does the problem of drunk driving persist? It's not easy to solve. College students are young and irresponsible, and drinking is part of their culture. Administrators have not wanted to abolish social houses and fraternities for fear that ending such beloved college traditions would lower alumni donations.   8

To college presidents, trustees and all college officials, I ask that you go home tonight and consider your love for your own son or daughter, your own brother or sister. Imagine the knock on your door at 3 A.M. when a uniformed police officer announces that your loved one has died. Then go to a mirror and look deep into your own eyes. Ask yourself the question: have I done enough to help solve this problem?   9

The choice is simple. You can choose to be a leader and an agent of change on a controversial issue. Or you can continue the annual practice of authoring one of your student's eulogies. My family, in its grief, begs you to do the former.   10

THE CRITICAL READER

Central Idea

1. What is the author's central idea, and in what paragraph is it stated? *Hint:* Look for the central idea near the middle of the essay, and look for a clue in the title.

Evidence

2. The author says that he is an "expert" on drinking and driving. What evidence does he provide to establish his qualifications to write on the topic of drunk driving?

3. According to the author, why does drunk driving among college students persist?

4. What reasons does the author give to explain why schools have been reluctant to address the problem of drunk driving?

Implications

5. In paragraph 5, the author says that a Middlebury student who was hospitalized for binge-drinking had a blood-alcohol level of .425 percent. In paragraph 7 he says that during the past year 15 percent of Middlebury's freshmen were brought to the infirmary as a result of being intoxicated. What purpose do these statistics serve?

Word Choice

6. What relationship do you see between the author's choice of words in paragraphs 3 and 9? What effect do these word choices have on readers?

SIGNALING CAUSE AND EFFECT

Recognizing the cause-and-effect pattern in others' writing and being able to use the pattern in your own writing depends upon your understanding of three common signals of causes and effects:

1. The question/answer signal

2. The act/consequence signal

3. The probability signal

The presence of these signals in introductory paragraphs, in thesis statements, and in topic sentences of paragraphs alerts you to causes or effects that follow. Using the signals in your own writing will let your readers know what to expect.

The Question/Answer Signal

As explained in Chapter 4, asking a question in an introductory paragraph is one of the devices writers use to build your interest in reading. The question may signal either a cause or an effect. Writers may state a question directly:

> Why do most Americans avoid sitting next to strangers in a theater when most Europeans will do just the opposite?

Or they may state the question indirectly:

> Many observers have wondered why Americans avoid sitting next to strangers in a theater while Europeans will do just the opposite.

An answer to either question would explain the reasons that Americans and Europeans differ in how close they are willing to sit to one another. Direct or indirect questions in the title, introduction, thesis statement, or topic sentences of paragraphs are signals of cause and effect. Some signal words to look for are *why, reason, cause, result,* and *because.*

In this excerpt from an essay by George Gallup, Jr., "The Faltering Family," Gallup asks a question that the rest of the essay answers. The question and the answer are underlined and annotated.

In a recent Sunday school class in a United Methodist Church in the Northeast, a group of eight- to ten-year-olds were in a deep discussion with their two teachers. When asked to choose which of ten stated possibilities they most feared happening, their response was unanimous. All the children most dreaded a divorce between their parents.   1

Later, as the teachers, a man and a woman in their late thirties, reflected on the lesson, they both agreed they'd been shocked at the response. When they were the same age as their students, they said, the possibility of their parents' being divorced never entered their heads. Yet in just one generation, children seemed to feel much less security in their family ties. . . .   2

What are the pressures that have emerged in the past twenty years that cause long-standing family bonds to be broken?   *Question*   3

Many now agree that the sexual revolution of the 1960s worked a profound change on our society's family values and personal relationships. Certainly, the seeds of upheaval were present before that critical decade. But a major change that occurred in the mid-sixties was an explicit widespread rejection of the common values about sexual and family relationships that most Americans in the past had held up as an ideal. . . .   *Answer*   4

          Answer

Gallup's essay goes on to explain four pressures that have caused the rejection of traditional family values: alternative lifestyles that have led to an increase in one-parent families; a change in our attitudes concerning sexual morality; the economic necessity for women to work outside the home; and the acceptance of feminist philosophy. Gallup analyzes the *effect* of the breakdown of family values by explaining the four pressures as possible *causes*.

EXERCISE **14.1**   Review Waldron's essay on pages 312–314. Where in the essay does he state questions and answer them? What are the questions and answers? What purpose do they serve? Share your findings with the rest of the class.

EXERCISE **14.2**   Think of a recent event that has some importance to you. It may be a personal event, such as an accident, or it may be something you have been reading or hearing about in the news. This event is an *effect*. To determine the causes, ask yourself the question "Why did this happen?" On a sheet of notebook paper, write down the effect, then underneath it list the causes. Save these notes as part of your brainstorming activities for planning an essay.

The Act/Consequence Signal

Scientists, journalists, historians, and others often write about actions and consequences. Consequences are the *results* of certain actions or *causes*. The assassination of John F. Kennedy in 1963 was a consequence that has aroused much controversy. That he died from gunshot wounds is unquestioned. But who fired the gun? Was there more than one killer? Who committed the action that resulted in the consequence of Kennedy's death is still being debated. One argument goes like this: If there were one gunman, one gun, one bullet, then there would not be three bullet wounds. This argument suggests that the consequence—three bullet wounds—could not be the result of one person firing one bullet. The act/consequence signal of cause and effect is easy to spot by the signal words *if . . . then*. Note in the following examples, however, that the same act/consequence relationship may be signaled by *if* alone, without the word *then* preceding the consequence statement.

If you do not brush and floss your teeth regularly, you may develop gingivitis or gum disease.

If you want people to treat you with respect, you must show them respect as well.

If you had not run that stop sign, you might have avoided the accident.

Some *if . . . then* relationships can be proven true—for example, the statement "If you do not water your houseplants, they will die" is verified by experience because you know that plants need water to survive. But the statement "If Bernard Bluff is elected president, there will be an end to the current economic crunch" can probably never be proven. Even if Bluff were elected, and even if the economy were to improve, there would still be differences of opinion concerning which actions resulted in an improved economy. Perhaps factors other than Bluff's election were at work. Therefore, when writing about causes and effects, keep in mind that an action may have consequences, and a consequence may be the result of several actions. Only through careful selection of evidence can you increase the likelihood that your *if . . . then* statement and its development will convince readers.

In the following excerpt from "Why Reading Aloud Makes Learning Fun," an article by Jim Trelease, the thesis is underlined, the *if . . . then* statement is bracketed, and the effects of reading to your children are annotated in the margin.

Thesis
Act/consequence
signal

It's really never too early to start reading to a child. [If a child is old enough to talk to—and parents talk to their children from Day 1—then he or she is old enough to be read to.] It doesn't matter that infants can't understand the words; the English language inside the covers of books is frequently a whole lot more organized, colorful and coherent than "koochie, koochie, koochie." Setting even a tiny child in front of a book and reading to him or her is

effect   intellectual stimulation.

effect   A visual competency is developing, too, because the child is being taught to focus attention on a picture on a page. This visual literacy is just as important as print literacy, and it is usually achieved before print literacy. At 18 months old, a child can identify a picture of a puppy and understand the word—and that's long before he can read it. . . .

1

2

effect   Next to hugging your child, reading aloud is probably the longest-lasting experience that you can put into your child's life. You will savor it long after he or she has grown up. Reading aloud is important for all the reasons
effects   that talking to children is important—to inspire them, to guide them, to educate them, to bond with them and to communicate your feelings, hopes and fears. You are giving children a piece of your mind and a piece of your time. They're more interested, really, in you than they are in the story—at least in the beginning. But it is not just you who are communicating but the author and illustrator. These are people who, in some cases, lived hundreds of
effect   years ago. So reading becomes a way to eavesdrop on history.

3

effects   Reading aloud to children on a routine basis improves their reading, writing, speaking, listening, and imagining skills. And it improves their attitudes toward learning Today attitude is the major stumbling block to literacy achievement. But what we do in this culture is teach
Source that   children how to read first; then we try to get them
supports the   interested in it. That's putting the cart before the horse.
thesis   Reading aloud is the primary focus for the national report *Becoming a Nation of Readers.* The first conclusion these people drew after two solid years of looking over all the research was: If you want to build readers, read aloud
Source that   to children early and often. Much the same conclusion
supports the   was reached in another national study, released in late
thesis   February, called *What Works: Research About Teaching and Learning.* . . .

4

Trelease goes on to say that too many children have a "workbook mentality" about reading, meaning they associate it with unpleasant schoolwork instead of regarding it positively as a leisure activity. He also sees a connection between the high percentage (75 percent) of boys in remedial classes and the lack of male involvement in their intellectual growth. He concludes that fathers, as well as mothers, should read to their children.

EXERCISE **14.3**   Skim Waldron's essay on pages 312–314 to find an *if . . . then* statement (remember, the word *then* may not always precede the consequence part of the statement). Determine what is the act and what is the consequence. Share your results with the rest of the class.

EXERCISE **14.4**   To help yourself think about causes and effects that operate in your life, make up three to five *if . . . then* statements like those on pages 317–318. Select the best one of your statements, and list the evidence you could use to support it if you were to develop it into an essay.

The Probability Signal

From time to time you may have wondered what would happen if you took a certain action or made a certain choice. *Probability* means *likelihood.* What is the probability that a seven will come up with any given roll of the dice? What is the likelihood that you will make an A on your next test, get the job you want, or that airline rates will go down before you decide to take your next trip? Scientists deal in probabilities every time they conduct experiments. Researchers now are trying to find a cure for AIDS. So far this deadly virus has eluded them, yet they keep asking "What if." What if we add this chemical, or that one? When you experiment with new study techniques, you are testing probabilities. You are looking for the cause that will produce the desired result. Words and terms that signal probable cause and effect relationships are: *probable, possible, likely, unlikely, may, might, perhaps,* and *what if.* The future tense is a probability signal also. Whenever writers predict causes or effects by explaining what people *will do* or what actions or events *will* take place, they are suggesting probable outcomes.

The following short passage describes a study in which a University of Kentucky researcher observed frog embryos to see what would happen to the ones attacked by predators. Probability signals are underlined.

Premature Ejection

When the going gets tough, some frog embryos get go-   1
ing. A new study shows that a red-eyed tree frog embryo
will hatch early if attacked.

Red-eyed tree frogs are found in tropical rain forests   2
from Mexico to Panama, and females lay masses of gelati-

nous eggs in plants over water. The eggs usually hatch around seven days later, and the tadpoles drop into the water. Karen Warkentin, a biologist at the University of Kentucky, observed clutches of frog eggs at ponds in Panama and noted the response to predators. When a wasp landed on the clutch and tried to bite open one of the eggs, the embryo frequently popped out and got away from its enemy.

"It's a pretty effective way to escape," says Warkentin,   3
noting that nearly 90 percent of the early-hatching embryos survived the attack.

Not all embryos are capable of such a response.   4
Warkentin notes: they <u>must be</u> at least four days old. Still, the ability of some unborn creatures to sense danger and take action is significant.

"People have not thought about embryos as actively   5
making decisions or responding to their environment," says Warkentin. "This tells us that embryos, at least in some cases, are not as helpless as we thought."

From *National Wildlife*, February/March 2001

According to Warkentin's research, frog embryos will hatch early if they are in danger. The significance of this finding is that it will affect the way we think about all embryos in the future. For example, if frog embryos can sense danger and take evasive action, then they may be able to respond to the environment in other ways as well. Moreover, Warkentin's findings may lead to similar research using the embryos of other species.

EXERCISE 14.5

Apply what you have learned about cause and effect signals by doing this exercise with group members. First, review the list of group roles and responsibilities as explained in Figure 1.6, page 28. Next, complete the activity that follows and share your results with the rest of the class. Then evaluate your group's performance.

1. Identify and discuss a problem on your campus such as inadequate parking, binge drinking at social events, cheating, sexual harassment, or some other issue that everyone in your group thinks is important.

2. State your problem, in writing, as a question such as "Why do students cheat?" This will help you determine your problem's *causes.*

3. State your problem as an action that has consequences, using the *if . . . then* format. For example, "If students cheat, then everyone is hurt in the following ways." This will help you determine your problem's *effects.*

4. Using the probability signal, write a sentence in which you state a desired solution to your problem. For example, "Cheating is everyone's problem, and we will have to work together to find a solution."

5. Choose either statement 2, 3, or 4 to develop more fully. For example, if you choose statement 2, answer your question by listing the causes. If you choose statement 3, list your problem's consequences. If you choose statement 4, list the steps involved in finding a solution to your problem.

6. Share your completed statement and list in a whole-class discussion that focuses on ways to use the three signals in thinking and writing about causes and effects.

GROUP EVALUATION

What did each person contribute to the group's activity? Was your group's performance successful? Why or why not? What additional questions do you have about cause and effect signals?

PLANNING YOUR CAUSE-AND-EFFECT ESSAY

If you think a topic you have chosen would benefit from a cause-and-effect pattern of organization, *the first step* in planning your essay is to brainstorm your topic, using the three signals as a guide:

1. *The question/answer signal:* Does your topic enable you to answer a question that has significance for both you and your readers? George Gallup, Jr., for example, asks the question "What are the pressures that have emerged in the past twenty years that cause long-standing family bonds to be broken?" The question is significant to anyone who is concerned about the high divorce rate in America and the effects of divorce on children.

2. *The act/consequence signal:* Does your topic enable you to explain an action and its consequences? Several famous people have written ar-

ticles and books about their drug addictions and how they overcame them. Some describe the act of taking drugs (cause) and the consequences, such as lost jobs and loss of self-respect (effects). Others explain how the consequences of taking drugs (cause) led them to take an action such as entering a drug rehabilitation program (effect).

3. *The probability signal:* Does your topic enable you to make a prediction about the future? For example, Warkentin's study suggests that biologists and others may have to change the way they think about an embryo's ability to respond to its environment. You could write an essay about a discovery that changed people's thinking or actions. You could also write an essay in which you predict what you will be doing in five or ten years based on the preparations you are making now.

The second step in planning your essay is to decide on a purpose for writing and determine your audience's needs. Suppose you choose as your topic "What causes math anxiety" and your purpose is to help readers identify the causes so they can overcome them. In addition to explaining the causes, you may also need to examine the effects of math anxiety so that readers will have a clear idea of why they should be concerned. Your audience may include readers who are math anxious and who already have a built-in interest in your topic. Your audience may also include readers who have never heard of math anxiety but who may be interested in learning about it since it may affect their friends and children.

The third step in planning your essay is to write a thesis statement that will control the development of your essay. Again, you can use the three signals as a guide. Remember to remain flexible in your choice of a thesis so that you can revise or rewrite it as needed. Following are examples of three possible thesis statements for an essay on the topic "Where I Live and Why." The cause and effect parts of each statement appear in parentheses.

The question/answer signal:	I live in Sweetwater (effect) because life in this small town embodies several of America's traditional values. (cause)
The act/consequence signal:	If you are seeking the pleasures of a coastal New England town (cause), then, like me, you might choose Sweetwater as your ideal place to live. (effect)

The probability signal: The move to Sweetwater (cause),
                                       will result in positive changes for
                                       my family. (effects)

The fourth step in planning your essay is to select and organize your
evidence to support your thesis. Though you can choose from among
many ways to organize your essay, you may want to start by using one of
the two methods diagrammed below.

Method 1: Several Causes, One Effect

Explain several causes that result in a single effect. The organizational
pattern of an essay developed from the thesis statement "I live in
Sweetwater because life in this small town embodies several of America's traditional values" might look like this:

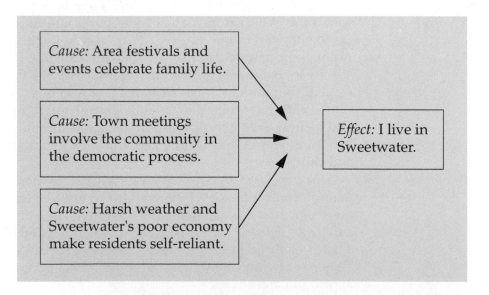

One paragraph could be devoted to explaining each of the three
causes. In the first paragraph, for example, you could describe one or
more festivals or events and tell *how* they celebrate family life.

Method 2: Several Effects, One Cause

Explain several *effects* of a single *cause.* The organizational pattern of an
essay developed from the thesis statement "The move to Sweetwater
will result in positive changes for my family" might look like this:

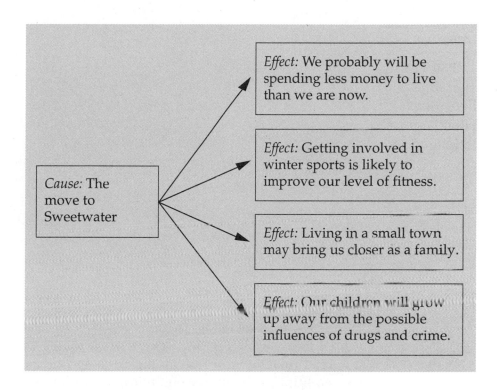

You could devote one paragraph to explaining each of the four effects. In the first body paragraph, for example, you could compare and contrast what it costs to live where you are living now with what it will cost you to live in Sweetwater.

To achieve coherence within and between paragraphs of your essay, use transitional words and phrases that signal cause-and-effect relationships, such as those listed in Figure 14.1. Choosing appropriate signal words will help readers follow your ideas.

EXERCISE 14.6

Facts and figures can be convincing details to use when explaining causes and effects. For example, what percentage of college students are binge-drinkers? What percentage of college students have been involved in alcohol-related accidents or deaths? What are the factors that put students at risk of becoming alcoholics? What are some guidelines for drinking responsibly? To answer these questions, use a search engine and type "binge drinking," "students," "alcohol abuse" in its dialog box. This group of words will turn up a list of sites for you to browse.

FIGURE 14.1

Transitions That Signal Cause-and-Effect Relationships

affect	for	solution
as a result	if . . . then	so
because	in order to	so that
cause	problem	then
consequently	reason	therefore
due to	result	
effect	since	

For best results, click on sites affiliated with a college or a well-known organization. One site to try is http://www.hsph.harvard.edu/cas the Harvard School of Public Health College Alcohol Study, which provides a list of articles on topics such as binge-drinking. To take a risk test, read guidelines for responsible drinking, and explore related topics, see http://www.glness.com/ndhs, a site funded by North Dakota Division of Alcohol and Drug. Remember that sites come and go. Your search may yield sites other than those mentioned here. Share your results in a class discussion.

TOPICS FOR WRITING

Either choose one of the topics below or make up your own topic. If you prefer, write an essay using the activities you did for Exercises 14.2, 14.4, and 14.5.

1. Answer a question that you think is important, such as:

   What is the organization SADD (Students Against Driving Drunk) doing to achieve its goals?

   Should high schools offer condoms to students as part of a sex education program?

   Why should you vote for a certain presidential candidate?

2. Explain an act and its consequences, such as:

What are the effects of a certain child-rearing practice?

What was the outcome of a choice you made?

What are the consequences of changing a career or quitting a job?

3. Explore a probability, such as:

What might happen if a certain law is passed or repealed?

What will be the employment opportunities for a graduate in your major?

How will solving a personal or family problem affect your life?

4. Review the most recent chapter you have read in the textbook of a favorite course. Look for causes and effects related to a topic that interests you. For example, in a psychology textbook you may find an explanation of the causes and effects of substance abuse. Then write an essay on your chosen topic and organize it by cause and effect.

Checklist for Revision

As you revise and edit your essay, check for the following:

1. Have you provided adequate background for your topic in the introductory paragraph?

2. Are your purpose and audience clear?

3. Do you have a clearly stated thesis?

4. Does your essay contain enough specific evidence to support your thesis?

5. Have you used as transitions one or more of the words and phrases that signal cause-and-effect relationships?

6. Are your sentences varied and error-free?

THE CRITICAL THINKER

To examine Rob Waldron's essay in more depth, think about and discuss the following questions. Then choose one of them as a topic for writing.

1. What introductory and concluding devices has the author used, and do you think he has used them effectively? Why or why not? To review introductions, see Chapter 4: to review conclusions, see Chapter 5.

2. To what extent does Waldron blame Ryan, the students at his college, and college administrators for Ryan's death? Explain your answer using evidence from the essay.

3. Waldron believes that colleges can do more to solve the problem of drinking and driving. What is your college doing to combat this problem or other problems of student alcohol abuse? What more do you think your college should do?

4. In paragraph 6, Waldron asks "What should we do about the Ryans of the world?" How would you answer this question?

YOUR DISCOVERY JOURNAL

For your next journal entry, think of a behavior people engage in that either makes you angry or makes you feel good. Comment on the causes and effects of the behavior. Save the notes for an essay on the topic "a behavior I wish people would or would not change."

Chapter 15

Using Definition

Writing often involves defining words or terms so that readers know exactly what you mean by them. Definitions are useful for explaining the meaning of a word or term that readers may be unfamiliar with or may misunderstand. Perhaps you want to redefine a word in terms of what it means to you, or you may need to clarify a term that has more than one meaning. Two types of definitions are useful in your writing: *simple definitions* and *extended definitions*. A simple definition is one that can be stated in a few words—for example, a simple definition of *fax machine* might be "a briefcase-sized piece of office equipment that can transmit copies of documents over telephone lines." A simple definition of *fax* might be "an abbreviation of *facsimile*, a word that means 'likeness' or 'copy'; *fax* can also be used as a verb meaning 'to send a copy.'" You can slip a simple definition into a piece of writing to define a term that may be unfamiliar to your audience without breaking the flow as in the following example:

Cherie remembered the secretarial assistant's job she had during the summer between her freshman and sophomore years. She had to learn her way around an unfamiliar office. Cherie learned how to operate a word processor and a *fax machine, which is a copier that transmits documents over telephone lines.* Though she has not had to *fax,* or send, anything since, she has used the word processors in her college's computer lab for writing essays and a research paper. Though the only reason Cherie took the summer job was to earn money for college, she now thinks that she learned a valuable skill.

You can find simple definitions in the dictionary, but rather than copy dictionary definitions, try to define terms in your own words. Use the dictionary to verify meanings and make corrections as needed. This process will help you come up with definitions that are meaningful not only because they are correct but because they relate directly to how you are using the words in context.

An *extended definition,* on the other hand, is longer, usually a paragraph or more, and can become the basis of a whole essay. As an organizational pattern, *definition* helps you explain the meaning of words, terms, or abstract ideas, such as *generosity* or *success,* and perhaps give your readers new insights into terms or ideas they take for granted. Definition is useful in academic writing also; for example, you may need to define a sociological term such as *crowd behavior* or a style of painting such as *cubism.*

AWARENESS CHECK

Before reading the following essay, explore your thoughts about families and family values. Think about the questions below and answer them either on your own or in a group discussion:

1. What does the word "family" mean to you?

2. What does the phrase "family values" mean to you?

3. Read the title, headnote, and first two paragraphs of the following essay. Based on this preview, what do you think will follow?

The Perfect Family
Alice Hoffman

Alice Hoffman is the author of thirteen novels, a book of short stories, and three children's books. Her essays have appeared in numerous magazines, newspapers, and anthologies. Her screenplay Independence

Day was made into a hit movie. In this essay, Hoffman challenges our ideas about family: what it means and how it has changed.

VOCABULARY CHECK

incriminating (4)	accusing, implicating, faulting
ministered (4)	took care of
righteous (6)	morally upright, just
encrusted (7)	caked with, covered
factoring out (8)	excluding, ignoring
deprived (11)	kept from owning or enjoying

When I was growing up in the 50's, there was only one sort of family, the one we watched on television every day. Right in front of us, in black and white, was everything we needed to know about family values: the neat patch of lawn, the apple tree, the mother who never once raised her voice, the three lovely children: a Princess, a Kitten, a Bud[1] and, always, the father who knew best.

1

People stayed married forever back then, and roses grew by the front door. We had glass bottles filled with lightning bugs and brand-new swing sets in the backyard, and softball games at dusk. We had summer nights that lasted forever and well-balanced meals, three times a day, in our identical houses, on our identical streets. There was only one small bargain we had to make to exist in this world: we were never to ask questions, never to think about people who didn't have as much or who were different in any way. We ignored desperate marriages and piercing loneliness. And we were never, ever, to wonder what might be hidden from view, behind the unlocked doors, in the privacy of our neighbors' bedrooms and knotty-pine-paneled dens.

2

This was a bargain my own mother could not make. Having once believed that her life would sort itself out to be like the television shows we watched, only real and in color, she'd been left to care for her children on her own, at a time when divorce was so uncommon I did not meet another child of divorced parents until 10 years later, when I went off to college.

3

[1]Princess, Kitten, and Bud are characters from *Father Knows Best,* a family sitcom that aired from 1954–1962.

Back then, it almost made sense when one of my best friends was   4
not allowed to come to my house; her parents did not approve of divorce
or my mother's life style. My mother, after all, had a job and a boyfriend
and, perhaps even more incriminating, she was the one who took the
silver-colored trash cans out to the curb on Monday nights. She did so
faithfully, on evenings when she had already balanced the checkbook
and paid the bills and ministered to sore throats and made certain we'd
had dinner; but all up and down the street everybody knew the truth:
taking out the trash was clearly a job for fathers.

When I was 10, my mother began to work for the Department of   5
Social Services, a world in which the simple rules of the suburbs did not
apply. She counseled young unwed mothers, girls and women who
were not allowed to make their own choices, most of whom had not
been allowed to finish high school or stay in their own homes, none of
whom had been allowed to decide not to continue their pregnancies.
Later, my mother placed most of these babies in foster care, and still
later, she moved to the protective-services department, investigating
charges of abuse and neglect, often having to search a child's back and
legs for bruises or welts.

She would have found some on my friend, left there by her right-   6
eous father, the one who wouldn't allow her to visit our home but
blackened her eye when, a few years later, he discovered that she was
dating a boy he didn't approve of. But none of his neighbors had dared
to report him. They would never have imagined that someone like my
friend's father, whose trash cans were always tidily placed at the curb,
whose lawn was always well cared for, might need watching.

To my mother, abuse was a clear-cut issue, if reported and found,   7
but neglect was more of a judgment call. It was, in effect, passing judgment on the nature of love. If my father had not sent the child-support
checks on time, if my mother hadn't been white and college-educated,
it could have easily been us in one of those apartments she visited,
where the heat didn't work on the coldest days, and the dirt was so en-
crusted you could mop all day and still be called a poor housekeeper,
and there was often nothing more for dinner than Frosted Flakes and
milk, or, if it was toward the end of the month, the cereal might be
served with tap water. Would that have meant my mother loved her
children any less, that we were less of a family?

My mother never once judged who was a fit mother on the basis   8
of a clean floor, or an unbalanced meal, or a boyfriend who sometimes
spent the night. But back then, there were good citizens who were only
too ready to set their standards for women and children, factoring out
poverty or exhaustion or simply a different set of beliefs.

There are always those who are ready to deal out judgment with   9
the ready fist of the righteous. I know this because before the age of 10

I was one of the righteous, too. I believed that mothers were meant to stay home and fathers should carry out the trash on Monday nights. I believed that parents could create a domestic life that was the next best thing to heaven, if they just tried. That is what I'd been told, that in the best of all worlds we would live identical lives in identical houses.

It's a simple view of the world, too simple even for childhood. Certainly, it's a vision that is much too limited for the lives we live now, when only one in 19 families are made up of a wage-earner father, a mother who doesn't work outside the home and two or more children. And even long ago, when I was growing up, we paid too high a price when we cut ourselves off from the rest of the world. We ourselves did not dare to be different. In the safety we created, we became trapped. 10

There are still places where softball games are played at dusk and roses grow by the front door. There are families with sons named Bud, with kind and generous fathers, and mothers who put up strawberry preserves every June and always have time to sing lullabies. But do these families love their children any more than the single mother who works all day? Are their lullabies any sweeter? If I felt deprived as a child, it was only when our family was measured against some notion of what we were supposed to be. The truth of it was, we lacked for little. 11

And now that I have children of my own, and am exhausted at the end of the day in which I've probably failed in a hundred different ways, I am amazed that women alone can manage. That they do, in spite of everything, is a simple fact. They rise from sleep in the middle of the night when their children call out to them. They rush for the cough syrup and cold washcloths and keep watch till dawn. These are real family values, the same ones we knew when we were children. As far as we were concerned our mother could cure a fever with a kiss. This may be the only thing we ever need to know about love. The rest, no one can judge. 12

THE CRITICAL READER

Central Idea

1. What is Alice Hoffman's thesis? Is it stated or implied?

Evidence

2. How does Hoffman describe the typical family of the 1950s when she was growing up?

3. In what way was Hoffman's family not typical?

4. What is Hoffman's idea of family?

Implications

5. Using evidence from the essay, what do you think is Hoffman's attitude toward mothers and fathers and their place, or role, in the family?

Word Choice

6. Hoffman makes use of repeated words and phrases throughout the essay: "righteous" is used once in paragraph 6 and twice in paragraph 9. "Judgment" is used twice in paragraph 7 and once in paragraph 9. "Judged" is used in paragraph 8, and the essay ends on the word "judge." What do you think is the significance of these word choices in relation to the author's thesis and to the title?

WRITING EXTENDED DEFINITIONS

Definitions should be linked to purpose and audience. For example, many writers define terms to call the reader's attention to a problem or an issue. *Burnout* is a term coined by social scientists in the 1970s to describe the psychological state of workers who had grown tired of their jobs to the point that they could no longer function successfully. Once the problem had a name, employers could begin to seek solutions. They began to offer incentives and develop programs to help employees overcome burnout or avoid it altogether.

The homeless is another term that calls our attention to a lingering social problem. Defining a group of people living without work and without homes keeps them visible so they cannot be ignored. Those who write about the homeless do so with the purpose of moving readers to do something about the plight of these people.

When you use definition in your writing, decide first what your purpose is and what your audience's beliefs and expectations are. For example, Alice Hoffman assumes that her readers are familiar with the ongoing debate about family values in the United States. Her purpose is to broaden the definition of family and to suggest that the perfect family does not exist. Much of her essay defines *family* and *family values* by contrasting real families versus ideal families.

To write extended definitions, ones that provide a lengthy explanation of the meaning of a word or term, you can choose from five common methods:

1. Define by giving examples.
2. Define by making comparisons.
3. Define by tracing history.
4. Define by narrating incidents.
5. Define by negation.

Define by Giving Examples

Examples illustrate what you mean by creating clear and vivid images in the reader's mind. Examples can come from personal experiences, observations, reading, and research. When you define a term by using examples, you explain it by describing it in a graphic way. The following excerpt from Art Carey's *The United States of Incompetence* defines *work*.

The excerpt begins by defining work as a four-letter word, thereby implying that work is dirty. The author further defines work by giving several brief examples that show what people think about work. Next are several examples of workers that illustrate ways people avoid work. The rest of the chapter from which this excerpt comes continues to define Americans' attitudes toward work and how these attitudes have changed. Carey defines work as "a dirty word," "a necessary evil," and "a terrible drudgery." In addition, he uses examples to illustrate situations in which people's work habits reveal how they feel about their jobs.

> The United States used to be famous for hard work. Now, *work* has become a four-letter word. Many Americans—whether stuck on an assembly line or in the ranks of middle management—consider work tedious, unsatisfying, a necessary evil that earns the paycheck and buys the food. In a society that idolizes wealth and worships leisure, work is the terrible drudgery that stands between the average American schmo and the weekend. *TGIF! It's Miller Time!*

> *The output of a factory is halved on Mondays as many workers call in "sick."*

> *Four men from the highway department stand around a pothole, laughing and drinking coffee. Everyone seems to be supervising; no one seems to be working.*

> *A sanitation crew squanders the afternoon in a bar when they're supposed to be picking up trash.*

A policeman spends the bulk of his shift flirting with waitresses and napping in his squad car instead of patrolling the streets.

A high-salaried executive whiles away the morning making personal phone calls and reading the paper rather than tending to business. . . .

Defining a word or term depends on a clear understanding of what it means. Exercise 15.1 takes you through three steps to accurate definitions.

EXERCISE 15.1   Select any five words or terms from the list below and experiment with three-step defining: First, define the word or term in your own words. Second, give one or more synonyms for the word or term, and verify your definition and synonym with the dictionary. Finally, write two graphic examples to illustrate your definition of the word. See the sample answer following the list. Share your results with the rest of the class.

poverty	prejudice	basketball fan
hobby	depression	pessimist
tightwad	optimist	slob
friend	leisure	art

Sample Answer:

Term: Self-control

Definition: Self-control is a quality of people who are able to set standards for themselves and live by them.

Synonym: Self-discipline

Example #1:   A student who refuses to sample drugs even though all his or her friends are doing it has self-control.

Example #2:   A person who is able to lose weight and keep it off has self-control.

Define by Making Comparisons

Another way to define a term is to compare or contrast it with one you think the reader already knows. To explain how a cellular phone works, you might compare it to a regular telephone: You operate the cellular phone the same way, but it is portable; you can use it in your car, and it gets its power from a battery. It does not have the same range as your home telephone, though, so you may not be able to use it everywhere you go. The following paragraph from the first chapter of Michael Korda's *Success!* defines success by comparing it to a journey:

> Try to think of success as a journey, an adventure, not a specific desti-nation. Your goals may change during the course of that journey, and your original ambitions may be superseded by different, larger ones. Success will certainly bring you the material things you want, and a good, healthy appetite for the comforts and luxuries of life is an excel-lent road to success, but basically you'll know you have reached your goal when you have gone that one step further, in wealth, fame or achievement, than you ever dreamed was possible.

Defining by comparison is also useful for explaining a complex term: one that has more than one meaning or one that can be applied to different categories of people or items. *Mental retardation*, for exam-ple, is difficult to define because there are different types of mental retardation.

In the following excerpt, the author defines two categories of men-tal retardation. The excerpt is from Sallie Tisdale's article "Neither Morons Nor Imbeciles Nor Idiots, In the Company of the Mentally Re-tarded" that appeared in *Harper's* magazine, June 1990:

> There are two widely accepted categories of retardation: organic and 1 nonorganic. Organic retardation has more than 250 known causes, among them Down syndrome and other chromosomal disorders, meta-bolic imbalances, tumors, brain malformations, and trauma. But re-searchers in the field commonly hold that only about 20 percent of all the people called retarded have an organic problem.
>
> The remaining 80 percent are affected by nonorganic retarda- 2 tion—retardation caused by, say, parental neglect or abuse, or by a baby's having eaten lead paint—and there is nothing physiologically wrong with them. Almost all the people classified as mentally retarded are considered to be nonorganically retarded. One of the more con-troversial questions in the field of mental retardation right now is whether the nonorganically retarded are—or should be labeled—retarded at all. . . .

Sallie Tisdale's purpose in the essay is to convince readers that we need a more descriptive definition of mental retardation. The excerpt above comes near the beginning of the essay where Tisdale illustrates the complexity of the term and shows why traditional definitions of mental retardation are inadequate.

EXERCISE 15.2   Add a comparison to the examples you wrote for the words or terms you defined in Exercise 15.1.

Sample Answer:

Term:	Self-control
Definition:	Self-control is a quality of people who are able to set standards for themselves and live by them.
Synonym:	Self-discipline
Example #1:	Students who refuse to sample drugs even though their friends are doing it have self-control.
Example #2:	A person who is able to lose weight and keep it off has self-control.
Comparison:	Self-control is like self-motivation. It is something you have to do for yourself: no one can do it for you.

Define by Tracing History

Sometimes it is helpful to show that a word or term you are defining has roots in the past. For example, rock and roll as defined by experts in the subject, is a term coined in the 1950s to mean a type of music that is a mix of jazz, blues, and country rhythms. As new trends in popular music have developed, writers have defined and explained them in terms of their roots in rock music of the 1950s. When you show how the definition of a word or term has connections to the past, you are tracing its history.

EXERCISE 15.3   Read the following excerpt from "Why People Are Rude," an essay by David A. Wiessler. In this essay, Wiessler defines *rudeness* both by using examples and by placing it in a historical context. Find and underline the part of the excerpt that defines by tracing the history.

Rudeness is becoming a common occurrence in American life. If you   1
don't like it, lump it. Or mind your own business. Or get out of the way.

That is the kind of talk and attitude that's cropping up more often   2
in almost every public experience—on the highways, in theater lines,
over the telephone, on public transit. The examples are almost endless:

Sitting in a New York movie theater, a man refuses to turn down his   3
radio despite requests from the usher and others watching the show.

An Atlanta newsstand operator is unable to wait on his customers   4
because passers-by shout at him for directions, information or change
without waiting their turns.

A woman stands in a Washington, D.C., supermarket line while her   5
children do the shopping. When the cart is full, she has the children
wheel it to the front of the line where she is standing ahead of
everyone else.

What's behind such incidents? Some experts say the trend began in   6
the 1960's when traditional values and manners came under fire. Others blame the fast-paced American lifestyle for creating a society that
has little time any more to be polite.

This is particularly true in big cities, where people are surrounded   7
by strangers. "In a small town, the person to whom you are rude is
more likely to be someone you are going to see again tomorrow," observed psychologist Stanley Milgram at the Graduate Center of the City
University of New York. "In the city, it is very unlikely you will ever again
encounter someone with whom you have a minor conflict. . . ."

Define by Narrating Incidents

Another way to define is to relate a brief story or incident that illustrates or reveals the meaning of a term as you see it. Suppose you want
to define the word *responsibility*. Perhaps this word has a special meaning for you because you remember when you first understood what it
means to be responsible. You decide to write an essay using as your extended definition the narration of an event in your life that made you
become a responsible person.

The following excerpt is from chapter 2 of *Superlearning* by Sheila
Ostrander and Lynn Schroeder with Nancy Ostrander, Dell, 1979. The
authors introduce and define the term *supermemory* by narrating an incident that reveals the qualities of this type of memory.

A ruggedly built, sandy-haired man in his sixties with a perpetually   1
wrinkled forehead walked quickly to the back of a large auditorium
crammed with scientists. It was at Dubna, near Moscow, the Soviet

Union's major atomic research center, and the prestigious audience included many world-renowned Soviet physicists.

This man, Mikhail Keuni, an artist, was going to show these famous physicists how to do math. "Cover that huge blackboard with circles," he told a volunteer on stage at the front of the room. "They can intersect. They can be inside one another. Draw them any way you wish."   2

As physicists spun the board around for Keuni to glance at, the audience laughed. It was totally white with circles. Keuni's eyes scarcely blinked. In two seconds he called out the total: "167!"   3

It took the Soviet Union's foremost brain trust over five minutes to do the calculations necessary to verify Keuni's instant and accurate answer.   4

Forty-digit numbers went up on the board and Keuni could recall them and calculate with them faster than a computer.   5

After his demonstration of numerical memory and wizardry, Keuni received a letter from scientists at the Joint Nuclear Research Institute: "If we weren't physicists, then it would be extremely difficult to verify that man's brain is capable of accomplishing such miracles." (Dubna, April 12, 1959.)   6

Mikhail Keuni possesses the gift of supermemory, that is, what allows him to do instant math faster than a calculator. It also allows him to learn with extraordinary speed. If something registers on Keuni's mind once, he can retrieve it whole. . . .   7

EXERCISE 15.4   What does the term *good friend* mean to you? Write a paragraph in which you define the meaning of this term by narrating an incident. For example, what happened? Who was involved? What did your friend do to demonstrate that he or she was a good friend? Your paragraph should answer these questions.

Define By Negation

As explained in previous sections, definitions can take many forms. First of all, you can define an object by telling what it *is*—the class of things to which it belongs. For example, a *kiwi* is a type of fruit known as a berry. Second, you can define an object by comparing it to other members of its class. For example, a *kiwi* is green and fleshy inside like a grape, has a taste similar to a strawberry, and it is about the size and shape of a large Italian tomato. Unlike these more familiar berries, however, a kiwi has a fuzzy brown inedible skin. Third, you can define an object by tracing its history. For example, the subtropical *kiwi* was originally available in the United States only as an imported luxury fruit, but now it is cultivated and marketed here. Fourth, you can define by narrating an incident, as in this brief passage:

> I remember the first time I saw a kiwi. It looked like a fuzzy brown egg. A friend showed me how to eat it by cutting it in half and scooping out the flesh with a spoon. "Don't eat the skin," she said. The flavor was sweet and familiar, a combination of strawberry and banana.

Finally, you can define an object by *negation,* which is an explanation of what the object *is not.* For example, a *kiwi* is not an aggregate fruit like a raspberry, not a single-seed fruit like a plum or a cherry, and not a segmented fruit like an orange. The fuzz on the kiwi's skin is neither soft nor stiff, but somewhere in between. In the following passage, *bagel* is defined mainly by negation:

> A bagel is not a dinner roll, not a sweet roll, not a bun nor a biscuit. It looks like a donut, but it is not. It is as hard as a sourdough roll, chewy as a French roll, but it is neither of these. It is not confined to any one use such as a breakfast food, lunch treat, or dessert snack. Though made of the same basic ingredients, not all bagels are alike. Round, chewy, and with a hole in the middle, a bagel is a type of hard bread that comes in many flavors and can be enjoyed any time of day.

EXERCISE 15.5

Apply what you have learned about the common methods of definition by doing this exercise with group members. First, review the list of group roles and responsibilities as explained in Figure 1.6, page 28. Next, complete the activity that follows and share your results with the rest of the class. Then evaluate your group's performance.

1. Review and discuss Alice Hoffman's essay on pages 330–333.

2. List several examples the author uses to define *family.*

3. Explain where and how the author uses comparison to define *family.*

4. Explain where and how the author defines *family* by tracing its history.

5. List one or more of the incidents the author narrates to expand her definition of *family.*

6. Explain where and how the author defines *family* or *family values* by negation.

GROUP EVALUATION

What did each person contribute to the group's activity? Was your group's performance successful? Why or why not? What additional questions do you have about the common methods of definition?

EXERCISE 15.6

Whether you are writing a simple definition or an extended definition, verify all definitions with a dictionary. Even if your definition is a personal one—for example, what *success* means to you—keep your readers' assumptions in mind by also acknowledging the term's conventional meaning. However, the dictionary is only the beginning. For historical background on a term or idea, encyclopedias and other reference works can be a big help. Two online resources to try are www.bartleby.com/reference and www.britannica.com. For example, to find the meaning of the Greek word *hubris,* the poetical term *sonnet,* or the anatomical term *cranium,* you could turn to either one of these resources. Browse the sites for a definition or any other information you can find on a term of your choice. Then share your results with the rest of the class.

PLANNING AND WRITING YOUR ESSAY

The following suggestions may help you plan and write an effective essay in which you have to define a word or term:

Have a Purpose for Writing

Determine a *purpose* for writing by asking yourself *what* you want to define and *why.* Do you want to define an unfamiliar term or a term that is easily misunderstood or confused with another? Do you want to redefine a word or clarify a term that has one or more meanings? Make your purpose clear in the introduction to your essay.

Understand Your Audience

Decide who your *audience* is. Also, determine what your audience's experiences might be concerning the word or term you define. If your definition of *freedom,* for example, is different from what you think most people mean by this term, begin by summarizing the popular definition before explaining how yours is different from it. If the subject you have chosen is a technical one—for example, "the advantages of using a spreadsheet"—then define *spreadsheet* and any other technical terms for uninitiated readers.

Limit Your Topic

If you decide to write a personal definition of an abstract term, such as *success* or *heroes,* make sure your topic is narrow enough to be specific. For example, *heroes* is too broad a topic. If you write about heroes, limit your discussion either to a specific kind of hero or to your beliefs and values concerning heroes. You could write about a war hero, such as General Norman Schwarzkopf of Desert Storm; a fictional hero, such as Batman or Cat Woman; a historical figure, such as Sir Thomas More or Joan of Arc; or an everyday hero, such as Christa McAuliffe, Concord, New Hampshire's teacher in space who died in the 1986 *Challenger* explosion. In your essay, limit your topic even further to explain exactly what makes the person or fictional character heroic or not heroic according to your definition.

On the other hand, instead of writing about one particular hero, you might decide to define the qualities of heroism using several people as examples. You could even write an essay explaining how the popular notion of what a hero is has changed, or whether there *are* any heroes today. After limiting your topic, write a thesis statement as in the following example:

> An everyday hero is one who overcomes hardship to be successful and whose success inspires others.

Support Your Thesis

Thoroughly explain your definition using one or more of the five common methods explained on pages 335–341: define by giving examples, by making comparisons, by tracing history, by narrating incidents, or by negation.

Organize Your Ideas

Use a clear pattern for organizing your evidence so that readers will understand your purpose and be able to follow your ideas. The informal outline on page 344 illustrates one possible way to organize an essay about a term whose meaning has changed.

Introductory paragraph:	Include thesis and simple definition of term.
First body paragraph:	Trace history of term—what it used to mean and what it means now.
Second body paragraph:	Give several examples to support your definition.
Third and fourth body paragraphs:	Narrate an incident that illustrates your definition.
Concluding paragraph:	Point to the future—predict what may happen as a result of the term's new meaning.

One last suggestion: avoid overworked beginnings, such as "Webster says" or "According to the dictionary." Instead of *quoting* the dictionary, use the dictionary only to verify and correct, if necessary, the definition that you write in your own words.

TOPICS FOR WRITING

Write an essay in which you define a word or term that interests you, or choose one of the topics below:

1. Develop an essay from the information you gathered in completing the exercises in this chapter.

2. Define one of the terms below; and remember to narrow your topic:

   maturity or immaturity

   manners (good or bad)

   a good (or bad) friend

   a good (or bad) marriage

   a good (or bad) parent

   a hero

   a technical or scientific term

3. Redefine an old term, such as *character, dating, family,* in light of current beliefs and practices.

4. Define a term from one of your courses such as *totalitarianism* (history), *perspective* (art), or *stimulus-response theory* (psychology).

Checklist for Revision

As you revise and edit your essay, check for the following:

1. Have you made your purpose clear to readers?

2. Is it clear from your introduction who your intended audience is?

3. Have you limited the topic sufficiently?

4. Have you defined by using examples, making comparisons, tracing history, or narrating incidents?

5. Is your essay organized logically so that readers can follow your ideas?

6. Are your sentences varied and error-free?

THE CRITICAL THINKER

To examine Alice Hoffman's essay in more depth, think about and discuss the following questions. Then choose one of them as a topic for writing.

1. What do you think is Hoffman's meaning in the first sentence of paragraph 3: "This was a bargain my own mother could not make," and what purpose does this sentence serve?

2. Why was one of Hoffman's best friends not allowed to come to her house, and in what way did that almost make sense as she says in paragraph 4?

3. Who is Hoffman's audience and what is her tone? Use evidence from the essay to explain your answer.

4. What are your hopes for your own family? Will your family values differ from or be similar to the family in which you grew up?

YOUR DISCOVERY JOURNAL

What is one quality that you consider essential in a good friend or mate? For example, is generosity, humor, loyalty, or another quality most important to you? Define the quality and write about it in your journal, using one of the five common methods of definition explained in this chapter.

Chapter 16

Arguing Persuasively

*N*o matter what you write, it is important to have a reason for writing. Of the two basic purposes, to inform or to persuade, your purpose in making an argument will always be to persuade your readers to think, feel, or act in a way that you think they should. *Argumentation* is an *attitude* toward writing rather than another pattern of organization, such as narration or cause and effect. When you argue for or against something that you think is important, you are taking a position on an issue. To argue effectively so that you will convince readers, support your position with evidence and use sound logic in doing so. To organize your evidence in an argumentative essay, you can choose any pattern or combination of patterns to fulfill your purpose and develop your thesis.

AWARENESS CHECK

Before reading the following essay, explore your thoughts about minority students. Think about the questions below, and answer them either on your own or in a group discussion:

1. Should teachers' expectations and academic standards be the same for all students? Explain your answer.

2. What are some of the problems minority students face as they pursue their degrees?

3. Read the title, headnote, and first two paragraphs of the following essay. Based on this preview, what do you think will follow?

Minority Student
Richard Rodriguez

Richard Rodriguez, the son of Mexican immigrants, lives and writes in San Francisco, where he grew up and received his education. His articles have appeared in Harper's, Saturday Review, *and* The American Scholar. *He is the author of* Hunger of Memory: The Education of Richard Rodriguez *from which this essay is taken. In the essay, Rodriguez argues against being labeled a minority student.*

VOCABULARY CHECK

clamored (2)	protested loudly
tally (2)	count
irony (3)	something contrary to what is expected
foisted (3)	forced
alienation (4)	emotional isolation
implicated (4)	connected
accessible (6)	within reach, easily attained
de facto (6)	not legally or officially established
plausible (8)	believable
contingents (9)	representative groups

MINORITY STUDENT—That was the label I bore in college at Stanford, then in graduate school at Columbia and Berkeley: a nonwhite reader of Spenser and Milton and Austen.   1

In the late 1960s nonwhite Americans clamored for access to higher   2 education, and I became a principal beneficiary of the academy's response, its programs of affirmative action. My presence was noted each fall by the campus press office in its proud tally of Hispanic-American students enrolled; my progress was followed by HEW statisticians. One of the lucky ones. Rewarded. Advanced for belonging to a racial group "underrepresented" in American institutional life. When I sought admission to graduate schools, when I applied for fellowships and summer study grants, when I needed a teaching assistantship, my Spanish surname or the dark mark in the space indicating my race—"check one"—nearly always got me whatever I asked for. When the time came for me to look for a college teaching job (the end of my years as a scholarship boy), potential employers came looking for me—a minority student.

Fittingly, it falls to me, as someone who so awkwardly carried the label, to question it now, its juxtaposition of terms—minority, student. For me there is no way to say it with grace. I say it rather with irony sharpened by self-pity. I say it with anger. It is a term that should never have been foisted on me. One I was wrong to accept. 3

In college one day a professor of English returned my term paper with this comment penciled just under the grade: "Maybe the reason you feel Dickens's sense of alienation so acutely is because you are a minority student." *Minority student.* It was the first time I had seen the expression; I remember sensing that it somehow referred to my race. Never before had a teacher suggested that my academic performance was linked to my racial identity. After class I re-read the remark several times. Around me other students were talking and leaving. The professor remained in front of the room, collecting his papers and books. I was about to go up and question his note. But I didn't. I let the comment pass; thus became implicated in the strange reform movement that followed. 4

The year was 1967. And what I did not realize was that my life would be radically changed by deceptively distant events. In 1967, their campaign against southern segregation laws successful at last, black civil rights leaders were turning their attention to the North, a North they no longer saw in contrast to the South. What they realized was that although no official restrictions denied blacks access to northern institutions of advancement and power, for most blacks this freedom was only theoretical. (The obstacle was "institutional racism.") Activists made their case against institutions of higher education. Schools like Wisconsin and Princeton long had been open to blacks. But the tiny number of nonwhite students and faculty members at such schools suggested that there was more than the issue of access to consider. Most blacks simply couldn't afford tuition for higher education. And, because the primary and secondary schooling blacks received was 5 usually poor, few qualified for admission. Many were so culturally alienated that they never thought to apply; they couldn't imagine themselves going to college.

I think—as I thought in 1967—that the black civil rights leaders were correct: Higher education was not, nor is it yet, accessible to many black Americans. I think now, however, that the activists tragically limited the impact of their movement with the reforms they proposed. Seeing the problem solely in racial terms (as a case of *de facto* segregation), they pressured universities and colleges to admit more black students and hire more black faculty members. There were demands for financial aid programs. And tutoring help. And more aggressive student recruitment. But this was all. The aim was to integrate higher education in the North. So no one seemed troubled by the fact that those who were in the best position to benefit from such reforms were those blacks least victimized by racism or any other social oppression—those culturally, if not always economically, of the middle class.

The lead established, other civil rights groups followed. Soon Hispanic-American activists began to complain that there were too few Hispanics in colleges. They concluded that this was the result of racism. They offered racial solutions. They demanded that Hispanic-American professors be hired. And that students with Spanish surnames be admitted in greater numbers to colleges. Shortly after, I was "recognized" on campus: a Hispanic-American, a "Latino," a Mexican-American, a "Chicano." No longer would people ask me, as I had been asked before, if I were a foreign student. (From India? Peru?) All of a sudden everyone seemed to know—as the professor of English had known—that I was a minority student.

I became a highly rewarded minority student. For campus officials came first to students like me with their numerous offers of aid. And why not? Administrators met their angriest critics' demands by promoting any plausible Hispanic on hand. They were able, moreover, to use the presence of conventionally qualified nonwhite students like me to prove that they were meeting the goals of their critics.

In 1968, the assassination of Dr. Martin Luther King, Jr., prompted many academic officials to commit themselves publicly to the goal of integrating their institutions. One day I watched the nationally televised funeral; a week later I received invitations to teach at community colleges. There were opportunities to travel to foreign countries with contingents of "minority group scholars." And I went to the financial aid office on campus and was handed special forms for minority student applicants. I was a minority student, wasn't I? the lady behind the counter asked me rhetorically. Yes, I said. Carelessly said. I completed the application. Was later awarded.

In a way, it was true. I was a minority. The word, as popularly used,

6

7

8

9

10

did describe me. In the sixties, *minority* became a synonym for socially disadvantaged Americans—but it was primarily a numerical designation. The word referred to entire races and nationalities of Americans, those numerically underrepresented in institutional life. (Thus, without contradiction, one could speak of "minority groups.") And who were they exactly? Blacks—all blacks—most obviously were minorities. And Hispanic-Americans. And American Indians. And some others. (It was left to federal statisticians, using elaborate surveys and charts, to determine which others precisely.)

I was a minority.   11

I believed it. For the first several years, I accepted the label. I certainly supported the racial civil rights movement; supported the goal of broadening access to higher education. But there was a problem: One day I listened approvingly to a government official defend affirmative action; the next day *I* realized the benefits of the program. I was the minority student the political activists shouted about at noon-time rallies. Against their rhetoric, I stood out in relief, unrelieved. *Knowing:* I was not disadvantaged like many of the new nonwhite students who were entering college, lacking good early schooling.   12

Nineteen sixty-nine. 1970. 1971. Slowly, slowly, the term *minority* became a source of unease. It would remind me of those boyhood years when I had felt myself alienated from public (majority) society— *los gringos. Minority. Minorities. Minority Groups.* The terms sounded in public to remind me in private of the truth: I was not—*in a cultural sense*—a minority, an alien from public life. (Not like *los pobres* I had encountered during my recent laboring summer.) The truth was summarized in the sense of irony I'd feel at hearing myself called a minority student: The reason I was no longer a minority was because I had become a student.   13

Minority student!   14

In conversations with faculty members I began to worry the issue, only to be told that my unease was unfounded. A dean said he was certain that after I graduated I would be able to work among "my people." A senior faculty member expressed in confidence that, though I was unrepresentative of lower-class Hispanics, I would serve as a role model for others of my race. Another faculty member was sure that I would be a valued counselor to incoming minority students. (He assumed that, because of my race, I retained a special capacity for communicating with nonwhite students.) I also heard academic officials say that minority students would someday form a leadership class in America. (From our probable positions of power, we would be able to lobby for reforms to benefit others of our race.)   15

In 1973 I wrote and had published two essays in which I said that I had been educated away from the culture of my mother and father. In   16

1974 I published an essay admitting unease over becoming the beneficiary of affirmative action. There was another article against affirmative
action in 1977. One more soon after. At times, I proposed contrary
ideas; consistent always was the admission that I was no longer like socially disadvantaged Hispanic-Americans. But this admission, made in
national magazines, only brought me a greater degree of success. A
published minority student, I won a kind of celebrity. In my mail were
admiring letters from right-wing politicians. There were also invitations
to address conferences of college administrators or government officials.

My essays served as my "authority" to speak at the Marriott Some-   17
thing or the Sheraton Somewhere. To stand at a ballroom podium and
hear my surprised echo sound from a microphone. I spoke. I started
getting angry letters from activists. One wrote to say that I was becoming the *gringos'* fawning pet. What "they" want all Hispanics to be. I
remembered the remark when I was introduced to an all-white audience and heard their applause so loud. I remembered the remark when
I stood in a university auditorium and saw an audience of brown and
black faces watching me. I publicly wondered whether a person like me
should really be termed a minority. But some members of the audience
thought I was denying racial pride, trying somehow to deny my racial
identity. They rose to protest. One Mexican-American said I was a minority whether I wanted to be or not. And he said that the reason I was
a beneficiary of affirmative action was simple: I was a Chicano. (Wasn't
I?) It was only an issue of race.

THE CRITICAL READER

Central Idea

1. What is Rodriguez's thesis and how does he introduce it?

Evidence

2. What minority group is Rodriguez a member of and where in the
   essay do you find the information?

3. Does Rodriguez's evidence consist mainly of facts or of opinions?
   Explain your answer.

Implications

4. According to Rodriguez, what are the disadvantages of being labeled a minority student? Use evidence from the essay to support your answer.

Word Choice

5. In this essay, Rodriguez asserts that he should not be the beneficiary of affirmative action because he is not *disadvantaged*. This term and the following terms are part of the language of affirmative action. What do the terms mean: *nonwhite, Hispanic-American, Latino, Chicano,* and *socially disadvantaged*? Use the context of the essay, then verify your definitions with a dictionary.

UNDERSTAND THE ELEMENTS OF ARGUMENT

To construct a persuasive argument, keep the following elements in mind:

1. The issue
2. The claim
3. The evidence
4. The opposing claims

The Issue

An *issue* is *a matter of public concern.* Gun control, abortion, affordable health care, and affirmative action are issues. An issue can be a problem that needs a solution or a question that requires an answer. Issues are often controversial; where issues are involved, people take sides. Smokers and nonsmokers are involved in an ongoing argument about the issue of smoking in public places. Pro-choice and pro-life groups debate with considerable heat the issue of abortion. Issues such as these are never resolved easily because people hold tenaciously to their opinions. If resolution does come, both sides must be willing to compromise. Some issues are of greater public concern than others, and people differ on what they think are the most important issues facing us today.

EXERCISE 16.1

Following is a list of issues for you and a partner to consider. Each of you should first think about the issues and then arrange them in their order of importance to you. Read each other's lists, and then talk about the issues. Choose one issue that you think public officials should expend the most energy trying to resolve. Share your results with the rest of the class.

the disposal of hazardous wastes

criminals' rights versus victims' rights

discrimination in the workplace against minorities, women, the aged, and the physically impaired

illegal drug trafficking and drug use

smokers' rights versus nonsmokers' rights

displays of racial intolerance, such as swastikas, burning crosses, and hate speech

athletic programs and problems

public mistrust of government

To define an issue suitable for writing an argumentative essay, first decide what is important to you. What are some of your social or private concerns? What matters of public concern do you talk or argue about with your friends and family? Issues can be the problems that affect a large segment of the public, such as those listed in Exercise 16.1, or they may affect a smaller, more narrowly defined public.

If you do not want to write about an issue that has a broad appeal, perhaps you can think of an issue that has a narrower, more personal appeal. For example, what matters of concern have caused arguments and differences of opinion on your campus, in your workplace, or in your family? Divorce is a personal issue many people face, and so is the problem of having to put a family member in a nursing home. One student defined the issue of inadequate police protection of residents in his neighborhood. Almost any subject might become the source of an issue from which you could construct a persuasive argument.

EXERCISE 16.2

Think about any discussions you have had during the past week; what were they about? What matters of public concern are being debated in the news, and which of these issues are important to you? What have you read lately that has caused you to agree or disagree with the author? After thinking about and answering these questions, define three or more issues that are important to you.

The Claim

A *claim* is either an *assertion,* or statement, of what you believe to be true, or a *demand* that something be done. "He injured me with his car" is an assertion. "He ought to pay my medical bills" is a demand. Both of these claims require proof if the injured person expects to convince a court that he or she was injured and should get paid. A *claim* is different from an *issue,* in that an issue is a matter of public concern or controversy, such as "gun control," but a claim is your position on the issue, the assertion or demand you make, such as "gun control denies citizens the right to protect themselves and ensures that only criminals will have guns." Many statements of claims will either include words such as *ought to, should, need,* and *must* or imply the idea that something should or ought to be done. Suppose you want to write about the issue of cheating on your campus. What claim can you make about this problem? Following is a list of possible claims about the issue of cheating:

The student government should establish an honor court to deal with cheating. (demand)

We should re-examine our college's policy on cheating. (demand)

The reasons college students cheat are more alarming than the cheating itself. (assertion)

The solution to cheating is everyone's responsibility. (assertion)

In the first paragraph of Rachel I. Barnes's essay "So You Want to Throw Out the Electoral College?", the issue is whether to keep or abolish the electoral college. *Note:* the claim is underlined.

Our presidential election system dates back to the founding fathers who established the Electoral College. Since that time scholars and others have wondered how willingly Americans would accept a president who lost the popular vote but won the electoral vote. Twice we have been put to the test: In 1888, Benjamin Harrison, a Republican, ran against Grover Cleveland, the Democratic incumbent. Although Harrison lost the popular vote, he beat Cleveland in the electoral vote to become president of a nation that largely accepted his win without complaint. Similarly, in the election of 2000, Republican George W. Bush lost the popular vote by a slim margin to Democrat Al Gore. However, Bush beat Gore in the electoral vote, a win that did not set well with many voters for two reasons. First of all, it seemed unfair that one state, Florida, could throw the election to a candidate who lost the popular vote. Second, Democrats questioned the legitimacy of the vote, calling for a recount that prolonged the election and led to legal wrangling on both sides. In the aftermath, Democrats and Republicans agreed on one point: that election reforms are needed. Proposals have included everything from requests for uniform election laws to abolition of the Electoral College. My own view is that we should think long and hard before scrapping a system that has failed to elect the majority candidate only twice in more than two centuries.

The claim is stated as a demand.

EXERCISE 16.3   Review Richard Rodriguez's article on pages 348–352, and then come up with your own definition of the issue and statement of the claim. Decide whether the claim is an assertion or a demand. Share your answers with the rest of the class.

To make a claim about an issue, ask yourself what can or should be done about this? What can I or anyone do? Should state or local government, police, individual citizens, or special groups take action? A statement that answers one or more of these questions is your claim.

EXERCISE 16.4   Select three issues either from the list in Exercise 16.1 or from your list in Exercise 16.2 and make a claim about them. State your claim in a complete sentence.

The Evidence

To convince readers, your argument needs to be well thought out and logical. Your proof should include each of the following:

1. Hard evidence (rational appeals)
2. Soft evidence (emotional appeals)

Hard evidence includes facts, examples, and authoritative opinion, and it makes a *rational appeal* to readers to use their reasoning powers. A nonsmoking ad on television that uses facts such as the percentage of smokers who die from heart and lung diseases is using hard evidence to get smokers to think about their chances of survival if they do not give up their habit. Suppose you want to argue that the salaries and benefits of nursing home health care workers are too low. You could support your claim with hard evidence such as the high turnover in personnel due to job dissatisfaction; the shortage of health care workers willing to work in nursing homes; and the number of employees who barely meet minimum qualifications for employment.

Soft evidence includes moral considerations, common-sense observations, personal opinions, and social values. It makes an *emotional appeal* to readers to listen to their hearts and consciences. Soft evidence can often be more powerful and persuasive than hard evidence. A non-smoking ad on television that uses social values and common sense might show attractive young people making such statements as: "Even a smart guy looks dumb with a cigarette hanging out of his mouth" or "I'm not interested in kissing a woman who has smoker's breath." An antidrug ad that uses a moral consideration to make an emotional appeal might show a teenaged boy hanging out with some children in a schoolyard; they are laughing and seem to be having a good time. A voice-over says, "This young man is making a living by hooking his friends on crack cocaine. He gives them the first few hits for free, then raises the price when they're hooked. He says 'This stuff won't hurt you; trust me.' Of course he'd never use crack himself; he's too smart." The moral consideration in this ad is trust. A friend is trustworthy; he or she will not lie to you. The ad's claim is that someone who tries to sell you drugs is not your friend.

Emotional appeals are often characterized by emotionally charged language, words and phrases that are carefully selected for their positive or negative connotations and for their power to evoke readers' feelings. Phrases such as "open-door policy," "equal access," and "equal opportunity" evoke our feelings against discrimination. Words such as "bigot," "privileged class," "elitist," and "good ol' boy" appeal to our prejudices. If you write an essay in which you make a claim in favor of a trade agreement between the United States and another country, you might include emotionally charged phrases such as "free trade" and "free market economy." But if your claim is against a trade agreement, you might choose phrases such as "fewer American jobs" or "cheap labor." The words you select should reinforce your claim.

Following are paragraphs 5–8 from Rachel I. Barnes's essay "So You Want to Throw Out the Electoral College?" These paragraphs explain why the author is against abolishing the Electoral College. The excerpt is annotated to show how the argument develops: Key ideas are underlined to make the author's claims and reasons stand out.

Claim

Despite critic's claims, the Electoral College is fundamentally more democratic than a than a one-person-one-vote system. For example, if the president were elected by popular vote, candidates would restrict their campaigning to the most densely populated states, ignoring the small

Reasons that support the claim

states. Because of the Electoral College, candidates are forced to campaign throughout the country. This, in turn, insures that the smaller states' interests are protected and that everyone—not just the voters in large urban areas—has a say in who gets elected. Minorities have made significant political gains as a result of forming huge voting blocs, particularly in northern states. In a one-person-one-vote system, these blocs would lose some of their power.

Claim

Far from discouraging people from voting, the 2000 election proves that every vote does count. If registered Republicans who did not vote in this election had voted for Bush, he would have won the popular vote and the

Reasons that support the claim

election without recounts and controversy. If more registered Democrats in Florida or in some of the other states that Bush carried had voted for Gore, then he would have been the winner. In either case, the number of people who vote in an election can be the deciding factor. This election's outcome should convince those who did not vote to show up at the polls in 2004.

Claim

Abolishing the Electoral College would not be easy. It would take a constitutional amendment—something that

Reasons that support the claim

has been tried and failed. Senator John F. Kennedy, who later became president, argued against a direct popular election proposal in the fifties. During both the Nixon and

5

6

7

Claim

Carter administrations, Congress rejected proposals for a direct popular election. Because small states benefit from the Electoral College, their senators are unlikely to vote for its abolition.

8

Probably the best reasons to keep the Electoral College lie in the lessons learned from the Florida debacle. Remember that only twice in our history has a candidate who lost the popular vote won the electoral vote. In every other presidential election, the system has elected the

Reasons that support the claim

majority candidate. Also, the 2000 election was our closest ever: Statisticians called it a tie, giving each candidate 49 percent of the popular vote. Many voters claimed a lack of excitement for either Bush or Gore and this may account for the fact that neither candidate emerged as a clear favorite nationwide. Finally, do not underestimate the fact that Bush carried the majority of the small states, which comprise a huge geographical area of the country. In this election, the Electoral College worked in their favor. In the previous two elections, other parts of the country stood to gain more from a Clinton win. Thus you could say that the Electoral College is a leveling factor, enabling all of the people to be represented some of the time. This is its greatest benefit and one that should guarantee its survival.

EXERCISE 16.5 Either on your own or in a small group discussion, find examples of hard and soft evidence in Richard Rodriguez's essay on pages 348–352.

EXERCISE 16.6 Choose one of your claims from Exercise 16.4, and do some brainstorming for evidence to support your claim. Make a list of both hard and soft evidence you could use.

The Opposing Claims

If all you do is make a claim and support it, your argument will be one-sided and therefore unconvincing. A persuasive argument will acknowledge differing opinions and answer opposing claims. For example, abortion is an issue that has been analyzed to near-exhaustion in the press and on television with no resolution in sight. Most people have chosen a side and consider themselves either pro-choice or pro-life. Whatever side you are on, your defense of your position will be weak unless you acknowledge what people on the other side think and the arguments they use to support their position.

Rachel I. Barnes answers opposing claims in paragraphs 2, 3 and 4 of her essay "So You Want to Throw Out the Electoral College?" The opposing claims are underlined and Barnes's answers are bracketed. Both claims and answers are annotated in the margin.

Claim Critics of the system call it outdated. They see the Electoral College as an indirect voting system rather than the direct "one person, one vote" principle of majority rule on which our system of government is based. For example, when voters cast their ballots, they are not voting for the candidate of their choice; instead, they are voting for a slate of *Answer* electors pledged to that candidate [Although voters indirectly elect the president through their electors, each voter's vote "counts" in the sense that it helps determine for whom the electors vote.] There are 538 electors in all: Each state gets one elector for each of its senators and representatives, and Washington D. C. gets three electors. To win in the Electoral College, a candidate must get a majority of the votes. What makes it possible for a candidate to lose the popular vote and win the electoral vote is the winner-take-all rule followed by 48 states. According to this rule, a candidate who wins a state's popular *Answer* vote gets all its electoral votes. [So, again, each person's vote in a particular state contributes toward a candidate's loss or victory in that state.] Although it may not be unconstitutional for an elector to break his or her pledge to vote for a candidate, that almost never happens. What happened in the 2000 election is that Bush lost the popular vote nationwide, but he carried more states than Gore did. As a result, the total number of electoral votes in the states Bush carried, including Florida, proved greater than the total number of electoral votes in the states Gore carried.

Claim Critics also point out that only 50 percent of registered voters voted in the 2000 election. Many voters believe that their vote does not count, and the 2000 election proved

2

3

Answer   them right, according to the critics. [However, pollsters have always complained about low voter turnout even in elections where a candidate won the popular vote and the electoral vote by huge margins. So it would seem that whether we retain or abolish the Electoral College, we might still have low voter turnout.]

Claim   Critics say that Americans want the Electoral College abolished, according to polls such as the Hart/Teeter poll of November 2000, which showed 57 percent of voters

Answer   favoring election of the president by a popular vote. [However, poll results are merely a barometer of the people's feelings at a given time and should not be the basis on which important issues having far-reaching consequences are decided.]

4

EXERCISE 16.7   Review Richard Rodriguez's essay, and decide whether he answers opposing claims. If you think he does, list the claims and answers on a sheet of notebook paper, or annotate them in the margin. Share your results with the rest of the class.

EXERCISE 16.8   Using your claim and support from Exercise 16.6, now list opposing claims and how you will answer them.

EXERCISE 16.9   No matter what issue you choose to write about—whether it is a social, environmental, political, cultural, or other issue that matters to you— your argument will be strengthened by evidence that includes facts and figures and expert opinion. Online newspapers, magazines, and topical websites provide a wealth of information. Following is a list of sites to explore. Choose one and browse it for information on an issue or topic that interests you. Keep in mind that websites change frequently. Your librarian can help you find the most up-to-date sites.

www.absolutetrivia.com   This site contains facts from such fields as sports, entertainment, and technology.

www.polisci.com/almanac/   U.S. government and political history, economics, and political

	systems of the world are some of the topics this website addresses.
abcnews.go.com/sections/science	Search this site for current headlines on popular science topics.
www.enn.com	On this site you will find articles from environmental journals and news headlines on the current state of the environment
www.geocities.com/-spanouldi/quote.html	Lists of quotations from poets, great leaders, and others are organized by author and subject.

Many newspapers have web pages containing the current day's headlines, lists of past stories, and other information. However, some of these sites may charge a subscription fee. Two sites to try are the *New York Times:* http://www.nytimes.com and the *Boston Globe:* http://www.boston.com.

PLAN YOUR ARGUMENT

Use the four essentials of argument to guide you in planning your essay by answering appropriate questions about them in writing, as shown in Figure 16.1. Your answers to these questions will help you define your

FIGURE 16.1

Using the Four Essentials of Argument to Plan an Essay

THE FOUR ESSENTIALS	QUESTIONS TO ASK YOURSELF
1. Define an issue.	1. What is my issue?
2. Make a claim.	2. What is my position? What will I demand or assert?
3. Prove your claim.	3. What support will I use—both rational and emotional appeals?
4. Answer opposing claims.	4. Who is my audience? What is their position? What are the opposing claims, and what are my answers?

issue, make a claim, prove your claim, and answer potential opposing claims from your intended audience.

Define an Issue

Ask yourself: What is my issue? Is it a pressing matter of concern in the news, in your workplace, or on campus that interests you? The issue you define is the topic of your essay. Your thesis statement should make clear what the issue is and what you think about it.

State Your Claim

Once you have selected a topic, ask yourself: What is my position? Start with who you are —your values and beliefs. The position you take on an issue is a direct result of your values and what you think is important. Ask yourself: What do I think about this issue? and What do I think should be done about it? The answers to these questions are your position. Also, what is your purpose for making the claim? Is it an assertion or a demand? Do you want to alert readers that a problem exists, or do you want them to take an action? Your purpose should take into account the effect you want your essay to have on your audience.

Prove Your Claim

How will you support your claim? What evidence will you use? The best arguments strike a balance between hard evidence (rational appeals) and soft evidence (emotional appeals). An argument that is strictly an emotional appeal will insult the intelligence of readers who might otherwise be convinced if you present them with some facts, statistics, and authoritative opinions. On the other hand, a strictly rational argument ignores readers' viewpoints, values, and attitudes. Reinforce your position with language carefully chosen for its effect. Select words whose connotations support your argument.

Answer Opposing Claims

Ask yourself these questions: Who is my audience? What is their position? What are their opposing claims and what are my answers? Consider your readers and the positions they hold on the issue you have chosen to write about. Those who agree with you will automatically be on your side. Those who oppose you will have to be convinced. Decide in advance what their arguments are and be able to answer them.

Though there are many ways to structure your argumentative essay, Figure 16.2 illustrates one good plan to follow.

DEVELOP YOUR ARGUMENT LOGICALLY

A logical argument is based on sound reasoning. Your reasoning will be sound if you have enough evidence to support your claim, if you answer opposing claims, and if you avoid the common fallacies that make an argument invalid. A *fallacy* is an error in reasoning. Fallacies fall into two categories: those that ignore issues and those that oversimplify issues.

Fallacies that ignore an issue distract your attention from the argument. For example, in recent elections, candidates have been criticized for attacking each other's character instead of debating the issues that concern voters. Writers may resort to emotional appeals when the facts alone are not convincing or when they think that by arousing your fears they can distract you from any rational attacks on their claims. Fallacies that oversimplify issues may present only one side of an argument, ignoring its complexity. Or they may reduce an argument to a choice be-

FIGURE 16.2

Structuring an Argumentative Essay

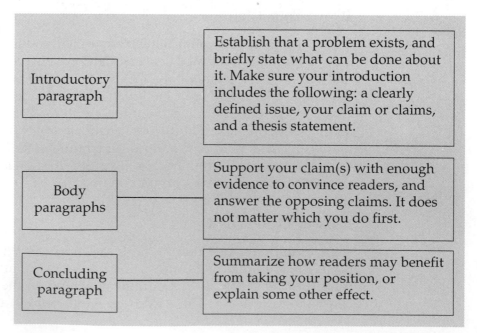

Introductory paragraph	Establish that a problem exists, and briefly state what can be done about it. Make sure your introduction includes the following: a clearly defined issue, your claim or claims, and a thesis statement.
Body paragraphs	Support your claim(s) with enough evidence to convince readers, and answer the opposing claims. It does not matter which you do first.
Concluding paragraph	Summarize how readers may benefit from taking your position, or explain some other effect.

tween two opposing sides when many other options may be valid. Both types of fallacies—those that ignore issues and those that oversimplify issues—are often the result of poor thinking habits such as jumping to conclusions before considering the evidence or rejecting evidence that does not support your opinion.

During your revision process, examine your evidence carefully for any fallacies that may weaken your argument. Then add whatever details are necessary to adequately support your claim. Figure 16.3 on page 366 and Figure 16.4 on page 368 list common fallacies with definitions, examples, and explanations of the thinking errors behind each fallacy.

EXERCISE 16.10

Apply what you have learned about fallacies that ignore or oversimplify issues by doing this exercise with group members. First, review the guidelines for group discussion explained in Chapter 1, page 28. Next, complete the activity that follows and share your results with the rest of the class. Then evaluate your group's performance.

Each item below is a fallacy. Read and discuss each fallacy, decide which fallacy it is, and explain the error in reasoning that led to the fallacy. Use Figures 16.3 and 16.4 as a resource. The first item is done as an example.

1. Everybody knows you can't get drunk on only one drink.

   The fallacy is begging the question. You can get drunk on one drink if the alcohol content is high enough. To say that "everybody knows" does not make a statement a fact.

2. You don't want to buy that dress; only a redneck would wear something like that.

3. The clerk was rude to me in that store, so I'll never go back.

4. "America: Love it or leave it."

5. The welfare bill that Congress passed will result in children starving.

6. Since we are both the same size and that shirt looks nice on you, I know it will look the same on me.

7. Ray is on academic probation, but his hours at work have changed so he'll do better in school now.

8. Everyone else is going to that new movie, so I will too.

FIGURE 16.3

Common Fallacies That Ignore Issues

FALLACY	DEFINITION	EXAMPLE	REASONING ERROR
Argument to the Person*	an attack on the person instead of the argument	calling someone a "racist" when race has nothing to do with the issue	Emotional words detract from the argument.
Argument to the People**	an appeal to the emotions instead of to reason	predicting dire consequences of an action without offering facts to support your claim	Predictions do not mean anything without facts to back them up.
Begging the Question	stating an opinion as if it were a fact	a city council member saying "Orlando is a beautiful city, as anyone can see."	Beauty is a matter of opinion.
Circular Reasoning	restating a claim as part of the evidence	saying that the roads are crowded because there are too many cars on the roads	*Why are the roads crowded? Why are there too many cars? The conditions are not explained.*
Non Sequitur	a conclusion that does not follow from the facts given	concluding that someone who is a good teacher would also be a good department chair	Being a good teacher does not necessarily make one a good leader.
Red Herring	changing the subject; distracting readers from the issue	answering "I'm for family values" to the question, "What is your stand on gun control?"	Family values and gun control are two different issues.

* Argument to the person is also called *argumentum ad hominem.*
**Argument to the people is also called *argumentum ad populem.*

9. Jay's girlfriend says, "Where were you last night?" Jay answers, "I sure am glad to see you."

10. Parents should prevent their children from watching violent TV programs because such programs are forceful and extreme.

11. I knew that question would be on the test because I didn't study for it.

GROUP EVALUATION

What did each person contribute to the group's activity? Was your group's performance successful? Why or why not? What additional questions do you have about the fallacies that ignore or oversimplify issues?

EXERCISE 16.11   The first passage below is from "Minority Student" on pages 348–352. The second passage is from "So You Want to Throw Out the Electoral College?" on pages 358–359. The third passage is from "Students are Dying: Colleges Can Do More" on pages 312–314. Choose one of the passages and write a paragraph in which you answer these questions about it: Do you agree or disagree with the idea expressed in the passage? Is the claim stated in each passage valid or invalid? Does the passage contain a fallacy?

1. I think—as I thought in 1967—that the black civil rights leaders were correct: Higher education was not, nor is it yet, accessible to many black Americans. (paragraph 6)

2. Because small states benefit from the Electoral College, their senators are unlikely to vote for its abolition. (paragraph 7)

3. The choice is simple. You can choose to be a leader and an agent of change on a controversial issue. Or you can continue the annual practice of authoring one of your student's eulogies. (paragraph 10).

TOPICS FOR WRITING

The best topic for an argumentative essay is an issue that you care deeply about. It is also helpful if you have had some direct experience with your topic or if you have researched it. Either make up your own topic, use your responses to the exercises in this chapter as

FIGURE 16.4

Common Fallacies That Oversimplify Issues

FALLACY	DEFINITION	EXAMPLE	REASONING ERROR
Bandwagon	an argument based on the idea that "everybody does it" or wants it	a teenager saying "Why can't I stay out past 10:00 P.M.? All my friends do."	The teenager's parents make the rules, not friends or their parents.
Either-or	reducing an issue to only two sides	reducing the abortion issue to pro-choice or pro-life	There are other possible positions to take on this issue.
Faulty Analogy	an inappropriate or inaccurate comparison	a parent saying "When I was your age I walked five miles to school in the snow, so why do you need a car?"	The conditions that existed when the parent was young are not the same as today's conditions.
Faulty Cause and Effect	believing that because one event follows another, the first event must be the cause of the other	someone saying "I left my window open last night, so now I have a cold."	Leaving the window open does not cause a cold; germs do.
Hasty Generalization	a conclusion drawn from insufficient evidence at hand	concluding that blind dates are a waste of time based on one bad experience	One bad experience on a blind date does not prove that all blind dates are bad.

a source for ideas, or take a position for or against an issue that has received public attention, such as one of the following:

> genetic research and engineering
>
> professional athletes' multimillion-dollar contracts
>
> whether the private life of a candidate influences his or her performance in office
>
> the benefits or drawbacks of living together before marriage

Write on the issue expressed in one of this chapter's readings.

> Agree or disagree with Richard Rodriguez's position on affirmative action.
>
> Agree or disagree with Rachel I. Barnes's claim that the Electoral College should not be abolished.

Checklist for Revision

As you revise and edit your essay check for the following:

1. Do you have a clearly stated or implied thesis, purpose, and audience?

2. Have you introduced your thesis by providing background information or by using some other strategy to interest readers?

3. Have you clearly defined an issue and made a claim?

4. Do you have enough evidence to support your claim and answer the opposition?

5. Is your essay logically organized and have you used transitions effectively?

6. Does the tone of your essay suit your purpose?

7. Are your sentences varied and error-free?

THE CRITICAL THINKER

To examine Richard Rodriguez's essay in more depth, think about and discuss the following questions. Then choose one of them as a topic for writing.

1. What does Rodriguez mean in paragraph 13 when he says that he was not a minority in a *cultural* sense?

2. In paragraph 15, Rodriguez says about a faculty member, "He assumed that, because of my race, I retained a special capacity for communicating with nonwhite students." What makes the professor's reasoning faulty? What fallacy has he committed? Explain your answer.

3. What assumptions did Rodriguez's professors have about minority students' ability to do academic work? Use evidence from the essay to explain your answer.

4. Do you agree or disagree with Rodriguez's position in this essay that higher education is not accessible to many black Americans? Explain your reasons.

YOUR DISCOVERY JOURNAL

Review the fallacies and their explanations in Figures 16.3 and 16.4 on pages 366 and 368. Which of these fallacies can you identify in your own thinking, conversation, or writing? Which of the fallacies have you noticed others using? Write in your journal about one statement you have heard or read recently that contains a fallacy. Explain why the statement is false or misleading.

Unit

3

More Choices:
A Collection of Readings

Selection
1

AWARENESS CHECK

Before reading the following essay, explore your thoughts about prejudice or discrimination. Think about the questions below, and answer them either on your own or in a group discussion:

1. What evidence of discrimination do you see today? Who is discriminated against and in what way?

2. What action can you take in support of those who are discriminated against?

3. Read the title, headnote, and first two paragraphs of the following selection. Based on this preview, what do you think will follow?

My Name Is Margaret
Maya Angelou

Maya Angelou is an author, performer, composer, and singer. In this selection from her autobiographical novel, I Know Why the Caged Bird Sings, *Angelou narrates an experience that reflects on the importance of her name to her identity. Angelou was born Marguerita Johnson in 1928.*

Recently a white woman from Texas, who would quickly describe herself as a liberal, asked me about my hometown. When I told her that in Stamps my grandmother had owned the only Negro general merchandise store since the turn of the century, she exclaimed, "Why, you were a debutante." Ridiculous and even ludicrous. But Negro girls in small Southern towns, whether poverty-stricken or just munching along on a few of life's necessities, were given as extensive and irrelevant preparations for adulthood as rich white girls shown in magazines. Admittedly the training was not the same. While white girls learned to waltz and sit gracefully with a tea cup balanced on their knees, we were lagging behind, learning the mid-Victorian values with very little money to indulge them. (Come and see Edna Lomax spending the money she made picking cotton on five balls of ecru tatting thread. Her fingers are bound to snag the work and she'll have to repeat the stitches time and time again. But she knows that when she buys the thread.)

1

We were required to embroider and I had trunkfuls of colorful dish-   2
towels, pillowcases, runners and handkerchiefs to my credit. I mastered
the art of crocheting and tatting, and there was a lifetime's supply of
dainty doilies that would never be used in sacheted dresser drawers. It
went without saying that all girls could iron and wash, but the finer
touches around the home, like setting a table with real silver, baking
roasts and cooking vegetables without meat, had to be learned elsewhere. Usually at the source of those habits. During my tenth year, a
white woman's kitchen became my finishing school.

Mrs. Viola Cullinan was a plump woman who lived in a three-   3
bedroom house somewhere behind the post office. She was singularly
unattractive until she smiled, and then the lines around her eyes and
mouth which made her look perpetually dirty disappeared, and her
face looked like the mask of an impish elf. She usually rested her smile
until late afternoon when her women friends dropped in and Miss
Glory, the cook, served them cold drinks on the closed-in porch.

The exactness of her house was inhuman. This glass went here and   4
only here. That cup had its place and it was an act of impudent rebellion to place it anywhere else. At twelve o'clock the table was set. At
12:15 Mrs. Cullinan sat down to dinner (whether her husband had arrived or not). At 12:16 Miss Glory brought out the food.

It took me a week to learn the difference between a salad plate, a   5
bread plate and a dessert plate.

Mrs. Cullinan kept up the tradition of her wealthy parents. She was   6
from Virginia. Miss Glory, who was a descendant of slaves that had
worked for the Cullinans, told me her history. She had married beneath
her (according to Miss Glory). Her husband's family hadn't had their
money very long and what they had "didn't 'mount to much."

As ugly as she was, I thought privately, she was lucky to get a hus-   7
band above or beneath her station. But Miss Glory wouldn't let me say
a thing against her mistress. She was very patient with me, however,
over the housework. She explained the dishware, silverware and ser-
vants' bells.

The large round bowl in which soup was served wasn't a soup   8
bowl, it was a tureen. There were goblets, sherbet glasses, ice cream
glasses, wine glasses, green glass coffee cups with matching saucers,
and water glasses. I had a glass to drink from, and it sat with Miss
Glory's on a separate shelf from the others. Soup spoons, gravy boat,
butter knives, salad forks and carving platter were additions to my vocabulary and in fact almost represented a new language. I was fasci-
nated with the novelty, with the fluttering Mrs. Cullinan and her
Alice-in-Wonderland house.

Her husband remains, in my memory, undefined. I lumped him   9
with all the other white men that I had ever seen and tried not to see.

On our way home one evening, Miss Glory told me that Mrs. Cullinan couldn't have children. She said that she was too delicate-boned. It was hard to imagine bones at all under those layers of fat. Miss Glory went on to say that the doctor had taken out all her lady organs. I reasoned that a pig's organs included the lungs, heart and liver, so if Mrs. Cullinan was walking around without those essentials, it explained why she drank alcohol out of unmarked bottles. She was keeping herself embalmed. 10

When I spoke to Bailey about it, he agreed that I was right, but he also informed me that Mr. Cullinan had two daughters by a colored lady and that I knew them very well. He added that the girls were the spitting image of their father. I was unable to remember what he looked like, although I had just left him a few hours before, but I thought of the Coleman girls. They were very light-skinned and certainly didn't look very much like their mother (no one ever mentioned Mr. Coleman). 11

My pity for Mrs. Cullinan preceded me the next morning like the Cheshire cat's smile. Those girls who could have been her daughters, were beautiful. They didn't have to straighten their hair. Even when they were caught in the rain, their braids still hung down straight like tamed snakes. Their mouths were pouty little cupid's bows. Mrs. Cullinan didn't know what she missed. Or maybe she did. Poor Mrs. Cullinan. 12

For weeks after, I arrived early, left late and tried very hard to make up for her barrenness. If she had had her own children, she wouldn't have had to ask me to run a thousand errands from her back door to the back door of her friends. Poor old Mrs. Cullinan. 13

Then one evening Miss Glory told me to serve the ladies on the porch. After I set the tray down and turned toward the kitchen, one of the women asked, "What's your name, girl?" It was the speckled-faced one. Mrs. Cullinan said, "She doesn't talk much. Her name's Margaret." 14

"Is she dumb?" 15

"No. As I understand it, she can talk when she wants to but she's usually quiet as a little mouse. Aren't you, Margaret?" 16

I smiled at her. Poor thing. No organs and couldn't even pronounce my name correctly. 17

"She's a sweet little thing, though." 18

"Well, that may be, but the name's too long. I'd never bother myself. I'd call her Mary if I was you." 19

I fumed into the kitchen. That horrible woman would never have the chance to call me Mary because if I was starving I'd never work for her. I decided I wouldn't pee on her if her heart was on fire. Giggles drifted in off the porch and into Miss Glory's pots. I wondered what they could be laughing about. 20

Whitefolks were so strange. Could they be talking about me? 21

Everybody knew that they stuck together better than the Negroes did. It was possible that Mrs. Cullinan had friends in St. Louis who heard about a girl from Stamps being in court and wrote to tell her. Maybe she knew about Mr. Freeman.

My lunch was in my mouth a second time and I went outside and relieved myself on the bed of four-o'clocks. Miss Glory thought I might be coming down with something and told me to go on home, that Momma would give me some herb tea, and she'd explain to her mistress. 22

I realized how foolish I was being before I reached the pond. Of course Mrs. Cullinan didn't know. Otherwise she wouldn't have given me the two nice dresses that Momma cut down, and she certainly wouldn't have called me a "sweet little thing." My stomach felt fine, and I didn't mention anything to Momma. 23

That evening I decided to write a poem on being white, fat, old and without children. It was going to be a tragic ballad. I would have to watch her carefully to capture the essence of her loneliness and pain. 24

The very next day, she called me by the wrong name. Miss Glory and I were washing up the lunch dishes when Mrs. Cullinan came to the doorway. "Mary?" 25

Miss Glory asked, "Who?" 26

Mrs. Cullinan, sagging a little, knew and I knew. "I want Mary to go down to Mrs. Randall's and take her some soup. She's not been feeling well for a few days." 27

Miss Glory's face was a wonder to me. "You mean Margaret, ma'am. Her name's Margaret." 28

"That's too long. She's Mary from now on. Heat that soup from last night and put it in the china tureen and, Mary, I want you to carry it carefully." 29

Every person I knew had a hellish horror of being "called out of his name." It was a dangerous practice to call a Negro anything that could be loosely construed as insulting because of the centuries of their having been called niggers, jigs, dinges, blackbirds, crows, boots and spooks. 30

Miss Glory had a fleeting second of feeling sorry for me. Then as she handed me the hot tureen she said, "Don't mind, don't pay that no mind. Sticks and stones may break your bones, but words . . . You know, I been working for her for twenty years." 31

She held the back door open for me. "Twenty years. I wasn't much older than you. My name used to be Hallelujah. That's what Ma named me, but my mistress give me 'Glory,' and it stuck. I likes it better too." 32

I was in the little path that ran behind the houses when Miss Glory shouted, "It's shorter too." 33

For a few seconds it was a tossup over whether I would laugh (imagine being named Hallelujah) or cry (imagine letting some white woman rename you for her convenience). My anger saved me from ei- 34 ther outburst. I had to quit the job, but the problem was going to be how to do it. Momma wouldn't allow me to quit for just any reason.

"She's a peach. That woman is a real peach." Mrs. Randall's maid 35
was talking as she took the soup from me, and I wondered what her name used to be and what she answered to now.

For a week I looked into Mrs. Cullinan's face as she called me Mary. 36
She ignored my coming late and leaving early. Miss Glory was a little annoyed because I had begun to leave egg yolk on the dishes and wasn't putting much heart in polishing the silver. I hoped that she would complain to our boss, but she didn't.

Then Bailey solved my dilemma. He had me describe the contents 37
of the cupboard and the particular plates she liked best. Her favorite piece was a casserole shaped like a fish and the green glass coffee cups. I kept his instructions in mind, so on the next day when Miss Glory was hanging out clothes and I had again been told to serve the old biddies on the porch, I dropped the empty serving tray. When I heard Mrs. Cullinan scream, "Mary!" I picked up the casserole and two of the green glass cups in readiness. As she rounded the kitchen door I let them fall on the tiled floor.

I could never absolutely describe to Bailey what happened next, be- 38
cause each time I got to the part where she fell on the floor and screwed up her ugly face to cry, we burst out laughing. She actually wobbled around on the floor and picked up shards of the cups and cried, "Oh, Momma. Oh, dear Gawd. It's Momma's china from Virginia. Oh, Momma, I sorry."

Miss Glory came running in from the yard and the women from 39
the porch crowded around. Miss Glory was almost as broken up as her mistress. "You mean to say she broke our Virginia dishes? What we gone do?"

Mrs. Cullinan cried louder, "That clumsy nigger. Clumsy little black 40
nigger."

Old speckled-face leaned down and asked, "Who did it, Viola? 41
Was it Mary? Who did it?"

Everything was happening so fast I can't remember whether her 42
action preceded her words, but I know that Mrs. Cullinan said, "Her name's Margaret, goddamn it, her name's Margaret!" And she threw a wedge of the broken plate at me. It could have been the hysteria which put her aim off, but the flying crockery caught Miss Glory right over her ear and she started screaming.

I left the front door wide open so all the neighbors could hear. 43

Mrs. Cullinan was right about one thing. My name wasn't Mary. 44

Suggestions for Thinking and Writing

1. Do you prefer to be called by your given name or by a nickname? Do you recall an experience when someone purposely called you by the wrong name or gave you a nickname you felt was uncomplimentary? How did you feel at the time, and what did you do about it? Write a narrative account of the experience.

2. Angelou's narration takes place during a time when girls were expected to marry, have children, and spend their lives as homemakers. Therefore, their preparation for adulthood involved learning how to manage a household and care for children. Think about the ways we prepare children for adulthood today. What training either in school or at home prepares boys or girls for the lives they will lead? Is the preparation adequate or not? Does it differ for boys and girls? Write about a strength or weakness in the way we prepare children for adulthood.

3. Do you know someone who, like the woman from Texas in Angelou's essay, describes himself or herself as a liberal but whose actions indicate differently? Do you know someone who doesn't think he or she is prejudiced but who really is? Write an essay about a way in which people who think they are not prejudiced may discriminate against others.

Selection
2

AWARENESS CHECK

Before reading the following essay, explore your thoughts about immigrant Americans. Think about the questions below, and answer them either on your own or in a group discussion:

1. What are some of the problems immigrants face as they try to adjust to their new homelands?

2. What special services or groups exist at your college to help students from other countries adjust to college life?

3. Read the title, headnote, and first two paragraphs of the following letter. Based on this preview, what do you think will follow?

Letter to My Mother

Tran Thi Nga

Tran Thi Nga was born in China. She was a social worker in Vietnam. In both Asia and the United States, she has worked as a journalist. The letter that follows is from Shallow Graves, *a book of poems written by Tran Thi Nga and Wendy Wilder. Tran Thi Nga's letter describes the experience of an immigrant whose family remains in Vietnam.*

Dear Mother,

1   I do not know if you are receiving my letters, but I will keep writing to you as you are always in my mind.

2   We have been here three years now. I have moved from Greenwich and have a wooden shingled house in Cos Cob. We have a garden in the back where we plant vegetables, flowers in the front the way we used to when we were together. I have a pink dogwood tree that blooms in spring. It looks like the Hoa dai tree, but has no leaves, only flowers.

3   We worked for months to clear away the poison ivy, a plant that turns your skin red and makes you itch.

4   We are near a beach, a school and a shopping center. Green lawns go down to the streets and there are many cars and garages. I am even learning to drive.

5   When we got our new house, people from the church came and took us to "Friendly's" for ice cream. Americans celebrate with ice cream. They have so many kinds—red like watermelon, green for pistachio, orange sherbet like Buddha's robes, mint chocolate chip. You buy it fast and take it away to eat.

6   Our house is small, but a place to be together and discuss our daily life. At every meal we stare at the dishes you used to fix for us and think about you. We are sorry for you and for ourselves.

7   If we work hard here, we have everything, but we fear you are hungry and cold and lonesome. Last week we made up a package of clothes. We all tried to figure out how thin you must be now. I do not know if you will ever receive that package wrapped with all our thoughts.

8   I remember the last days when you encouraged us to leave the country and refused to go yourself. You said you were too old, did not want to leave your home and would be a burden to us. We realize now that you sacrificed yourself for our well-being.

9   You have a new grandson born in the United States. Thanh looked beautiful at her wedding in a red velvet dress and white veil, a yellow turban in her dark hair. She carried the chrysanthemums you love.

10   You always loved the fall in Hanoi. You like the cold. We don't. We

have just had the worst winter in a century, snow piled everywhere. I must wear a heavy coat, boots, fur gloves, and a hat. I look like a ball running to the train station. I feel that if I fell down, I could never get up.

Your grandson is three, in nursery school. He speaks English so well   11
that we are sad. We made a rule. We must speak Vietnamese at home so that the children will not forget their mother tongue.

We have made an altar to Father. We try to keep up our traditions   12
so that we can look forward to the day we can return to our country, although we do not know when that will be.

Here we are materially well off, but spiritually deprived. We miss   13
our country. Most of all we miss you. Should Buddha exist, we should keep praying to be reunited.

Dear Mother, keep up your mind. Pray to Buddha silently. We will   14
have a future and I hope it will be soon.

We want to swim in our own pond.
Clear or stinky, still it is ours.

Your daughter,
Nga

Suggestions for Thinking and Writing

1. Have you ever been separated from a family member? What were your feelings? How did you keep in touch with this person? Write about what you did to cope with the separation.

2. What advice do you have for Tran Thi Nga? Write an essay in which you suggest ways for her to adjust to her new country while maintaining ties with home.

3. Anyone who has ever moved to a new town, taken a new job, or transferred to a new school can understand what it feels like to be an outsider. Write about such a time in your life. How did you feel? Who helped you? How did you finally become comfortable in your new town, job, or school?

Selection
3

AWARENESS CHECK

Before reading the following essay, explore your ideas about the First Amendment right to freedom of speech. Think about the questions below, and answer them either on your own or in a group discussion:

1. What does the phrase "freedom of speech" mean to you?

2. Do you believe that Americans' freedom of speech is limited today? Why or why not?

3. Read the title, headnote, and first two paragraphs of the following excerpt. Based on this preview, what do you think will follow?

Speech Wars Among Women
Nat Hentoff

Nat Hentoff is a celebrated columnist whose articles have appeared in the Washington Post *and the* Village Voice. *This essay is excerpted from his book* Free Speech For Me But Not For Thee.

At Arizona State University, Nichet Smith—a junior majoring in justice studies—was going with three friends to visit a student in the Cholla Apartments on campus. 1

The four women, all of them black, stopped suddenly in front of the door of one of the rooms. On it was a flyer: 2

WORK APPLICATION

(Simplified form for Minority Applicants).

The next line said: BLACK APPLICANTS—It is not necessary to attach a photo since you all look alike. 3

Among the questions on the form were: 4

NUMBER OF CHILDREN CLAIMED FOR WELFARE

NUMBER OF LEGITIMATE CHILDREN (if any)

LIST APPROXIMATE ESTIMATE OF INCOME AND INDICATE SOURCE—THEFT: _____

WELFARE: _____ UNEMPLOYMENT: _____

MARITAL STATUS: _____ COMMON LAW: _____ SHACKED UP: _____

OTHER _____

"It hurt real big-time," Nichet Smith said. "I wonder how many people actually feel that way." 5

Along with hurt, there was rage. The four black women went to   6
the resident adviser at Cholla and said they intended to confront the
students who had put that poster on their door. And that is just what
they did.

The women, it should be emphasized, did not turn to the adminis-   7
tration to "protect" them. They did not demand that Arizona State's
anti-harrassment speech code be invoked. (The code is as afraid of free
speech as all of its many equivalents around the country.)

The four black women, powered by their own anger, knocked at   8
the door of the apartment and found one of its inhabitants, who as-
sured them he'd had nothing to do with putting up that flyer. And yes,
he understood why they were so furious and yes, yes, he would take it
down right away.

It didn't end there. The four women spread the word and were the   9
main force in organizing and leading an open meeting the next evening
at the Cholla Apartments. About fifty students, half of whom were
white, showed up. One of the whites on hand, Tami Trawhells, said:
"It's offensive for me as a white person because it looks like all white
people feel that way."

Also present was Charles Calleros, a laid-back, shrewd assistant   10
dean of the law school and a professor there. Some of the students
wondered why the hell the administration—rather than letting the four
women do it—had not ordered the poster taken down.

Arizona State, however, is a public university. And so the First   11
Amendment applies. Calleros carefully explained to the students that
the First Amendment protects even the most offensive speech. Furthermore, the rules of the Cholla Apartments make it clear that students living there can post whatever they like on their doors. There was no
constitutional way, therefore, for officials of Arizona State to rip that
flyer from the door.

The four black women, however, are not agents of the state, and   12
so they got it done.

Professor Calleros pointed out—as the women had already   13
demonstrated—that the First Amendment did not prevent anyone offended by the poster from telling the offending students and anyone
else how they felt about it.

The four women delivered that message very clearly. And repeat-   14
edly. And black students organized a rally and a press conference,
along with an evening program at Cholla on African-American history.
Rather than rhetoric, the evening was focused on a compelling Public
Broadcasting program about the black lawyers, headed by Charles
Houston of Howard University Law School, who fought to end seg-
regated schools during the twenty years preceding *Brown* v. *Board
of Education.*

There were also a march and rally and a session organized by students members of the NAACP at which race relations at Arizona State were forcefully discussed before a hundred or so students. A strong thread through all these discussions was the need for more multicultural education at Arizona State. Not propaganda in the guise of education, but the real stuff. 15

As for the black women, one of their themes, as described by Charles Calleros, was: 16

"They expressed pride in being identified not just as persons but as black women; yet they demanded that others recognize that each of them is unique rather thatn a collection of stereotypical physical and emotional characteristics."

An obbligato to these dialogues on campus—sparked by the Work Application poster—was a stream, sometimes a torrent, of letters in the college paper, the *State Press*. 17

One of the letters ("names withheld upon request") read: 18

"We would like to extend our sincerest and deepest apologies to anyone and everyone who was offended by the tasteless flyer that was displayed on our front door. . . . and was mentioned on the front page of the *State Press*. . . .

"We did not realize the hurt that would come of this flyer. We now know that we caused great distress among many different people and we would again like to apologize to whomever was offended."

When I was at Stanford a couple of months later, I told the Arizona State story to a number of black and Latino students, many of whom believe that speech codes—including severe punishments for offensive speech—are necessary to protect them from racists and sexists on campus. 19

I told them what the four black women at Arizona State had done about the flyer on the door and what happened afterward. At the meeting on campus, the four women had emphasized that at first—when the pain of seeing that flyer hit them—they felt like victims. But after confronting the perpetrators of the flyer and then creating much of the momentum for what followed at the university, they no longer felt like victims. They now felt empowered. 20

Speech codes, on the other hand, weaken those they ostensibly protect by not enabling them to protect themselves. 21

Charles Calleros made another useful point. Because they were not punished, those who were responsible for the flyer were not—he emphasized—turned into "First Amendment martyrs." Had they been made into martyrs for free speech, much attention would have been diverted from the racism on campus and how to deal with it. 22

As for the students who had put that flyer on their door, Charles Calleros tells me that some time later, the director of the residence hall 23 came into their room and saw two of them watching a program on Martin Luther King with great interest.

Some of the most lasting education takes place outside the classroom. As, for further instance, what happened during a student rally where a student of color recalled what Eleanor Roosevelt once said: "No one can make you feel inferior without your consent." 24

Those four black women not only refused to consent but made those who tried to make them feel inferior recognize where the sense of inferiority properly belonged. 25

In April, Arizona State's chapter of the NAACP presented its annual Image Awards to those students "who exhibit positivity where negativity once prevailed." 26

One of the recipients of the award had helped bring Malcolm X's daughter to campus. Other winners included the four black women who had refused to be victims of racism. 27

But still, the University Student Code—which was *not* invoked by the self-empowered four black women—remains in effect. It includes speech as a form of harassment, and the term "harassment" is so broad and vague that the code is in contempt of the First Amendment. Professor Calleros is trying to "improve" the code but does not understand that the only way to protect free speech—as Justice William Brennan told me in an interview after his retirement—is to abolish *all* speech codes. Not "improve." Abolish. 28

In a letter to the president of the university—published in April in the *Devil's Advocate,* the law school student newspaper—Mark Morita took a scornful look at the code, which reads: 29

"It shall be a violation of university policy for any faculty member, staff member, administrator or student to act on the basis of another's status, with the purpose or effect of creating an intimidating, hostile, or offensive working, residential, or educational environment. Status means race, sex, color, national origin, religion, age, sexual orientation, handicap, or Vietnam-era status."

The way to deal with this impenetrable fog, says Morita, is "get rid of it." And he cited the "chilling effect" of the Correctness Code: 30

"Last semester, during Ethnic Food Day, I jokingly suggested forming a White Men's Law Student Association, so we could serve baloney on white bread with mayonnaise! My companions, with genuine fear in their eyes, hushed me up. 'Don't even make jokes,' they whispered. 'If someone hears you, you could get into big trouble.'"

Also in the *Devil's Advocate,* there was a letter by Arizona State law professor Fernando R. Teson about the dangers of speech codes to free expression: 31

". . . Every week I hear colleagues in different parts of the country tell me they prefer to conduct their classes in a bland and noncontroversial manner because they just don't want the headache of having to defend themselves against . . . zealots."

Professors also need to be empowered themselves.   32

Suggestions for Thinking and Writing

1. Why did the University of Arizona not order that the offensive poster be taken down? Write a paragraph in which you answer this question using evidence from the essay.

2. How did the four black women turn a potentially dangerous situation into a positive force for racial harmony? What were the positive results of their confrontation with those who had posted the offensive sign?

3. In paragraph 21, the author says "Speech codes, on the other hand, weaken those they ostensibly protect by not enabling them to protect themselves." Do you agree or disagree with the author that all speech codes should be abolished? Write an essay in which you explain your reasons.

Selection
4

AWARENESS CHECK

Before reading the following essay, explore your thoughts about what it means to be a "junior." Think about the questions below, and answer them either on your own or in a group discussion:

1. What do you think is the source of the tradition of naming sons after their fathers? Why do you suppose there is not a similar tradition for naming girls?

2. What effect does being named a "junior" have on a boy growing up?

3. Read the title, headnote, and the first two paragraphs of the following essay. Based on this preview, what do you think will follow?

Being a Jr.

Rafael A. Suarez, Jr.

Rafael A. Suarez, Jr., is a journalist and television reporter whose articles have been published in newspapers and magazines. The following essay from the New York Times *explains what being a "junior" means to the author.*

There is a photograph in my parents' house in Brooklyn which never fails to grab a gaze as I pass by. It was taken in 1958, on the beach in Jacksonville, Florida. My father, trim, smiling, tan, holds his first-born, a little over a year old. That's me. On that sunny day in Florida, my sailor father is a few months past his twentieth birthday. I think of myself at twenty, a senior in college living in my first apartment, and laugh at the idea of my having had a child at that age.

My father looks happy in the photo. I look happy, too. Today I have a face something like his, a body much like his, and a name *exactly* like his. Exactly the same, except for two letters and a period on my birth certificate, diploma, driver's license and credit cards: Jr. At the risk of sounding a little syrupy, I'd say his name is one of the nicest things my father has ever given me. Rafael is one of the seven archangels, and he is known as God's healer for his role in restoring the sight of Tobit in that Apocryphal book. Thus Angel, my father's middle name, and mine, is fitting.

There are hundreds, perhaps thousands of names for men. There are plenty of other names in my own family that would have worked perfectly well. My brothers got them. My father and mother could have given me a different middle name. Then I would have been named for my father, but not a Jr.

When friends first see my byline, or look over my shoulder as I sign a register, and they see the "Jr." at the end, there are several reactions. "I wouldn't like that," said one. "I like having my *own* name." Some men say, "You're a junior? Me too!"

Only men get to say that, because only men get to be juniors. Women with feminized versions of their fathers' names don't get a legal tag to reflect the fact and neither do women named for their mothers. Besides, the attitudes that go with having "junior children" seem to be more closely associated with boys than girls. Though customs are changing, carrying on the family name is still something done by boys and very effectively done by "juniors."

In addition to the sexual exclusivity of juniorism, there is a cultural one. Though there is no religious reason for it, Eastern European Ashkenazic Jews will not name children for their fathers or mothers, except in the unlikely event that the father is dead at a boy's birth. There are exceptions to this generalization, but none of the guys with whom I played ball at the Jewish Community House in Bensonhurst were juniors. Most of my Jewish buddies are carrying a dead relative's initials around, or some rough English cognate of a Hebrew name. It seems a shame that not only dad but *all* of the living are excluded from the thrill of having a namesake.

I'm happy with my name, and I like being a junior, but there is a down side. Mail meant for me still somehow ends up at my father's house. When I still lived at home I got half my mail "pre-opened." I can still remember the look on my father's face when my friends on the phone, asking for me and getting him, would launch into personal conversation. Family members finally got into the habit of asking "junior or senior?" when callers weren't specific enough.

In the world of juniors, I was one of the lucky ones. I was never called "Junior" as a nickname. I knew one Junior for years without ever knowing his real name. He and many other Juniors will tell you that Junior is their real name and sign it that way on a greeting card or a letter. These are the guys people probably have in mind when they ask me if I have a fragile sense of identity because of my juniorhood.

Identity is not a problem. In addition to being me, I get the privilege of having my name attached to something longer-lived than just me. When I introduce myself, I don't say "My name is . . ." or "I am called . . ." I say "I am Rafael." The difference is important, because a name doesn't only tell people what to call you, it tells them who you are.

I often think about my life as being not only a gift from my parents to me, but as being a gift from me to them. It must be a special gift for my father, since we have the same name. I think of the kick he probably gets when he sees my byline in a magazine or newspaper, or when he sees my name, *our* name, under my face when I report on television. He loves my brothers and is proud of them. But it can't be the same as seeing his name, his son's name, in a prominent place.

Of the three brothers, am I the most like my father? Maybe. I think that when I was named for my father, the intention was that my name not be simply a utile thing, not be just a handy sound to summon a boy when the garbage needs to be taken down. When a child is named, it is an attempt to define the child. And my definition is my father. I thank my parents for their vote of confidence, and I hope I live up to my name.

Still, there are complications of juniorhood, and they don't end at the age of majority or when a boy moves away from home. I will be a junior until the day I die, no matter how long my father lives. If I ever have a son, he can be named for me, but he can't be "Jr." We would have to begin the numbers game, which somehow doesn't

7

8

9

10

11

12

have the intimacy of "Sr." and "Jr." This theoretical manchild would have "3d" (pronounced "the third") at the end of his name, and I'm not sure how I feel about that. My wife says, unequivocally, "No way." A friend suggested that the resulting name would be a "little too Waspy." But I don't think Rafael Angel Suarez 3d has to worry about being too Waspy.

Suggestions for Thinking and Writing

1. In paragraph 2, Suarez explains the meaning of his name and why he thinks it suits him. He says that Rafael is one of the seven archangels and that the name means "God's healer." To find the meaning of your name, or any name, look in a dictionary of names in the reference section of your library. Write an essay in which you explain the meaning of your name or a friend's or relative's name. Explain how the name either does or does not fit the personality of its owner.

2. In paragraph 9, Suarez says ". . . a name doesn't only tell people what to call you, it tells them who you are." Write a paragraph in which you explain the author's meaning.

3. Names are closely tied to a person's identity: his or her sense of self. Review and compare the essays "My Name is Margaret," pages 373–377, and "Being a Jr.", 386. Using evidence from these essays, write an essay in which you explain what each author's name has to do with his or her identity.

Selection
5

AWARENESS CHECK

Before reading the following essay, explore your thoughts about adopting a baby. Think about the questions below, and answer them either on your own or in a group discussion:

1. Would you ever consider adopting a child? Why or why not?

2. Would you consider adopting a child of a different race, nationality, or ethnic group? Why or why not?

3. Read the title, headnote, and the first two paragraphs of the following essay. Based on this preview, what do you think will follow?

The Chosen One

Laura Cunningham

In this essay, originally published in the New York Times Magazine, *the author explains her concerns about adopting a Chinese baby and the choice she made.*

A year ago, I boarded a flight to Shanghai during a gale force wind. The plane shivered and taxied back to the hangar twice before taking off. It is testimony to my anxiety about the purpose of my journey that I felt no fear of flying. I carried with me an empty infant car bed (aptly named the Dream Ride), a three-week supply of diapers, wipes, pediatric antibiotics, bottles and disposable nipples. I was on my way to adopt one of the tens of thousands of baby girls abandoned in China each year.   1

Today as I write, my 1-year-old daughter sleeps in a crib in the next room. She lies in the position of trust—on her back, her arms wide-spread, her face tip-tilted as if for the next kiss.   2

A happy ending, so far, for my darling Chinese daughter, and for me. But the journey to Shanghai has somehow not ended. Many nights, I wake at 3 A.M.—yanked from my dream, my heart hammering alarms. At that silent, moonlit time, I remember my choice.   3

I am embarrassed now to recall the doubt that accompanied me to China. The orphanage had sent a fax (yes, in the new China, orphanages send faxes): "We have a baby for you. We would have taken her picture but it was too cold."   4

My concern, if I can articulate the chill gut slide of panic as a "concern," was that somehow I would walk into the orphanage and fail to respond to the baby; that somehow she would not feel like "the right one." I would have to go ahead with the adoption out of momentum, some grim sense of decency, but without the hoped-for love at first sight.   5

The baby, it seemed from the fax, was already chosen. And while I claimed to love all babies, in my secret, cowering heart I had to admit that I was more drawn to some babies than to others. It wasn't beauty or even intelligence that I required of a baby, but some sign of being, well, simpatico.   6

I could not see her until the orphanage opened Monday morning.   7

I had arrived in Shanghai on Saturday night. The interval was the high tide of my fear—suspense seemed hydraulic; blood rushed through me at unprecedented speed.

Until Monday I had only the ambiguous answers of Ms. Zhang, the orphanage's emissary who had greeted me at the airport. When I asked: "How old is the baby? How big?" Ms. Zhang answered only with another question: "What size baby clothes have you brought with you?"   8

Her response raised some possibility of control, or at least influence. Maybe the baby was *not* yet chosen. In my sneaking secret chicken heart, I could still pick the best and the brightest star of abandoned baby girlhood in Shanghai.   9

Passing the time until I could meet "my baby," I met another baby at the hotel, already adopted by a single man. (China permits adoptions by foreigners, whether married or unmarried. Its adoption policy is unusual in that citizens, as well as foreigners, must be at least 35 years old to adopt.) She struck me, however, as not meant to be my baby. She did seem just right for her new father, an American psychologist, who carried with him a sitcom's supply of baby paraphernalia.   10

Next I went to the nearest tourist attraction, the Temple of the Jade Buddha, where there was said to be a Buddha to whom mothers pray for a good baby.   11

The Buddha glowed in the dim temple. It wasn't jet lag that sent me reeling to my knees before the Buddha. Half-Jewish, half-Southern Baptist, all doubt, I knelt in truest prayer. *Let the baby be one I can truly love.*   12

At 9 sharp the next morning I waited in the orphanage, wearing my winter coat indoors (now I understood the fax). Even in midwinter there was no heat. Vapor rose from the thermoses of hot tea carried by the female employees. The translator announced that the baby was being carried in from the nursery building.   13

"You will have a choice," she said.   14

I looked out the window as she pointed across a courtyard filled with dead bamboo and gray laundry. The window itself was grimy, but through it I saw two women in blue smocks, running toward me. Each held a bundle. There were *two* babies.   15

They were swaddled in comforters, their heads completely draped in towels. The first baby was unveiled. There was a staccato of Chinese translated as: "Pick this one. She is more beautiful. She is more intelligent." Baby No. 1 was the nurses' favorite, a 2-month-old of unsurpassed good looks and robust health. She smiled.   16

But I couldn't take my eyes from the second baby, who was revealed almost as an afterthought. She was thin, piteous, a green-complexioned elf, with low-set ears that stuck out. She wheezed. In a   17 pocket of my coat, I held a vial of antibiotics, carried on good advice from a friend.

I had no choice. The second baby was sick. I had medicine impossible to obtain here. I accepted the tiny green baby, gasping and oozing, into my arms. I noticed she also had a bald spot, from lying unmoved in her crib. 18

Shame over my earlier indecision blew from the room like a fetid draft of disease and poverty. 19

Was it love at first sight? I knew in that instant that we were at the start of our life together. 20

Love overtakes you at odd moments. I was trying to collect a urine sample, required for a medical test. I held her, her little purple fanny over a rice bowl, in my arms all night. I drew the blankets around us both as a tent to keep away the cold. We waited, silently, all night, until she took a literal "tinkle." Her eyes met mine, on the other side of the world, and I knew Little-Miss-Ears-Stick-Out, With-Tears-in-Her-Eyes was mine, all right. 21

Within 24 hours, the medicine had taken effect: she turned ivory pink; her eyes cleared. She was beyond my dreams, exquisite, a luminous old soul with contemporary wit. I gazed at her and saw the fatefulness of every mother's choice. It is not the beautiful baby who is chosen, but the chosen baby who becomes beautiful. 22

To enter a house filled with unwanted babies is to pass through a door that you can never shut. At 3 A.M., I see the others—the aisles of green cribs holding bundled babies. I try to close my eyes to them, but they refuse to disappear. They are lying there. They are cold; they are damp. I see one baby girl especially. She had an odd genetic defect: the skin of her body was coal black, but her face had no color; she looked as if she were wearing the white theatrical mask of tragedy. 23

Last Christmas, I was able to choose the green, sick baby over the laughing, healthy one. Would I have had the courage to take one of the others? Would someone? I wake up and see the small faces. They are lying there waiting, waiting to be chosen. 24

Suggestions for Thinking and Writing

1. Write a paragraph in which you explain what the author means by "it is not the beautiful baby who is chosen, but the chosen baby who becomes beautiful." (paragraph 22)

2. Under what conditions would you adopt a child? As a possible parent of an adopted child, what would you have to offer? What reservations or fears about adopting a child would you have? Explain your answers in an essay.

3. Write an essay from the point of view of an adopted child. Imagine you are a child who needs a home. What would you hope for in a family that might adopt you? What are the advantages and disadvantages of being adopted?

Selection 6

AWARENESS CHECK

Before reading the following essay, explore your thoughts about what makes a good leader. Think about the questions below, and answer them either on your own or in a group discussion:

1. What do you think are the qualities that make a good leader?

2. Who were Ulysses S. Grant and Robert E. Lee?

3. Read the title, headnote, and the first two paragraphs of the following essay. Based on this preview, what do you think will follow?

Grant and Lee: A Study in Contrasts
Bruce Catton

Bruce Catton (1899–1978) had an illustrious career. He was a newspaper columnist, speechwriter, information director for government agencies, the author of eighteen books, and from 1954 until his death he was the editor of American Heritage *magazine. America's best-known Civil War historian, Catton was awarded the Medal of Freedom for his accomplishments.*

When Ulysses S. Grant and Robert E. Lee met in the parlor of a modest house at Appomattox Court House, Virginia, on April 9, 1865, to work out the terms for the surrender of Lee's Army of Northern Virginia, a great chapter in American life came to a close, and a great new chapter began.   1

These men were bringing the civil war to its virtual finish. To be sure, other armies had yet to surrender, and for a few days the fugitive Confederate government would struggle desperately and vainly, trying to find some way to go on living now that its chief support was gone.   2

But in effect it was all over when Grant and Lee signed the papers. And the little room where they wrote out the terms was the scene of one of the poignant, dramatic contrasts in American history.

They were two strong men, these oddly different generals, and they represented the strengths of two conflicting currents that, through them, had come into final collision.   3

Back of Robert E. Lee was the notion that the old aristocratic concept might somehow survive and be dominant in American life.   4

Lee was tidewater Virginia, and in his background were family, culture, and tradition . . . the age of chivalry transplanted to a New World which was making its own legends and its own myths. He embodied a way of life that had come down through the age of knighthood and the English country squire. America was a land that was beginning all over again, dedicated to nothing much more complicated than the rather hazy belief that all men had equal rights, and should have an equal chance in the world. In such a land Lee stood for the feeling that it was somehow of advantage to human society to have a pronounced inequality in the social structure. There should be a leisure class, backed by ownership of land; in turn, society itself should be keyed to the land as the chief source of wealth and influence. It would bring forth (according to this ideal) a class of men with a strong sense of obligation to the community; men who lived not to gain advantage for themselves, but to meet the solemn obligations which had been laid on them by the very fact that they were privileged. From them the country would get its leadership; to them it could look for the higher values—of thought, of conduct, of personal deportment—to give it strength and virtue.   5

Lee embodied the noblest elements of this aristocratic ideal. Through him, the landed nobility justified itself. For four years, the Southern states had fought a desperate war to uphold the ideals for which Lee stood. In the end, it almost seemed as if the Confederacy fought for Lee; as if he himself was the Confederacy . . . the best thing that the way of life for which the Confederacy stood could ever have to offer. He had passed into legend before Appomattox. Thousands of tired, underfed, poorly clothed Confederate soldiers, long-since past the simple enthusiasm of the early days of the struggle, somehow considered Lee the symbol of everything for which they had been willing to die. But they could not quite put this feeling into words. If the Lost Cause, sanctified by so much heroism and so many deaths, had a living justification, its justification was General Lee.   6

Grant, the son of a tanner on the Western frontier, was everything Lee was not. He had come up the hard way, and embodied nothing in particular except the eternal toughness and sinewy fiber of the men who grew up beyond the mountains. He was one of a body of men who owed reverence and obeisance to no one, who were self-reliant   7 to a fault, who cared hardly anything for the past but who had a sharp eye for the future.

These frontier men were the precise opposites of the tidewater aristocrats. Back of them, in the great surge that had taken people over the Alleghenies and into the opening Western country, there was a deep, implicit dissatisfaction with a past that had settled into grooves. They stood for democracy, not from any reasoned conclusion about the proper ordering of human society, but simply because they had grown up in the middle of democracy and knew how it worked. Their society might have privileges, but they would be privileges each man had won for himself. Forms and patterns meant nothing. No man was born to anything, except perhaps to a chance to show how far he could rise. Life was competition.

8

Yet along with this feeling had come a deep sense of belonging to a national community. The Westerner who developed a farm, opened a shop, or set up in business as a trader could hope to prosper only as his own community prospered—and his community ran from the Atlantic to the Pacific and from Canada down to Mexico. If the land was settled, with towns and highways and accessible markets, he could better himself. He saw his fate in terms of the nation's own destiny. As its horizons expanded, so did his. He had, in other words, an acute dollars-and-cents stake in the continued growth and development of his country.

9

And that, perhaps, is where the contrast between Grant and Lee becomes most striking. The Virginia aristocrat, inevitably, saw himself in relation to his own region. He lived in a static society which could endure almost anything except change. Instinctively, his first loyalty would go to the locality in which that society existed. He would fight to the limit of endurance to defend it, because in defending it he was defending everything that gave his own life its deepest meaning.

10

The Westerner, on the other hand, would fight with an equal tenacity for the broader concept of society. He fought so because everything he lived by was tied to growth, expansion, and a constantly widening horizon. What he lived by would survive or fall with the nation itself. He could not possibly stand by unmoved in the face of an attempt to destroy the Union. He would come at it with everything he had, because he could see it as an effort to cut the ground out from under his feet.

11

So Grant and Lee were in complete contrast, representing two diametrically opposed elements in American life. Grant was the modern man emerging; beyond him, ready to come on the stage, was the great age of steel and machinery, of crowded cities and a restless, burgeoning vitality. Lee might have ridden down from the old age of chivalry, lance in hand, silken banner fluttering over his head. Each man was the

12

perfect champion of his cause, drawing both his strengths and his weaknesses from the people he led.

Yet it was not all contrast, after all. Different as they were—in background, in personality, in underlying aspiration—these two great soldiers had much in common. Under everything else, they were marvelous fighters. Furthermore, their fighting qualities were really very much alike.   13

Each man had, to begin with, the great virtue of utter tenacity and fidelity. Grant fought his way down the Mississippi Valley in spite of acute personal discouragement and profound military handicaps. Lee hung on in the trenches at Petersburg after hope itself had died. In each man there was an indomitable quality . . . the born fighter's refusal to give up as long as he can still remain on his feet and lift his two fists.   14

Daring and resourcefulness they had, too; the ability to think faster and move faster than the enemy. These were the qualities which gave Lee the dazzling campaigns of Second Manassas and Chancellorsville and won Vicksburg for Grant.   15

Lastly, and perhaps greatest of all, there was the ability, at the end, to turn quickly from war to peace once the fighting was over. Out of the way these two men behaved at Appomattox came the possibility of a peace of reconciliation. It was a possibility not wholly realized, in the years to come, but which did, in the end, help the two sections to become one nation again . . . after a war whose bitterness might have seemed to make such a reunion wholly impossible. No part of either man's life became him more than the part he played in their brief meeting in the McLean house at Appomattox. Their behavior there put all succeeding generations of Americans in their debt. Two great Americans, Grant and Lee—very different, yet under everything very much alike. Their encounter at Appomattox was one of the great moments of American history.   16

Suggestions for Thinking and Writing

1. Which paragraphs of Catton's essay are organized by contrast? Which paragraphs are organized by comparison? Does he devote more space to comparison or to contrast, and why? How does Catton's choice of an organizational pattern support his purpose? Write a paragraph in which you answer these questions.

2. According to Catton, what were the different ideals that each man represented? What traits did they share, and which trait does Catton

think is most important? Write a paragraph in which you answer these questions.

3. Do the ways of life that Grant and Lee stood for still exist in some parts of today's society? Would you describe yourself as a Grant or a Lee? Write a paragraph in which you answer these questions.

Selection
7

AWARENESS CHECK

Before reading the following essay, explore your thoughts about animals. Think about the questions below, and answer them either on your own or in a group discussion:

1. Which animals either disgust or fascinate you? Why?

2. What human qualities do you see reflected in the behavior of animals?

3. Read the title, headnote, and the first two paragraphs of the following essay. Based on this preview, what do you think will follow?

The Dead Chameleon
Robin Simmons

Robin Simmons is a writer and professor at Valencia Community College. In the following essay, she describes an encounter with a dead chameleon and teaches us something about our connection to all living things.

One day I discovered a dead chameleon in my mailbox. He was lying on   1
the black metal bottom under a deluge of envelopes and sales circulars; no nudging with the corner of my phone bill would stir him to life. As I have an aversion to touching dead things, I left him there, naively hoping that the mailman would pluck him out or that a clean-up crew of ants would carry him off.

　　The following day, after grabbing my mail, I realized the dead rep-   2
tile would remain in his overlarge coffin until I removed him myself. A

better option than extracting the little lizard, I rationalized, would be watching the process of decay. Already his fawn coloring was darkening to chocolate, and his eyes, once round with life, had collapsed. As the weather was dry November cool, I imagined that he would slowly crisp up like the Indian corn hung on the front door for the holidays.

After my next trip to the mailbox, however, I had to rethink the relatively antiseptic decomposition I had anticipated. For now death had aggressively claimed the corpse: the chameleon's blackened, bloated body sat in a dark puddle of escaping juices while tiny flies, attracted by the putrefaction, floated around the mailbox lid, which a clothespin propped open. So that my mail would not soak up the liquid oozing from the dead lizard, I hastily laid a folded section of newspaper on top of him.

For many days afterward, each time I reached inside, the mailbox exhaled decay. I held my breath as I retrieved the envelopes and did not dare pull back the sheets of newspaper to observe what was happening underneath.

When both the stench and the insects disappeared a week later, I gingerly lifted a corner of the newspaper shroud. What a mistake that was. Fat, white fly hatchlings, their segmented wormy bodies squirming in the light, littered the mailbox floor as they fed on the chameleon carcass. Gagging, I dropped the corner, vowing never to lift the paper again.

My curiosity was as dead as the little lizard, and I retrieved my mail for weeks without thought of the chameleon. Not until, that is, a two-inch long cockroach took up residence in the box. At first, I thought the hairy-legged bug had come to die there as well, a victim of monthly Terminex sprayings. The lively roach, however, had no intention of joining Brother Chameleon in Pest Heaven. As soon as I opened the lid, he would recklessly circle the inside of the mailbox, just as a daredevil skateboarder does an empty swimming pool. Cockroach droppings covered the newspaper that lined the mailbox.

Four days later, the kamikaze cockroach disappeared. What had kept him there so long, I wondered. Then it dawned on me that insect excrement might be all that remained of the dead chameleon. Tentatively, I pulled back the newspaper. More cockroach droppings, clinging tenaciously to the underside of the yellowed sheets, began to rain down on the mailbox floor, making dry "pings" as they struck the metal.

There on the floor were the scattered bones of the little lizard, nibbled clean by the snacking cockroach. For a moment, the perfect skeleton did not seem to be five inches under my nose; rather, I felt as if I were on a museum balcony several stories above, watching the under-construction assembly of a fossilized dinosaur.

The bones, each so tiny and delicate, had the same definition and   9
detail as the remains of a towering *Tyrannosaurus rex.* Little teeth, previously used to choke down dusty-winged moths, lined the jaws; the
two pin holes on the snout had once sucked in air as the chameleon
sat soaking in the sun. Past the gaping eye sockets, a row of spiky
vertebrae tapered off the skull. Leg bones, resembling the miniature
leftovers from a Kentucky Fried Chicken pig-out, littered the floor of
the mailbox.

What should have seemed repulsive, I found beautiful instead. In   10
its minuscule detail, the skeleton became more real for me than the live
lizards that dashed out of my way as I approached the front walk. Here,
splendidly defined, was the framework that *allowed* the chameleon
his mobility. The lizard's existence was layered. Formerly, I could only
appreciate the chameleon's surface, an understanding as transitory
and incomplete as a sunrise painting by Monet; now, though, I knew
the center.

It was death and decomposition that had finally allowed me to see   11
life, for under my own preppie clothing and Ivory-washed skin existed
this same basic structure of bone, flesh, and skin—all with the potential
for decay. No longer was I just the person a mirror reflected; I was a
multi-layered creature whose own life and mobility depended upon all
the strata underneath the facade everyone else superficially gleaned.

Suggestions for Thinking and Writing

1. Which details in Simmons's essay suggest that she is, at first, dis-
   gusted by the decomposition process going on in her mailbox?
   Where in the essay does her attitude change? What has she learned
   from the dead chameleon? Write a paragraph in which you answer
   these questions.

2. Just as Simmons learned an important lesson from the chameleon,
   you may have learned an important lesson from an encounter with
   an animal. Or you may have read or heard about such an encounter
   and its consequences. Write an essay about the encounter and what
   it taught you or can teach others.

3. Environmentalists believe that every animal has an important role to
   play in the life of our planet. They believe that humans must protect
   animals because we are all connected. Do you think Simmons would
   share these beliefs? Do you share them? Why or why not? Write an
   essay in which you answer these questions.

Selection
8

AWARENESS CHECK

Before reading the following essay, explore your thoughts about homosexuality. Think about the questions below, and answer them either on your own or in a group discussion:

1. How would you react to the news that your son or daughter is a homosexual?

2. Why is homosexuality a difficult topic for some parents and children to discuss? What other topics present difficulties? Why?

3. Read the title, headnote, and the first two paragraphs of the following essay. Based on this preview, what do you think will follow?

Gay

Anna Quindlen

Anna Quindlen is the author of several books, and for many years she was a columnist for The New York Times. *She now writes for* Newsweek. *In the following essay from* Living Out Loud, *Quindlen writes about a family who has difficulty coping with a son's death from AIDS.*

When he went home last year he realized for the first time that he 1 would be buried there, in the small, gritty industrial town he had loathed for as long as he could remember. He looked out the window of his bedroom and saw the siding on the house next door and knew that he was trapped, as surely as if he had never left for the city. Late one night, before he was to go back to his own apartment, his father tried to have a conversation with him, halting and slow, about drug use and the damage it could do to your body. At that moment he understood that it would be more soothing to his parents to think that he was a heroin addict than that he was a homosexual.

This is part of the story of a friend of a friend of mine. She went to 2 his funeral not too long ago. The funeral home forced the family to pay extra to embalm him. Luckily, the local paper did not need to print the cause of death. His parents' friends did not ask what killed him, and his parents didn't talk about it. He had AIDS. His parents had figured out at the same time that he was dying and that he slept with men. He tried to talk to them about his illness; he didn't want to discuss his homosexuality. That would have been too hard for them all.

Never have the lines between sex and death been so close, the chasm between parent and child so wide. His parents hoped almost until the end that some nice girl would "cure" him. They even hinted broadly that my friend might be that nice girl. After the funeral, as she helped with the dishes in their small kitchen with the window onto the backyard, she lost her temper at the subterfuge and said to his mother: "He was gay. Why is that more terrible than that he is dead?" The mother did not speak, but raised her hands from the soapy water and held them up as though to ward off the words.

I suppose this is true of many parents. For some it is simply that they think homosexuality is against God, against nature, condemns their sons to hell. For others it is something else, more difficult to put into words. It makes their children too different from them. We do not want our children to be too different—so different that they face social disapprobation and ostracism, so different that they die before we do. His parents did not know any homosexuals, or at least they did not believe they did. His parents did not know what homosexuals were like.

They are like us. They are us. Isn't that true? And yet, there is a difference. Perhaps mothers sometimes have an easier time accepting this. After all, they must accept early on that there are profound sexual differences between them and their sons. Fathers think their boys will be basically like them. Sometimes they are. And sometimes, in a way that comes to mean so much, they are not.

I have thought of this a fair amount because I am the mother of sons. I have managed to convince myself that I love my children so much that nothing they could do would turn me against them, or away from them, that nothing would make me take their pictures off the bureau and hide them in a drawer. A friend says I am fooling myself, that I would at least be disappointed and perhaps distressed if, like his, my sons' sexual orientation was not hetero. Maybe he's right. There are some obvious reasons to feel that way. If the incidence of AIDS remains higher among homosexuals than among heterosexuals, it would be one less thing they could die of. If societal prejudices remain constant, it would be one less thing they could be ostracized for.

But this I think I know: I think I could live with having a son who was homosexual. But it would break my heart if he was homosexual and felt that he could not tell me so, felt that I was not the kind of mother who could hear that particular truth. That is a kind of death, too, and it kills both your life with your child and all you have left after

3

4

5

6

7

the funeral: the relationship that can live on inside you, if you have nur-   8
tured it.

In the days following his death, the mother of my friend's friend
mourned the fact that she had known little of his life, had not wanted
to know. "I spent too much time worrying about what he was," she
said. Not who. What. And it turned out that there was not enough
time, not with almost daily obituaries of people barely three decades
old, dead of a disease she had never heard of when she first wondered
about the kind of friends her boy had and why he didn't date more.

It reminded me that often we take our sweet time dealing with the   9
things that we do not like about our children: the marriage we could
not accept, the profession we disapproved of, the sexual orientation
we may hate and fear. Sometimes we vow that we will never, never accept those things. The stories my friend told me about the illness, the
death, the funeral and, especially, about the parents reminded me that
sometimes we do not have all the time we think to make our peace
with who our children are. It reminded me that "never" can last a long,
long time, perhaps much longer than we intended, deep in our hearts,
when we first invoked its terrible endless power.

Suggestions for Thinking and Writing

1. When Quindlen says "We do not want our children to be too different," she means that we hope our children will grow up to be like us
   and that we worry about what may happen to them if they do not.
   Based on your experience, do you think this is true? Write an essay
   in which you explain your reasons.

2. Young people have far greater access to birth control devices and information than ever before. At the same time, teen pregnancy, date
   rape, and AIDS have become social problems that many college students' parents never had to face. Write an essay about the effects of
   these developments on today's dating practices.

3. Quindlen quotes the mother of her friend's friend as saying, "I
   spent too much time worrying about what he was, not who." This
   statement addresses the issue of stereotyping. Homosexuals, minority students, the disabled, and many others may well think that
   people "spend too much time worrying about what I am, not who."
   Write an essay in which you respond to this statement.

Selection
9

AWARENESS CHECK

Before reading the following essay, explore your thoughts about heroes and role models. Think about the questions below, and answer them either on your own or in a group discussion:

1. In the past, schools taught children about the exemplary lives of heroes and role models. What heroes and role models do you remember from your own early school years?

2. If you were teaching history to a class of young students, what hero or role model would you want to include in one of your lessons? What is exemplary about this person's life?

3. Read the title, headnote, and first two paragraphs of the following essay. Based on this preview, what do you think will follow?

In Search of Heroes
Peter H. Gibbon

Peter H. Gibbon is headmaster at Hackley School in Tarrytown, New York. The following article appeared in Newsweek's *"My Turn" column in 1993. Gibbon believes that the tradition of educating children by teaching them about the exemplary lives of others has ended. What has replaced it, he says, is a culture that emphasizes history's mistakes and provides no role models.*

To teach about exemplary lives has been a goal of American and European education for hundreds of years. Schools automatically offered young people heroes and role models. How else to combat the ambiguities and temptations of adult life? Where else to find the good to be imitated and the evil to be avoided? And so young people read Plutarch's "Lives," were saturated in the pious maxims of McGuffey's "Readers" and inculcated with the triumphs of Washington, Jefferson and Lincoln.

    Did this force-feeding of idealism in youth make our grandparents and great-grandparents better people? I couldn't say whether this is

1

2

the case. I can say only that the tradition of education by exemplary lives has ended.

The end may have come during the '60s, with the counterculture, the youth rebellion and the questioning of authority. Certainly Vietnam, the assassinations and Watergate gave many an excuse for cynicism.

It may be partly the new trend in biographies, which looks into all corners of a subject's life and pitilessly probes for ordinariness and weakness. The private lives of our leaders are fair game, and we expect (some even hope) to find dirt. Thus we learn that John F. Kennedy was sexually compulsive, that Lyndon Johnson was more often than not devious and that Sir Thomas More, one of my heroes, was vindictive, disputatious and vain.

It may be a new approach to history, which stresses that violence and exploitation were endemic in our past. The discovery of America and the settlement of our West, for example, do not represent the opening of opportunity or the creation of wealth but genocide, environmental rape and the injection of lawlessness, greed and materialism into Eden. Columbus becomes a killer instead of a discoverer.

If new trends in biography and history make it difficult to have heroes, what about our popular culture and the media? My students are inundated with images and bombarded with information. Has this increase in information given them heroes?

My generation was raised on "The Adventures of Ozzie and Harriet." My students watch "Married with Children." We admired Rock Hudson and even thought that was his name; my students know he died of AIDS. We loved "Shane" and "Gunsmoke"; they watch "Blazing Saddles" and "Saturday Night Live." We subscribed to Boys' Life. Even junior-high school students relish National Lampoon and "Doonesbury." We listened to preachers like Billy Graham. They were amused by Tammy and Jimmy. I liked Elvis Presley. They like him, too, but they know he died bloated and drug-infected.

Because we read Boys' Life, were we Boy Scouts? Hardly. But I do think we were more trusting, naive, sentimental and less cynical. We had greater faith in the adult world (perhaps knowing less about it) and were more deferential to authority. We had some heroes.

While irreverence among the young is inevitable and, in some ways, desirable, I would argue that today irreverence, skepticism and mockery permeate our scholarship and culture to such a degree that the tradition of exemplary lives is destroyed and that it is difficult for the young to have heroes. In schools we offer students lives that are seriously flawed, juvenile novels that emphasize "reality" and a history that is uncertain and blemished. At home they roam among dozens of channels and videos that do not intend to uplift and offer no role models.

3

4

5

6

7

8

9

Disappearing heroes: Sir Richard Livingstone, a 20th-century ed-   10
ucator, tells us, "True education is the habitual vision of greatness." I
am afraid that we have lost the vision of greatness in our schools and
culture. We have traded exemplary lives and heroes for information,
irony and reality. I am terrified that our children are not being raised by
exemplary lives and confident schools; nor by high culture, vigilant
communities, families, churches and temples, but rather by an all-
enveloping enemy culture interested in amusement, titillation and con-
sumerism.

I have no easy answers for disappearing heroes and increasing ir-   11
reverence, only a few modest suggestions. Portray old heroes as human
beings, but let them remain heroic. Yes, Lincoln liked bawdy stories,
was politically calculating and suffered from depression. But he also ex-
hibited astonishing political and moral courage and always appealed to
"the better angels of our nature."

For a shabby age, find new heroes and heroines. I recently discov-   12
ered the letters and diaries of the German sculptor Käthe Kollwitz, who
died in 1945. She endures personal despair, a world war and fascism;
still she paints and draws, has compassion and thinks lofty thoughts.

In schools, give moral and ethical education the same importance   13
as the presentation of reality. Teachers need to be more cautious and
selective about introducing messiness and complexity to our children.
Presenting "reality" is a rather empty educational goal if our reading
lists and assignments produce disillusioned, dispirited students.

Intellectuals and columnists could be less mocking and disdainful   14
of those in authority. Too often they look for weakness, find fault and
are confident of easy answers for complex problems; and American
young people conclude that there is only corruption and shallowness in
high places and no heroes.

Hollywood and popular culture must be fought. The movies, the   15
media and the popular-music industry offer their own heroes—most of
whom are disdainful of normal life, hard work and fidelity. Instead, they
glorify violence, excitement and aberration. The cumulative effect of
such indoctrination is incalculable but frightening.

Of course, parents need not be victims of Hollywood, of pundits,   16
of negligent schools or a cynical age. They are the first and most important educators. If they try to make their lives exemplary, so will
their children.

Suggestions for Thinking and Writing

1. Gibbon says that we need to find new heroes. Who are some of today's role models that lead exemplary lives? Write an essay about a
   hero for our times.

2. Gibbon says that movies, the media, and the music industry offer heroes that reject normal life and hard work. Instead, they glorify violence, excitement, and what is abnormal or aberrant. Think of a popular entertainment figure who either does or does not fit this description. Then write an essay in which you explain why this person is or is not a good role model for young people.

3. Think about the following quotation from Gibbon's article. Do you agree or disagree with it? Write an essay in which you either support or reject the quotation and explain why.

> I am terrified that our children are not being raised by exemplary lives and confident schools; nor by high culture, vigilant communities, families, churches and temples, but rather by an all-enveloping enemy culture interested in amusement, titillation, and consumerism.

Selection 10

AWARENESS CHECK

Before reading the following essay, explore your thoughts about a favorite place to visit. Think about the questions below, and answer them either on your own or in a group discussion:

1. What is your favorite place to visit? Why do you like it, and what do you like to do there?

2. If you could travel to any place in the world, where would you go and why? Whom would you take with you?

3. Read the title, headnote, and the first two paragraphs of the following essay. Based on this preview, what do you think will follow?

Once More to the Lake

E.B. White

Elwyn Brooks White (1899–1985) is the author of the popular children's books Stuart Little *and* Charlotte's Web. *He wrote numerous essays for the* New Yorker *and a monthly column for* Harper's Magazine. *His writings are collected in several anthologies. In "Once More to the Lake," a classic piece written in 1941, White's descriptive details and vivid language recreate the lake he visited with his son. The essay is reprinted from* **One Man's Meat.**

One summer, along about 1904, my father rented a camp on a lake in   1
Maine and took us all there for the month of August. We all got ring-
worm from some kittens and had to rub Pond's Extract on our arms and
legs night and morning, and my father rolled over in a canoe with all
his clothes on; but outside of that the vacation was a success and from
then on none of us ever thought there was any place in the world like
that lake in Maine. We returned summer after summer—always on August 1st for one month. I have since become a salt-water man, but
sometimes in summer there are days when the restlessness of the tides
and the fearful cold of the sea water and the incessant wind which
blows across the afternoon and into the evening make me wish for the
placidity of a lake in the woods. A few weeks ago this feeling got so
strong I bought myself a couple of bass hooks and a spinner and returned to the lake where we used to go, for a week's fishing and to re-
visit old haunts.

I took along my son, who had never had any fresh water up his   2
nose and who had seen lily pads only from train windows. On the journey over to the lake I began to wonder what it would be like. I wondered how time would have marred this unique, this holy spot—the
coves and streams, the hills that the sun set behind, the camps and the
paths behind the camps. I was sure that the tarred road would have
found it out and I wondered in what other ways it would be desolated.
It is strange how much you can remember about places like that once
you allow your mind to return into the grooves which lead back. You
remember one thing, and that suddenly reminds you of another thing.
I guess I remembered clearest of all the early mornings, when the lake
was cool and motionless, remembered how the bedroom smelled of
the lumber it was made of and of the wet woods whose scent entered
through the screen. The partitions in the camp were thin and did not
extend clear to the top of the rooms, and as I was always the first up I
would dress softly so as not to wake the others, and sneak out into the
sweet outdoors and start out in the canoe, keeping close along the
shore in the long shadows of the pines. I remembered being very careful never to rub my paddle against the gunwale for fear of disturbing
the stillness of the cathedral.

The lake had never been what you would call a wild lake. There   3
were cottages sprinkled around the shores, and it was in farming country although the shores of the lake were quite heavily wooded. Some of
the cottages were owned by nearby farmers, and you would live at the
shore and eat your meals at the farmhouse. That's what our family did.

But although it wasn't wild, it was a fairly large and undisturbed lake and there were places in it which, to a child at least, seemed infinitely remote and primeval.

I was right about the tar: it led to within a half a mile of the shore. But when I got back there, with my boy, and we settled into a camp near a farmhouse and into the kind of summertime I had known, I could tell that it was going to be pretty much the same as it had been before—I knew it, lying in bed the first morning, smelling the bedroom, and hearing the boy sneak quietly out and go off along the shore in a boat. I began to sustain the illusion that he was I, and therefore, by simple transposition, that I was my father. This sensation persisted, kept cropping up all the time we were there. It was not an entirely new feeling, but in this setting it grew much stronger. I seemed to be living a dual existence. I would be in the middle of some simple act, I would be picking up a bait box or laying down a table fork, or I would be saying something, and suddenly it would not be I but my father who was saying the words or making the gesture. It gave me a creepy sensation. 4

We went fishing the first morning. I felt the same damp moss covering the worms in the bait can, and saw the dragonfly alight on the tip of my rod as it hovered a few inches from the surface of the water. It was the arrival of this fly that convinced me beyond any doubt that everything was as it always had been, that the years were a mirage and there had been no years. The small waves were the same, chucking the rowboat under the chin as we fished at anchor, and the boat was the same boat, the same color green and the ribs broken in the same places, and under the floor-boards the same freshwater leavings and débris—the dead helgramite, the wisps of moss, the rusty discarded fishhook, the dried blood from yesterday's catch. We stared silently at the tips of our rods, at the dragonflies that came and went. I lowered the tip of mine into the water, tentatively, pensively dislodging the fly, which darted two feet away, poised, darted two feet back, and came to rest again a little farther up the rod. There had been no years between the ducking of this dragonfly and the other one—the one that was part of memory. I looked at the boy, who was silently watching his fly, and it was my hands that held his rod, my eyes watching. I felt dizzy and didn't know which rod I was at the end of. 5

We caught two bass, hauling them in briskly as though they were mackerel, pulling them over the side of the boat in a businesslike manner without any landing net, and stunning them with a blow on the back of the head. When we got back for a swim before lunch, the lake was exactly where we had left it, the same number of inches from the dock, and there was only the merest suggestion of a breeze. This seemed an utterly enchanted sea, this lake you could leave to its own devices for a few hours and come back to, and find that it had not 6 stirred, this constant and trustworthy body of water. In the shallows, the dark, water-soaked sticks and twigs, smooth and old, were undulating in clusters on the bottom against the clean ribbed sand, and by the track of the mussel was plain. A school of minnows swam by, each minnow with its small individual shadow, doubling the attendance, so clear and sharp in the sunlight. Some of the other campers were in swimming, along the shore, one of them with a cake of soap, and the water felt thin and clear and unsubstantial. Over the years there had been this person with the cake of soap, this cultist, and here he was. There had been no years.

Up to the farmhouse to dinner through the teeming, dusty field, the road under our sneakers was only a two-track road. The middle track was missing, the one with the marks of the hooves and the splotches of dried, flaky manure. There had always been three tracks to choose from in choosing which track to walk in; now the choice was narrowed down to two. For a moment I missed terribly the middle alternative. But the way led past the tennis court, and something about the way it lay there in the sun reassured me; the tape had loosened along the backline, the alleys were green with plantains and other weeds, and the net (installed in June and removed in September) sagged in the dry noon, and the whole place steamed with midday heat and hunger and emptiness. There was a choice of pie for dessert, and one was blueberry and one was apple, and the waitresses were the same country girls, there having been no passage of time, only the illusion of it as in a dropped curtain—the waitresses were still fifteen; their hair had been washed, that was the only difference—they had been to the movies and seen the pretty girls with the clean hair.

Summertime, or summertime, pattern of life indelible, the fade-proof lake, the woods unshatterable, the pasture with the sweetfern and the juniper forever and ever, summer without end; this was the background, and the life along the shore was the design, the cottages with their innocent and tranquil design, their tiny docks with the flagpole and the American flag floating against the white clouds in the blue sky, the little paths over the roots of the trees leading from camp to camp and the paths leading back to the outhouses and the can of lime for sprinkling, and at the souvenir counters at the store the miniature birch-bark canoes and the post cards that showed things looking a little better than they looked. This was the American family at play, escaping the city heat, wondering whether the newcomers in the camp at the head of the cove were "common" or "nice," wondering whether it was true that the people who drove up for Sunday dinner at the farmhouse were turned away because there wasn't enough chicken.

It seemed to me, as I kept remembering all this, that those times

7

8

9

and those summers had been infinitely precious and worth saving. There had been jollity and peace and goodness. The arriving (at the beginning of August) had been so big a business in itself, at the railway station the farm wagon drawn up, the first smell of the pine-laden air, the first glimpse of the smiling farmer, and the great importance of the trunks and your father's enormous authority in such matters, and the feel of the wagon under you for the long ten-mile haul, and at the top of the last long hill catching the first view of the lake after eleven months of not seeing this cherished body of water. The shouts and cries of the other campers when they saw you, and the trunks to be unpacked, to give up their rich burden. (Arriving was less exciting nowadays, when you sneaked up in your car and parked it under a tree near the camp and took out the bags and in five minutes it was all over, no fuss, no loud wonderful fuss about trunks.)

Peace and goodness and jollity. The only thing that was wrong   10 now, really, was the sound of the place, an unfamiliar nervous sound of the outboard motors. This was the note that jarred, the one thing that would sometimes break the illusion and set the years moving. In those other summertimes all motors were inboard; and when they were at a little distance, the noise they made was a sedative, an ingredient of summer sleep. They were one-cylinder and two-cylinder engines, and some were make-and-break and some were jump-spark, but they all made a sleepy sound across the lake. The one-lungers throbbed and fluttered, and the two-cylinder ones purred and purred, and that was a quiet sound too. But now the campers all had outboards. In the daytime, in the hot mornings, these motors made a petulant, irritable sound; at night, in the still evening when the afterglow lit the water, they whined about one's ears like mosquitoes. My boy loved our rented outboard, and his great desire was to achieve singlehanded mastery over it, and authority, and he soon learned the trick of choking it a little (but not too much), and the adjustment of the needle valve. Watching him I would remember the things you could do with the old one-cylinder engine with the heavy flywheel, how you could have it eating out of your hand if you got really close to it spiritually. Motor boats in those days didn't have clutches, and you would make a landing by shutting off the motor at the proper time and coasting in with a dead rudder. But there was a way of reversing them, if you learned the trick, by cutting the switch and putting it on again exactly on the final dying revolution of the flywheel, so that it would kick back against compression and begin reversing. Approaching a dock in a strong following breeze, it was difficult to slow up sufficiently by the ordinary coasting method, and if a boy felt he had complete mastery over his motor, he was tempted to keep it running beyond its time and then reverse it a few feet from the dock. It took a cool nerve, because if you threw the switch a twentieth of a second too soon you could catch the flywheel when it still had speed enough to go up past center, and the boat would leap ahead, charging bull-fashion at the dock.

We had a good week at the camp. The bass were biting well and the sun shone endlessly, day after day. We would be tired at night and lie down on the accumulated heat of the little bedrooms after the long hot day and the breeze would stir almost imperceptibly outside and the smell of the swamp drift in through the rusty screens. Sleep would come easily and in the morning the red squirrel would be on the roof, tapping out his gay routine. I kept remembering everything, lying in bed in the mornings—the small steamboat that had a long rounded stern like the lip of a Ubangi, and how quietly she ran on the moonlight sails, when the older boys played their mandolins and the girls sang and we ate doughnuts dipped in sugar, and how sweet the music was on the water in the shining night, and what it had felt like to think about girls then. After breakfast we would go up to the store and the things were in the same place—the minnows in a bottle, the plugs and spinners disarranged and pawed over by the youngsters from the boys' camp, the fig newtons and the Beeman's gum. Outside, the road was tarred and cars stood in front of the store. Inside, all was just as it had always been, except there was more Coca-Cola and not so much Moxie and root beer and birch beer and sarsaparilla. We would walk out with a bottle of pop apiece and sometimes the pop would backfire up our noses and hurt. We explored the streams, quietly, where the turtles slid off the sunny logs and dug their way into the soft bottom; and we lay on the town wharf and fed worms to the tame bass. Everywhere we went I had trouble making out which was I, the one walking at my side, the one walking in my pants.   11

One afternoon while we were there at that lake a thunderstorm came up. It was like the revival of an old melodrama that I had seen long ago with childish awe. The second-act climax of the drama of the electrical disturbance over a lake in America had not changed in any important respect. This was the big scene, still the big scene. The whole thing was so familiar, the first feeling of oppression and heat and a general air around camp of not wanting to go very far away. In midafternoon (it was all the same) a curious darkening of the sky, and a lull in everything that had made life tick; and then the way the boats suddenly swung the other way at their moorings with the coming of a breeze out of the new quarter, and the premonitory rumble. Then the kettle drum, then the snare, then the bass drum and cymbals, then crackling light against the dark, and the gods grinning and licking their chops in the hills. Afterward the calm, the rain steadily rustling in the calm lake, the return of light and hope and spirits, and the campers running out in joy and relief to go swimming in the rain, their bright   12

cries perpetuating the deathless joke about how they were getting simply drenched, and the children screaming with delight at the new sensation of bathing in the rain, and the joke about getting drenched
linking the generations in a strong indestructible chain. And the come-
dian who waded in carrying an umbrella.

When the others went swimming my son said he was going in too.   13
He pulled his dripping trunks from the line where they had hung all
through the shower, and wrung them out. Languidly, and with no
thought of going in, I watched him, his hard little body, skinny and
bare, saw him wince slightly as he pulled up around his vitals the small,
soggy, icy garment. As he buckled the swollen belt suddenly my groin
felt the chill of death.

Suggestions for Thinking and Writing

1. Using descriptive details that appeal to all five senses, write a paragraph about a place you have visited. Select details that will enable
   your readers to visualize the place and imagine what it would be like
   to visit there.

2. One of the reasons the lake is important to White is because it reminds him of his childhood. Do you recall any special places from
   your childhood such as a summer home, vacation spot, or relative's
   home that you visited regularly? Write an essay in which you explain
   why this place is important to you.

3. White uses both description and comparison as organizational patterns. White compares the lake when he was a boy to the lake as it
   was when he revisited it with his son. What has changed? What has
   stayed the same? Think of a place you used to visit as a child that you
   still visit now. Write an essay about the changes that have occurred.
   Use comparison as your organizational pattern.

Unit

4

The Selective Writer

*U*nit 4 is about *grammar.* If you are like many students, the mention of that word may cause you to have visions of difficult terms, confusing rules, and papers marked in red. However, grammar is more than a set of rules to be followed or broken. It is a system that describes how language works: how we use words and sentences to construct meaning and express our ideas.

Without question, grammar can be complicated, but it has its practical side. By understanding just a few basics, you can begin to eliminate surface errors and improve your writing. The ability to communicate in clear, correct language is an asset not only in college but in the workplace. Employers in every field value effective communication skills and usually require job applicants to have them.

Unit 4 does not cover every aspect of grammar. It focuses instead on the skills you need now and the problems that are most likely to trouble you as a beginning writer. To get the most you can out of Unit 4, think of grammar as another facet of the writing process. For example, Units 1 and 2 describe writing as a series of choices you make about purpose, audience, thesis, evidence, and organization. Grammar introduces another set of choices about what words to use, how to put them together in sentences, how to connect ideas, and how to correct errors. The more choices you have as a writer, the more selective you can be.

Section A
Basic Choices:
The Parts of Speech

To understand the rest of the topics covered in Unit 4, you need to review the parts of speech. Words are the most basic units of meaning. Each word in a sentence functions as one of eight parts of speech: *nouns, pronouns, verbs, adjectives, adverbs, prepositions, conjunctions,* and *interjections.* How a word is used determines what part of speech it is. Knowing the parts of speech and how they function helps you to select the right words and put them together correctly. During the revision process, if you can identify the parts of speech within a sentence that is giving you difficulty, you may be able to figure out what is wrong and improve your sentence by making better choices.

A.1 NOUNS

You learned long ago that a noun is the name of a person, place, or thing. Nouns also name ideas. See the following chart for examples.

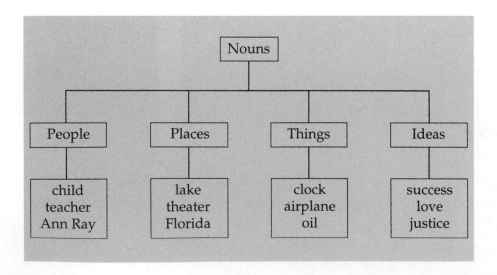

Nouns can change their gender (actor, actress) and number (dog, dogs). Nouns have a *subjective case,* meaning they refer to the person, place, thing, or idea itself as in "Harry." Nouns also have a *possessive case,* meaning they suggest ownership as in "Harry's."

Nouns are classified in five categories: (1) *Proper names* are specific and are always capitalized as in *General Colin Powell, Lake Michigan,* and *AT&T.* (2) *Common nouns* are general and are not capitalized as in *teachers, country,* and *cookware.* (3) *Collective nouns* refer to groups such as *team, squad, club,* and *committee.* (4) *Abstract nouns* name ideas such as *kindness, humor,* and *disease.* (5) *Concrete nouns* name things you can experience through your five senses such as *cookie, music,* and *fragrance.* Read the following two sentences in which the nouns are labeled.

    proper name   **common nouns**   **concrete noun**

1. <u>Maria Cortez,</u> a <u>decorator,</u> chooses <u>fabrics</u> for their <u>colors</u> and

   concrete noun

   <u>textures.</u>

    collective noun   **proper name**   **common noun**

2. Our <u>committee</u> has invited <u>Jake Stevens</u> to be our <u>speaker</u> because

          abstract nouns

   of his <u>experience</u> and <u>humor.</u>

Why is it important to know that nouns have gender, number, case, and categories? These qualities of nouns are essential to your understanding of other grammatical concepts covered in Unit 4. For example, number is an essential part of subject-verb agreement. Case and number are essential parts of pronoun-antecedent agreement. Knowing the gender and categories of nouns can help you make more precise, accurate, and effective word choices and may also help you determine the reasoning behind an author's word choices.

EXERCISE 1

Use what you have learned about the categories of nouns to complete the following sentences. The first one is done as an example.

1. I am a member of the chess ____club____. (collective noun)

2. Adam's _____ is a quality I admire. (abstract noun)

3. _____ is a place I enjoy visiting. (proper name)

4. My desk is littered with _____, _____, and _____.
(common nouns)

5. For holiday dinners we often serve _____ and _____
(concrete nouns)

6. Ed is captain of the football _____.(collective noun)

EXERCISE 2

Examine a paragraph from one of your returned papers. Identify and circle all the nouns in the paragraph. Determine the category of each noun and decide whether your choices could be improved. Compare your results with those of a partner.

A.2 PRONOUNS

A *pronoun* is a word that is used in place of a noun. For example, *he* replaces George, *she* replaces Mary Jo, and *it* replaces car. Pronouns enable you to avoid excessive repetition of the names of people, places, and things. Pronouns are useful also in maintaining point of view. For example, you may recall from Chapter 9 the explanation of the first-person, second-person, and third-person points of view and the pronouns required to establish and maintain them. A good understanding of pronouns and their uses can help you avoid one of the most common errors in writing: lack of agreement between a pronoun and its *antecedent* (a previously mentioned noun that the pronoun replaces). For an explanation of this error and how to correct it, see section D.1 on pages 485–493.

Characteristics of Pronouns

The four characteristics of pronouns are *person, gender, number,* and *case.* For example, the pronoun *she* is a third-person pronoun, it expresses the female gender, and it refers to one person. As you can see, *person* identifies the pronoun, *gender* describes the sex of the pronoun, and *number* classifies the pronoun as singular or plural. A pronoun's case indicates how it is used in a sentence, as in the following examples.

She threw the ball.

She threw it.

She threw his ball over the fence.

In the first sentence, *she* is in the *subjective case* because *she* is the subject of the sentence: the one who performs an action. In the second sentence, *it* is in the *objective case* because this pronoun receives the subject's action. In the third sentence, *his* is in the *possessive case* because this pronoun indicates ownership.

Types of Pronouns

To select the right pronoun, ask yourself two questions: (1) What is the pronoun's case or function in the sentence? (2) What are the person, gender, and number of the noun (antecedent) that the pronoun either refers to or replaces? In addition, being able to identify a pronoun's type may aid your selection. Pronouns are classified according to eight types: *personal, possessive, demonstrative, reflexive, intensive, interrogative, relative,* and *indefinite.* Figure A-2.1 lists types of pronouns with explanations, examples, and uses.

EXERCISE 3   To check your understanding of pronouns, read the paragraph below and answer the questions that follow it. Use Figure A-2.1 as a reference.

> (1) Ellen wanted to do something different, so she decided to ask a friend to go with her to Busch Gardens. (2) Ellen's friend, Soo Yin, asked, "What is there to do at Busch Gardens?" (3) Ellen told her that the attraction had rides, jungle animals, food, and souvenirs. (4) "Those should be enough to keep us entertained," said Soo Yin. (5) "In fact," she said, "I'm always ready to do whatever comes along." (6) When they arrived at the gate, they saw some friends. (7) Ellen and Soo Yin decided to join them. (8) Then Soo Yin remembered that she had left her sweater in the car. (9) The air was a little chilly, and Ellen said, "Would you bring mine too?" (10) In a few minutes they caught up with the rest of the group, and everyone had a good time. (11) Ellen herself was glad she had suggested the trip.

1. List the personal pronouns in sentence 1.

2. Identify the interrogative pronoun in sentence 2.

3. To what group of words does *that* refer in sentence 3?

4. What kind of pronoun is *those* in sentence 4, and to what does it refer?

FIGURE A-2.1

Types of Pronouns

PRONOUN TYPE	EXPLANATION	EXAMPLES	USE
Personal	They replace nouns that name people or things.	I, you, he, she, it, we, they, me, him, her, us, them	Susan, the gift is perfect. I sent you a note about it.
Possessive	These pronouns show ownership.	my, mine, your, yours, his, hers, its, our, ours, their, theirs	This gift is yours. The other one is mine.
Demonstrative	They refer to certain people or things.	this, that, these, those	Whose book is this? (this refers to book.)
Reflexive	They indicate the subject (person or thing) acting on, by, or for itself.	myself, yourself, himself, herself, itself, ourselves, yourselves, themselves	John cut himself a piece of cake.
Intensive	The intensive pronoun is a reflexive pronoun used for emphasis.	any reflexive pronoun with antecedent in the same sentence	Stephen King himself spoke at our convention.
Interrogative	These pronouns are for asking questions.	who, whom, whoever, whomever, what, which, whose	Which one should I open first?
Relative	The relative pronouns are the same as the interrogatives but are used to relate groups of words to a noun or pronoun.	For people: who, whom, whoever, whomever, whose; For things: that, what, which, whatever	Where is the present that you gave me? Joe invited Carlos, who is my best friend.
Indefinite*	These pronouns have no antecedents but refer to people or things in general.	someone, many, few, another, everything, any, neither, most, something, all, both	I would love to date him, but I belong to another.

*For a more complete list of examples, see section D.1, page 491.

5. What are the antecedents of *she* (sentence 5), *they* (sentence 6), and *them* (sentence 7)?

6. Find the relative pronoun in sentence 5.

7. Find the possessive pronouns in sentences 8 and 9.

8. What is the indefinite pronoun in sentence 10?

9. What kind of pronoun is *herself* in sentence 11?

10. In which sentence do you find a second-person pronoun, and what is the pronoun?

A.3 VERBS

A *verb* is a word that expresses an action or a state of being. For example, *walk* is an action. You can visualize someone walking. On the other hand, *feel* or *seem* are verbs that describe states of being or conditions as in these sentences:

The child <u>seems</u> happy.

I <u>feel</u> tired today.

Notice the words on either side of the verbs in these sentences. The noun *child* and the pronoun *I* tell you whose condition is being described. The words *happy* and *tired* tell you what each condition is.

Types of Verbs

Verbs like *walk* are called *action verbs*. Verbs like *seem* and *feel* are called *linking verbs* because they link, or connect, the noun or pronoun with the words that describe it. In addition to action verbs and linking verbs, there are *helping verbs*, which are also called *auxiliary verbs*.

Helping verbs have two functions: Used with a main verb, a helping verb can express tense (the time an action or condition occurs) or form a question, as in the following examples:

I <u>have</u> mailed the letter. (a past action)

<u>Have</u> you mailed the letter? (a question)

To be complete, a sentence must have at least one verb. Leaving out the verb can result in a *fragment*, or incomplete sentence, one of the common types of errors students make. Therefore, it is important to

FIGURE A-3.1

Types of Verbs

Action Verbs	walk, run, see, fly, put, sit, catch, follow, flow, sing, dictate, deliver
Linking Verbs	all forms of *to be* (is, am, are, was, were, be, being, been), become, feel, grow, look, remain, seem
Helping Verbs	all forms of *to be,* have, has, had, do, does, did, can, could, may, might, must, shall, should, will, would

recognize verbs. Figure A-3.1 lists the three types of verbs and a few examples of each.

Verb Tense

Tense refers to the time period a verb represents, such as past, present, or future. Figure A-3.2 on page 423 gives examples of all the verb tenses. You do not need to memorize the grammatical terms for the tenses. They are listed here only to help you see that all the tenses except the simple present, past, and future require some form of the verbs *to be* or *to have* as helping verbs that precede the main verb.

A verb can be *regular* or *irregular. Regular verbs* form the past tense and the past participle—the form of the verb used with auxiliary verbs in the present perfect, past perfect, and future perfect tenses—by adding *-d* or *-ed* to the simple verb form:

Simple Verb	Simple Past Tense	Past Participle
expire	expired	expired
offend	offended	offended

Irregular verbs do not form the simple past tense and the past participle by adding *-d* or *-ed*. Instead, they change their spelling, often by changing an internal vowel:

Simple Verb	Simple Past Tense	Past Participle
feel	felt	felt
ring	rang	rung
bring	brought	brought

FIGURE A-3.2
Verb Tenses

TENSE	EXAMPLE (REGULAR VERBS)
Simple present	I *applaud.*
Simple past	I *applauded* yesterday.
Simple future	I will *applaud* this afternoon.
Present perfect	I have *applauded* before.
Past perfect	I had *applauded* for several days.
Future perfect	By tomorrow I *will have applauded* for twenty-two hours.
Present progressive	I *am applauding* now.
Past progressive	I *was applauding* last week.
Future progressive	I *will be applauding* when I go on vacation next month.
Present perfect progressive	I *have been applauding* all night.
Past perfect progressive	Before we left the theater, I *had been applauding* the actors.
Future perfect progressive	By the time you leave the theater, I *will have been applauding* for several minutes.

Figure A-3.3 on pages 424–425 lists some common irregular verbs with their simple-past and past-participle forms.

EXERCISE 4   In each of the following sentences, the verb is in the present tense. First, circle the verb in each sentence. Then rewrite the sentence in the tense indicated in parentheses. Use Figures A-3.2 and A-3.3 as needed for reference. The first sentence is done as an example.

FIGURE A-3.3

Some
Common
Irregular
Verbs

SIMPLE VERB	SIMPLE PAST TENSE	PAST PARTICIPLE
arise	arose	arisen
become	became	become
begin	began	begun
blow	blew	blown
break	broke	broken
build	built	built
choose	chose	chosen
cost	cost	cost
do	did	done
draw	drew	drawn
drink	drank	drunk
eat	ate	eaten
feed	fed	fed
fight	fought	fought

1. I take the math test. (simple future)

   I will take the math test next week.
2. The sculptor molds statues out of clay. (simple past)
3. The plane arrives at 8:00 P.M. (present progressive)
4. The Stuart Gallery shows the work of local artists. (present perfect)
5. Don Johnson produces *Nash Bridges*. (past perfect)
6. The secretary types the letter. (past perfect progressive)
7. I lie on the couch in the afternoon. (simple past)
8. The photographer develops his own film. (past progressive)

FIGURE A-3.3 (CONT.)

Some Common Irregular Verbs

SIMPLE VERB	SIMPLE PAST TENSE	PAST PARTICIPLE
fly	flew	flown
give	gave	given
have	had	had
hold	held	held
keep	kept	kept
know	knew	known
lay (to place)	laid	laid
lead	led	led
lie (to recline)	lay	lain
ride	rode	ridden
see	saw	seen
shake	shook	shaken
steal	stole	stolen
take	took	taken

9. My sister goes to church each Sunday. (simple future)

10. We choose only the ripest pears. (future progressive)

A.4 ADJECTIVES AND ADVERBS

Adjectives modify, or change, the meanings of nouns and pronouns by explaining what kind, which one, how many, or whose. Read the following sentences from Steven D. Stark's "Would Scarlett Accept 'First, Save Yourself'"?, and notice what the underlined adjectives tell you about the words they modify.

What kind?	"Both *Titanic* and *Gone With the Wind* center on the survival of <u>privileged</u>, <u>rebellious</u> heroines (played by <u>British</u> actresses), caught in a <u>tragic</u> love triangle."
Which one?	"The Civil War was <u>the</u> great event that forged this nation. . . ."
How many?	"<u>A few</u> nights aboard ship changed Rose's love life."
Whose?	". . . . it's clear that *Titanic* is the blockbuster film of <u>our</u> age."

Adverbs modify the meaning of verbs, adjectives, and other adverbs by explaining how, when, where, how often, or to what extent. Notice how Steven D. Stark uses the following adverbs in "Would Scarlett Accept 'First, Save Yourself'"?

How?	"'<u>Frankly</u>, my dear, I don't give a damn.'"
When?	"Each is set against the sweeping panorama of a well-known American historical event that occurred about 78 to 85 years <u>before</u> it was made."
Where?	"A few nights <u>aboard</u> ship changed Rose's love life."
How often?	". . . a musical soundtrack that features at least one song that can be played <u>endlessly</u> on MTV."
To what extent?	"The whole premise of *Gone With the Wind* is that the <u>most</u> meaningful relationships are those that can survive a lifetime of hardships. . . ."

Suppose you want to make a judgment that one job is more interesting than another, or one boss is easier to work with than another, or a decision to change jobs was the hardest one you have ever made? To write about these judgments, you have to use *degrees of comparison*. Adjectives and adverbs have three degrees of comparison: positive, comparative, and superlative:

Positive	To make no comparison	The job is *hard*.
Comparative	To compare two things: use *-er, more,* or *less*	This job is *harder* than that one. My job is *more* difficult than yours.
Superlative	To compare three or more things: use *-est, most,* or *least*	This is the *easiest* job I have ever had. This job is the *least* difficult one.

In the following sentence Steven D. Stark uses the superlative degree to suggest that, compared with other books, the book on which *Gone With the Wind* was based was the most popular book of all: "Finally, *Gone With the Wind* was based on the <u>most</u> popular book of its era." Practice using adjectives, adverbs, and degrees of comparison by completing the next two exercises.

EXERCISE 5

Read the following paragraph. Fill in the blanks with the proper adjectives and comparative forms. Choose from the list below:

dusty	darkest	bright	sharper	paler
youngest	quiet	narrow	healthiest	unfortunate
scariest	palest	musty	small	

Count Dracula lived in a 1 _____, _____ castle in a 2 _____ town in Hungary called Transylvania. Dracula was the 3 _____ vampire of them all. During the day, he slept in his 4 _____ box of earth because he could not stand the 5 _____ sunlight. At night he would roam the village looking for his most 6 _____ victims, the 7 _____ and 8 _____ women, who would become his brides. He would drink their blood by piercing two 9 _____ holes in their necks with fangs 10 _____ than steel. He might visit the same victim several nights in a row. The morning after the first bite, she would be drained of color. The next morning someone might say to her, "You have a 11 _____ face than usual." When the victim died from the loss of blood, someone would be sure to say, "That is the 12 _____ face I've ever seen." Of course the story of Count Dracula is only a legend, so you need not be afraid to go out even on the 13 _____ night.

EXERCISE 6 Read the following paragraph. Fill in the blanks with the proper adverbs and comparative forms. Choose from the list below:

slowly	carelessly	more easily	regularly
usually	carefully	more efficiently	lately
really	harder	extremely	

Andrea 1 _____ did well in math, but 2 _____ she was having trouble in her algebra class. She had not done the homework 3 _____ , so she was getting behind. Algebra was not an easy course for her. Maybe she needed to learn how to study 4 _____. Then she could do her homework 5 _____ and start to make better grades. Her instructor suggested that she work 6 _____ and 7 _____ when doing practice problems and proofread her work. He suggested that Andrea's errors were from working 8 _____. "You are 9 _____ quiet in class; perhaps you need to ask more questions," he said. "Well, there are some things I don't 10 _____ understand," Andrea answered. She decided to try 11 _____ to get over her fear of speaking in class.

Irregular Adjectives and Adverbs

Some adjectives and adverbs are *irregular;* that is, their comparative and superlative degrees are not formed in the usual way. Figure A-4.1 on page 429 lists the comparative and superlative degrees of some common irregular adjectives and adverbs. Words that have no comparative degrees are *unique, dead,* and *perfect.* Something that is unique is one of a kind. Since it takes two to make a comparison, it is not possible for one of a kind to be more or less unique. Similarly, it is not correct to say *this is the most perfect day I have ever seen.* The day is either perfect or not perfect; there is no degree of perfection. You may have heard the cliché "deader than a doornail." Not only is it a worn-out phrase, it is also illogical. Dead is dead; whatever is not dead is alive.

EXERCISE 7 Examine a piece of your own writing, either an essay that has been marked and returned to you or some work in progress. Underline all the adjectives and adverbs in one of your paragraphs. Correct any comparative forms that you have used incorrectly. Substitute better, more

FIGURE A-4.1

Comparison of Irregular Adjectives and Adverbs

POSITIVE	COMPARATIVE	SUPERLATIVE
bad	worse	worst
good	better	best
little	less	least
many	more	most
much	more	most
some	more	most

precise, or more interesting adjectives and adverbs for the ones you have underlined.

EXERCISE 8

Read the following paragraph and edit it for incorrect use of adjectives and adverbs.

It is more easier to flunk a course than to pass it if you remember three things: attendance, grades, and social life. First of all, when you wake up in the morning, just stay in bed. Something is sure to happen in class that will ruin your day. Since it is most beneficial to stay home or go to the beach than to attend class, your absence will put you more farther along the road to failure. Also, forget grades. Grades make you sweat. Getting good grades takes more harder work than making F's. You can make an F without any effort at all. Finally, everyone needs a social life. That is the most importantest reason for attending college in the first place. There is a newest saying that applies here: pass up a party and pass a test. Of course, if you insist on being a confident, successful student, just ignore everything I have said.

A.5 PREPOSITIONS

A *preposition* is one of many common words such as *in, out, over, under, beside,* or *within.* A *prepositional phrase* is a group of words that consists of a preposition plus its *object* (noun or pronoun). Prepositions and prepositional phrases link the object to the rest of the sentence. Prepositions have three characteristics.

1. They show relationships of time, space, direction, and condition.

> prep.   object
> The art festival occurs in the spring. (time)

> prep. object
> You can sit between us. (space)

> prep.   object
> He sunk the ball through the hoop. (direction)

> prep. object
> I like all vegetables except broccoli. (condition)

2. A preposition usually comes before its object as in the example sentences above. However, in some sentences the preposition follows the object as in the next two sentences.

> object   prep
> Love is something I cannot do without.

> object prep.
> Would you please let the cat in?

3. Prepositions that consist of more than one word are called *compound prepositions*. See Figure A-5.1 on page 421 for a list of some common and compound prepositions.

> compound prep. object
> The game was called because of rain. (condition)

EXERCISE 9   Underline prepositional phrases and label prepositions and objects in the following sentences excerpted from Robin Simmons's "Give Mine to the Birds" (page 150). In addition, explain the relationship each preposition or prepositional phrase suggests. The first one is done as an example.

> prep.   ——object———
> 1. "Initially, I would be repelled by the worms' unappetizing
>
>   ——object———
>   characteristics."
>
>   *The prepositional phrase explains what she would be repelled by.*

FIGURE A-5.1

Prepositions

COMMON PREPOSITIONS

against	down	past
along	during	since
among	except	through
around	for	till
at	from	to
before	in	toward
behind	near	under
below	of	underneath
beneath	off	until
beside	on	up
between	onto	upon
beyond	out	with
by	outside	within
despite	over	without

COMPOUND PREPOSITIONS

according to	in place of
aside from	in regard to
as of	in spite of
as well as	instead of
because of	on account of
by means of	out of
due to	prior to
in addition to	with regard to
in front of	with respect to

2. "I am not used to seeing my pork chops writhing on my plate, so wiggling worms would make me queasy."

3. "Because they are mucous-coated on the outside, they would slip around in my mouth, sliming my tongue."

4. "On the inside, worms are gritty from all the dirt in their digestive tract, so my teeth would grind annoyingly as I chewed."

5. "These colors remind me of chewing gum stuck to the undersides of school desks, a rather distasteful association."

6. "The last time I perused the meat section of Winn-Dixie, there were no cellophane-packaged worms snuggled between the chicken legs and cube steaks."

7. "Nor can I buy prepared worms at a deli as I do chicken salad and baked beans."

8. "Are worms most tasty scrambled with eggs for breakfast, chopped and sprinkled over ice cream, served as an appetizer on Hi Ho crackers, or heaped like fried onions on hot sandwiches?"

9. "I would similarly be shunned by my coworkers."

10. "Until McDonald's creates a McWorm item for its menu, I will leave worms for early birds."

A.6 CONJUNCTIONS

A *conjunction* connects words, phrases, or clauses. A *phrase* is a group of words that lacks a subject, predicate (verb plus auxiliaries), or both. A *clause* is a group of words that contains a subject and predicate. Clauses, phrases, and the uses of conjunctions are explained in greater detail in Section B. For now, let's review three types of conjunctions that provide you with numerous choices for connecting your ideas: *coordinating, correlative,* and *subordinating.*

The *coordinating conjunctions* are easy to remember because there are only seven: *for, and, nor, but, or, yet,* and *so.* The acronym FANBOYS, made from their first letters, will help you remember them. These conjunctions connect words or word groups of the same kind, for example, two nouns, two verbs, or two *independent clauses* (word groups that contain a subject and predicate and that can stand alone as complete in themselves). Coordinating conjunctions express relationships of addition, contrast, cause, effect, choice, and negative choice. To learn more about combining sentences with coordination, see Figure B-4.1 on pages 448–449.

We walk and swim each morning before breakfast. (*and* joins two verbs and relates them by *addition*)

You can take biology or physics to complete your program. (*or* joins two nouns and relates them by *choice*)

I would like to go to the movies with you, but I have to study. (*but* joins two independent clauses and relates them by *contrast*)

The *correlative conjunctions* work in pairs to link parts of a sentence that are alike. Some common correlative conjunctions are *either . . . or, neither . . . nor, both . . . and, not only . . . but also,* and *whether . . . or.* To learn more about correlation, see pages 495–497.

College graduates who can speak both English and another language may have an edge in tomorrow's workplace.

Either I have gained weight, or this shirt has shrunk.

The *subordinating conjunctions* introduce *dependent clauses* (those that cannot stand alone as sentences) and connect clauses. Subordinating conjunctions include such words as *after, because, that, if, although,* and *where.* Subordinating conjunctions express relationships of time, cause, effect, condition, contrast, location, and choice. To learn more about combining sentences with subordination, see section B.5, pages 450–457.

Although I want to go to the party, I have studying to do. (The clauses are related by *contrast*.)

You can usually find a fast-food restaurant wherever you travel in the United States. (The clauses are related by *location*.)

A.7 INTERJECTIONS

An *interjection* is a word or expression that indicates surprise or another strong emotion. When it stands alone, the interjection is punctuated with an exclamation point. Within a sentence, an interjection is set off by one or more commas. In formal writing, you should use interjections sparingly, if at all.

Wow! You look great.

Oh, it's you.

So, what else is new?

Hooray! I got an A on the test.

Well, I expected as much.

EXERCISE 10   In the following paragraph, identify the part of speech for each numbered and underlined word. Choose from: noun, pronoun, verb, adjective, adverb, preposition, conjunction, or interjection.

Savannah, Georgia, is a great place to spend a weekend. Several hotels and inns <u>along</u> the river offer tourists many opportunities for shopping
[1]
and dining. Whether <u>you</u> want a quick snack or a leisurely meal, you can
[2]
find a restaurant to suit your budget. The riverfront shops offer everything
from the usual t-shirts to the unusual custom kites and <u>handcrafted</u>
[3]
candles. If you have a sweet tooth, <u>try</u> a pecan praline from one of several
[4]   [5]
candy stores. Back at your hotel, step <u>out</u> on the balcony to watch the
[6]
huge oil tankers and barges <u>slowly</u> navigate the river. If outdoor activities
[7]
are your <u>passion</u>, rent a bicycle and pedal around Savannah's quaint
[8]
squares or spend a day at the beach. If tours turn you on, visit <u>historic</u>
mansions or the low country. Fans of John Berendt's bestseller *Midnight in
the Garden of Good and Evil* will enjoy a tour that explores the book's
[9]
points of interest. As one traveler remarked, "<u>Oh</u>, I've been here eleven
[10]
times, <u>and</u> I still haven't seen it all."

Section B
Sentence Effectiveness Choices

A *sentence* is a group of words that starts with a capital letter and ends with a period, question mark, or exclamation point. A sentence is a basic unit of meaning that contains a subject and predicate. A sentence is an *independent clause* that can stand alone as a unit of meaning. A sentence is a group of words, complete in itself, that needs no further explanation. These definitions describe the parts and functions of a sentence. You can also define a sentence by purpose and type.

Three things determine the effectiveness of your sentences: (1) the way you put together the parts of a sentence, (2) your choice of sentence types that can add interest and variety to your writing, and (3) your identification and elimination of surface errors that interfere with communication.

B.1   SENTENCE PARTS, PURPOSES, AND TYPES

A sentence has two basic parts: the *subject* and the *predicate*. To be complete, a sentence must have at least one subject and one predicate. The *subject* tells who or what the sentence is about. A sentence may have a *simple subject* (one) or a *compound subject* (more than one). The simple subject plus its modifiers is called the *complete subject*. The *predicate* tells what the subject is doing, what is happening to the subject, or what state of being the subject is in. The predicate contains one or more verbs and may include auxiliary (helping) verbs such as *has* or *have*. The *simple predicate* consists of the main verb plus auxiliaries. The *compound predicate* consists of two or more verbs joined by a conjunction.

In the following example sentences, subjects and predicates are underlined and annotated.

simple   simple
sub.   pred.
<u>Jade</u> <u>laughed</u>.

compound   simple
   sub.   pred.

Jade and Jake were laughing.

compound   simple
   sub.   pred.

Jade and Jake laughed and talked incessantly.

compound   simple
   sub.   pred.

The happy young couple decided to buy a house.

Purposes of Sentences

Sentences are classified according to purpose as indicated in Figure B-1.1.

EXERCISE 11   Underline and label the subjects and predicates in each of the following sentences.

1. Diana Ross and the Supremes performed throughout the United States and the world.

2. Today many fans of Elvis Presley still celebrate his birthday on January 8.

3. Every generation has its own music.

FIGURE B-1.1

Purposes of the Sentence

PURPOSE	EXPLANATION	EXAMPLE
DECLARATIVE	To make a statement	Tennis is a popular sport.
INTERROGATIVE	To ask a question	Do you play tennis?
IMPERATIVE	To make a request or give a command	Wear proper clothing on the court.
EXCLAMATORY	To express strong feeling	What a great serve!

4. Music brings people together and gives them something in common to share.

5. However, generations can be torn apart by differences of opinion concerning music.

6. Music appreciation courses explore different types of music and teach students how to evaluate them.

7. Similarly, their children often do not respond to music from the big band era.

8. Country music, on the other hand, has enjoyed a cross-generational appeal.

9. Many World War II generation parents cannot understand their children's music.

10. Who knows what the next musical trend will be?

Types of Sentences

Sentences are made up of *clauses* and *phrases* (word groups). Clauses can be *independent* or *dependent*. An independent clause contains a subject and predicate and can stand alone as a unit of meaning. A dependent clause also contains a subject and predicate, but it cannot stand alone. It must be connected to an independent clause to make complete sense. A *phrase* is a group of words that does not contain a subject and predicate. The number of clauses and how they are connected determines sentence type. There are four types of sentences: *simple, compound, complex,* and *compound-complex.*

Simple Sentence This type of sentence has one independent clause that contains at least one subject and one predicate. It may also contain one or more phrases.

$$\underline{\overset{\text{S} \quad \text{P}}{\text{Snow melts.}}}$$
independent clause

$$\underline{\text{In mud season,}} \ \underline{\text{the snow }\overset{\text{S}}{}\text{melts and }\overset{\text{compound pred.}}{\text{becomes slushy and dirty.}}}$$
  phrase   **independent clause**

Compound Sentence This type of sentence has at least two independent clauses but no dependent clauses. The clauses can be joined in three ways: with a comma plus coordinating conjunction (*and, but, nor, or, for, so,* or *yet*); with a semicolon and no conjunction; or with a semicolon plus conjunctive adverb (such as *however, next, instead*) followed by a comma. For more on compound sentences, see sections B.4, B.6, and C.5.

joined by coordinating conjunction

S P   S   P
I like to read mystery novels, (and) I especially enjoy Randy Wayne
   independent clause   independent

White's thrillers.
   clause

joined by semicolon

S P   S   P
I like to read mystery novels; I especially enjoy Randy Wayne
   independent clause   independent

White's thrillers.
   clause

joined by conjunctive adverb

S P   S   P
I like to read mystery novels; (moreover,) I especially enjoy Randy Wayne
   independent clause   independent

White's thrillers.
   clause

Complex Sentence This type of sentence has one independent clause and one or more dependent clauses. In a complex sentence, a subordinating conjunction (such as *after, although,* and *since*) or a relative pronoun (such as *who, whom, that,* or *what*) is used to connect clauses. For more on complex sentences, see sections B.5 and B.6.

subordinating conjunction

She likes to watch television while she exercises
   independent clause   dependent clause

relative pronoun

The treadmill belongs to Maria, who won it in a contest.
   independent clause   dependent clause

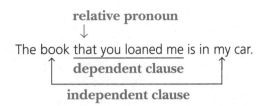

relative pronoun
↓
The book that you loaned me is in my car.
      dependent clause
independent clause

Compound-Complex Sentence This type of sentence has at least two independent clauses and one or more dependent clauses.

subordinating conjunction   coordinating conjunction
↓   ↓
While my father was in the hospital, he quit smoking, and he lost several
    dependent clause   independent clause   independent
pounds
    clause

EXERCISE 12   Apply what you have learned about independent and dependent clauses and sentence types. Combine each pair of sentences below into one sentence. The first one is done as an example.

1. The forecast is for warm dry weather.
   I think I will go to the beach.

   The forecast is for warm dry weather, so I think I will go to

   the beach.

2. Terry sings in the church choir.
   Terry plays a clarinet in the university band.

3. My car has 50,000 miles on it.
   My car is in perfect shape.

4. Chris fought learning to use a computer.
   Chris couldn't get along without it now.

5. The concert was cancelled.
   Hundreds of angry fans protested.

6. I am definitely not a morning person.
   Eight A.M. classes are not for me.

B.2 ELIMINATING SENTENCE FRAGMENTS

Clear and complete sentences are essential to good writing. Complete sentences effectively communicate ideas; incomplete sentences do not. Being able to recognize an incomplete sentence and knowing how to correct it will make you a more confident writer. An incomplete sentence is called a *fragment* because it is only part of an idea and is not complete in itself. Read the fragment below:

Because I could not get up this morning.

This fragment is a dependent clause. By itself, it does not express a complete thought. If you were to walk up to a friend of yours and say, "Because I couldn't get up this morning," your friend would probably look puzzled and say something like "So?" or "because of what?" Your friend would be left hanging because you had not completed your thought. To complete the thought, you must connect the fragment to an independent clause.

dependent clause   **independent clause**
Because I could not get up this morning, I was late for work.

independent clause   **dependent clause**
I missed breakfast because I could not get up this morning.

Three features make a sentence complete: a *subject,* a *verb* (*predicate*), and a *complete thought*. If one or more of these elements is missing, a fragment results. Remember that the *subject* tells *who* or *what* the sentence is about. The *verb* tells what the subject is doing or what is happening to the subject. A thought is *complete* if it communicates an idea that needs no further explanation.

Relative pronouns such as *who, which, that,* and *what* and subordinating conjunctions such as *because, although,* and *while* often appear at the beginning of a dependent clause and serve to connect it to an independent clause. When you edit your essays, reread any sentence that begins with one of these words to check it for completeness. See the following examples:

What the dentist told me.

This is a dependent clause beginning with a relative pronoun, and it is a fragment.

What the dentist told me is to floss every day.

What the dentist told me is a dependent clause that acts as the *subject* of an independent clause, so the sentence is complete.

Although I am very tired.

A dependent clause that begins with a subordinating conjunction is a fragment.

Although I am very tired, I will go to the movie with you.

The dependent clause *although I am very tired* is now connected to an independent clause, so the sentence is complete.

Another way to correct dependent clause fragments such as the ones in these examples is to remove the relative pronoun or subordinating conjunction if the group of words that follows can stand by itself as a sentence:

~~That~~ a great place to take children is Disney World.

~~Although~~ I am very tired.

Now the sentences are complete because they contain subject and verb, and the ideas they express are complete in themselves.

To correct a sentence fragment, determine whether you need to add a subject or a verb to complete the thought. Figure B-2.1 lists features of a sentence and questions that can help identify them. Figure B-2.2 shows you how to correct a fragment by adding the missing feature needed to make a complete sentence.

FIGURE B-2.1

Identifying the Features of a Sentence

FEATURES	QUESTIONS TO ASK YOURSELF
Subject	*Who* or *what* is the sentence about?
Verb	What is the subject *doing, feeling,* or *being*? What is *happening* to the subject?
Complete thought	What *idea* is communicated? Is the idea *complete*? Does the sentence begin with a *subordinating conjunction* or a *relative pronoun: when, because, who,* etc.?

EXERCISE 13

Test each of the word groups below for completeness. If a word group is a complete sentence, leave it alone. If you find any fragments, rewrite them to make them into complete sentences.

1. Because the car had 80,000 miles on it.

2. She needed to return the books to the library.

3. Such as hunting, fishing, and hiking.

4. That met in the auditorium last week.

FIGURE B-2.2

Making Fragments into Complete Sentences

FRAGMENT	WHAT IS MISSING?	COMPLETE SENTENCE
Tourists from all over the world.	A *verb* is missing. What do the tourists *do*?	Tourists from all over the world *come* to New Orleans.
Sing and dance in the streets.	A *subject* is missing. *Who* or *what* sing and dance?	*People* dressed in brightly colored costumes sing and dance in the streets
When the King and Queen are crowned.	The *thought* is incomplete. What *explanation* is needed?	*Everyone celebrates* when the King and Queen are crowned.

5. So many obligations and responsibilities.

6. Working and attending classes at the same time.

7. What the dog needed most.

8. Not wanting to let them down.

9. Since he had always been a procrastinator.

10. If you do not study for the exam.

EXERCISE 14   The following paragraph contains five sentence fragments. Underline them, decide what is missing, then rewrite the paragraph so that there are no fragments.

> Luis and Silvana went mountain climbing in the Andes. Their trip took three weeks. They had to plan ahead and take enough food, water, and other supplies. Because there were no stores where they were going. They, another couple, and their two guides could not carry enough supplies for the six of them. A helicopter to drop off supplies at certain points along the way. Temperatures were often below zero. At night, they had to build a wall of snow to protect their tents from the wind. Once when Luis was walking across a frozen river. The ice cracked, and he fell into the freezing water. Silvana and the others helped him remove his wet clothes. Wrapped him in sleeping bags until his clothes could dry, and then they resumed their journey. At the top of the mountain, they laughed, cried, and hugged each other. Rested before the long trip back down.

B.3 ELIMINATING FUSED SENTENCES AND COMMA SPLICES

When you edit your essays, you need to proofread them to find and correct any errors. Two errors to check for are the *fused* sentence and the *comma splice*. You should strive to eliminate these errors from *all* your writing. A *fused* sentence is one that contains two or more independent clauses without any mark of punctuation to separate them. Read the next sentence:

> Yvette spent the whole day registering for classes she did not even have time for lunch.

A *comma splice* error occurs when one sentence contains two or more independent clauses, and they are incorrectly separated by a comma. Read the sentence again.

> Yvette spent the whole day registering for classes, she did not even have time for lunch.

With or without the comma, the sentence expresses *two* complete thoughts:

1. Yvette spent the whole day registering for classes.

2. She did not even have time for lunch.

One way to correct a fused sentence or to eliminate a comma splice is to *state each complete thought in a separate sentence* as in the example above. Suppose, however, that you think it would be more effective to express both these ideas about Yvette in one sentence; there is a correct way to connect them. The chart in Figure B-3.1 on pages 445–446 explains five ways to correct fused sentences and comma splices.

As a writer, you are free to choose the method of correction you prefer. Do not get stuck on any one method, however. To add some variety to your writing, experiment with all the ways to correct your sentences. It *does* matter which conjunctions or relative pronouns you use to connect two complete thoughts or to connect a dependent clause to an independent clause. For one thing, determine how one thought relates to another; also, learn what each conjunction means so you can choose the best one. For more on conjunctions and how to use them, see sections B.4 and B.5.

EXERCISE 15

The first sentence below is a fused sentence; the second one contains a comma splice. Rewrite each sentence five different ways so that you can try all five ways to correct the sentences. When you finish, you will have a total of ten sentences. Refer to the chart in Figure B-3.1 for help.

1. Mark stayed up all night cramming for a statistics test it didn't cover what he had studied.

2. Linda was well prepared for the test, she was sure she had made an A or a B.

FIGURE B-3.1

Five Ways to Correct Fused Sentences and Comma Splices

1. Use a period to separate complete thoughts within a fused sentence or sentence containing a comma splice.

    Fused: Reynaldo got off the Metro at the wrong stop he had to walk several blocks to the museum.

    Comma splice: Reynaldo got off the Metro at the wrong stop, he had to walk several blocks to the museum.

    Correct: Reynaldo got off the Metro at the wrong stop. He had to walk several blocks to the museum.

2. Make a compound sentence by using a comma + a coordinating conjunction (*for, and, nor, but, or, yet, so*) to connect complete thoughts.

    Reynaldo got off the Metro at the wrong stop, **so** he had to walk several blocks to the museum.

3. Make a compound sentence by using a semicolon to connect complete thoughts that are closely related.

    Reynaldo got off the Metro at the wrong stop; he had to walk several blocks to the museum.

4. Make a compound sentence by using a semicolon + conjunctive adverb + comma to connect complete thoughts. (*however, therefore, furthermore, instead, in addition, also, moreover, as a result, consequently*, etc., are conjunctive adverbs.)

    Reynaldo got off the Metro at the wrong stop; **therefore,** he had to walk several blocks to the museum.

5. Make a complex sentence by using a subordinating conjunction (*because, since, although, after, when, before, until, as, that, if, unless*) or relative pronoun (*who, which, that*) to create a dependent clause and connect it to the independent clause.

**FIGURE B-3.1
(cont.)**

**Five Ways to
Correct Fused
Sentences and
Comma
Splices**

First use a subordinating conjunction to create a dependent clause:

Because Reynaldo got off the Metro at the wrong stop . . .

Then connect the dependent clause to the independent clause:

Because Reynaldo got off the Metro at the wrong stop, he had to walk several blocks to the museum.

HINT: Always put a comma after the dependent clause when you connect it to an independent clause.

EXERCISE 16

Read the following paragraph and edit it for fused sentences and comma splices.

> The electricity went off at my house several inconvenient things happened. My clock is electric, so the alarm did not go off luckily I wake up at about 5:30 every morning anyway. I had to take a cold shower, that was not the worst of it I could not use my blow dryer. "A good breakfast will make up for everything," I thought. I had forgotten that the stove and coffeemaker would not work without electricity, I had to go to class without my coffee. It looked like rain outside, but there was no way to know for sure I could not tune in The Weather Channel on TV. On the way to work, I realized that I take electricity and many other things I use every day for granted I expect them to always be there. Now our state officials are telling us we have to conserve water I have already started.

B.4 SENTENCE COMBINING: COORDINATION

As you revise your essays, you may find opportunities for sentence combining. Sometimes the ideas expressed in two separate sentences may be more effectively stated in a compound sentence that combines the ideas. One way to create a compound sentence is by *coordination*. The term *coordination* comes from a Latin word meaning "of equal rank." When you use coordination to combine independent clauses of equal importance, you join them with connecting words called *coordinating conjunctions*.

There are seven coordinating conjunctions: *for, and, nor, but, or, yet,* and *so.* Each of the coordinating conjunctions establishes a different relationship between the independent clauses. Your choice of which coordinating conjunction to use thus depends on the relationship you want to express. For example, *for* and *so* establish a cause-and-effect relationship. *For* introduces a reason; *so* introduces a result. Suppose you wrote the following two sentences:

1. Today would be a good day to go to the beach.

2. The weather is clear and sunny.

You can combine the sentences to establish a cause-and-effect relationship between the weather and a good day at the beach by joining them with either *for* or *so:*

reason

1. Today would be a good day to go to the beach, <u>for</u> the weather is clear and sunny.

result

2. The weather is clear and sunny, <u>so</u> today would be a good day to go to the beach.

In each sentence, the good weather is the *cause,* or reason; the *effect,* or result, of the good weather is that today is a good day to go to the beach.

Note that both sentences have a *comma* before the coordinating conjunction. When you use a coordinating conjunction to combine independent clauses, *put a comma before the coordinating conjunction.* This is rule 5 of the six rules for using commas explained in section C.6 on pages 475–480.

Figure B-4.1 on pages 448–449 shows how to use the seven coordinating conjunctions. Study the chart, paying special attention to the relationship each conjunction creates between the two independent clauses in each sentence. Then complete Exercises 17 and 18.

EXERCISE 17   Combine each pair of sentences on page 449 into one sentence. First, decide how the sentences are related. Then connect them by using an appropriate coordinating conjunction. Refer to Figure B-4.1 if you need help remembering the conjunctions or the relationships they imply.

FIGURE B-4.1

Coordinating Conjunctions and Sentence Relationships

CONJUNCTION	RELATIONSHIP	EXAMPLE SENTENCE
For	cause and effect (reason)	Lupe was excited about the party, for she had not been to one in a long time. (The fact that Lupe had not been to a party in a while was the *cause* of her excitement.)
And	addition	Carlos and Janet gave a party, and they invited all their friends. (Giving a party and inviting friends *add* up to two *equally* important things that Carlos and Janet did.)
Nor	no choice	Jackie said she didn't want to eat inside, nor did she want to eat outside. (Jackie made *no choice* between eating inside or outside.)
But	exception, contrast	Kurt hoped that he would be back in town in time for the party, but he did not think he could make it. (The fact that Kurt did not think he could make it is an *exception* to his hope that he would.)
Or	choice	Party guests could select items from the buffet and eat inside, or they could take their food outside. (Guests could make a choice to eat either inside or outside.)

FIGURE B-4.1

Coordinating Conjunctions and Sentence Relationships

CONJUNCTION	RELATIONSHIP	EXAMPLE SENTENCE
Yet	exception, contrast	Lucious said he would not be at the party, yet he showed up anyway. (Lucious came to the party *in contrast* to what he said.)
So	cause and effect (result)	Jack arrived at the party fifteen minutes before it was scheduled to begin, so he was the first one there. (Being the first one at the party was the *result* of arriving fifteen minutes early.)

1. Robert B. Parker is a popular writer of detective novels. Most of his books are about Spenser, a private eye.

2. Spenser lives and works in Boston, Massachusetts. His work often takes him to other states.

3. Susan Silverman is Spenser's girlfriend. Hawk is Spencer's associate and a good friend.

4. Susan and Hawk must be regular characters in the stories. They would not appear in all the novels.

5. Susan is a psychiatrist. She does not always understand what motivates Spenser.

6. Spenser would not think of getting out of shape. Hawk would not think of getting out of shape.

7. Cooking is another of Spenser's accomplishments. He can put a meal together on short notice.

8. In *Pastime* Parker introduced Pearl, Spenser's dog. Following novels have included her.

9. Parker's mysteries are also travel guides. They inform readers about restaurants and other places of interest in Boston.

EXERCISE 18   Complete the sentences by adding your own independent clause after the comma and coordinating conjunction.

1. I have a pet boa constrictor, *and* . . .
2. I would love to sing at your wedding, *but* . . .
3. This cellular telephone does not work anymore, *so* . . .
4. Rick would either like to be a trapeze artist, *or* . . .
5. Myra wore a sequined cat-suit to the party, *yet* . . .
6. I cannot afford a new car right now, *for* . . .
7. The children did not want to go to the zoo, *nor* . . .
8. Please do not go bungee jumping today, *for* . . .
9. The job I really want would give me plenty of vacation time, *and* . . .
10. While rummaging in the attic, Mark found his old tuxedo, which was now too small, *so* . . .

EXERCISE 19   Most of the sentences in the following paragraph are short and choppy. Using coordinating conjunctions, combine some of them to create a more effective paragraph.

> For a long time, I refused to use a computer. I thought typing was easier and faster. I did not think a computer could do anything my typewriter could not do. I was wrong. I discovered word processing. Now typographical errors are no problem. I can erase with the touch of a key. I am through with messy liquid correcting fluid and crumbly erasers. If I want to take out a paragraph, I do not have to retype the whole page. I especially like the spell-check feature. I miss some errors when proofreading. The computer finds them for me. Word processing has saved me hours of time. I will never go back to typing.

B.5 SENTENCE COMBINING: SUBORDINATION

Subordination involves joining two clauses in such a way that one clause is clearly more important than the other. One clause remains independent, and the other is joined to it by a connecting word that shows the second clause is subordinate to, or dependent on, the main, independent clause. The resulting sentence is a *complex sentence.* The connecting word can be either a *subordinating conjunction* or a *relative pronoun,* and it always introduces the dependent clause.

The most common subordinating conjunctions are:

although	provided that
as	since
as if	so that
as long as	than
as though	though
because	until
before	when
even though	where
if	wherever
in order that (to)	whether
once	while

The meaning of the subordinating conjunction you choose establishes how the dependent and independent clauses are related. Figure B-5.1 on page 452 lists six commonly used subordinating conjunctions—*because, since, so that* and *in order that* establish cause-and-effect relationships between the dependent and independent clauses. *Because* and *since* introduce a reason; *so that* and *in order that* introduce a result. Suppose you wrote the following two sentences:

1. I am going to wash my car.

2. It is dirty.

You can combine the sentences to establish a cause-and-effect relationship between the two ideas by subordinating one of them with *because* or *since.* The examples below show two ways you can do this. The dependent clause is underlined.

1. <u>Because it is dirty</u>, I am going to wash my car.

2. I am going to wash my car <u>since it is dirty</u>.

FIGURE B-5.1

Subordinating Conjunctions and Sentence Relationships

CONJUNCTION	RELATIONSHIP	EXAMPLE SENTENCE
After	Following	Carlos and Janet began cleaning up *after* the guests went home. (Cleaning up is an act that *followed* when the guests left.)
How	Process	Carlos and Janet did not know *how* they would get the spots out of the carpet. (The *process* they would use to get the spots out is what they didn't know.)
Even though	Although	Carlos started cleaning now *even though* he would rather wait until later. (Carlos will do the cleaning *although* he would rather wait.)
Unless	Except	*Unless* Janet agreed to help, Carlos would have to finish by himself. (Janet's agreeing to help would be an *exception* to Carlos's having to finish by himself.)
Whenever	Indefinite time	Janet said she would make breakfast *whenever* they got finished. (Janet will fix breakfast at some *indefinite time* in the future.)
While	During, at the same time	*While* Janet worked on the spots in the carpet, Carlos vacuumed the furniture. (Cleaning the spots took place *during* the vacuuming of the carpet.)

In both sentences, "dirty" is the *cause* of the *effect* of washing the car. Also, "I am going to wash my car" is the most important idea, and "because it is dirty" is subordinate to it. *The independent clause always states the most important idea. The dependent clause states the subordinate, or less important idea.* It does not matter whether the dependent clause begins the sentence or ends it; the idea expressed in the dependent clause is still *subordinate* to, or *less important* than, the idea expressed in the independent clause. Also, when the dependent clause is at the beginning of the sentence, a *comma* follows it. If the dependent clause comes at the end of the sentence, there is *no comma* before the subordinating conjunction.

The next example illustrates how to combine the four sentences below into one sentence by using a subordinating conjunction. The dependent clause is underlined.

1. The Weather Channel predicts a hurricane.
2. The hurricane is coming this way.
3. Residents should prepare for the storm.
4. Residents should buy candles, canned goods, flashlight batteries, and bottled water.

<u>Because the Weather Channel predicts that a hurricane is coming this way</u>, residents should prepare for the storm by buying candles, canned goods, flashlight batteries, and bottled water.

The new sentence is more effective than the four original sentences because it eliminates repetitive words and phrases.

When combining sentences, it is all right to change the wording or eliminate some words as long as the new sentence has the same meaning as the original group of sentences. Also, there are many possibilities for combining sentences. Although you and someone else might combine a group of sentences in entirely different ways, both of your new sentences might be equally effective.

EXERCISE 20

Combine each pair of sentences into one sentence by using subordination.

1. a. Mid-May through mid-November is hurricane season in Florida.

   b. Florida residents prepare for the season.

2. a. Florida residents keep track of the weather.

   b. Florida residents use a hurricane tracking map or watch the local weather forecast on television.

3. a. Hardware stores stock hurricane supplies.

   b. Hardware stores usually run out of supplies.

4. a. Hurricanes used to have women's names, such as Donna or Alice.

   b. Hurricanes now have men's names, such as Hugo or Andrew.

5. a. Naming hurricanes only after women was considered sexist.

   b. Men's names were added to avoid sexism.

EXERCISE 21   Combine each group of sentences into one sentence by using subordination.

1. a. Nancy wants an unusual pet.

   b. Macaws are unusual.

   c. Macaws are a kind of parrot.

   d. Nancy is going to buy a macaw.

2. a. Electric eels live in South America.

   b. Electric eels carry a charge that is equal to about 160 volts.

   c. Electric eels can defend themselves against predators.

3. a. Dragonflies are harmless to humans.

   b. Dragonflies are useful.

   c. Dragonflies eat mosquitoes.

   d. Dragonflies have been used in research that has led to improvements in aircraft.

4. a. Roaches do not live only in filthy places.

   b. Hospitals have to exterminate roaches.

   c. Many clean, respectable restaurants have to exterminate roaches.

   d. Roaches are not choosy about where they live.

When a *relative pronoun* joins clauses in a relationship of subordination, the dependent clause is called a *relative clause*. The information contained in the relative clause is less important than that in the independent clause. Following is a list of the most commonly used relative pronouns and when to use them:

who	refers to people
that	usually refers to things but can refer to people
which	refers to things

If the relative clause comes at the end of the sentence, a comma precedes the relative pronoun only if the information contained in the clause can be omitted with no loss in meaning. If the information is essential, however, then no comma precedes the relative pronoun. When the relative clause interrupts the independent clause, and if the clause contains nonessential information, it is surrounded by commas. The annotated examples below illustrate these features of the relative clause within a relationship of subordination.

1. Betty Friedan, who has been called the mother of the women's movement, wrote *The Feminine Mystique.*

2. *Iron John,* which is a best-selling book by Robert Bly, is a male's response to feminism.

3. The first women who became members of the National Organization for Women were pioneers in women's rights.

4. *The Feminine Mystique* is the book that started the feminist movement.

5. Can you name the woman who was the first president of the National Organization for Women?

In the first two sentences, the relative clauses *interrupt* the independent clauses. The relative clauses in each of these sentences contain information not essential to the meaning of the sentence, so they are surrounded by commas. In the first sentence, the relative clause is nonessential because the independent clause names the woman who is the subject of the sentence. The relative clause in the second sentence is nonessential because the independent clause names the book that is the subject of the sentence.

In the third sentence, unlike sentences 1 and 2, the relative clause that modifies the independent clause does contain essential information that you need to identify the women who were pioneers. Commas do not surround this clause.

In the fourth and fifth sentences, the relative clauses *follow* the independent clauses. In the fourth sentence, there is no comma at the beginning of the relative clause because the information it contains is essential to the meaning of the independent clause. The relative clause specifies the book's importance. In the fifth sentence, the relative clause is essential because it provides information needed to identify the women referred to in the independent clause. You do not need a comma before the relative clause in the fifth sentence.

EXERCISE 22   Use relative pronouns to combine the following sentences. Add commas where necessary.

1. Mary McCarthy is an author.
   Mary McCarthy wrote *The Group*.

2. *The Group* is about a group of young women.
   The women go to the same college.

3. Some colleges used to be men's colleges.
   These colleges now admit women.

4. I remember the old chapel.
   The old chapel has been torn down.

5. Beverages are not permitted in the department store.
   Beverages are permitted in the lounge.

EXERCISE 23   Most of the sentences in the following paragraph are short and choppy. Using subordinating conjunctions, combine some of the sentences to create a more effective paragraph. Also, add transitions where necessary to give your paragraph coherence.

Ireland is a great place to spend a vacation. Most people travel in southern Ireland. Southern Ireland has rocky coastlines, scattered villages, castles, and other interesting sights to see. The Cliffs of Mohr are a breathtaking sight. It is a long walk to the edge of the cliffs. It is a steep drop from the cliffs to the ocean. Waves thunder against the cliffs. Taking a country drive is like stepping back in time. A farmer will stop traffic to take his herd of sheep across the road. Thatch-roofed cottages dot the countryside. Northern Ireland is also an interesting place. Not many tourists go into northern Ireland. They have heard about the IRA activity there. They miss an opportunity to see another part of the country. White's Island is the site of pre-Christian ruins. This remote island is accessible only by boat. You can rent a small rowboat from a farmer. He lives across the lake from the island. There is nothing on the island but the ruins and grazing cattle. The silence and natural beauty add to the enchantment of the place. Some tourists believe that a trip into northern Ireland is worth the trouble and the risk.

B.6 EXPANDING YOUR SENTENCES: PHRASES AND CLAUSES

As you write and rewrite, sentences will become the focus of much of your revision: how to change, rearrange, combine, and correct them so that they express your ideas clearly and effectively. One way to get more detail into your sentences is to expand subjects and predicates by adding descriptive words, phrases, and clauses.

Phrases

Expanding subjects and predicates by adding words, phrases, and clauses gives you still more choices as a writer. A *phrase* is a group of words that is not a sentence because it lacks either one or both of the two basic parts: subject and predicate. To be a phrase the group of words must function together as a single part of speech. Phrases can function as nouns, verbs, adjectives, or adverbs. If a phrase explains *who* or *what*, it acts as a *noun*. Phrases that explain *which* or *what kind* function as *adjectives*. A phrase that tells *when, where,* or *how* functions as an *adverb*.

Phrases add detail to your sentences. The following examples explain several types of phrases and illustrate how they function in sentences:

Prepositional phrases	They begin with prepositions: *for, to, around, through, over,* etc. They describe relationships such as time, place, or direction.

After failing to stop, Maria's car skidded into a telephone pole.

Both phrases are functioning as *adverbs*, telling *when* and *where* the car skidded.

Verbal phrases	They are forms of verbs that cannot stand alone as the main verb of a sentence. They act as nouns, adjectives, or adverbs.

Maria decided <u>to call a wrecker</u>.

The phrase functions as a *noun* explaining *what* Maria decided.

<u>Tired and depressed</u>, Maria wondered how she would get to work the next day.

The phrase functions as an *adjective* describing Maria.

<u>Getting the car fixed</u> was the only thing on Maria's mind.

The phrase functions as a *noun* describing *what* Maria was thinking.

An absolute phrase	Contains a noun or pronoun, *-ing* or *-ed* verb form, and modifiers. It frequently modifies an entire sentence rather than a single word.

<u>The car having been hauled away</u>, Maria waited for her sister to pick her up.

The phrase modifies the whole sentence, explaining why Maria had to wait.

The car was a mess, its windshield <u>smashed into pieces</u> and its front end <u>crushed to bits</u>.

These phrases function as adjectives, describing what happened to the windshield and front end.

Appositive phrase	Placed next to a noun or pronoun to identify or rename it, the appositive phrase acts as a noun modifying another noun.

Maria, <u>a college student</u>, did not know where she would get the money to pay for the car.

The phrase identifies Maria. It is a nonrestrictive phrase since it does not add essential information to the sentence. Nonrestrictive phrases are set off with commas.

> Maria went home and read the book *Sex, Drink, & Fast Cars* by Stephen Bayley.

The phrase identifies the book's title. It is a restrictive phrase because it provides essential information; therefore, the phrase is *not* set off with commas.

Remember that a phrase is a group of words, acting together as a single part of speech that cannot stand alone as a sentence because it lacks either a subject, predicate, or both. Phrases are sentence expanders that add interest and detail to your sentences.

EXERCISE 24   Expand each of the following sentences by adding phrases.

1. The telephone rang. (Add a *verbal phrase* that tells how the phone rang.)

2. Toby sounded angry. (Add an *appositive phrase* that tells who Toby is.)

3. I gave Lisa the phone. (Add an *appositive phrase* that tells who Lisa is.)

4. She slammed it down. (Add a *verbal phrase* that describes how she slammed it down.)

5. I turned on the answering machine. (Add an *absolute phrase* that describes how the machine was turned on.)

6. Lisa turned it off. (Add a *prepositional phrase* that tells *when* she turned the machine off.)

Clauses

Clauses are a group of words containing a subject and a predicate. There are two types: *independent* and *dependent* (or *subordinate*).

Independent clause   It can stand alone as a sentence because it expresses a complete thought.

> Amigos is a new Mexican restaurant.

Dependent (subordinate) clause	It cannot stand alone as a sentence because the thought it expresses requires completion or connection to something more.

that opened in our neighborhood

The following sentence shows the relationship of an independent and a dependent clause:

independent clause   **dependent clause**

My brother owns the restaurant that opened in our neighborhood.

The dependent clause explains which restaurant my brother owns.

Dependent clauses usually begin with a relative pronoun (such as *which, that, what, whatever, who, whose, whom, whoever,* and *whomever*) or a subordinating conjunction (such as *after, because, rather than,* and *when*). Section B.5 explains how to use these conjunctions and others like them to establish relationships within sentences. The following examples illustrate how to use dependent clauses to expand your sentences:

1. Maria wants a car. (unexpanded independent clause)

   Maria wants a car that gets good gas mileage and has a high safety rating.
   dependent clause

The dependent clause expands the sentence by telling you what kind of car Maria wants.

2. Maria wants a Volvo. (unexpanded independent clause)

   dependent clause   **dependent**

   Because safety is a high priority, Maria wants a Volvo that has a high safety rating.

   clause

The first dependent clause explains why Maria wants a Volvo. The second dependent clause describes the Volvo.

3. Maria will buy a Volvo. (unexpanded independent clause)

dependent clause

When she wins the lottery, Maria will buy a Volvo.

The dependent clause explains when Maria will buy a Volvo.

Notice how in the three examples above, adding dependent clauses expands the original sentences by adding information to them.

EXERCISE 25

Expand the sentences by adding clauses either at the beginning or the end as indicated in the examples above.

1. A good friend is one *who*...

2. I would like to have a car *that*...

3. *Until*... I will have to put up with his behavior.

4. *When*... the kitchen flooded.

5. I believe I will get the job *because*...

EXERCISE 26

Working with a partner, read the following paragraph. Identify phrases and clauses the writer has used to expand the basic sentence parts of subject and predicate.

My cousin, Ned, is a great swimmer. The first summer he visited us in Florida, he saved a girl from drowning in the ocean. We had spent the morning at the beach. In the afternoon, Ned was sunbathing beside me when a young girl started splashing in the water. Then she started waving her arms over her head. She would disappear under the water, then come up to the surface. At first, we thought she was playing. Through his binoculars, Ned could see that she was in trouble. Ned raced to the water and dove into the waves. He swam hand over hand in long strokes until he reached her. She was almost drowned. After he got her on shore, he gave her mouth-to-mouth resuscitation, breathing air into her lungs. Fortunately, she revived. She said my cousin had saved her life. Ned said it was his swimming ability that had saved them both. He had taken a lifesaving course and knew how to keep her head above the water while slowly working his way back to shore. The girl's parents offered him money, but he would not take it. To that girl, Ned was more than a great swimmer. He was a hero.

B.7 VARYING YOUR SENTENCES

You can improve your style by writing sentences that are more interesting and varied. To achieve sentence variety, try these four common methods:

1. Use a variety of sentence lengths.
2. Use a variety of sentence types.
3. Use a variety of sentence beginnings.
4. Use a variety of sentence relationships.

Use a Variety of Sentence Lengths

Sentences are either short, medium, or long. The best short sentences are simple and direct. Though too many may make your writing sound choppy and monotonous, a few carefully placed ones can give your writing balance and help you emphasize important ideas. Medium-length sentences occur most frequently, probably because it seems logical and more effective to combine related ideas from two or more simple sentences into one sentence. Long sentences are detail filled and can help clarify complex ideas and relationships. However, too many of them may make your writing seem unnecessarily wordy. The four previous sentences in this paragraph illustrate all three sentence lengths. The first two sentences are short; the third and fourth sentences are long, and the fifth and sixth sentences are medium. Following are additional examples. The first sentence is from Donald Murray's essay on pages 180–183, and the second and third sentences are from Robin Simmons's essay on page 150.

Short	"We fear that writing will prove us ignorant."
Medium	"I am not used to seeing my pork chops writhing on my plate, so wiggling worms would make me queasy."
Long	"Are worms most tasty scrambled with eggs for breakfast, chopped and sprinkled over ice cream, served as an appetizer on Hi-Ho crackers, or heaped like fried onions on hot sandwiches?"

Should you have an equal mix of short, medium, and long sentences in your essays? Not necessarily: short sentences are characteristic of Ernest Hemingway's bold, spare style. Another of America's greatest writers, William Faulkner, favored long sentences. They seemed to fit the complexity of his stories and his characters' lives. Sentence length is as much a part of the writing style of the nonfiction writer as it is of the fiction writer. The editorial pages of the newspaper contain the work of many fine writers: Bob Greene, George Will, Ellen Goodman, Barbara Erenreich, and William Raspberry, to name a few. Though their writing differs in other ways, these writers use more medium-length sentences than short or long. Goodman and Raspberry use short sentences for emphasis, often near the end of their pieces. Erenreich's and Will's long sentences add depth to their writing and help them clarify complex issues.

Sentence length is a matter of choice as are the other aspects of style. Your style will develop with time and practice. For now, try to use all three sentence lengths in your writing.

EXERCISE 27   Examine one or more of your essays to determine whether your sentence length is varied. See how many examples you can find of short, medium, and long sentences; then decide what you need to do to vary your sentence length.

Use a Variety of Sentence Types

Sentences may be *loose, periodic,* or *balanced.* In a *loose* sentence, the subject and verb come first and are followed by information that helps to clarify them. Loose sentences are straightforward and easy to read because the subject and verb at the beginning let you know what the sentence is about. The *loose* sentence is also the most common type. The following example of a loose sentence is from Simmons's essay on page 150. The subject and predicate are labeled and underlined:

>   s   p
> These <u>colors</u> <u>remind</u> me of chewing gum stuck to the undersides of school desks, a rather distasteful association.

The rest of the sentence clarifies what object the colors remind Simmons of and that the association is distasteful.

In a *periodic* sentence, the subject, the verb, or subject and verb come near the end of the sentence. Because the explanatory information comes first, readers have to wait to get to the key idea of the sentence. Writers use periodic sentences to build suspense, to add emphasis, or to create drama. The following example of a periodic sentence is also from Simmons's essay. The subject and predicate of the independent clause are labeled and underlined.

> Since ground beef goes for $2.49 a pound,
> <u>worms</u> <u>would</u> be a considerable savings.
>   s   P

By placing a dependent clause first—which, by definition, is an incomplete thought—the writer creates suspense as to how she is going to complete the thought when she gets to the main subject and verb. As you read the next example, notice the suspense that you feel while you are waiting to see what the sentence is about.

> Spewing blue oily smoke from its exhaust, squealing its
> tires on the slick pavement, rumbling ominously in the
> bowels of its engine before it finally quit, the old
> <u>Chevrolet</u> <u>came</u> to a halt.
>   s   P

The delayed subject and predicate in the above periodic sentence create a more dramatic scene for the reader than if the subject and verb had come at the beginning.

EXERCISE 28   Select a paragraph from an essay you have written, and either add a periodic sentence to it or revise one of your sentences to make it a periodic sentence.

A *balanced* sentence contains parallel words, phrases, or clauses in a series. Elements within sentences are *parallel* when they are used in similar ways or when they appear in the same grammatical form. In each pair of the following sentences, the first sentence contains an italicized element that is not parallel. The second sentence in each pair is a revised version in which all elements are parallel.

WORDS

a. The pasta was soggy, limp, and *it had been cooked too long.* (Not balanced: *soggy* and *limp* are adjectives; *it had been cooked too long* is not parallel because it is a clause.)

b. The pasta was soggy, limp, and overcooked. (Balanced: now all three modifiers are adjectives.)

PHRASES

a. Dr. Fractal is a caring teacher, *an expert in math,* and a reliable colleague. (Not balanced: *caring teacher* and *reliable colleague* each consist of a noun modified by a preceding adjective; *an expert in math* is not parallel because it is a noun modified by a prepositional phrase.)

b. Dr. Fractal is a caring teacher, an expert mathematician, and a reliable colleague. (Balanced: now all three phrases are parallel.)

CLAUSES

a. When Victor played the piano and sang, everyone *applauds* and asked for more. (Not balanced: *played the piano and sang* is in the past tense; *applauds* is not parallel because it is in the present tense.)

b. When Victor played the piano and sang, everyone applauded and asked for more. (Balanced: now both clauses are in the past tense.)

EXERCISE 29   Select a paragraph from an essay you have written, and either add a balanced sentence to it or revise one of your sentences to make it balanced.

Use a Variety of Sentence Beginnings

Varying the way you begin your sentences is another way to improve your style. Basically, the way you begin a sentence depends upon how you want to introduce the subject and predicate. You have already learned that the *type* of sentence you use will create a difference in the way your sentences begin: In *loose* sentences, the subject and verb come first; in *periodic* sentences, the subject and verb are delayed until near the end of the sentence. You can also begin your sentences with *adjectives, adverbs, modifying phrases, prepositional phrases, transitional words and phrases,* or *dependent clauses.* Following are examples of each type. The subjects and predicates are labeled and underlined.

Adjective	Tired and hot, the <u>dog</u> <u>dug</u> a hole in the wet dirt and <u>lay down</u>. ◄— compound predicate Crimson and gold, the fall <u>leaves</u> <u>made</u> a colorful backdrop for the white <u>house</u>.
Adverb	Carefully the <u>prowler</u> <u>eased</u> open a basement window. Quietly the <u>children</u> <u>crept</u> out of bed to spy on the teenagers having a party downstairs.
Modifying phrases	Fearful of making any noise, <u>Nancy</u> <u>called</u> the police to report that she heard a prowler. To reach a verdict of guilty, the <u>jury</u> <u>would have</u> to believe the prosecuting attorney's evidence.
Prepositional phrases	"Over the river and through the woods, to Grandmother's house <u>we</u> <u>go</u>." Before taking off, the <u>pilot</u> <u>completed</u> his pre-flight checklist.
Transitional words and phrases	For example, a <u>vote</u> for this candidate <u>might split</u> the ticket, resulting in a vote for the other party. Consequently, <u>Ed</u> <u>made</u> a better grade on the test than he had thought he would.
Dependent clauses	Because there was a snack bar built right into the pool, the <u>swimmers</u> <u>ate</u> lunch in the water. After the game was over, <u>everyone</u> <u>went</u> to a restaurant.

EXERCISE 30   Revise one of your essays for sentence variety by changing the beginnings of your sentences so that you have at least one of each type.

Use a Variety of Sentence Relationships

As you learned in sections B.4 and B.5, you can use *coordination* and *subordination* to combine sentences in a variety of relationships shown by the coordinating and subordinating conjunctions and the relative pronouns you choose. Be careful, however, not to overuse any one of the coordinating or subordinating conjunctions. It is easy to get hooked on a favorite conjunction, such as *and* or *but,* and use it several times in one paragraph. To vary your sentence structure vary your use of conjunctions.

Sentence relationships are of two types: those that occur *within* sentences, and those that occur *between* sentences. Coordination and subordination help you combine independent clauses to express their relationship within a single sentence. *Transitional phrases* and adverbs such as *therefore, however,* and *nevertheless* can show relationships within or between sentences. By establishing clear sentence relationships you are able to achieve coherence. The following examples show how transitional phrases and certain adverbs establish relationships between sentences. The transitions and adverbs are underlined. Relationships are italicized.

Transitional phrases

Did you know that you have three types of memory? One type is your sensory memory. Another type is short-term memory. Your long-term memory is the third type. (The transitional phrases establish a *part-whole* relationship between the first sentence and the three sentences that follow; memory is broken down into three types.)

I wish I had a computer that was more convenient to use than my large desk model. For example, I would like to have one of the portable laptop models. (The transitional phrase establishes a relationship of *clarification* between the first sentence, which is a general statement and the second sentence, which is an example.)

I did not study enough for the exam. As a result, I did not make a very good grade. (The transitional phrase sets up a *cause* and *effect* relationship between the two sentences.)

The computer has all but replaced the typewriter in today's offices. <u>On the other hand</u>, a typewriter may still be indispensable for small jobs such as typing addresses on envelopes and filling in forms. (The transitional phrase establishes a relationship of *contrast* between the two sentences.)

Adverbs
:   I really would love to go swimming with you at Rock Springs. <u>However</u>, I have a bad cold. (The adverb sets up a relationship of *contrast* between the two sentences.)

The painters did not do a very good job of painting my house. <u>Moreover</u>, they did not clean up the mess they made. (The adverb establishes a relationship of *addition;* the second sentence adds one more thing that the painters in the first sentence did not do well.)

You forgot my birthday, and you did not even call me until two weeks after you got back from your vacation. <u>Therefore</u>, I think our relationship is over. (The adverb establishes a *cause* and *effect* relationship between sentences.)

You forgot my birthday, and you did not even call me until two weeks after you got back from your vacation. <u>Nevertheless</u>, I will give you one more chance to show you care. (The adverb sets up a relationship of *opposition* or *contrast* between the first and second sentences.)

EXERCISE 31
:   Examine an essay in progress to see whether you have used coordination and subordination to add variety to your sentences. Determine whether you are overusing any one of the conjunctions. Revise a paragraph or a whole essay to improve your use of coordination and subordination and to eliminate overuse of a conjunction.

EXERCISE 32
:   Examine an essay that you are working on. See whether you have used a variety of transitional phrases and adverbs to achieve coherence between sentences. Revise a paragraph or the whole essay to vary your use of transitional phrases and adverbs and to establish clearer relationships between sentences.

EXERCISE 33   The following paragraph is composed exclusively of short simple sentences. In addition, the paragraph is not very well organized. Revise it to improve the organization and to add sentence variety, using all the methods explained in this section.

> Rick is a carpenter. Rick is forty-eight years old. Rick has been doing carpentry for more than twenty years. He is tired of building cabinets. He is tired of doing the finish work on houses. The work is hard. The work is time consuming. Rick no longer finds the work challenging. He wants to do something else. Rick likes to grow plants. He also likes to cook. He enjoys using a variety of herbs and spices. He cannot always find fresh herbs and spices. He has to use dried ones. Rick thinks there is a market for fresh herbs and spices. He would like to start an herb and spice business. He has the land. He knows how to build greenhouses. He has good business sense. The work would be challenging. He could get out of carpentry. He could start a new career.

Section C
Punctuation Choices

Correct use of punctuation can help you communicate confidently and without confusion. Readers expect you to follow the rules and conventions of punctuation because errors can interfere with your message. What are your choices for effective punctuation? Section C reviews the marks and rules of punctuation.

C.1 END PUNCTUATION MARKS

Choose an appropriate punctuation mark to end a sentence.

The *period, question mark,* and *exclamation point* are marks of punctuation that you probably use correctly most of the time. Because these end marks are so familiar, it is easy to take them for granted. Following is a quick review of the three ways to end a sentence.

1. *Place a period at the end of a sentence that either makes a statement or issues a command:*

   Maria took her bicycle to the repair shop for an estimate.

   Fill out one of these forms.

2. *Place a question mark at the end of a sentence that asks a direct question, but place a period at the end of a statement that indirectly asks a question:*

   How soon can you fix my bicycle?

   Maria asked the mechanic how soon the bicycle would be ready.

   Maria wanted to know when the mechanic could fix her bicycle.

3. *Place an exclamation point at the end of a statement to indicate surprise or intense feeling:*

I must have my bicycle by next Friday!

What an outrageous price!

I cannot believe it will cost that much!

TIP: Exclamations can be forceful and effective if used very sparingly, but if you overuse them, they lose their punch. Use an exclamation point only when the intensity of feeling or surprise expressed in your writing justifies it.

C.2 THE COLON

Place a colon at the end of a statement if what follows is a list, quotation, explanation, or word needing special emphasis:

I will have to repair or replace the following: a wheel, the tire and tube, and the handlebars.

Maria thought of two proverbs that applied to her recent accident with the bicycle: "an ounce of prevention is worth a pound of cure" and "better safe than sorry."

Here is what you can do if I do not finish repairing your bicycle in time: use our loaner, but this time watch out for chuckholes.

At this point, Maria could think of only one thing to do: cry.

C.3 THE DASH

Place a dash before and after words that interrupt the flow of thought or before words that create a dramatic effect:

Maria was unhappy enough as it was, but the fact that her bicycle was brand new—she had bought it only two weeks ago—added to her despair.

When the mechanic presented Maria with an estimate, he told her that there was only one way to look at it—sitting down.

Dashes, like exclamation points, should be used sparingly and only when there is a good reason for doing so.

C.4 THE HYPHEN

1. *If two or more words that describe a noun function as a unit, connect them with a hyphen:*

   Maria showed that she still had a sense of humor when she asked if the shop had a lay-away plan.

   The mechanic laughed but told her the shop did have a time-payment plan.

   Considering what the bill would do to her bank account, Maria wondered whether she would get into a charge-it-as-a-way-of-life routine.

2. *When you have to divide a word at the end of a line, use a hyphen. Break the word at the end of a syllable. If you do not know how to divide a certain word into syllables, consult your dictionary. Figure C-4.1 on page 473 lists rules for hyphenating words at the end of a line.*

EXERCISE 34

Correctly place hyphens or dashes in the sentences below. Words in parentheses following each sentence tell you what to do.

1. The fight or flight response that is typical of animals who are confronted by an aggressor has also been observed in humans. (Use hyphens to connect words functioning as a unit.)

2. When an animal is backed into a corner so that he cannot retreat, he will do the only thing left to him fight back. (Use a dash for dramatic effect.)

3. Grizzly bears have a reputation for aggressiveness they actually prefer to avoid confrontation but they will often flee rather than fight if there is an escape route. (Use dashes to set off words that interrupt the flow of thought.)

4. Most people try to avoid physical conflict unless backed into a corner. (Use a dash for dramatic effect.)

FIGURE C-4.1

How to Hyphenate at the End of a Line

1. Do not hyphenate short words, one-syllable words, or words pronounced as one syllable.

2. Do not leave only one or two letters at the end of a line or carry over one or two letters to the next line.

3. Hyphenate only at the end of a syllable.

4. If a word already has a hyphen (self-confident, all-inclusive), divide it only after the hyphen.

5. Hyphenate two-word numbers from twenty one through ninety-nine.

6. Hyphenate compound words formed from a number plus another word (three-mile walk, thirty-day time limit).

7. Hyphenate two-word fractions (one-half, two-thirds).

5. Even the most mild mannered people, however, may react physically if they feel their lives or their children's lives are threatened. (Use a hyphen to connect words functioning as a unit.)

C.5 THE SEMICOLON

1. *Place a semicolon between two sentences that are closely related:*

   Maria worried about the results of her bicycle repairs; would she be able to tell that her new bike had been in an accident?

2. *Place a semicolon before a conjunctive adverb that joins two independent clauses. See Figure C-5.1 on page 474 for a list of conjunctive adverbs and the relationships they signal.*

   On Friday, Maria's bike was ready; moreover, it looked as good as it did on the day she bought it.

FIGURE C-5.1

Conjunctive Adverbs and Sentence Relationships

RELATIONSHIPS	CONJUNCTIVE ADVERBS
Addition	also, besides, furthermore, moreover
Contrast	however, instead, nevertheless, nonetheless, otherwise, still
Comparison	likewise, similarly
Result	accordingly, consequently, hence, then, therefore
Time	finally, meanwhile, next, subsequently, then
Emphasis	certainly, indeed

3. *Use a semicolon to separate items in a series, if the items already contain commas:*

Listening to the shop radio, Maria heard three "oldies" that made her wish she had a car: "409," by the Beach Boys; "Oh Lord Won't You Buy Me a Mercedes Benz," by Janis Joplin; and "Little GTO," by Ronnie and the Daytonas.

EXERCISE 35

Examine your returned papers for errors in the use of the semicolon and other punctuation markers. Using what you have learned in this chapter, correct your errors.

EXERCISE 36

In the following paragraph, all marks of punctuation except commas have been left out. Read the paragraph and supply the missing marks of punctuation.

Far from being merely a means of sweetening your breath, mouthwash in the United States has taken on a deeper meaning Mouthwashes have acquired certain images in consumers' minds no one knows this better than advertisers who use these images to sell their products According to some psychologists, a person's choice of mouthwash may be influenced by the image the mouthwash projects Product A projects a no-nonsense germ fighting image Product B, on the other hand, projects a sexual image clean breath is sexy breath Product B's latest ads show couples getting out of bed in the morning afraid to kiss each other until they've used their mouthwash Product A's purchasers may see themselves as sensible people, more concerned about the germs that can cause bad breath than about being kissable however, Product B's users may see themselves as lovers whose mouthwash is just one more weapon in the arsenal of love which mouthwash do you think more people buy

C.6 THE COMMA

In some cases, a comma is like a little pause in a conversation. The comma, or the pause, gives readers or listeners a chance to think about what is being said and the relation of one idea to another. Sometimes you can tell where a comma should go by reading your sentence aloud and listening for the natural pause that indicates a break in the flow of thought. In cases where this practical suggestion does not work, a familiarity with the comma's common uses may help.

1. *Commas separate items in a series.*

If you have three or more items in a series, separate them with commas.

Blake had bruises, lacerations, and contusions following his accident at work.

He had a cast on his arm, several bandages on his leg, and a brace on his neck.

In the first example, commas separate single words in a series. In the second example, commas separate phrases in a series.

2. *Commas separate two adjectives that modify the same word if the adjectives are coordinate and belong to the same class.*

The tired, overworked nurses worked on Blake for several hours.

but

One big black bruise covered most of Blake's face.

Adjectives are *coordinate* when they modify the same word and when they belong to the same class of ideas. In the first example, the adjectives *tired* and *overworked* are coordinate because they both modify *nurses* by telling how the nurses felt. Since both words describe feelings, they are of the same class, and they need a comma to separate them. In the second example, the adjectives *big* and *black* are not coordinate. Although they both modify *bruise,* they tell you two different things about the bruise. *Big* describes its size and *black* describes its color. *Size* and *color* belong to different classes of ideas, so they do not need a comma to separate them.

If you have trouble deciding when to place a comma between two adjectives that modify the same word, try this classic method. Say the words with "and" between them, then say them in reverse. If they sound o.k. either way, put a comma between them. If they sound odd, leave the comma out. For example, "tired and overworked nurses" sounds o.k.; so does "overworked and tired nurses." However, "big and black bruise" sounds odd; so does "black and big bruise."

3. *A comma follows introductory words, phrases, and clauses.*

> Fortunately, Blake's workman's compensation insurance covered the costs of his injuries.

> On the other hand, he had already spent some money before he was able to file the claim.

> Even after he had recovered from his injuries, Blake had occasional soreness.

In the first example, the comma follows an introductory word. In the second example, the comma follows an introductory phrase. In the third example, the comma follows an introductory dependent clause.

Commas also follow introductory transitions, as in the next four examples.

> First, Blake was rushed to the hospital.

> After that, emergency room personnel took care of him.

> When they were finished, Blake was admitted to the hospital for a few days.

> Finally, he was allowed to go home.

If you introduce a sentence with a transition, or any other introductory material, be sure to follow it with a comma.

4. *Commas come before and after interrupting words, phrases, and clauses that are not restrictive in meaning.*

Several coworkers, fortunately, were close by when Blake's accident happened.

Blake, hurt and frightened, lay in the ambulance wondering what would happen next.

The emergency room, which Blake had been to once before, was an efficiently run place.

In the first example, a word interrupts the sentence. In the second example, a phrase interrupts. In the third, a dependent clause interrupts. In each example, the interrupter is not restrictive (essential to the meaning of the sentence). It is set off with commas to show that it is simply added information that does not affect the meaning of the sentence as a whole. To test this out, either cross out or cover up the interrupter, and read what is left of the sentence. You will find that in each example the sentence makes sense without the interrupter. The insertion of interrupters provides you, the writer, with another option for constructing sentences. The use of interrupters can add interest to your sentences and can increase your sentence variety.

Restrictive phrases and clauses sometimes act as interrupters, but because they *are* essential to the meaning of a sentence, they are not set off by commas:

Blake remembered that the song *Benny and the Jets* was playing on the radio while he was in the emergency room.

The nurses *who were on duty* did their best to make Blake comfortable.

The phrase in the first example and the clause in the second example are both *restrictive* because they are essential to the meaning of the sentence. Therefore, they are not set off by commas. In the first example, the phrase "Benny and the Jets" identifies the song that was playing. In the second example, the clause "who were on duty" identifies which nurses took care of Blake.

5. *A comma comes before a coordinating conjunction joining two independent clauses.*

Blake fully recovered from his accident, *and* he returned to his job.

The company instituted new rules that they hoped would prevent accidents like Blake's in the future, *but* they would have to wait and see.

In each example, the coordinating conjunction joins two independent clauses. The comma before the coordinating conjunction signals the beginning of a new independent clause with its own subject and verb. There are seven coordinating conjunctions: *for, and, nor, or, but, yet,* and *so.* Each of these conjunctions has a different meaning and expresses a different relationship between two clauses. For a review of coordination, see section B.4 on pages 446–450.

6. *Commas set off certain ordinary material.*

Commas set off the names of people who are addressed directly:

This may hurt a little, Blake, when I remove the cast.

Can you move all of your fingers, Blake?

Commas separate the parts of a date and divisions of numerical expressions:

Blake's accident happened on Friday, March 27, 1998.

Blake's insurance covered more than $5,000 in medical bills.

Commas separate the parts of an address:

The hospital is at 1500 Mercy Drive, Bloodworth, MA 02123.

Note that there is no comma between the state and the zip code.

Commas follow informal greetings and the closing in letters:

Dear Blake,

Sincerely,

In some formal letters, a colon (:) follows the greeting.

EXERCISE **37**   Place commas where needed in the sentences below:

1. Marta I want you to follow these steps exactly to use our new word processor.

2. First turn on the monitor.

3. When a list of icons appears, click on your program's icon.

4. Wait for a blank screen a little flashing line in the upper left corner and some icons across the top and bottom of the screen.

5. Now you are ready to use the keyboard which works just like a type-writer to type whatever you want.

6. There are more things you will need to know but I cannot tell you all of them today.

7. I will be out of the office until Tuesday April 21.

8. A list of these instructions which I have typed out for you should help you remember the steps.

9. Also you can request a free manual from the downtown office at 1600 West Central Street Clarksville OK 32102.

10. I hope you have an interesting rewarding learning experience.

EXERCISE **38**   Read the following paragraph and insert commas where needed:

When you have found the right place for your home office you are ready to select the furniture you will need. How much space you have will determine your choice of a desk or table. If your office is in a spare room you can choose almost any type of desk. You might want a desk that is big enough to hold a computer a printer and a fax machine. If you are converting a closet into an office you might want to install a pull-out shelf that can serve as a desktop. A sturdy comfortable chair is another piece of furniture you will want to consider. Make sure the chair has firm back support and that it is comfortable to sit in for long periods of time. As important as the desk and chair is the kind of lighting you have. If you are converting closet space hang a fluorescent light above your pull-out shelf. If you have a conventional desk you can position it under an existing light fixture or you can buy a lamp. Select one that does not take up too much space and that gives strong bright light. A bookcase and file cabinet are two other pieces of furniture you should have if space is unlimited. Use the bookcase for books supplies or other items. A file cabinet that you can lock is a good storage place for important papers and documents. If your office is in the closet simply install one or more shelves above your pull-out desktop for easy convenient storage. Cardboard file boxes are small stackable and affordable organizers for your closet workplace.

C.7 THE APOSTROPHE

The *apostrophe* (') has two functions: to show possession and to indicate omitted letters or numbers.

1. *To show possession add* 's *to the end of a singular noun even if the noun ends in* -s:

> a student's book
>
> Bob Jones's dog
>
> Beethoven's Ninth Symphony
>
> the car's transmission
>
> the bat's wings

If a noun is plural, add only an apostrophe at the end.

> several girls' dresses
>
> hundreds of voters' wishes
>
> two doctors' patients

If a noun is plural but does not end in -s, add 's.

> women's friends

children's toys

men's watches

Do not use an apostrophe with possessive case pronouns.

The book is <u>hers</u>.

I forgot my pencil; may I borrow one of <u>yours</u>?

<u>Whose</u> backpack is this?

Every college has <u>its</u> rules.

2. *Use an apostrophe when making contractions. A* contraction *is a word or number that contains one or more missing letters or numerals. An apostrophe takes the place of what is omitted.*

they're (they are)

you'd (you would)

class of '97 (1997)

a '67 Chevy (1967)

To choose between a contraction and the expression it stands for, consider your audience and how informal you want to be. Generally speaking, contractions are inappropriate in academic or other formal writing. Figure C-7.1 on page 482 lists commonly used contractions.

C.8   QUOTATION MARKS

Use double *quotation marks* (" ") to enclose direct quotations, and always use them in pairs. Use single quotation marks (' ') for a quotation within a quotation. Use quotation marks to enclose songs, short stories, articles, essays, and poems. (Underline or italicize longer works such as

**Commonly
Used
Contractions**

aren't = are not	she's = she is
can't = cannot	there's = there is
didn't = did not	they'd = they would, they had
don't = do not	they're = they are
he'd = he would, he had	wasn't = was not
he's = he is	weren't = were not
I'd = I would, I had	we'd = we would, we had
it's = it is	we're = we are
I'm = I am	we've = we have
isn't = is not	who's = who is
let's = let us	won't = will not
she'd = she would, she had	you're = you are

books, movies, and television series.) Remember to punctuate quotations correctly. These rules are illustrated below.

1. *Use quotation marks in pairs—at the beginning and end of the quotation.*

   "Hand in your papers," said the instructor.

   Chris said, "I'm not finished."

2. *For a quotation within a quotation, use single quotation marks.*

   "'A Person Worthy of Admiration' is the title of my essay," said the student.

RESEARCH TIP: Long passages of more than four typed lines should not be enclosed in quotation marks. Instead, indent each line of the quotation ten spaces from the left margin.

3. *Enclose titles of songs, short stories, articles, essays, and poems in quotation marks.*

"Love Me Tender" (song made popular by Elvis Presley)

"The Open Boat" (short story by Stephen Crane)

"On Liberty" (essay by John Stuart Mill)

"Stuck in an Elevator With a Dead Body? Here's What to Do" (newspaper article in *Wall Street Journal,* March 11, 1997)

"Those Winter Sundays" (poem by Robert Hayden)

4. *To punctuate quotations correctly, follow the guidelines in Figure C-8.1.*

FIGURE C-8.1

Punctuate Quotations Correctly

PUNCTUATION MARK	CORRECT PLACEMENT	EXAMPLE SENTENCE
PERIOD, COMMA	inside quotation marks	"Thank goodness," said Russ, "My essay is finished."
COMMA	after a phrase that introduces a quotation	The speaker asked, "Can you hear me in the back of the room?"
COMMA	before and after interrupting words	"If I can borrow some paper," said Than, "I'll pay you back tomorrow."
COLON, SEMICOLON	outside quotation marks	Tara said, "I'd like to go to the concert"; however, she did not have a ticket.
EXCLAMATION POINT, QUESTION MARK	inside quotation marks unless they apply to the whole sentence	Juan said, "Hurry up!" Do you recall the song "I'll Be Seeing You"?

EXERCISE 39   In the following sentences, add apostrophes and quotation marks where they are needed.

1. Have you read the poem Loveliest of Trees?

2. Whos going with you to the dance?

3. Dont tell me you wouldnt like to have a chocolate shake.

4. This car gets poor gas mileage, said Boomer, I wish I could afford a new one.

5. Bill's article, Matadors Secure Another Win, appeared in the college newspaper.

6. Six boys coats need cleaning, and two girls shoes need polishing.

7. My dad has a 57 Thunderbird that he has restored.

8. Joan's favorite Beatles song is Love Me Do.

9. Ouch! the child cried.

10. The instructor always asks, May I have a volunteer?

Section D
Choices for Special Problems

This section deals with a few special problems that can cause difficulty for beginning writers. For example, agreement errors and misplaced and dangling modifiers distract and confuse readers. Articles can be especially troublesome for the person who speaks English as a second language. Many students say they need a review of the rules concerning the use of numbers in writing.

As you know, there are many ways to put words together to create sentences and paragraphs. Knowing how to overcome your problem areas will help you make more successful choices.

D.1 PRONOUN CASE, REFERENCE, AND AGREEMENT

Choosing a point of view and maintaining it throughout your essay depends upon a solid understanding of pronouns and how to use them. *Pronouns* are words used in place of nouns. They can help you avoid needless repetition, and they can also serve as a coherence device. The three essentials of pronoun usage are *case, reference,* and *agreement.* See section A.2 on pages 418–421 if you need a quick review of pronouns.

Pronoun Case

Pronoun case refers to a pronoun's function in a sentence. Since pronouns replace nouns, they can function in all the ways nouns function: as subjects, objects, or possessive modifiers.

Subjective case pronouns function as *subjects* and can replace noun subjects:

Edmundo could not find his backpack.

He could not find his backpack.

Objective case pronouns function as objects of verbs or prepositions and can replace noun objects:

Sue and Latrisha loaned <u>Edmundo</u> a pen and some paper.

Sue and Latrisha loaned <u>him</u> a pen and some paper.

They gave the pen and paper to <u>Edmundo</u>.

They gave the pen and paper to <u>him</u>.

Possessive case pronouns can appear anywhere in a sentence as modifiers; they show ownership and can replace possessive nouns:

<u>Edmundo's</u> backpack had been stolen.

<u>His</u> backpack had been stolen.

Edmundo used <u>Sue's</u> pen and <u>Latrisha's</u> paper.

<u>Edmundo</u> used <u>their</u> pen and paper.

Notice that personal pronouns also have different forms depending on whether they are singular or plural. Before doing the following exercise, study Figure D-1.1 on page 487, which lists all the forms of the personal pronouns.

EXERCISE 40

Replace the underlined nouns in each sentence with the appropriate subjective, objective, or possessive case of personal pronouns.

1. Elena bought a used camper; <u>Elena</u> had wanted <u>a camper</u> for a long time.

2. <u>Elena</u> bought the camper from someone who needed to get rid of it so <u>Elena</u> got an unbelievably good deal.

3. Elena felt great behind the wheel of <u>Elena's</u> camper.

4. Elena took <u>Elena's</u> family for a ride, and <u>the family</u> congratulated <u>Elena</u> for finding such a good camper at such a low cost.

FIGURE D-1.1

Cases of Personal Pronouns

	SUBJECTIVE	OBJECTIVE	POSSESSIVE
1st person singular	I	me	my, mine
1st person plural	we	us	our, ours
2nd person singular	you	you	your, yours
2nd person plural	you	you	your, yours
3rd person singular	he, she, it	him, her, it	his, hers, its
3rd person plural	they	them	their, theirs

5. When the previous owner called Elena a week later, the previous owner asked Elena how Elena liked the camper, and Elena answered, "Just fine."

Pronoun Reference

Always make clear which noun a pronoun refers to. If the *antecedent*—literally, the word that "goes before"—of your pronoun is unclear, your sentence will be confusing.

UNCLEAR	**CLEAR**
Bob told Richard that his garbage disposal would not run.	Bob said to Richard, "My garbage disposal will not run." (The pronoun *my* tells you that the garbage disposal belongs to Bob.)
(Was it Bob's or Richard's garbage disposal? The reference is unclear.)	
Bob was sure that they had sold him a faulty garbage disposal. (Nothing in the sentence tells you who *they* are.)	Bob was sure that Ace Appliances had sold him a faulty garbage disposal. (Now it is clear who *they* are.)
Bob wanted to know what the store was going to do about it. (You cannot tell from the sentence what *it* means.)	Bob wanted to know what the store was going to do about the garbage disposal. (Now you can tell that *it* is the *garbage disposal*.)

EXERCISE 41   Either rewrite the sentence or replace the underlined pronouns with words that make the reference clear.

1. Amy went with Nga to the department store to return <u>her</u> blouse.

2. Although it was Memorial Day, Amy thought that <u>they</u> would be open.

3. Amy was right, so she and Nga went inside to ask <u>them</u> to exchange the blouse for a smaller size.

4. The clerk said, "I'm sorry, but we're out of those. Do you want to exchange <u>it</u> for a different one or take a refund?"

5. <u>She</u> decided to take the money and go somewhere for lunch.

Whether to use *who, whom, whoever,* and *whomever* can be confusing for some students. As explained on pages 419–421, these pronouns are both *relative pronouns* (useful for referring to a noun within a clause) and *interrogative pronouns* (useful for asking questions.) They can be either singular or plural as in the following sentences:

Janice is the only one <u>who</u> is talking.

Janice and Jeremiah are the only ones <u>who</u> are talking.

Finally, *who* and *whoever* also function as *subjective case pronouns* but *whom* and *whomever* function as *objective case pronouns*. Several rules may help you to avoid confusion.

Use *who* or *whoever* as the subject of a sentence, clause, or question. To test whether you have used *who* or *whoever* correctly, you should be able to replace it with *he, she, they, I,* or *we* in the sentence or clause in which it appears.

<u>Who</u> is having the party? (<u>She</u> is having the party.)

<u>Who</u> should we say invited us? (We should say <u>she</u> invited us.)

<u>Whoever</u> brings the food should know how many are coming. (<u>He</u> brings the food.)

Please give an invitation to <u>whoever</u> might want to come. (<u>They</u> might want to come.)

Use *whom* or *whomever* as the object of a verb or the object of a preposition. To test whether you have used *whom* or *whomever* correctly, you should be able to replace it with *him, her, them, me,* or *us.* If you still are unsure, mentally rearrange the words in the sentence or clause so that the subject and verb are in the proper relationship; then substitute the appropriate pronoun for *whom* or *whomever* as in the following sentences.

<u>Whom</u> did you invite to the party? (You did invite <u>him</u> to the party.)

To <u>whom</u> did you give the invitations? (You did give the invitations to <u>them</u>.)

She will invite <u>whomever</u> she likes. (She likes <u>them</u>.)

We will accept money from <u>whomever</u> we can get to contribute. (We can get <u>them</u> to contribute.)

EXERCISE 42

Read each sentence. Then underline the appropriate pronoun in parentheses. Remember that *who* and *whoever* function as subjects, but *whom* and *whomever* function as objects.

1. The National Wildlife Federation is an organization that was founded to help people (who or whom) want to protect endangered species from abuse and extinction.

2. The organization awards research grants to (whoever, whomever) it chooses.

3. The photographer (who, whom) we invited to speak at our garden club meeting has been a frequent contributor to *National Wildlife* magazine.

4. For a small fee, anyone (who, whom) wants to support the organization's work can become a member of The National Wildlife Federation.

5. (Whoever/whomever) wants to help animals can serve in other ways as well.

6. Local groups, such as an animal shelter in your community, are always looking for people to (who, whom) they can turn for financial or other kinds of support.

7. Dick Morgan is someone (who, whom) my community praises for his work with injured birds.

8. (Who/whom) do you know in your community (who/whom) is a friend to animals?

Pronoun Agreement

A pronoun must *agree* in number and gender with its antecedent. Use a singular pronoun to refer to a singular antecedent; use a plural pronoun to refer to a plural antecedent. The gender of your pronouns (masculine: *he, his, him;* feminine: *she, hers, her;* or neuter: *it, its*) should also agree with that of their antecedents. For a quick review of pronoun types, see Figure A-2.1 on page 421.

> Because Parrish had studied for his test, he was prepared to do well.

> Because the students had studied for their test, they were prepared to do well.

In the first example, the singular masculine pronoun *his* and *he* refer to the singular masculine antecedent *Parrish*. In the second example, the plural pronouns *their* and *they* refer to the plural antecedent *students*.

Sometimes the antecedent of a personal pronoun is an indefinite pronoun, such as *everyone, someone, each,* or *one.*

> Has anyone left her coat behind?

Indefinite pronouns do not specify the things or individuals they refer to and therefore can cause some problems in agreement. In the above example, both the verb *has left* and the personal pronoun *her* are singular. Indefinite pronouns are singular, and you should refer to them with singular personal pronouns. Avoid using the plural *their* to refer to an indefinite pronoun.

> Incorrect: Has anyone left their coat behind?

Another agreement problem with indefinite pronouns is that, because they are *indefinite,* their gender is unknown. Do not automatically use a masculine personal pronoun like *he, his,* or *him* unless you are specifically referring just to men. Either substitute *he or she, his or hers, him or her* or, if these sound awkward, rewrite your sentence to avoid using them:

Someone has left <u>his or her</u> answer sheet on the desk.

Someone has left <u>an</u> answer sheet on the desk.

I found <u>an</u> answer sheet on the desk.

Before doing the following exercise, review the list of indefinite pronouns in Figure D-1.2 below.

EXERCISE 43   Choose the pronoun in parentheses that agrees in number and gender with its antecedent.

1. Some students believe that algebra is (his, their) hardest course.
2. José, like many students, becomes anxious before (he, they) takes a test.
3. But if José goes into a test prepared, he will usually make a good grade on (them, it).
4. "Just between you and (I, me), I don't like algebra," said José.
5. "Then you and (I, me) agree on at least one thing," said his friend, Rose.

FIGURE D-1.2

Indefinite Pronouns

anybody	neither
anyone	nobody
each	no one
either	one
everybody	somebody
everyone	someone

6. Of Rose and José, it is (her, she) who makes better grades.

7. José and (her, she) often study together.

8. Unfortunately, a student who does not prepare sufficiently for a test will usually not do (his, his or her, their) best work.

9. Anyone who is willing to prepare for (his or her, their) tests has a good chance of succeeding.

10. Rewrite sentences 4 and 5 to eliminate the need for personal pronouns.

If the antecedent consists of two singular pronouns joined by the correlative conjunctions *either . . . or, neither . . . nor,* or *not only . . . but also,* use a singular pronoun. If the antecedent consists of two plural nouns joined by these conjunctions, use a plural pronoun:

Either <u>Mary</u> or <u>Carrie</u> will bring <u>her</u> notes to the meeting (<u>Mary</u>, <u>Carrie</u>, and <u>her</u> are singular)

Neither the <u>men</u> nor the <u>women</u> want to give up <u>their</u> places in line. (<u>Men</u>, <u>women</u>, and <u>their</u> are plural.)

Not only the group's <u>president</u> but also the other <u>officers</u> will give their reports.

What if a correlative conjunction joins a singular noun and a plural noun as in the third example above? The rule for this type of sentence construction is that the pronoun should agree with the noun that is closer to it. However, following the rule can sometimes cause confusion as in the following sentence:

Either the students or the teacher will correct her answers.

This sentence follows the rule of making the pronoun agree with the closest noun, but the meaning is confused. The students, not the teacher, are the ones whose answers should be corrected. To preserve this meaning and to follow the rule, simply reverse the order of the nouns:

Either the teacher or the students will correct their answers.

To avoid confusion in your own writing when using correlative conjunctions, place the plural noun closer to the pronoun as in the previous example.

EXERCISE **44**

Choose the pronoun in parentheses that agrees in number and gender with its antecedent.

1. Neither Larry nor Leroy wants to do (their, his) work.

2. Not only my aunt but also my cousins will bring (her, their) car.

3. We were upset because neither the dog nor the cats would eat (its, their) food.

4. My grandmother thinks that either an apple or some nuts would add (its, their) distinct flavor to the salad.

5. We asked neither this speaker nor that speaker to limit (their, his or her) time.

EXERCISE **45**

Read the following paragraph and correct any errors you find in pronoun case, reference, or agreement, either by changing the pronoun or by rewriting the sentence.

Tinsey's job as a registered nurse is very demanding. She works in an intermediate care center where many of the patients are bedridden, so Tinsey has to bathe, change, and feed him or her. Others may be on tube feedings, and Tinsey must see that his or her pump is working properly, the lines are clear, and a new bottle of food is attached as soon as they are empty. Monitoring a patient's vital signs is also a part of Tinsey's job. She takes their temperature, pulse, and blood pressure several times during her shift. If a patient is on oxygen, Tinsey must make sure that the line remains attached to the oxygen supply and that they do not dislodge the tube. When a patient rings for their nurse, Tinsey must answer the call and attend to their needs. In addition to all her other tasks, Tinsey writes reports and attends staff meetings. At the end of her shift she has earned her rest.

D.2 VERB TENSE CONSISTENCY AND AGREEMENT

Mistakes in verb tense consistency and agreement are among the most common types of errors college students make in writing. Before reading this section, see section A.3 on pages 421–425 for a quick review of verbs.

Tense Consistency

The verb in a dependent clause of a sentence should be *in the same tense* as the verb in the independent clause. If the verb in the independent clause of a sentence is in past tense, then the verb in the dependent clause should also express past time:

> Darryl <u>wished</u> (past) that he <u>had bought</u> (past perfect) the jacket when it <u>was</u> (past) on sale.

> Darryl <u>missed</u> (past) the sale because he <u>was working</u> (past progressive) late.

If the verb in the independent clause of a sentence is in the present tense, the verb in the dependent clause should also express present time:

> Darryl <u>now thinks</u> (present) that he <u>is going</u> (present progressive) to buy the jacket anyway.

> Darryl <u>says</u> (present) that he <u>has</u> never <u>seen</u> (present perfect) a jacket that he <u>likes</u> (present) as well.

> Darryl <u>hopes</u> (present) that the store <u>will have</u> (future: *will* plus present tense form of verb) some jackets left.

> Darryl <u>thought</u> (past) that the store <u>would have</u> (past tense form of *will have*) some jackets left.

EXERCISE 46

Circle the appropriate verb tense in the sentences that follow.

1. Linda (takes, took) Freshman Composition at 8:00 on Tuesdays and Thursdays this semester.

2. She (likes, liked) this class, but she (does not, do not) like to write.

3. At least that is how she (felt, has felt) when the semester began.

4. Now she (thinks, was thinking) that she (likes, liked) to write a little better than she used to.

5. In fact, she (is looking, was looking) forward to her next writing class.

6. Chuck, a friend of Linda's, (attends, attended) a creative writing class this semester.

7. He (wants, wanted) Linda to sit in on it sometime because he (knows, knew) she will like it.

8. Chuck (has talked, had talked) so much about this class that Linda has already decided to sign up for it.

9. She (worries, worried) that the class may be too hard for her.

10. "Don't worry," Chuck says. "The class (is, was) for beginners."

Verb Agreement

The subject and verb of a sentence must agree in number. If the subject is singular (one person or thing), the verb form must be singular. If the subject is plural (two or more persons or things), the verb form must be plural. Note that the present tense of a verb in the third-person *singular* always ends in *-s* or *-es*, whereas the third-person plural form of the verb in the present tense has no *-s* or *-es*. This is just the opposite from nouns: nouns normally form their *plural* by adding *-s* or *-es*.

The rain falls. (*Rain* is singular; the verb adds *-s*.)

Heavy rains fall. (*Rains* is plural; the verb drops the *-s*.)

Careta plays the violin. (*Careta* is singular; the verb adds *-s*.)

Careta teaches music. (*Careta* is singular; the verb adds *-es*.)

Where a correlative conjunction joins two nouns, not only must a pronoun agree with the closer antecedent but the verb must also agree in number with the closer subject. Where one noun is plural and the other is singular, place the plural noun closer to the verb to avoid confusion. If the subjects are two different personal pronouns, then make the verb agree in person and in number with the subject closer to it. When meaning may be in doubt, write your sentences so that the plural subject is closer to the verb, and make the verb agree.

> Neither Ron nor Rita has brought a lunch today. (Singular subjects agree with singular verb.)

> Not only the students but also the teachers eat here. (Plural subjects agree with plural verb.)

> Neither Raymond nor his sisters have eaten yet. (A plural and a singular subject: Verb agrees with closer subject.)

> Either my brother or I fix dinner. (Third person subject and first-person subject: Verb agrees with closer subject.)

> Not only fruit juices but also the fruit itself adds flavor to recipes. (A plural subject and a singular subject: Verb agrees with closer subject.)

EXERCISE 47   At the end of each sentence are paired verbs. Pick the correct one to fill in the blank by first underlining the subject of the sentence or clause and then choosing the verb form that agrees with the subject.

1. Margaret and Steve _____ at the San Diego Zoo at 9:00 in the morning. (arrives, arrive)

2. They _____ to go their separate ways and meet back at the entrance for lunch. (decides, decide)

3. Margaret _____ on the skylift to get a view of the whole zoo. (rides, ride)

4. While she is riding, she _____ a strange animal. (spots, spot)

5. There are several others like it, and they _____ like pigs with long faces. (looks, look)

6. They have crooked little horns that _____ up from the bottom of their mouths. (curls, curl)

7. The person that _____ the skylift says, "That's Charlie, the warthog." (operates, operate)

8. Steve _____ so much time looking at the timber wolves that he misses most of the other animals. (spends, spend)

9. After lunch, Margaret and Steve take each other to see the animals that each _____ best. (likes, like)

10. The wolves _____ no attention, but the warthog looks at Margaret and Steve and _____. (pays, pay) and (snorts, snort)

The following sentences contain subjects joined by correlative conjunctions. Read each sentence. Then underline the correct verb within parentheses.

1. Neither the employees nor their manager (like, likes) the store's new working hours.

2. Not only consumers but also employees (prefer, prefers) a store that is clean and up-to-date.

3. Either a department store or a specialty store (sell, sells) the items most consumers want.

4. Neither the mall's food court or the various stand-alone restaurants surrounding the property (serve, serves) exactly what we want.

5. Not only my friends, but also my family (like, likes) our area's newest movie theater.

Read the paragraph that follows and correct any tense or agreement errors that you find.

A few years ago, a really strange thing happens. A woman bought a wallet made out of eelskin and the next thing she knew, her Mastercard would not works. The clerk at the store where she tried to use the card said that something must have demagnetized it. The woman also had some gasoline credit cards that she kept in the back of her checkbook; these were working fine. While she was waiting to receive a replacement credit card, she heard on the news that other people is having the same problem. The rumor was that the wallets were made of the skin from electric eels and that they still contained traces of electricity which had destroyed the credit cards. The company got so many complaints that they did some research. As it happened, the wallets were not even made of the skin of electric eels at all. They were made of hagfish skin. The mystery were solved by researchers who pointed out that some of the wallets had metal clips which could have demagnetized the cards. Not only that, they said that if you lays a wallet down on a VCR, that could demagnetize the card as well.

D.3 MISPLACED AND DANGLING MODIFIERS

Modifiers are words, phrases, or clauses that describe or limit other words within sentences. Good descriptive writing contains numerous modifiers that specify *what* something looks, sounds, smells, tastes, and feels like and *how* it acts. The usual position for a modifier is next to the word it modifies. If modifiers are out of place, they can create confusion in your sentences, making it difficult for readers to understand what you mean. *Misplaced modifiers* and *dangling modifiers* are two common sentence errors you can learn to recognize and correct.

Misplaced Modifiers

A *misplaced modifier* is one that is not placed next to the word it describes. Figure D-3.1 on page 499 illustrates how to correct misplaced modifiers. Study the figure before you do Exercise 50.

EXERCISE 50

Each sentence below has a misplaced modifier. Underline the misplaced word or word group in each sentence, and then rewrite the sentence so that the modifier is next to the word it modifies.

Misplaced Modifier: We <u>nearly</u> had eight inches of rain last week. (The writer's intent is to explain how much rain.)

Correction We had <u>nearly</u> eight inches of rain last week. (Now the writer's intent is clear.)

1. For the person who needs to only lose a few pounds, exercise and a balanced diet will do the job.

2. Jack, however, wanted results fast because he did not want to go to the fraternity dance with his girlfriend wearing a tuxedo that was too small.

3. Jack tried the Super Skinny Diet advertised by a famous rock star who lost 30 pounds on television.

FIGURE D-3.1

Misplaced Modifiers and How to Correct Them

MISPLACED MODIFIER	CORRECTLY PLACED MODIFIER
My brother keeps the trophy that he won for playing soccer <u>in the bookcase.</u> (My *brother* did not play soccer in the bookcase.)	The trophy <u>in the bookcase</u> is the one my brother won for playing soccer. (The *trophy* is in the bookcase.)
We bought the car from a salesman <u>that has a five-year warranty.</u> (The *salesman* does not have a five-year warranty.)	The salesman sold us a car <u>that has a five-year warranty.</u> (The *car* has a five-year warranty.)
We <u>almost</u> had fifty people come to our party. (The writer *does not* mean that fifty people were expected, but none of them came.)	We had <u>almost</u> fifty people come to our party. (The writer *does* mean that about fifty people came to the party.)

Rule: *Place modifying words and word groups next to the words they modify.*

4. "All you have to do," the rock star said, "is drink a Super Skinny shake after being mixed up in a blender three times a day."

5. By the end of the first day, Jack was so hungry that he ate three hamburgers driving home in a pickup truck.

6. Jack's father, who was a nutritionist, told him to exercise and eat sensibly with his stationary bicycle.

7. Jack tried this plan and by the end of three weeks had nearly lost six pounds.

8. He returned the rest of the Super Skinny shake mix to the store where he had bought it for a refund.

9. The manager took the shake mix and gave Jack a refund after throwing it in the trash can.

10. Jack went to the dance with his girl wearing a tuxedo that fit just right.

Dangling Modifiers

A modifier that begins a sentence but does not modify the subject of the sentence is a *dangling modifier.* Dangling modifiers confuse readers and, like misplaced modifiers, create errors in logic:

> Flying upside down, we watched the Blue Angels.

The sentence is illogical because the wording of it suggests that *we* are flying upside down, not the Blue Angels. You can correct the dangling modifier in two ways:

> Flying upside down, the Blue Angels performed for us. (The intended subject follows the modifier that begins the sentence.)

> We watched the Blue Angels, who were flying upside down. (The modifier becomes a dependent clause.)

Figure D-3.2 on page 501 provides additional examples of dangling modifiers and how to correct them.

EXERCISE 51

Each sentence below has a dangling modifier. Underline the dangling modifier in each sentence, and then rewrite the sentence so that the word or subject the modifier describes follows it, or make the modifier into a dependent clause.

1. Studying for the algebra exam, the chair was so uncomfortable that Maria couldn't concentrate.
2. Finding another chair, now the temperature seemed too cool.
3. After adjusting the temperature, the light bulb in the desk lamp burned out.
4. Feeling hungry after all this work, a snack seemed like a good idea.
5. Trying once more to study, her concentration still wandered.
6. To do well on the test, studying was absolutely essential.
7. Ringing on the table beside her bed, Maria got up from her desk to answer the phone.

FIGURE D-3.2

Dangling Modifiers and How to Correct Them

DANGLING MODIFIER	CORRECTED MODIFIER
Sitting in the bookcase, my brother won the trophy for playing soccer. (My *brother* is not sitting in the bookcase.)	The trophy sitting in the bookcase is the one my brother won for playing soccer. (The *trophy* is sitting in the bookcase.)
With a five-year warranty, the salesman sold me the used car. (The *salesman* does not have a five-year warranty.)	The salesman sold me a car that has a five-year warranty. (The *car* has a five-year warranty.)
To guarantee winning the lottery, tickets in every possible number combination are necessary. (*Who* needs the tickets to guarantee winning?	To guarantee winning the lottery, you need tickets in every possible number combination. (*You* need the tickets to guarantee winning.)

Rule 1: *Follow a modifier at the beginning of a sentence with the word or subject it modifies.*

or

Rule 2: *Make the modifier into a dependent clause. (You may need to change the verb also.)*

8. Telling her friend she had to study, going out was a great temptation.

9. Sitting down once more, her roommate came in from class and started to play the stereo.

10. Deciding she needed a better study place, the library seemed inviting.

EXERCISE 52   Find and correct the misplaced and dangling modifiers in the paragraph below.

Mr. Dohrmat decided to have a pool installed with his Christmas bonus. Hoping for a healthful summer of swimming laps every morning, a pool seemed like a great idea. Judy and Jimmy Dohrmat were distracted by the construction doing their homework. Finally the pool was filled, and all the neighborhood children came over for a look in their bathing suits. That afternoon Mrs. Dohrmat's relatives, the Freeloaders, called to say they were coming to spend their vacation in their camper with their three kids. For the next month, the Freeloaders' children, the neighborhood kids, and the two little Dohrmats monopolized the pool. Just when Mr. Dohrmat would start to relax on his air mattress, one of the children would capsize him by jumping in with the dog wearing an innertube around his waist. One morning Mr. Dohrmat told his wife he should have invested his Christmas bonus during breakfast. His wife said, "Never mind; the kids only are young once." Bobbing with children, Mr. Dohrmat eyed the pool wistfully. "I suppose you are right," he said.

D.4   ARTICLES

Articles are also adjectives, and there are only three: *the, a,* and *an. The* is a *definite article; a* and *an* are *indefinite articles.* The following rules will help you choose articles correctly.

1. *Choose the definite article when referring to a specific item that is either known to the reader or has been mentioned before:*

   <u>the</u> club that I joined

   <u>the</u> boy wearing the blue shirt

   <u>the</u> captain of the team

   <u>the</u> flowers in my garden

2. *Use* the *with certain proper nouns and with gerunds (verbs ending in -ing that function as nouns). Figure D-5.1 on page 503 lists some examples.*

TIP: Although the proper nouns listed in Figure D-5.1 and certain others like them require articles, many do not. For example, *Mount Fuji, Mount St. Helens,* and *Mount Palomar* do not require the article. However, *the Rocky Mountains* and *the Himalayas* do. Compare also *The Bahama Islands* and *Bikini Island, The University of Maine* and *Brown University.*

3. *Choose an indefinite article when referring to a general item, not one in particular.*

a shelter for the homeless

a city in Florida

an automatic teller machine

an elephant in the zoo

4. *Choose* a *when the word that follows starts with a consonant sound.*

a kiss	a quiet evening
a paper lantern	a blast furnace
a laughing hyena	a tuba player

FIGURE D-5.1

Definite Article *the* With Proper Nouns and Gerunds

USE *THE* WITH	EXAMPLES
PLURAL PROPER NOUNS	*the* Great Lakes *the* Canary Islands *the* Phoenix Suns *the* Smoky Mountains
COLLECTIVE PROPER NOUNS	*the* Automobile Association of America *the* Knights of Columbus
SOME GEOGRAPHICAL PLACE NAMES	*the* Mediterranean Sea *the* Mojave Desert *the* Rio Grande
NAMES THAT CONTAIN *the . . . of*	*the* District *of* Columbia *the* University *of* Florida *the* President *of* the United States *the* Fourth *of* July *the* War *of* the Roses
GERUNDS	The *skiing* at Snowmass is great. I'll do the *cutting;* you do the *sewing.* Leave the *knitting* to Grandma.

5. *Choose* an *when the word that follows starts with a vowel sound.*

<u>an</u> antique chair   <u>an</u> organization

<u>an</u> empty cup   <u>an</u> upright piano

<u>an</u> iron   <u>an</u> honor

EXERCISE 53   Read the following paragraph. Then choose *the, a,* or *an* to fill in each blank.

Nepal is 1 _____ kingdom in India. It has 2 _____ population of 20,827,000. 3 _____ capital of Nepal is Kathmandu. Nepali is 4 _____ official language, but Maithir and Bhojpuri are also spoken. Nepal is 5 _____ only official Hindu state in the world. Hindus make up 90 percent of 6 _____ population in 7 _____ country that is also 5 percent Buddhist, 3 percent Muslim, and 2 percent Christian. Nepal has hot, humid summers and mild winters. It is bounded by 8 _____ Himalayas, whose peaks are permanently covered with snow. 9 _____ monsoon season lasts from June to September. Nepal has 10 _____ annual rainfall of 56 inches. Agriculture is 11 _____ mainstay of the economy, but tourism is 12 _____ rapidly developing industry.

D.5 NUMBERS

Numbers can be expressed in words or figures. The choice depends on how many numbers appear in your paper and what they signify. If you use only a few numbers, and if they can be expressed in one or two words, spell them: *fifty* percent, a population of *six thousand, twenty-five* copies. Remember to hyphenate numbers from twenty-one through ninety-nine. However, if numbers occur frequently in your paper, spell out those from one to nine, but use figures for 10 or higher. When writing papers for the humanities, do not begin a sentence with a number. Either spell the number or revise your sentence so that the number does not come first. Figure D-6.1 lists guidelines for using numbers.

FIGURE D-6.1

Guidelines for Using Numbers

Dates	February 9, 1945 1918–1992
Addresses	33 Poplar Avenue 6509 Grapevine Road Mt. Dora, FL 32726
Times	3:02 P.M.; three o'clock
Mathematical Expressions	3.1416; 2 1/2; one-third; 50 percent
Chapters and Pages	Volume 4, page 21; Chapter 8, page 102
Scores and Statistics	3–1 odds; a score of 14–0
Identification Numbers	radio station 105.9; (telephone numbers, social security numbers, zip codes)
Measurements	36 inches; 120 pounds; 16 liters; 4 tablespoons; 3"×5"
Act, Scene, Line	Act II, scene 3, lines 10–17
Temperatures	212°F; 100°C
Money	10 cents; $3.2 million; $12.00

Section E
Word Choice

As a writer, you have many choices, but your word choice is your most important one. What words will you choose? What combinations of words will result in the best sentences you can write? What words and the ideas they represent will appeal to your readers? Three strategies can help you make these decisions: knowing a word's stated and implied meanings, being able to choose among words that look or sound alike, and learning a few spelling tips so that spelling does not become a stumbling block.

E.1 DENOTATION AND CONNOTATION

To make effective word choices, understand the difference between a word's *denotation* and its *connotation*. The dictionary definition is a word's *denotation*. The emotional associations that a word evokes are its *connotations*. For example, *thin, slender, slim, skinny,* and *emaciated* all have the same denotation: weight that falls below the average. However, each of these words has different connotations. *Skinny* connotes unattractiveness; *emaciated* connotes malnourished; and *thin, slim,* and *slender* usually connote degrees of attractiveness. However, people may disagree about a word's connotation. Some people might say that fashion models are skinny, whereas others would call them slender. Your choice of one of these words to describe a fashion model would depend upon whether you think that a typical model's size and body type are attractive.

Connotations also can change over time. For example, *awesome,* an adjective that denotes mixed feelings of wonder, reverence, and dread, used to be reserved for use in a spiritual context. The word still has this connotation in the following two sentences:

As Greta listened to the <u>awesome</u> strains of Beethoven's *Ninth Symphony,* her eyes filled with tears.

Some people say that while standing before El Greco's <u>awesome</u> painting The Crucifixion, they can feel the presence of God.

Beginning in the seventies, *awesome* developed a new usage as a slang term and therefore new connotations, as in the following two sentences:

Mikey whipped out the plastic minicar from the cereal box and said, "Wow, this is <u>awesome</u>!"

Jennifer said to Angela, "Wear your red leather miniskirt to the party; it looks <u>awesome</u> on you."

Used as slang, *awesome* still carries connotations of wonder, but the wonder is more generalized to cover anything that might be called "great" or "terrific."

Understanding the difference between denotation and connotation can help you select the words that will most effectively communicate your ideas.

EXERCISE 54

Each of the word groups in the following exercise contains three words that have approximately the same *denotation* but different *connotations*. For each word group, do the following:

1. Write a single *denotative* definition for the word group.

2. Write the *connotative* meanings of each of the three words.

3. Rate each of the three words as positive, neutral, or negative in its connotation.

Example:	pre-owned, used, worn-out
Denotation:	The terms all mean "not new."
Connotation:	<u>Worn-out</u> suggests "unusable" and is the negative term. <u>Used</u> means "not new" though there may be some use left. <u>Used</u> is the neutral term, and <u>pre-owned</u> is the positive term. It suggests that an item had a prior owner but is neither used up nor worn out.

WORD GROUPS

a. obese, large, plump

b. persistent, stubborn, unyielding

c. synthetic, fake, artificial

d. act, stunt, trick

e. stroll, swagger, walk

f. to boss, to control, to manage

g. disrobe, strip, undress

h. cheap, bargain-priced, inexpensive

i. crippled, differently abled, handicapped

j. show, expose, display

EXERCISE 55   Because of their connotations, the six underlined words in the following paragraph do not match the tone of the rest of the paragraph. First determine why each of the six words is inappropriate, then replace each one with a word that has an appropriate connotation.

Three friends meet once a week to play poker. Although they play for only pennies, the game can get very intense, with heated arguments on all sides. Before they know it, one is accusing the other of cheating. To solve these problems so they can all relax and have an enjoyable game, they have come up with some new rules. First of all, they have to wear ski masks so that the expressions on their mugs will not reveal the cards they are hugging. Second, they have to keep their mitts above the table at all times. In addition, they play at a glass-topped table to prevent anyone from sneaking a hand underneath to pluck a hidden card. Also, they always play with a new pack of cards so that no one can mark the cards ahead of time or cram extras into the deck. The friends find their game amusing and think they are wonderfully creative to have come up with a way to play it and avoid getting peeved.

E.2 MAKING SENSE OF CONFUSING WORDS

Words can be confusing when they look alike or sound alike. It is easy to write one word when you really mean another one that happens to look or sound like it. Though many of the most commonly confused words are simple ones whose meanings you know when you stop to think about them, it is easy to confuse them when you are writing. Call it a slip of the pen or the computer key. Two things can help you make sense of confusing words. First, review their meanings. Secondly, proofread your essays for any of the following words you may have confused.

advice, advise

Advice is a noun meaning "opinion concerning what to do." *Advise* is a verb meaning "to give advice or an opinion."

> My counselor gave me some good advice (opinion) about what course to take.

> My counselor advised me (gave an opinion) to take a study skills course.

affect, effect

Affect used as a verb means "to influence." *Effect* used as a verb means "to bring about." *Effect* used as a noun means "a result."

> *affect* and *effect* used as verbs:

> Your jokes affect (influence) me in a negative way.

> The new fertilizer will effect (bring about) new growth.

> *effect* used as a noun:

> We do not know what effect (result) this new drug will have.

accept, except

Accept is a verb meaning "to receive with pleasure." *Except* is most commonly used as a preposition meaning "excluding."

I <u>accept</u> (receive with pleasure) your apology.

Everyone <u>except</u> (excluding) Roxanne is invited.

brake, break

Brake used as a verb means "to stop." *Break* used as a verb means "to crack, smash, or shatter."

I <u>brake</u> (stop) for animals.

To <u>break</u> (shatter) a mirror is to invite bad luck.

choose, chose

Choose is the present-tense form of the verb *to choose,* meaning "to select." *Chose* is the past-tense form of the same verb.

Every four years voters <u>choose</u> (select) a new president of the United States.

After an election, pollsters try to determine why voters <u>chose</u> (selected) their candidates.

coarse, course

Coarse is an adjective meaning "rough" or "vulgar." *Course* is a noun meaning "subject" or "direction."

Burlap is a <u>coarse</u> (rough) material.

Some people do not like to hear <u>coarse</u> (vulgar) jokes.

Algebra is a required <u>course</u> (subject) at most colleges.

The explorers followed the river's <u>course</u> (direction).

everyday, every day

Everyday is an adjective meaning "ordinary." *Every day* is an adverbial phrase meaning "each day."

A tornado is not an <u>everyday</u> (ordinary) weather condition.

The mail arrives <u>every day</u> (each day) at 10:30 a.m.

its, it's

Its is a possessive pronoun meaning "belonging to." *It's* is a contraction of "it is."

The dog buried <u>its</u> (belonging to, his) bone in the yard.

Because <u>it's</u> (it is) raining, you will need your umbrella.

loose, lose

Loose is an adjective meaning "not tight." *Lose* is a present-tense form of the verb "to lose," meaning "to misplace."

<u>Loose</u> (not tight) clothing is comfortable on hot days.

Every time I lay down my keys, I <u>lose</u> (misplace) them.

peace, piece

Peace is a noun meaning "harmony." *Piece* is a noun meaning "part."

We would like all nations to live in <u>peace</u> (harmony).

I would like another <u>piece</u> (part) of pie.

passed, past

Passed is the past-tense form of the verb "to pass," meaning "to move on or ahead." *Past* used as an adjective means "over and done." *Past* used as a noun means "a former time."

We <u>passed</u> (moved ahead of) the cars on the right.

There is no use crying over <u>past</u> (over and done) mistakes.

Some people enjoy thinking about the <u>past</u> (a former time).

quiet, quite, quit

Quiet used as an adjective means "silent"; used as a verb, it means "to silence." *Quite* is an adverb meaning "completely." *Quit* is a verb meaning "to stop" or "to leave."

After the storm, it was <u>quiet</u> (silent).

Is there no way to <u>quiet</u> (to silence) that noisy dog?

I am not <u>quite</u> (completely) finished with this essay.

Do not <u>quit</u> (leave) your job unless you find a better one.

their, there, they're

Their is a possessive pronoun meaning "belonging to them." *There* is an adverb meaning "in that place." *They're* is a contraction of "they are."

These are <u>their</u> (belonging to them) books.

Put your jacket over <u>there</u> (in that place).

<u>They're</u> (they are) noisy today.

to, too, two

To is commonly used as a preposition meaning "in a direction toward." *Too* is an adverb meaning "also" and "more than enough." *Two* is a noun meaning "the sum of one plus one."

Send the check <u>to</u> (toward) me.

I like chocolate ice cream <u>too</u> (also).

You have paid <u>too</u> much (more than enough) for this VCR.

There will be <u>two</u> (one plus one) for dinner.

wear, where, were, we're

Wear is a verb meaning "to have on." *Where* is an adverb meaning "at what place." *Were* is a past-tense form of the verb "to be." *We're* is a contraction of "we are."

I wish you would <u>wear</u> (have on) your new suit to the wedding.

<u>Where</u> (at what place) did you put my new suit?

I did not know you <u>were</u> (to be) going to the reception.

<u>We're</u> (we are) a cute couple.

who's, whose

Who's is a contraction meaning "who is." *Whose* is a possessive pronoun meaning "belonging to whom."

<u>Who's</u> (who is) ready for a swim?

<u>Whose</u> (belonging to whom) swimming trunks are these?

your, you're

Your is a possessive pronoun meaning "belonging to you." *You're* is a contraction of "you are."

This must be <u>your</u> (belonging to you) sister.

I hope <u>you're</u> (you are) not intending to eat these doughnuts.

EXERCISE 56   Edit the following paragraph by finding and correcting any confusing words.

Having a rat die in you're office is an experience you will not forget. In the first place, you do not always know where the rat is. It may be in the attic caught in a trap you put up their the last time one died, or it may be decaying inside a wall were it crawled to try to escape. Secondly, the smell is so strong its hard to concentrate on anything else. It really disrupts the piece of the office. Passed experience may have shown you that if this rat has died, another probably will to, so you had better call a construction company and try to find out how there getting in the building. If someone can find the holes and seal them up, then you're problems will be over. If not, then you will just have to except the situation as it is and realize that once the air is clear, you may have to go through all this again.

E.3 SPELLING TIPS

Careless errors, especially in spelling, can interrupt the flow of even the most well-organized and logically supported essay because they call attention to themselves. When you proofread your essays to catch and correct surface errors, don't forget spelling. Following are some common spelling rules and tips for improving your spelling.

1. *You may have learned this rule long ago:* i *before* e *except after* c *or when pronounced* ay, *as in* neighbor *and* weigh.

   bel<u>ie</u>ve, gr<u>ie</u>ve   (use <u>i</u> before <u>e</u>)

   rec<u>ei</u>ve, perc<u>ei</u>ve   (except after <u>c</u>)

   Some exceptions: either, foreign, forfeit, height, leisure, neither, seize, weird

2. *When adding an ending to a word that ends in* e: *keep the* e *before a consonant; drop it before a vowel. (Vowels are* a, e, i, o, u, *and sometimes* y; *all the other letters are consonants.)*

   hop<u>e</u> + <u>f</u>ul = hop<u>e</u>ful   (keep <u>e</u> before a consonant)

   cop<u>e</u> + <u>i</u>ng = cop<u>i</u>ng   (drop <u>e</u> before a vowel)

Some exceptions: argue + ment = argument

judge + ment = judgment or judgement

true + ly = truly

damage + able = damageable

advantage + ous = advantageous

3. *When adding an ending to a word that ends in* y: *if the* y *is preceded by a vowel, keep the* y; *if the* y *is preceded by a consonant, change the* y *to* i.

bu̲y + ing = buy̲ing   (vowel u̲ precedes y̲)

co̲py + ed = co̲pied   (consonant p̲ precedes y̲)

4. *Generally, when adding an ending to a one-syllable word that ends in a consonant: double the final consonant if it is preceded by a single vowel; leave it alone if it is preceded by two vowels:*

shi̲p + ed = shi̲pped   (p̲ preceded by single vowel i̲)

se̲a̲t + ed = se̲a̲ted   (t̲ preceded by two vowels e̲a̲)

5. *Generally, when adding an ending to a multi-syllable word that ends in a consonant: double the final consonant if it is preceded by a single vowel; leave it alone if it is preceded by two vowels or by a consonant + vowel.*

commi̲t + ing = commi̲tting   (t̲ preceded by single vowel i̲)

despa̲i̲r + ing = despa̲i̲ring   (r̲ preceded by two vowels a̲i̲)

benef̲i̲t + ed = benef̲i̲ted   (t̲ preceded by consonant + vowel f̲i̲)

Some exceptions: quitting, cancellation, excellent, questionnaire

6. *To form plurals of nouns, add* -s *to most nouns; add* -es *to most nouns ending in* o, ch, sh, ss, x, *or* zz.

plan + s = plans

star + s = stars

her<u>o</u> + es = heroes

lun<u>ch</u> + es = lunches

toothbru<u>sh</u> + es = toothbrushes

sph<u>in</u>x + es = sphinxes

mi<u>x</u> + es = mixes

Some exceptions: words that end in two vowels, such as *radios* and *zoos*.

EXERCISE 57   Examine several of your returned essays for spelling errors that have been marked. Make a list of your errors and try to determine which of the six rules you need to review.

Tips for Improving Your Spelling

1. Keep lists of words you misspell and that you frequently look up in the dictionary. Try to learn the spelling of these words by figuring out which rule applies.

2. Use a memory aid. For example, choose a word you commonly misspell and memorize some spelling points about it—for example:

    accommodate contains two *c*'s, two *m*'s, two *o*'s, and *a date*.

    There is <u>a rat</u> in separate.

3. Try the following method for learning the spelling of difficult words: pronounce the word; spell it aloud one letter at a time; write the

word without looking at it; check your spelling; repeat the steps until you can spell the word from memory.

4. Use the dictionary; keep it handy when you write.

5. Review basic spelling rules; seek extra help from your college library or learning lab, which may have programmed materials you can check out for improving spelling.

6. If you use a word processor, use the spelling check feature.

Acknowledgments

Chapter 1

DYMPNA UGWU-OJU From *Newsweek*, December 4, 2000. All rights reserved. Reprinted by permission.

Chapter 2

ROBERT M. PIRSIG From *Zen and the Art of Motorcycle Maintenance* by Robert Pirsig. Copyright © 1974 by Robert M. Pirsig. Reprinted with permission of HarperCollins Publishers, Inc. and William Morrow & Company, Inc.

Chapter 3

SARA GILBERT Gilbert, Sara D. "The Different Ways of Being Smart," from *Using Your Head: The Many Ways of Being Smart* (Macmillian, 1984, pp. 55–62). Reprinted by permission Sara D. Gilbert, the author of more than a score of other nonfiction self-help books for adults, teenagers, and children.

N. SCOTT MOMADAY Momaday, N. Scott: *The Names: A Memoir.* Copyright © 1976. Reprinted with permission of the author.

LINDA PASTAN "Marks," from *The Five Stages of Grief* by Linda Pastan. Copyright © 1978 by Linda Pastan. Used by permission of W.W. Norton & Company, Inc.

Chapter 4

GREGG EASTERBROOK Copyright © 1981 by The New York Times Co. Reprinted with permission. All rights reserved.

STEPHEN KING Reprinted With Permission. © Stephen King. All rights reserved. Originally appeared in *The New York Times Book Review* (1987).

ROBERT MACNEIL Robert MacNeil, "The Trouble With Television" from a speech "Is Television Narrowing Our Minds" delivered at the Presidents Leadership Forum, SUNY, Purchase, 11/13/84. Reprinted with permission from the March 1985 *Reader's Digest.*

JOE QUEENAN Queenan, Joe, "I Married An Accountant," *Newsweek*, November 14, 1988. Used with Permission.

CAROLINE SUTTON From *How Did They Do That?* by Caroline Sutton. Copyright © 1984 by Hilltown Books. Reprinted by permission of HarperCollins Publishers, Inc. and William Morrow & Company, Inc.

ELLIOT WEST Reprinted by permission of *American Heritage,* Inc.

Chapter 5

JESS STEIN From The Word-A-Day Vocabulary Builder by Bergen Evans. Copyright 1963 by Bergen Evans. Reprinted by permission of Random House, Inc.

PHYLLIS THEROUX Phyllis Theroux, "Shopping with Children" from *Night Lights* (New York: Viking Penguin, 1987). Copyright © 1987 by Phyllis Theroux. Reprinted by permission of the Aaron M. Priest Literary Agency, Inc.

Chapter 6

STEVEN J. HACKNEY Reprinted by permission of the author.

ROBIN SIMMONS Kanar, Carol, *The Confident Student.* Copyright © 1991 by Houghton Mifflin Company. Used with permission.

Chapter 7

WILLIAM ZINSSER Copyright © 1976, 1980, 1985, 1988, 1990, 1994, 1998 by William K. Zinsser. Reprinted by permission of the author.

Chapter 8

CRUMP AND CARBONE   From *Writing On-line,* Updated Second Edition, by Crump/Carbone. Copyright © 1998 by Houghton Mifflin Company. Reprinted with permission.

ENCYCLOPAEDIA BRITANNICA   Reprinted with permission from *Encyclopaedia Britannica,* 15th edition, Copyright © 1992 by Encyclopaedia Britannica, Inc.

DONALD MURRAY   "Where Do You Find Information?" from *The Craft of Revision* by Donald M. Murray, copyright © 1991 by Holt, Rinehart, and Winston, reprinted by permission of the publisher.

Chapter 9

TOM BODETT   From *Small Comforts* © 1987 by Tom Bodett. Reprinted by permission of Perseus Books Publishers, a member of Perseus Books, L.L.C.

LANGSTON HUGHES "Salvation" from *The Big Sea* by Langston Hughes. Copyright © 1940 by Langston Hughes. Copyright renewed 1968 by Anna Bontemps and George Houston Bass. Reprinted by permission of Hill and Wang, a division of Farrar, Strauss & Giroux, LLC.

MAXINE HONG KINGSTON From *The Woman Warrior* by Maxine Hong Kingston. Copyright © 1975, 1976 by Maxine Hong Kingston. Reprinted by permission of Alfred A. Knopf, Inc.

DANIEL MEIER   Copyright © 1987 by The New York Times Co. Reprinted by permission. All rights reserved.

CARIN C. QUINN   Reprinted by permission of *American Heritage* Inc.

CAROLINE SUTTON   From *How Did They Do That?* by Caroline Sutton. Copyright © 1984 by Hilltown Books. Reprinted by permis-

sion of HarperCollins Publishers, Inc. and William Morrow & Company, Inc.

GRACE MING-YEE WAI   "Chinese Puzzle" by Grace Ming-Yee Wai. Reprinted by permission *MS.* Magazine, copyright © 1988.

Chapter 10

BRETT LOTT   Copyright © 1993 by the Antioch Review, Inc. First appeared in the *Antioch Review,* Vol. 51. No. 1. Reprinted by permission of the Editors.

Chapter 11

ANDY ROONEY   "How to Put Off Doing a Job," from *Word for Word* by Andrew A. Rooney, copyright © 1984, 1985, 1986 by Essay Production, Inc. Used by permission of G.P. Putnam's Sons, a division of Penguin Putnam, Inc.

LAURA TOMASHEK   Reprinted by permission from Laura Tomashek.

Chapter 12

TOM BODETT   From *Small Comforts* © 1987 by Tom Bodett. Reprinted by permission of Perseus Books Publishers, a member of Perseus Books, L.L.C.

Chapter 13

STEVEN D. STARK   Reprinted by permission from Steven D. Stark.

Chapter 14

NATIONAL WILDLIFE   © 2001 National Wildlife Federation. Reprinted from the Feb/Mar issue of *National Wildlife Magazine.*

JIM TRELEASE   Trelease, Jim. "Why Reading Aloud Makes Learning Fun," from *U.S. News & World Report* (March 17, 1986, pp. 66–67). Reprinted by permission.

ROB WALDRON   From *Newsweek,* October 30, 2000. All rights reserved. Reprinted by permission.

Index

Instructor's Resource Manual

The Confident Writer

Third Edition

Carol C. Kanar

Valencia Community College
Emeritus

Houghton Mifflin Company   Boston   New York

Senior Sponsoring Editor: Mary Jo Southern
Senior Associate Editor: Kellie Cardone
Senior Project Editor: Fred Burns
Manufacturing Coordinator: Florence Cadran
Marketing Manager: Annamarie L. Rice

Printed in the U.S.A.

ISBN: 0-618-13114-0

123456789-QF-06 05 04 03 02

Contents

To the Instructor

Thank you for selecting *The Confident Writer,* Third Edition. I wish you and your students a productive and successful semester or quarter. Whether you are a new teacher or a seasoned veteran, you know, or are about to learn, that the first day of class opens on a vista of infinite possibility. Each student enters your class with the hope that he or she will succeed. Establish a tone of hopeful confidence on the first day and watch it build during the weeks ahead.

We know that writing is an essential communication skill necessary to success in college and the workplace. Being able to write effectively is a career asset that may lead to a promotion or a better job. We recognize the value of critical reading and thinking and their relationship to the writing process. We also know that reading is the foundation of every course, a source for ideas, and a springboard to critical thought and action. To help you challenge your student writers to reach for those higher levels of thought and to build and sustain their confidence through a steady acquisition of skill, *The Confident Writer,* Third Edition, does the following:

- It teaches writing as a recursive process that operates through three stages that are neither discrete nor always sequential: *prewriting, drafting* and *organizing,* and *rewriting* (revising and editing).

- It emphasizes the importance of *audience awareness* and a *purpose* for writing so that students come to see writing as growing out of a need to communicate ideas, beliefs, feelings, and information, and not as a skill for classroom use only.

- It conceptualizes writing as a series of choices the writer makes so that limiting a topic, formulating a thesis, selecting and organizing evidence, and choosing a logical framework for the presentation of ideas are controlled only by the writer's purpose, audience, and desire to communicate.

- It teaches grammar not as a set of inflexible rules that are incidental to the writing process but as a series of logical choices the writer makes to communicate ideas effectively.

- It provides essays, several of which are new to the third edition, written by a culturally diverse group of writers on a variety of interesting topics. It uses prereading, reading, and postreading activities to establish a context for reading and a motivation for writing; and, at the same time, it provides reinforcement and practice of critical reading skills.

Using the Features

Following is a brief guide to the features and how to use them. For more specific suggestions on how to use the features within the context of each chapter, see Suggestions for Each Chapter on pages 22–34.

Awareness Check

The Awareness Check serves several purposes: to establish a context for reading the chapter opening essay, to assess students' prior knowledge of the topic, and to make some assumptions or predictions about the essay. You can use the Awareness Check as a group activity within class to promote active reading, or you can have students do it on their own. Many instructors like to build students' interest in an essay before assigning the reading for homework. Some do the Awareness Check with students near the end of a class meeting so they can begin the next class with a discussion of the essay.

Vocabulary Check

The Vocabulary Check is a new feature whose purpose is to help students identify words in the chapter-opening essays that may be difficult or unfamiliar. The Awareness Check and the Vocabulary Check used together are prereading activities that help students establish a background for reading by focusing their attention on terms and ideas that may be essential to their understanding of the reading selections that follow.

Essays

The essays that come near the beginning of the chapter relate either in structure or content to the topic covered in the chapter. For example, one of the topics covered in Chapter 7, "Editing Your Essays," is how to trim and tighten an essay by eliminating wordiness, passive voice, and tired expressions. The essay that opens the chapter is William Zinsser's "Clutter," which is about eliminating the language that clutters writing. The essays both in unit 3 and in each chapter represent a variety of cultural perspectives and themes. In addition, throughout most chapters, there are examples and exercises that use excerpts from other essays to illustrate writing strategies or processes. These excerpts are usually related to the chapter-opening essay according to structure, topic, or theme. The Rhetorical Table of Contents lists all essays and excerpts according to their rhetorical patterns. For the third edition, 30 percent of the essays and other readings have been replaced.

The Critical Reader

The Critical Reader is a postreading activity that follows each essay. It is designed to promote critical analysis of the author's strategy and development. Students can do the activity on their own, in small groups, or as a general class discussion. The questions are divided into four sections: *central idea, evidence, implications,* and *word choice. Central idea* asks students to identify the author's thesis, purpose, or both. *Evidence* asks them to identify the author's support and determine how it is organized. *Implications* asks them to make inferences from the essay to interpret the writer's meaning. *Word choice* asks them about specific words, terms, or phrases and how they serve the author's purpose or establish the tone. The questions in each critical reader vary because they are geared to reflect both the essay's structure and content and the chapter's topic and concepts. The overall effect of prereading and prewriting activities is to encourage students to read actively, that is, to do something with the reading, whether it be to analyze it in order to understand how the writer's purpose was achieved or relate it to their own lives and experiences as a springboard for thinking and writing.

Exercises

The exercises in each chapter increase in difficulty as the chapter progresses. Most of the exercises ask students to generate their own writing. Many exercises follow a progression so that by the time a student has completed three exercises in a row, that student has drafted an essay. Every chapter contains exercises that students can do on their own and at least one that is designed for collaborative learning. Use the exercises as you see fit. It is not necessary that all students complete all exercises. You may decide that your students have already mastered a skill addressed in an exercise, so you might choose to skip that one. You may decide that an exercise designated as a group activity would work better for your class as an individual exercise. Feel free to choose or adapt exercises to suit your students' needs. One reason each chapter contains so many exercises on different levels of difficulty is to provide the flexibility you need to make the text meet the demands of your course objectives and your students' abilities.

New in every chapter is an Internet exercise, which is especially useful for instructors who want to add computer applications to their courses. These exercises take students to authors' websites, writing center websites, and other useful sites to accomplish a variety of tasks. Cumulatively, the exercises provide an introduction to using the Internet for research.

Topics for Writing

A list of topics for writing completes each chapter's discussion of the writing process as related to the chapter's overall topic. The topics are meant as suggestions only; this text assumes that students and their instructors may prefer to generate their own topics. Each list includes some of the following kinds of topics:

- topics that pick up on a theme or idea suggested by the chapter-opening essay

- topics of general interest

- academic topics that allow students to apply knowledge gained from one of their other courses

- topics that call for a personal response

Checklist for Revision

To get good revisions from students, teach them how to revise and then make revision an important part of your course objectives. *The Confident Writer,* Third Edition, offers specific suggestions on how to revise for content, organization, and style. The checklist for revision that comes near the end of every chapter focuses on such basics as thesis, purpose, evidence, and organization, but modifies these slightly in each chapter to incorporate a consideration of whatever topic a chapter covers. Thus, the Checklist for Revision is also a summary feature.

The Critical Thinker

The Critical Thinker near the end of each chapter has been completely revised. This feature now consists of four questions that encourage in-depth thinking about the chapter-opening essay. These questions focus on various aspects of the essay's structure or the author's meaning. The directions ask students to think about and discuss all four questions; then choose one as a topic for writing. However, instructors should feel free to use these questions as they wish. Any of them would make good topics for collaborative discussion and reporting.

Your Discovery Journal

A journal is a storehouse of ideas. Many professional writers keep journals in which they record their thoughts on the day's events, reflections on their reading, snippets of conversations, details of events and experiences—anything that may become a topic for writing.

Instructors use journals in many ways. Some instructors treat them as a way to establish a personal relationship with their students. They require students to keep journals, and they collect them periodically, read them, and make encouraging comments. Others make journal writing optional. Some see the journal as a way to monitor their students' learning, believing that the journal comments provide an insight into whether students understand course content. Some have even altered their presentation of material or retaught concepts that journal responses make clear the students are not getting.

If journal writing is a required activity in your class, or if you would like to try it, you will find that the topics provided in each chapter's Your Discovery Journal are thought provoking and lead to critical thinking and self-discovery. Or you can simply introduce this feature, explain that some writers have collected thoughts in their journals and have later turned them into topics for writing, and encourage students to try journal writing as an optional activity.

The Selective Writer, Unit 4

The title of unit 4 reflects *The Confident Writer,* Third Edition, assumption that writing is a series of choices, and correct grammar is the choice for clear communication. An idea can be expressed in any number of ways, but the more ways students know to combine sentence elements, or to expand sentences, the more options they have for framing ideas.

The Selective Writer, though by no means a comprehensive discussion of all grammatical concepts, is a mini-handbook of grammar that covers the common errors most beginning writers make and provides enough instruction to help students make good choices. Principles are explained briefly and simply with some exceptions to the rules noted.

The pronoun section has been expanded in the third edition. This section now includes discussions and exercises on the use of *who, whom, whoever,* and *whomever*; sentences of the "between you and me" variety; and pronoun-antecedent agreement with correlative conjunctions. The verb section has been expanded with a discussion and exercises on subject-verb agreement with correlative conjunctions. For those instructors who prefer a more integrative approach, the following chart suggests a way to integrate the topics covered in The Selective Writer with chapter content.

Integrating Selective Writer Topics with Chapter Content

Unit 4 Topic	Chapter	Chapter Topics	How They Integrate
B.1 sentence parts, types, and purposes	1	Overview of essay and introduction to writing process	Sentences are the foundation of paragraphs and essays.

Unit 4 Topic	Chapter	Chapter Topics	How They Integrate
B.2 sentence fragments	2	Prewriting strategies	Prewriting may result in fragments, which will need correcting as students draft and revise.
B.3 fused sentence, comma splice	3	Writing paragraphs	Topic sentences should be complete sentences, neither fragments nor run-ons.
B.4 coordination	4	Writing the thesis statement	Students need to correctly connect clauses when writing thesis statements and supporting sentences.
B.5 subordination	5	Supporting the thesis	
B.7 sentence variety	6	Revising for content, organization, and style	Writing varied sentences is one way to revise for style.
E.2 confused words	7	Editing	Confused words are one thing to check when editing.
C.1–C.6 punctuation	8	Library and research skills	Citing sources requires correct punctuation.
D.1 pronouns and C.8 quotation marks	9	Narration	Pronouns help achieve point of view. Quotation marks are used for dialogue.
D.3 modifiers	10	Description	Correctly placed modifiers are essential to description.
A.3, D.2 verbs	11	Process	Verbs establish time, and processes move through time.
D.5 numbers	12	Classification and division	Numbers and numerical transitions may clarify the explanation.
A.4 adjectives, adverbs, degrees of comparison	13	Comparison and contrast	Comparative words and phrases must be used correctly.

Unit 4 Topic	Chapter	Chapter Topics	How They Integrate
A.6 conjunctions, B.4–B.5 coordination and subordination	14	Cause and effect	Conjunctions and transition words help establish the cause-and-effect relationship.
E.1 denotation and connotation	15	Definition	Accurate word choice is an important part of defining.
E.3 spelling rules	16	Argument	Tone and word choice strengthen an argument. Words must be spelled correctly.

The Student-Centered Writing Class

Student-centeredness is more than a teaching style; it is an attitude those of us who love teaching probably already have in the sense that we care about our students and we try earnestly to reach them in whatever ways we have found that work. Some colleagues perceive the student-centered class as one that lacks structure. Others are skeptical of collaborative learning on the grounds that small group activity can degenerate into socializing. On the contrary, a student-centered class must be carefully structured to wean students from dependence on the instructor to the development of independent learning strategies. Group activity also requires structure so that each person is aware of learning outcomes and has a task to perform within the group.

A student-centered class is one in which the instructor, though an expert and the final authority, allows students to assume much of the responsibility for learning. In a student-centered class, students spend some time listening, some time working together and sharing ideas, and some time working independently. Student-centered classes are characterized by mini-lectures followed by immediate application of what is learned, rather than lectures that last almost the whole class period and are followed by a brief question-and-answer period or free-for-all discussion. In a student-centered class, nobody gets by with "winging it." Students are expected to know what the course objectives are and how each day's lesson fits into an overall plan for meeting those objectives. Finally, the students in a student-centered class take part in the evaluation process. The instructor grades their work, but the students also evaluate their own and each other's performance.

Establishing a Learning Community

A learning community is simply a group of people who share goals and objectives and who are actively and cooperatively engaged in learning activities that will help them achieve their goals. How do you turn your writing class into a learning community?

One way to begin is by asking students what they want to get out of the course. Though some may say they are just there to meet a requirement, treat that as a valid goal and list it on the board. Then ask them what else they would like to learn. Explore what writing is, and the uses of writing. Try to elicit your students' personal goals. If your course syllabus lists course objectives, have students compare what is on the syllabus with their comments and suggestions you have written on the board. You may find that many of them match. Those students who say they are just there to meet a requirement should be led through the syllabus to find out what the requirements are. This approach lets students know from the first day that everyone's responses get fair consideration and that everyone must be an active participant.

Instead of zeroing in on objectives and requirements on the first day, some of my colleagues like to reserve the first day for introductions. They use ice-breakers and other creative activities to help students get to know each other and feel comfortable in the class. My colleagues who use this approach also spend considerable class time throughout the term having students read and evaluate each other's writing. For them, first-day introductions are a step toward developing audience awareness.

Whatever you do to encourage involvement and interpretation, keep it going throughout the term. In a community of learners, everyone participates. Continually seek ways to involve students in activities that require everyone to contribute a meaningful part.

The Uses of Collaborative Learning

Many advocates of collaborative learning believe that students learn best from each other. Whether or not you share this belief, you probably value group activities for what can be some very positive outcomes. Working together encourages cooperation and compromise, skills valued in most workplaces.

Productive group activity has two requirements: The assignment and outcome must be clear, and everyone must take part. Make sure students know what their group is expected to find, achieve, or produce. It may be helpful to prepare a worksheet on which you list a series of questions to be answered about a reading, for example. If your students are evaluating each other's essays, a checklist or some other type of guide might be helpful. To ensure that everyone participates, limit the number of group members to four and try this simple division of tasks:

The *leader's* job is to keep everyone on task and make sure that each person contributes.

The *recorder* writes down the group's responses.

The *researcher* has charge of the dictionary, textbook, or other resource needed to answer questions or verify information.

The *reciter* summarizes the group's findings for the whole class.

Encourage, perhaps require, your students to take a different role each time they participate so they gain experience in the different types of group interaction.

Understanding Your Students' Needs

Your students have a variety of strengths and weaknesses. Though you probably have course objectives that you expect all students to meet, you probably also have allowed for some flexibility to provide for individual differences. During the first week or two of class, assess your students' writing skills. Many instructors find the *writing sample* an effective assessment tool. Before you begin instruction, have your students write an essay on a general topic. Tell them that the essay is for assessment purposes only and will not be graded. Do the writing sample in class so that there is no opportunity for students to get "help" from someone else. Use the sample to determine where your students are at the beginning of the course in relation to where you want them to be at the end. Do not mark up the essays. Instead, return each student's essay with two comments: 1. something the student has done well (a skill to build upon); 2. something that needs work (a skill that needs developing). Finally, make a tally of the group's strengths and weaknesses and share this information with the class. Following are two topic suggestions for writing samples:

Who I am and how I got to be that way

Why I have always liked or hated writing

As you collect and mark essays throughout the term, continue to do a tally of the group's strengths and weaknesses so that they can see their progress, not only as individuals, but as members of their learning community.

Reading in the Writing Class

Writing is meant to be read. All writers write for an audience, either imagined or real. A common complaint among instructors of writing is that students lack audience awareness. Perhaps this is because students do not always see themselves as readers or as the intended audience for a writer's message. With the exception of a glance at the morning paper, a quick once-over of an assigned textbook chapter, or some hastily conducted research in the library, many of our students simply do not read. They lack the experience we take for granted of reading a well-crafted essay and becoming thoroughly engaged by it or of reading the op-ed page in the newspaper and having our ire aroused.

The Reading and Writing Connection

Reading and writing are two facets of the same thinking process by which we construct, interpret, and evaluate meaning. If, as in *The Confident Writer,* Third Edition, the subject of the reading and writing is the essay, then the objective is to teach students to look for the same things in their reading that they try to achieve in their writing. Every writing skill we teach has a corresponding reading skill.

Making the connection between reading and writing is as simple as saying, for example, "Your essay's thesis is its central idea, what the whole essay is about. Just as you try to come up with a thesis when you are writing, you also try to figure out what the author's central, or main, idea is when you are reading. As a reader, you want to know what the author's thesis, is. As a writer, you try to state your own thesis clearly so that readers know what it is." Even instructors who say, "I do not have time to teach reading in the writing class" are probably teaching reading without realizing it. Whenever they talk about *audience* and what the audience knows, assumes, or expects, they are talking about readers and the reading process. Following is a chart that lists common writing skills most instructors teach and the reading skills that correspond to them.

Writing	Reading
Writing a thesis statement for an essay	Finding the central idea of a passage
Writing a topic sentence of a paragraph	Reading for the main idea of a paragraph

Understanding your audience's assumptions, expectations	Being aware of yourself as part of an author's audience, your assumptions and expectations as a reader
Having a purpose for writing	Determining an author's purpose
Selecting evidence to support your thesis	Finding the evidence that supports the author's point
Selecting a specific type of evidence such as facts, opinions, reasons, and examples	Being able to distinguish between facts and opinions as you read
Organizing your evidence in a logical, meaningful way	Following an author's ideas by recognizing common organizational patterns
Concluding your essay; making implications for readers	Being able to make inferences, draw conclusions from, and make judgments about what you read
Using coordination and subordination to vary sentence structure and connect ideas	Seeing relationships within and between sentences

Literal and Critical Comprehension Skills

Reading takes place on two levels, the *literal* level, which involves recognition of what the writer *says* or *states directly,* and the *critical* level, which involves interpretation of what the writer *implies* or *suggests indirectly.* If your students' papers lack insight, it may be because they have trouble reading and thinking at the critical level. Following is a list of literal and critical comprehension skills. Look over the list and determine how many of these skills most of your students possess.

Literal Comprehension Skills

- Finding the stated main idea of a given passage
- Finding specific information that supports a main idea
- Using the context of a passage to determine the meaning of an unfamiliar word within it

Critical Comprehension Skills

- Finding unstated main ideas by using stated information

- Determining an author's purpose

- Distinguishing between fact and opinion

- Distinguishing among different types of evidence

- Finding and following an author's pattern of organization

- Understanding how one sentence relates to another, or how an idea expressed in one part of a sentence relates to an idea expressed in another part of the same sentence

- Understanding how an argument develops from premise to conclusion

- Being able to make valid inferences and draw logical conclusions

- Being able to apply knowledge gained in one situation to another situation (for example, applying skills learned in writing class to writing an essay for another class)

- Being able to synthesize knowledge or information gained from several sources to come up with new findings

Many instructors complain that some students' papers are vacuous, that students cannot handle difficult topics that require them to *analyze* what they have read, to *apply* knowledge, or to *synthesize* information. Some complain that student writing is cliché-ridden and lacks originality. Students whose reading and thinking have not progressed much beyond a literal level usually do write this way. How do you get students to think more critically so that they can write the kinds of papers that are interesting and meaningful?

Critical Thinking

Critical thinking simply means doing those things listed under the aforementioned "critical comprehension skills," although some researchers may come up with a more exhaustive list than mine. As you can see from the list, you probably require your students to use one or more critical comprehension skills at every class meeting and on each assignment. Of course, some students are better at thinking critically than others, and some of those who do it well know neither what they are doing nor why. Though some people possess a greater capacity for critical thinking than others, everyone can improve his or her critical thinking skills.

Teaching critical thinking means helping your students see *why* and *how* the things you have asked them to do are part of the writing process.

To evaluate your students' grasp of critical thinking skills, ask them to explain to you why they selected a certain piece of evidence to support a thesis, or to explain their purpose for writing, or to describe the audience they had in mind for an essay they have written. The Critical Thinker in each chapter of *The Confident Writer,* Third Edition, contains questions that ask students to apply one or more of the critical comprehension skills listed on pages 12–13 to their in-depth analysis of the chapter-opening essay. For the specific critical comprehension skills addressed in each chapter's The Critical Thinker, see Suggestions for Each Chapter on pages 22–34 of this resource manual.

How to Read an Essay

Critical reading is the application of critical thinking to the reading process. To understand an essay requires reading on both the literal and critical levels of comprehension. Students should plan to read each assigned essay at least twice. The first reading is for pleasure, to get a sense of what the whole piece is about and to get a feeling for the writer's style and tone. The second reading is for study, to determine the writer's meaning and strategy. The second reading will probably take longer than the first, so students should plan their study time accordingly. You could ask them to prepare written answers to the questions like those in The Critical Reader and share them in small groups; or you could cover the questions in a class discussion. Remind them to underline or annotate in the margin the thesis statement, if they find one, and where each new piece of evidence begins. They should be prepared to discuss the writer's purpose and intended audience, and to underline or mark portions of the text that help them determine audience and purpose. This prepares them for discussion and prevents them from having to hunt for information in class. Suggest that they read with a dictionary at hand so they can look up words whose meanings they cannot figure out by using the context. In addition, ask them to put a question mark beside any phrase, idea, or piece of information they do not understand so that they will not forget to ask about it later.

If students read and mark the essay as explained above, they should have little trouble answering the questions that follow in The Critical Reader. Though there are probably many ways to read an essay, it is important that students use some kind of system for reading and annotating the text. Otherwise, their reading is likely to be only cursory and passive.

Before reading a chapter-opening essay, spend a few minutes in class preparing for the reading by briefly determining what the essay is about and who the author is. Ask students a few questions to activate their prior knowledge about the author's topic and any assumptions they may have about it. This prereading activity establishes a background, or context, for the reading. If you do this near the end of class, you can assign the essay for homework and for discussion at the next class meeting.

Discussion of an essay is a postreading activity that allows students to apply critical thinking skills to the task of reading. During discussion, ask your students these questions:

- What is the author's central idea?

- What evidence did the author use to support it?

- What implications do you see?

- (What is your interpretation of the author's meaning?) How has the author used words effectively to get the message across?

The Critical Reader that follows each essay addresses these questions under the headings of: *central idea, evidence, implications,* and *word choice.*

To summarize, introduce your students to the system in Table 1 as one effective way to read an essay and to apply the knowledge gained from it to the writing process. The first column in the table lists steps to follow, the second column lists what to do at each step, and the third column lists chapter features or parts that address each step. If you think the table is helpful and would like your students to try this system, you are welcome to reproduce it as a handout. The table also reminds students of some of the textbook features and their uses.

Table 1.   How to Read an Essay

Steps Feature/Part	What to Do	Textbook
1. Preread:	Establish context for reading; formulate questions to be answered by reading; check your assumptions and prior knowledge about the topic; find out what you can about the author; identify difficult or unfamiliar words and their meanings.	Awareness Check headnote that precedes essay Vocabulary Check
2. Read essay:	Read for pleasure and an overall sense of topic, style, and tone.	chapter-opening essay
3. Read essay again:	Determine meaning and strategy; underline or annotate essay; mark trouble spots with "?".	
4. Postread:	Review essay for *central idea, evidence, implications,* and *word choice.*	The Critical Reader
5. Apply:	Use the essay as a source for topics. Use skills modeled in the essay in your own writing.	Topics for Writing and The Critical Thinker

Study Skills for Student Writers

As you well know, many students do not apply the skills they learn in one class to similar work required in another without some continued reinforcement of those skills. We can do much to help our writing students develop good study habits that will not only help them be successful in our writing classes but will help them confidently tackle the tasks of writing that they have after they leave us. In addition to having a reading-study system as explained on pages 14–16 of this manual, these study skills are necessary for success in the writing class: *motivation, preparation, time management,* and *listening* and *note taking*.

Motivation and Student Responsibility

Students are either internally or externally motivated. Internally motivated students are self-motivated, and they accept responsibility for their successes and failures. They know that effort leads to achievement, and they see the connection between study and grades. These students rarely make excuses. They usually arrive on time, are prepared for class, and know what the requirements are. They know when tests are scheduled, and they keep up with the syllabus. Externally motivated students make excuses and do not accept responsibility for their success or failure. They believe it is your job to motivate them. They do not see the connection between effort and achievement, study and grades. Instead, they often believe that good grades are the result of luck or of having a good instructor. They are often late, absent, and unprepared. They may appear to be in the dark concerning tests and assignments, and they often do not keep up with the syllabus.

The behavioral problems of externally motivated students that keep them from being successful can all be traced to their belief that they do not control what happens in their lives. It is not that they lack motivation, but that they expect motivation to come from others. They depend on us to give it to them. How do we get these students to accept responsibility for their own motivation and perform-ance? One way is to provide opportunities for them to *be* responsible. For example, in a small group activity, the student must assume one of the assigned tasks such as *recorder* or *reciter.* The other students provide the peer pressure needed to keep the student on track. When students do contribute something significant to the group, they feel successful and thus experience one of the rewards of being responsible. Gradually, they learn that effort pays off.

It is important not to give up on your externally motivated students. When they come in after an absence and ask you if they can make up work, refer them to your syllabus for your stated policy on make-up work instead of repeating it every time they ask. The same is true of homework and deadlines for turning in papers. If you print due dates in your syllabus, you can hold your students responsible for keeping up with them and insist that they make the effort to do so.

Because writing is a process of building skill and skill requires practice, motivation is essential in the writing class. Motivation is a *student* responsibility. Continually seek ways to help your externally motivated students become aware of the behaviors that are holding them back. As students begin to see the connection between effort and success, they also develop self-motivation.

Preparation and Performance

In a writing class, there is a gradual development of skill that can only be gained through practice. To learn to write, students must write. They also need to see the connection among textbook assignments, class activities and discussion, and writing assignments. You can make this connection in your syllabus and in the way you structure your class. You can also suggest ways for students to go about doing the assignments, giving them tips and hints that you know other students have used successfully. Though preparation is their responsibility, you can do a few things to remind students of ways to prepare for your class. For example, you can begin the class by writing the day's objective on the board. Do a little review by asking your students why this objective is important and how it relates to what you did at the last class meeting. End the class by stating the objective for the next class meeting. Through this type of modeling exercise, you are teaching your students to integrate new knowledge with previously learned material and to anticipate what comes next.

Managing Time Effectively

How much time do you expect students to spend writing and revising each essay? How many essays do you expect them to write during the term? What is your schedule for marking and returning essays? What reading or other daily assignments do you plan to make, and how long should it take a college student to complete them? Of course, the obvious answer to any of these questions is, "It varies." Some of the variables include: how much time is available for study; how many assignments your students have to complete for their other courses; how often reading assignments and papers are due.

The obvious conclusion is that students are more likely to be successful in your writing class if they schedule time for completing essays and other assignments. Your syllabus can be a big help. Suggest that your students make a calendar of the term's work, enter on the calendar the due dates that are on your syllabus, then stay on schedule. The purpose of making and following a schedule is to prevent waiting until the night before to write an essay that is due on the next day. A calendar may not work for everyone, but making one is a positive step students can take toward managing their time. During the first weeks of class, they should keep track of how much time it takes to read, do assignments, and write an essay, then adjust their calendars accordingly.

Listening and Taking Notes

To encourage good listening and note-taking skills, model the kind of notes you want students to take. Plan your lectures and outline them. At the beginning of the semester, either list main ideas and major details on the board as you go, or put up the outline on the overhead projector so students can follow and take notes from it. When they become accustomed to your style, lecture without board notes or the overhead. Sometimes, at the end of the lecture, have them compare notes with each other to fill in gaps and ask questions, or summarize main ideas and examples so they can check their notes. Encourage students to keep a notebook and to title and date their notes. Enumerate when you are lecturing and use a lot of transitional words and phrases. To help students improve listening skills, tell them what to listen for: the words, phrases, and other signals you frequently use.

You probably use many of these techniques or have other ones that work better for you. In any case, we cannot assume that students know how to take notes. If we want students to learn and remember the writing strategies we are teaching, we have to suggest effective ways to take notes and provide clues that will aid their listening.

Assessment and Learning

There is no one best way to evaluate student essays, but a variety of assessment measures may provide a more complete picture of a student's progress and acquisition of skill. Though you may be familiar with all four of the methods below, I will briefly review their advantages and disadvantages. Whatever assessment measures you use, make sure they are clear to your students, that you state your grading policy in the syllabus, and that you do not change your policy during the term.

Analytical Grading

An analytical grading scheme is one that specifies point values for the A, B, C, D, and F grades and explains the characteristics of each grade. The advantage of this system is that it is fair. The standard is an objective one, and the bases for assigning a grade are spelled out. A disadvantage is that some students may quibble over points, becoming more grade-oriented and less progress-oriented in their writing than we would like.

Holistic Scoring

Holistic scoring is based upon a quick reading of an essay to get an overall impression of its competence. Essays are holistically scored on a scale of 1 to 6, for example, with 1 being the lowest and 6 being the highest. The essay is not marked. Two people read the essay independently, and their scores are compared. If they do not agree, a third reader reads the essay and determines the score. Scores are based on predetermined characteristics, or descriptors, that all readers who participate in a holistic scoring session have been trained to use. Both writers and readers are unidentified, making this probably the fairest of assessment measures. Another advantage is that the quick reading and lack of written comments on the essays enable an instructor to read many papers in a short time. A disadvantage of holistic scoring is that students have no comments or marks on their papers that point out strengths and weaknesses.

If you use holistic scoring, it should not be your only measure of assessment. For example, you could use holistic scoring for exam essays such as a midterm and final essay. For all other essays, you could use analytical grading. With holistic scoring as with analytical grading, it is important that students know the characteristics of the scores you assign to their papers.

Peer Evaluation

Many instructors believe that students learn much about writing through reading and evaluating each other's essays. A peer evaluation is a student reading of an essay with the reader's assessment of how well the essay meets certain established criteria. Some instructors develop peer evaluation sheets that list the criteria. Some have students read and comment on only one or two aspects of the paper. For example, a class might break up into pairs and evaluate each other's essays for a clear statement of thesis and sufficient evidence to support it. Whether or not the peer evaluation counts as a grade is up to the instructor. An advantage of peer evaluation is that students develop audience awareness through reading each other's essays and by seeing how others respond to their essays. Also, some students take advice more readily from their peers than from instructors. They may ask each other questions that they would not want to raise in front of the whole class or that they feel uncomfortable discussing with you. Disadvantages of peer evaluation are that some students may not take it seriously and that some students may not be able to give an effective and meaningful evaluation.

Self-Evaluation

A neglected area of assessment may be the self-evaluation. We probably do not spend enough time teaching students how to find and evaluate their own strengths and weaknesses because so many of them either over- or underestimate their strengths. Again, a clear set of criteria for evaluation makes it possible for students to know what we expect from their writing. A self-evaluation goal should be to help all students become capable of reading their essays and determining what they did well, what needs improving, and how much progress they are making without our having to write A, B, or C on every paper. Though we may never reach this goal, it is well worth our time to encourage, even require, our students to do a periodic self-evaluation. Checklists and progress charts are helpful self-evaluation tools.

Suggestions for Each Chapter

The following suggestions offer specific ways to use each chapter's features and exercises. You are the best judge of what your students' writing strengths and weaknesses are, what you need to focus on in each chapter, and what you can conveniently leave out. In general, a good plan to follow is to assign a chapter for reading, then choose the sections or exercises you want to emphasize in class.

Unit 1   The Writing Process

Chapter 1
Understanding the Essay: An Overview

This chapter explains what an essay is and introduces students to the three stages of the writing process: (1) prewriting, (2) drafting and organizing, and (3) rewriting. Although I believe that writing is a holistic, recursive process, I also believe that separating the process into stages, however artificial, makes it easier to explain and easier for students to grasp. Every writer probably approaches writing tasks in a slightly different way. Some would not dream of beginning without an outline. Others draft first and outline later to discover what they have written and what they need to add or leave out. Throughout the process, there is much starting and stopping, rethinking, and rewriting. But, whatever they do and however they do it, most writers do the following at some point in their process: they think about their topics and try to generate ideas for writing (prewriting); they write a rough draft and begin to experiment with selecting and organizing evidence to support a thesis (drafting and organizing); and they revise and edit until they are satisfied with what they have written (rewriting).

Assign the whole chapter for reading, then select the sections, concepts, or exercises you want to emphasize. For example, you might want to engage students in a discussion of how to read an essay, emphasizing active reading habits over passive reading habits. Then you could use Dympna Ugwu-Oju's essay "Should My Tribal Past Shape Delia's Future" as an example of good writing. Build a context for reading the essay by discussing the Awareness Check's three questions. Ask students to share what they know about the problems parents face when raising children in a culture that differs from their own. Use The Critical Reader and The Critical

Thinker to guide your students through a critical analysis of the essay's structure and the author's meaning and strategy.

Another goal in the first chapter is to help students see themselves as writers and to overcome any negative thoughts they may have about writing or about their abilities. Keeping a journal is a confidence-building activity. If you want your students to keep journals, now would be a good time to introduce Your Discovery Journal along with whatever criteria you want your students to follow. Knowing where to find help can also build confidence. Exercise 1.4 asks students to find out what online resources are available to student writers. If your writing course contains a computer component, you probably will want your students to do this exercise.

For a thematic approach, build your discussion of this chapter around family: What are some of the beliefs and attitudes we want our children to have? From a cultural standpoint, what are some similarities and differences among these beliefs?

To integrate a grammar topic with this chapter, try section B.1, Unit 4. This section is an overview of sentence parts, types, and purposes. Since sentences are the foundation of paragraphs and essays, it makes sense to include a review of sentences with your overview of the essay and introduction to the writing process.

Chapter 2
Using Prewriting Strategies

A common student complaint is, "I don't know what to write." Chapter 2 focuses on three basic ways to help students get started. First, they need to develop confidence in the self they bring to writing. Students come to us with a wealth of experiences; diverse social, racial, ethnic, and cultural backgrounds; and a variety of interests, values, and goals. They tend to undervalue this experience as a source of topics and ideas for writing. Exercise 2.1 lists several categories of experience and asks students to list as many items as they can about themselves that will fit into each category to come up with a profile that defines who they are. This is a self-discovery exercise that addresses the question, "What do I bring to the writing process?"

A second way we can help students get started is to show them how to limit a topic. If a topic is not limited sufficiently, it is either too broad and general or too narrow to be meaningful. Robert M. Pirsig's essay, which is excerpted from *Zen and the Art of Motorcycle Maintenance*, illustrates how one teacher got his student to focus her writing on one brick instead of the whole building. Have your students read the essay and answer The Critical Reader questions that follow as an introduction to your discussion of how to limit topics.

Teaching students prewriting strategies is a third way to help students get started, and this chapter covers brainstorming, freewriting, the journalist's questions, and clustering. To these familiar strategies, Chapter 2 adds a new one: START.

This acronym stands for Self, Topic, Audience, Reason (purpose), and Tone. Have your students try all the strategies with the objective of settling on the one that works best for them and making it their own. Try this exercise on tone to supplement those in the text: search the letters to the editor pages of your newspaper. Though not always well-written, they are often excellent examples of tones that students can readily identify. Look for letters written on the same topic that have different tones. Have your students bring in letters to share with the class or their own letters to the editor. If your students want to experiment with freewriting, assign Exercise 2.5, which explains how to freewrite on computer. The blank-screen technique explained in this exercise promotes spontaneity and the free flowing of ideas by making it impossible to edit as you go.

To integrate a grammar topic with this chapter, try section B.2, Unit 4. This section covers sentence fragments, which are among the most frequent errors students make. Clear, correct sentences are the foundation of good writing. If you integrated a discussion of sentence parts, types, and purposes with Chapter 1, it may seem logical to continue with a discussion of ways to eliminate sentence errors as you move into this chapter and the next one.

Chapter 3
Improving Your Paragraph Skills

Chapter 3 covers three keys to confident paragraph writing: main idea, support, and organization. "Main Idea" covers stated and implied main ideas. "Supporting the Main Idea" covers how to support the main idea with specific evidence in the form of facts, reasons, and examples. "Organizing the Evidence" covers unity and three coherence patterns: time order, spatial order, and emphatic order. Review with your students Figure 3.2, which lists and briefly explains coherence patterns. Have them mark the page in their books for quick reference to the figure, or point out that the inside back cover of *The Confident Writer* contains a quick guide to many of the book's figures, with page references. The chapter also covers signal words and phrases that help achieve coherence between sentences.

This chapter focuses on the paragraph, not as an isolated unit, but as a part of an essay. Though it probably will be a refresher for most, it may be new information for some. Introduce the three keys as guides for how to revise paragraphs that need more or better development.

Sara Gilbert's essay "The Many Ways of Being Smart," which begins the chapter, is one that your students will enjoy, and it also is an excellent model of good paragraph development. It will be easy for your students to find Gilbert's topic sentences and to determine that examples are her primary choice of evidence. The essay's positive thesis, that we are all intelligent in some ways, is very encouraging to students. For an in-depth analysis of this essay, assign The Critical Thinker's four questions. In addition, have your students do Exercise 3.1, which is an online search for information on other theories of intelligence; Howard Gardners' multiple intelligence theory is given as an example. For writing assignments based on this essay, see The Critical Thinker.

Because a focus on paragraph improvement leads to a focus on the individual sentences that make up the paragraph, you can easily integrate grammar instruction into the discussion of the paragraph. For example, a topic sentence must be a complete sentence. Students should check topic sentences for completeness and to eliminate fused sentence and comma splice errors, which are covered in section B.3, Unit 4.

Chapter 4
Stating Your Thesis

Chapter 4 shows students how to write clear thesis statements that limit, control, and direct what they will say in their essays. Begin it by helping students recognize the difference between a thesis statement and a simple statement of fact using Exercise 4.2. Also, Stephen King's essay "Ever Et Raw Meat?" has a clearly stated thesis that students can usually find with little help. The thesis makes clear how King intends to develop his central idea. Exercise 4.1 illustrates how to find an author on the Internet by taking students to King's website and by suggesting other sites they might try. Students' searches and results could form the basis of a class discussion not only on King and his writing but on researching an author in general.

Exercises 4.2–4.5 lead students through the process of constructing a thesis that clearly states or implies a topic, the writer's opinion about the topic, the purpose for writing, and the parts, or divisions, of the essay. These exercises will have some of your students writing good thesis statements within one or two class meetings.

Chapter 4 presents the thesis statement within the context of an introductory paragraph and covers five ways to introduce the thesis: with an anecdote, with a revealing question, with background information, with a quotation and explanation, or with interesting facts or figures. In addition to the chapter exercises, try this classroom exercise: Have students get into groups of four and take out whatever textbooks from other classes they have with them. Turn to a chapter in one of these books that they are currently working on. Read the paragraph that introduces the whole chapter or that introduces a section of the chapter, and try to determine the writer's thesis and which of the five common methods of introduction the writer has used. Most students will be able to find one or more of the introductory devices you have taught them. The exercise is helpful for two reasons: They get to see how other writers use the strategies you are teaching them, and they experience themselves as readers responding to the writer's strategy. One more benefit is that, in your writing class, you are teaching them a reading skill that they can apply critically in other classes: to look for the writer's thesis (central idea) and how it is introduced.

Organization in writing is often a matter of setting up and maintaining logical relationships within and between sentences. Students can learn to do this by using transitional words and phrases, and by using coordination and subordination. Section B.4, Unit 4, covers coordination and the relationships that the coordinating conjunctions establish between clauses. One way to integrate coordination with instruction on how to write thesis statements is to put some of your students' thesis statements on the board and show how they can be improved by coordination. Or you can show students how coordination can help them combine sentences to improve their introductory paragraphs.

Chapter 5
Supporting Your Thesis

Chapter 5 covers selecting and arranging evidence and organizing the essay so that it follows the direction of development from introduction through the body paragraphs to a conclusion. Principles of organization can be difficult for students to grasp, so this chapter suggests three ways to help students deal with the problem.

First, have them experiment with making informal outlines that specify the broad divisions of their paper. If they have written thesis statements that divide their topic into parts, then they already know what their divisions will be. The broad divisions may become body paragraphs that they can develop with the evidence they generated from a brainstorming list or other prewriting activity.

Try teaching them the three levels of development as represented on a formal outline: from general to specific, from main idea to major detail to minor detail. Students tend to stay at the first level of development, writing one general statement after another, so that their body paragraphs lack concrete details. If you believe that outlines are too prescriptive, introduce them as a revision device. After students have written their drafts, have them outline them to determine how they have organized their evidence and to expose weak development.

Teach students signal words and the other coherence devices explained in Chapter 5 to help them connect paragraphs. Subordination, as explained in section B.6, Unit 4, is one way to set up and maintain relationships between sentences and paragraphs. If you choose to integrate section B.6 with Chapter 5, give students practice in determining how a sentence that begins with a subordinating conjunction relates to the ones preceding and following it.

Students must be taught strategies for concluding their essays. Have them examine writing from their textbooks, and examples you bring in for the writer's use of a concluding device. Devices covered in this chapter are summary, prediction, and challenge. Four of the introductory strategies covered in Chapter 4 also work well as concluding devices: anecdote, quotation and explanation, facts and figures, and revealing question. In addition, have your students search the Internet for more information on unity and coherence. See Exercise 5.6 for suggestions.

Chapter 6
Revising Your Essays

How do we get students to spend more time revising their essays? One way is by providing them with revision strategies and supervising and commenting on their application of those strategies. This chapter explains *what* to revise and *how* to revise.

Spend some time on revision. When you cover this topic, run your class like a workshop. Explain the strategies, return essays that need revising, and have your students work either individually or in small groups, leaving you free to answer questions and supervise the activity. Have them do three revisions: one each for content, organization, and style. Though you want them to do three separate revisions the first time to learn the strategies, they may not need to do three separate revisions every time they write.

A revision for style means rewriting to improve diction, tone, and sentence variety. Sentence variety is covered in section B.7, Unit 4. You may find this to be one of the most useful grammar lessons in Unit 4 because it unlocks the mystery of style for students by teaching them that, in part, style has to do with sentence length and type, two aspects of sentence structure that are easy for students to understand and control.

Refer to the student essay that opens the chapter and Robin Simmons's essay on page 150 as resources for students who write strings of general statements and need to revise for content. Figure 6.1 lists questions to ask about organization, and students can use it as a checklist when they are revising to achieve better organization. Exercise 6.6 takes students to the Strunk and White website to find more information on tone.

Chapter 7
Editing Your Essays

Editing consists of proofreading to find mistakes in grammar, punctuation, and spelling as well as eliminating the "clutter" of wordiness, passive voice, and tired expressions. William Zinsser's essay "Clutter" introduces the chapter and is the basis for The Critical Thinker topic that asks students to write about the clutter they find in newspaper articles. To find the clutter, they have to apply the proofreading skills explained in the chapter.

Spend some time going over Figures 7.1 and 7.2. Figure 7.1 is a list of common grammatical errors that students can use as a starting point to determine what their most frequent errors are. A review of their returned essays may reveal a pattern of errors. Figure 7.2 is an editing checklist students can use either for group editing activities or for editing drafts of their essays on their own. Exercise 7.2 suggests writing-center websites students can use for searching out information and practice material on the specific types of errors they make.

Encourage students to buy, use, and bring to class a dictionary, a thesaurus, and other helpful tools, such as a bad speller's dictionary if they have a spelling problem.

Confusing words and word pairs are the subject of section E.2, Unit 4, which covers thirty-nine of the words students most often confuse. When editing their essays, students should also check for any confused look-alike and sound-alike words.

Chapter 8
Using the Library, Doing Research

Chapter 8 addresses library and research skills. Only you can determine whether this chapter is appropriate for your classes. Many instructors introduce research and library skills to beginning writers. Many prefer to postpone these for more advanced classes, after students have mastered the basics of writing. One good argument for introducing these skills early is that students may be required to conduct research and write research papers or reports in one or more of their classes before having had an opportunity to take an advanced composition course in which these skills are traditionally taught. Chapter 8 introduces students to the basics of using the library, researching, writing, and documenting papers and may give them a jump-start in learning these important skills before they are required to explore them in more depth in subsequent courses.

Since correct punctuation is an essential part of both citing sources and compiling a bibliography, you could integrate a review of punctuation with Chapter 8. Sections C.1–C.6 of Unit 4 cover punctuation. Use Exercise 8.3, an online card catalog activity, as part of your introduction to using your library's resources.

Unit 2   Patterns as Options

Chapter 9
Using Narration

Chapter 9 begins with Langston Hughes's "Salvation," a classic narrative essay about a conversion experience. This essay exemplifies all the characteristics of narration covered in the chapter: It follows a time sequence to explain the event; it makes clear what the event's significance is; it makes use of dialogue and descriptive details to bring the event to life; and its point of view is the one best suited to telling this story.

Narration is the easiest pattern for many students to master because they have written narrative essays for high school classes, so they may already know that narration is about relating events and that time order is its primary organizational principle. They most likely will need help in choosing descriptive details, maintaining a consistent point of view, determining the significance of the event they want to describe, and using dialogue.

Tracing events through time is a feature of narration that textbook writers use to explain events such as "The Battle of Britain" or what happens during mitosis. In a science lab, students conduct experiments in which they observe certain chemical reactions that occur over a period of time, and they have to recount these events in their notes. Acquainting students with these other uses of narration may help them to make the connection between what they do in your class and the reading and writing they do in other classes. Being able to recognize and follow common thought patterns is a critical reading skill that you can integrate into your instruction on the uses of patterns in writing.

You may also want to emphasize that answering the journalist's questions—*who, what, where, when, why, how,* and *what if?* is a good prewriting activity for planning a narrative essay, and that Figure 9.1 lists common transitions useful for alerting readers to a time sequence.

Section D.1, Unit 4, covers pronoun case, reference, and agreement. The discussion and exercises in this section tie in with the explanation of point of view on pages 224–227. Since maintaining a consistent point of view in a narrative essay is often difficult for students, you may want to integrate this section with Chapter 9. Section C.8, Unit 4, on quotation marks also integrates well with this chapter, particularly with the discussion on using dialogue in a narrative essay.

For an interesting writing assignment, have students complete Exercise 9.9, which takes them to the Gallery of Achievers website. This site lists high achievers in many areas such as sports, science, art, education, and architecture. Have students write about a person they admire using information from this site. To add depth to the assignment, have them consult other resources, in addition to this one, for information about their person of choice.

Chapter 10
Using Description

The Zora Neale Hurston excerpt and Brett Lott's essay that begin this chapter abound with sensory details. Have students use Figure 10.1, the sensory detail chart, to analyze the Hurston and Wong pieces for descriptive details. Encourage them to use details in their writing that appeal to all five senses.

Description depends upon making careful observations and having a purpose and controlling idea for your description. All of these are covered in the chapter with appropriate exercises, but you may want to come up with additional exercises of your own that take students out of the classroom to do some observing and note taking. When discussing the purpose of description, be sure to emphasize the difference between the objective and subjective purposes as explained in the chapter. Also, make the connection between objective purpose and academic writing. Science writers, for example, provide detailed descriptions of plant and animal life for the purpose of distinguishing one species from another. A good exercise is to have students examine several different types of writing both for sensory details and for descriptive purpose. You could use textbook passages, newspaper or magazine articles, and excerpts from books that either you or the students bring in. Also try Exercise 10.7, which takes students to www.photovault.com, a collection of photographs they can use as a resource for writing. Photographs test students' powers of observation, forcing them to report exactly what they see in the photo, and testing their ability to make inferences from what they observe.

Descriptive details are largely constructed through the use of adjectives, adverbs, concrete nouns, and the placement of modifying words, phrases, and clauses. Therefore, section D.3, Unit 4, integrates well with this chapter.

Chapter 11
Explaining a Process

Andy Rooney's essay "How to Put Off Doing a Job" is a humorous twist on self-help manifestos of the evils of procrastination and how to get things done. Not only is Rooney's essay a good example of process, it is a lighthearted way to approach the subject of procrastination and perhaps even generate a serious discussion of the problem that will lead to a writing assignment.

The difference between an informational and directional process is one you will want to emphasize. When students have trouble with writing about processes, it is often because their purpose for writing is not clear.

Use Figure 11.1 to help students see the connection among purpose, process, and outcome. Audience awareness is important in writing about processes. Students need to determine how familiar with the process readers already are and what more they need to be told. Central also to good process writing are the identification, organization, and explanation of steps or stages in the process. Chapter exercises cover these points, but you may want to try additional exercises. Have students form groups of four and list and explain the steps in the registration process. Then compare the groups' lists. Most students think they know all there is to know about this process, and maybe they do, but can they explain it accurately to someone who has never done it? The problems they encounter as they try to do this exercise illustrate the pitfalls of writing about processes: determining how many steps or stages there are; getting them in the proper sequence; breaking them down into meaningful substeps; and providing enough detail for readers to follow the process.

Figure 11.2 is a list of transitions that signal steps or stages in processes, and the section on thesis statement explains how to signal process, purpose, and parts of your essay in the thesis statement. Use the figure to supplement your discussion on coherence. Use the suggestions for writing thesis statements both to help your students get started and as a refresher for those who still have trouble with stating their essay's central idea.

Since processes often involve stages that move through time and since verb tenses indicate when actions take place, sections A.3 and D.2, Unit 4, on verbs, tense consistency, and agreement integrate well with this chapter, as does Exercise 11.9, which is an Internet search activity involving paragraph skills and transitions.

Chapter 12
Choosing Classification or Division

Like comparing and contrasting, classifying comes naturally to students. They have all had practice using classification systems, whether to sort and arrange their belongings, look for a video to rent, or set up a budget.

You can use some of these homely examples to introduce classification and have students come up with their own. See whether they can determine the basis for their classifications: How are the items in a kitchen arranged and why? What would happen if you did not have a certain drawer for the cooking utensils?

Use the dividing and sorting exercises in the chapter to help students grasp the concept that there are two ways to classify: by dividing one thing into its parts or by sorting many things into categories. Tom Bodett's "dish demeanor" provides an excellent example of a classification broken down into categories and subcategories that are easy for students to identify. Bodett also mixes process with classification, and you can use this essay to illustrate how mixed patterns work. If your students are interested in learning more about Tom Bodett, have them do Exercise 12.7, which takes them to his website.

Section D.5, Unit 4, is one you could integrate with your explanation of classification and division. This section covers the correct use of numbers. Transition words that express numbers or numbers themselves often appear in an author's explanation of a classification or division system.

Chapter 13
Comparing and Contrasting

Two problems you may encounter in teaching comparison and contrast are that students may try to compare two unrelated subjects, or they may have trouble selecting and organizing their points or characteristics of comparison. To overcome the problem of choosing unrelated subjects, emphasize that the subjects should be members of the same class of items: two types of computers, two different teachers, or two different films, as in Steven D. Stark's essay on pages 293–296. Also, point out that they should have a purpose for comparing subjects: either to distinguish between them, or to make a judgment about them, for example, that one is better or more advantageous than the other. Use Figure 13.1, which lists several pairs of subjects, their relationship, and two different topics that illustrate both kinds of purposes.

To overcome the problem of selecting and organizing evidence, have students make two-columned lists for brainstorming their subjects side by side. They should compare subjects on the basis of several common characteristics and end up with about the same amount and kind of information. Placing the lists side by side visually demonstrates gaps in the lists. Use Figures 13.2 and 13.3, which illustrate two ways to organize comparative details: a point-by-point or subject-by-subject analysis. The thesis statement can also serve as an organizing feature of the essay if it clearly states or implies the purpose and subjects or terms of comparison. Have students read and complete the exercises in the section "Write a Thesis That Sets Up the Pattern."

An effective comparison requires the use of adjectives that specify *what kind*, *which one*, *how many*, and *whose*. It also requires the use of adverbs that specify *how*, *when*, *where*, *how often*, and *to what extent*. In addition, it requires an understanding of the degrees of comparison: positive, comparative, and superlative. Section A.4, Unit 4, covers adjectives, adverbs, and the degrees of comparison, and you may want to emphasize the examples that show how Stark uses adjectives and adverbs, and have students try to find more of them either in Stark's essay in this chapter or in other pieces of writing they or you bring to class. Exercise 13.5 lists two helpful websites students can visit to gather information for writing an essay in which they compare two films.

Chapter 14
Explaining Causes and Effects

Understanding causes and effects can be troublesome for students, but you can help them overcome their difficulties by introducing the three signals of a cause-and-effect analysis that are explained in this chapter: the question-and-answer signal, the act/consequence signal, and the probability signal.

Use Figure 14.1 to explain transitions that signal cause-and-effect relationships, and teach your students two methods of organization for analyzing causes and effects: Explain causes that produce a single effect, or explain several effects that result from one cause.

Rob Waldron's essay "Students are Dying: Colleges Can Do More" is about the causes and effects of alcohol abuse among college students. It is a topic that interests many students who have struggled with alcohol abuse, either their own or that of someone close to them. Furthermore, Spring Break and the binge drinking that accompanies this celebration is a fact of many college students' lives. The essay, therefore, should generate some lively discussion and writing topics on alcohol or drug abuse. As a follow-up to Waldron's essay, have students complete the Internet activity on binge drinking in Exercise 14.6.

Section A.6, Unit 4, on conjunctions integrates well with this chapter. You could also do a brief review of sections B.4 and B.5 on coordination and subordination. Conjunctions establish relationships within and between sentences—among them the cause-and-effect relationship.

Chapter 15
Using Definition

Chapter 15 explains how to write extended definitions using five common methods: example, comparing, tracing history, narrating incidents, and negation. Alice Hoffman's "The Perfect Family" defines *family* in all these ways.

Make sure your students understand the roles purpose and audience play in a good definition of a word or term. Some of the best definitions give readers a new meaning for a familiar term. To write a good definition, students must have a good reason for defining a word, or a term, and a clear understanding both of how readers define the term and how they expect readers to change or add to their definitions.

Exercise 15.6 is an activity involving the use of two online reference tools that can help students with writing definitions.

Section E.1, Unit 4, on denotation and connotation integrates well with the chapter's topic. To write good definitions, students need to know their way through a dictionary and thesaurus, and they need to be aware of the emotional associations attached to many words and terms, which are not always explained in the dictionary. Use the exercises in this section for practice in using denotation and connotation.

Chapter 16
Arguing Persuasively

This chapter does not distinguish between argument and persuasion as separate rhetorical modes because it is intended as an introduction to the features of argumentative writing: defining an issue, making a claim, proving your claim, and answering opposing claims. The underlying assumption of the chapter is that argument is an *attitude* rather than a pattern; it is a position the writer takes toward a subject that can be explained or defended with evidence. The evidence may be organized using any of the patterns explained in Chapters 9–15. Exercise 16.9 is a search activity that takes students to several websites they can use as resources for finding information on a variety of issues, one of which may interest them as an essay topic.

Richard Rodriguez's essay "Minority Student" illustrates these principles of argument. He argues that affirmative action programs may do more harm than good and may not be in the best interests of minority students. As one means of advancing his argument, he writes an extended definition of *minority*.

Introduce Figures 16.1 and 16.2 as helpful guides for planning and writing an argumentative essay. Figure 16.1 lists questions to ask to brainstorm your topic, and Figure 16.2 illustrates one way to structure an argumentative essay. When teaching this topic, suggest ways that students can apply everything else they have learned in the course to the writing of an argumentative essay. Use Figures 16.3 and 16.4 to teach the common fallacies that ignore or oversimplify issues and make an argument invalid.

Section E.3, Unit 4, covers six rules of spelling improvement. If it is appropriate in your course to cover spelling, have students examine some or all of their returned essays for spelling errors, list the misspelled words, and determine which of the rules they need to review. This exercise generally reveals a pattern of errors that reflects one or more of the rules covered in this section. If you do not plan to cover spelling, you could instead introduce a grammar concept that you have not previously addressed.

Preparing Your Syllabus

Students who lack good study habits may ignore the syllabus unless you make a point of reading it with them in class and referring to it often during the first few weeks. For some students, using the syllabus may be their first step toward becoming independent learners. To encourage independence, require students to bring the syllabus to class every day. Throughout the course, when they ask questions that your syllabus answers, refer them to the appropriate section. Insisting that students use the syllabus is one way to help them develop responsibility for their progress in class.

In compiling your syllabus for *The Confident Writer*, Third Edition, keep in mind that the flexible organization of the text has been designed to enable you to tailor your course to your students' needs.

Sample Syllabus A below is for a sixteen-week course. Because course descriptions and instructors' policies vary, only the assignment schedule is included. This syllabus allows for maximum flexibility in that it does not specify which exercises students must do. It is a general guideline that allows you to decide how much to cover in a class period and to assign exercises and essays accordingly. As you decide which exercises you want students to complete and when you want them to hand in final drafts of essays for grading, have them write the information in the syllabus on lines you provide. Each week focuses on a single chapter and one or more major topics. The first half of the semester is devoted to the writing process, and the second half is devoted to rhetorical patterns.

Sample Syllabus A (sixteen-week course)

Week 1   Reading assignment: Chapter 1
              Topics: An Introduction to the Course
                             An Overview of the Essay
                             The Process of Writing

              Exercises: _____

              Writing assignment: _____

Week 2   Reading assignment: Chapter 2
                Topic: Getting Started
                Exercises: _____
                Writing assignment: _____

Week 3   Reading assignment: Chapter 3
                Topic: The Paragraph (a review)
                Exercises: _____
                Writing assignment: _____

Week 4   Reading assignment: Chapter 4
                Topics: Thesis Statements
                              Introductions
                Exercises: _____
                Writing assignment: _____

Week 5   Reading assignment: Chapter 5
                Topics: Evidence
                              Conclusions
                Exercises: _____
                Writing assignment: _____

Week 6   Reading assignment: Chapter 6
                Topic: The Revision Process
                Exercises: _____
                Writing assignment: _____

Week 7   Reading assignment: Chapter 7
                Topic: The Editing Process
                Exercises: _____
                Writing assignment: _____

Week 8   Reading assignment: Chapter 8
                Topics: Library Skills
                            Researching and Writing
                Exercises: _____
                Writing assignment: _____

Week 9   Reading assignment: Chapters 9 and 10
                Topics: Narration and Description
                Exercises: _____
                Writing assignment: _____

Week 10   Reading assignment: Chapter 11
                Topic: Process
                Exercises: _____
                Writing assignment: _____

Week 11   Reading assignment: Chapter 12
                Topic: Classification and Division
                Exercises: _____
                Writing assignment: _____

Week 12   Reading assignment: Chapter 13
                Topic: Comparison and Contrast
                Exercises: _____
                Writing assignment: _____

Week 13   Reading assignment: Chapter 14
                Topic: Cause and Effect
                Exercises: _____
                Writing assignment: _____

Week 14   Reading assignment: Chapter 15
                Topic: Definition
                Exercises: _____
                Writing assignment: _____

Week 15   Reading assignment: Chapter 16
               Topic: Making Arguments
               Exercises: _____
               Writing assignment: _____

Week 16   Reading assignment: Selected essays and topics from Units 3 and 4
               Topics: Review of Process, Writing Strategies,
                            and Selected Grammar Topics
               Exercises: _____
               Writing assignment: _____

    Sample Syllabus B below, like Sample Syllabus A, is for a sixteen-week course. This syllabus places greater emphasis on the writing process than on rhetorical patterns.

Sample Syllabus B (sixteen-week course)

Week 1   Reading assignment: Chapter 1
               Topics: An Introduction to the Course
                            An Overview of the Essay
               Exercises: _____
               Writing assignment: _____

Week 2   Reading assignment: Chapter 1 continued
               Topic: The Process of Writing
               Exercises: _____
               Writing assignment: _____

Week 3   Reading assignment: Chapter 2
               Topic: Getting Started
               Exercises: _____
               Writing assignment: _____

Week 4   Reading assignment: Chapter 3
                Topic: The Paragraph (main idea and supporting evidence)
                Exercises: _____
                Writing assignment: _____

Week 5   Reading assignment: Chapter 3 continued
                Topic: The Paragraph (organizing the evidence)
                Exercises: _____
                Writing assignment: _____

Week 6   Reading assignment: Chapter 4
                Topic: Thesis Statements
                Exercises: _____
                Writing assignment: _____

Week 7   Reading assignment: Chapter 4 continued
                Topic: Writing Good Introductions
                Exercises: _____
                Writing assignment: _____

Week 8   Reading assignment: Chapter 5
                Topic: Evidence
                Exercises: _____
                Writing assignment: _____

Week 9   Reading assignment: Chapter 5 continued
                Topic: Writing Good Conclusions
                Exercises: _____
                Writing assignment: _____

Week 10   Reading assignment: Chapters 6 and 7
                Topic: The Revision and Editing Processes
                Exercises: _____
                Writing assignment: _____

Week 11   Reading assignment: Chapter 8
           Topic: The Research Process
           Exercises: _____
           Writing assignment: _____

Week 12   Reading assignment: Chapters 9 and 10
           Topics: Understanding Thought Patterns
                         Narration
                         Description
           Exercises: _____
           Writing assignment: _____

Week 13   Reading assignment: Chapters 11 and 12
           Topics: Process
                         Classification and Division
           Exercises: _____
           Writing assignment: _____

Week 14   Reading assignment: Chapters 13 and 14
           Topics: Comparison and Contrast
                         Cause and Effect
           Exercises: _____
           Writing assignment: _____

Week 15   Reading assignment: Chapters 15 and 16
           Topics: Definition
                         Making an Argument
           Exercises: _____
           Writing assignment: _____

Week 16   Reading assignment: Selected essays and topics from Units 3 and 4
           Topics: Review of Process and Writing Strategies
                         Review of Common Grammatical Problems
           Exercises: _____
           Writing assignment: _____

Sample Syllabus C below is intended for a ten-week course. This syllabus provides more structure than Syllabus A or B in that it specifies the number of essays to be collected for grading and when they are due for grading. On a syllabus of this type, you might also specify which exercises you want done in class and which you want done as homework. Since instructors' choices of exercises may vary, write-on lines indicate where exercises could be typed before handing out the syllabus. Like Syllabus B, Syllabus C emphasizes process over pattern.

Sample Syllabus C (ten-week course)

Week 1   Reading assignment: Chapter 1

     Topics: Introduction to Course

     Overview of the Essay

     Understanding the Writing Process

     Exercises (in class): _____

     Exercises (homework): _____

Week 2   Reading assignment: Chapter 2

     Topic: Getting Started

     Exercises (in class): _____

     Exercises (homework): _____

     Essay #1 due at the end of the week

Week 3   Reading assignment: Chapter 3

     Topic: The Paragraph (a review)

     Exercises (in class): _____

     Exercises (homework): _____

     Essay #2 due at the end of the week

Week 4   Reading assignment: Chapter 4

     Topic: Thesis and Introduction

     Exercises (in class): _____

     Exercises (homework): _____

     Essay #3 due at the end of the week

Week 5   Reading assignment: Chapter 5
                Topic: Evidence and Conclusion
                Exercises (in class): _____
                Exercises (homework): _____
                Essay #4 due at the end of the week

Week 6   Reading assignment: Chapters 6–8
                Topic: Revising, Editing, and Researching
                Exercises (in class): _____
                Exercises (homework): _____

Week 7   Reading assignment: Chapters 9–11
                Topics: Understanding Thought Patterns
                                Narration, Description, Process
                Exercises (in class): _____
                Exercises (homework): _____
                Essay #5 due at the end of the week

Week 8   Reading assignment: Chapters 12–14
                Topics: Classification and Division, Comparison and Contrast,
                                Cause and Effect
                Exercises (in class): _____
                Exercises (homework): _____
                Essay #6 due at the end of the week

Week 9   Reading assignment: Chapters 15–16
                Topics: Definition and Making Arguments
                Exercises (in class): _____
                Exercises (homework): _____

Week 10   Reading assignment: Selected essays and topics from Units 3 and 4
                Topics: Review of Process, Strategies, and Grammar
                Exercises (in class): _____
                Exercises (homework): _____
                Essay #7 due at the end of the week

As you prepare your syllabus, bear in mind that the chapters of *The Confident Writer,* Third Edition, contain many exercises. Your choices will reflect your course objectives and your students' needs. The number and variety of exercises allow you plenty of options for structuring your course.

Answer Key

Chapter 1
Understanding the Essay: An Overview

The Critical Reader

1. The central idea is stated in the second sentence of paragraph 9: "Every decision involving Delia is a tug of war between Ibo and American traditions."

2. To be an asset to her husband the author believed she had to cater to him and to her children and to become educated in both the Ibo and Western cultures so as to raise the bride price.

3. In paragraph 3, the author says that both she and her husband are professionals and that they go to PTA meetings. These examples support her statement, "I'm as American as anyone else." She also says in paragraph 3 that her Ibo customs influence her decision making in her private life.

4. The issues with which the author has struggled in raising her daughter are whether to turn Delia into the kind of woman her grandmothers want her to be or to let her be an independent woman, whether to applaud her academic and athletic victories or belittle her for being "only a woman," and whether Delia will consider her mother's feelings in choosing a spouse.

5. Answers will vary.

6. The word choices in paragraph 9 are effective because "struggled," "tug of war," and "vacillated" all suggest the difficulty the author is having in deciding how to raise her daughter. These word choices also clearly illustrate that she is torn between the Ibo and American value systems.

Exercise 1.1

Answers will vary.

Exercise 1.2

Answers will vary.

Exercise 1.3

Answers will vary, but the thesis statement should be a complete sentence and should make clear two things: the writer's topic and what the writer wants to say about it.

Exercise 1.4

Because computer support for writing varies from campus to campus, the results of student searches will also vary.

Exercise 1.5

Answers will vary but should look something like this:

1. a personal letter
   a. Purpose: to update my reader on the events in my life
   b. Audience: a friend or relative who knows me well
2. an invitation to a party
   a. Purpose: to tell them the purpose, time, and place of the party
   b. Audience: those invited to the party
3. a résumé
   a. Purpose: to explain your experience and qualifications for the job
   b. Audience: prospective employers
4. a letter to the editor of your local newspaper
   a. Purpose: to express your views on an issue of current interest
   b. Audience: readers of the paper
5. a letter of complaint
   a. Purpose: to explain what the complaint is and what you want done about it
   b. Audience: the person to whom you are making the complaint
6. an essay for a writing class
   a. Purpose: to make and support a point; to fulfill an assignment
   b. Audience: instructor and classmates or an imagined audience
7. an essay test for one of your courses
   a. Purpose: to demonstrate your knowledge of the subject
   b. Audience: instructor

Exercise 1.6

The author's purpose is to express the difficulty she is having as an Ibo woman raising an American daughter. She writes for a general audience of readers that may include parents who are having similar difficulties and interested others.

Exercise 1.7

Answers will vary.

Exercise 1.8

Answers will vary, but the lists of evidence students come up with should support their thesis statements.

Exercise 1.9

Answers will vary.

Exercise 1.10

Answers will vary.

Exercise 1.11

Reports will vary.

The Critical Thinker

1. Students' viewpoints will vary. However, the author's meaning of "I was only a woman" is that in Ibo society women are devalued. This idea is reinforced by the author's details concerning the ways women are expected to cater to their parents', husbands', and children's needs.

2. The author is an Ibo woman. Although she lives in the United States, tribal values and traditions are very much a part of her life. She asks whether her tribal past should shape Delia's future, but is unable to answer this question. She appreciates the independence American women have, and to some extent she wants her daughter to have the same opportunities as other American women. At the same time, she would also like to pass on her Ibo culture. She is torn between these two desires.

3. Students' answers will vary, but many parents—perhaps most—believe that there is some part of the child-rearing process that they could have done better.

4. Students' essays will vary.

Chapter 2
Using Prewriting Strategies

The Critical Reader

1. Pirsig's central idea about teachers and writing is that teachers need to encourage student writers to see for themselves. Good writing results from original thinking.

2. Pirsig's three examples of writing assignments that made students do original thinking are: write about one brick, write about the back of your thumb, write about a coin.

3. Neither the teacher nor the girl had anything to say because they had already heard instead of seeing for themselves.

4. The fact that "everyone" was able to write something on the teacher's topics suggests that he believes everyone is capable of original thinking. Also, he did not give up on the girl who could not think of anything to say, even though her other teachers had.

5. Answers will vary.

Exercise 2.1

Answers will vary.

Exercise 2.2

Answers will vary, but they should look like the one in the following sample:

    Topic: friends
    Limited topic: the most important quality of a good friend

Exercise 2.3

Answers will vary.

Exercise 2.4

Students' brainstorming lists will vary, but they should look like the example on pages 40–41.

Exercise 2.5

Answers will vary, but students' responses should resemble freewriting as explained on page 42.

Exercise 2.6

Answers will vary, but students' articles should be about 200 words in length and should answer the journalist's questions: *who, what, where, when, why, how,* and *what if.*

Exercise 2.7

Students' underlinings may vary from the suggested underlining below:

1. From his <u>broad, flat</u> bill to his <u>webbed feet</u>, the <u>furry</u> duck-billed platypus is an <u>odd</u> animal. <u>Awkward on land</u>, he's a <u>graceful swimmer</u>. Shrimp are the platypus's favorite food, but you might wonder how he ever finds them since he <u>swims with his eyes closed</u>. <u>Electric sensors</u> on his bill can <u>detect</u> the tiny <u>electric current</u> given off by the movement of the shrimp's tail. <u>Not only do the receptors</u> in the platypus's bill <u>help him find dinner</u>, but they <u>help him navigate</u> too. Flowing waters create electric fields through which the platypus glides with ease. (inform)

2. The <u>last thing we need</u> in our area is a baseball stadium. We already have two convention centers and one sports arena, which the taxpayers have financed— never mind the fact that whenever we were given the chance, <u>we voted against</u> such a <u>waste</u> of our tax dollars. For one thing, these places are private businesses and <u>should</u> be paid for with private funding. Second, their owners, who care about nothing but making a profit, have <u>gouged</u> consumers to the point that many of us cannot afford to attend events taking place in buildings that we bought. For example, one ticket to a basketball game can cost as much as $150, parking costs fifteen dollars, and a soft drink is five dollars. Third, in every case we were told that the center or arena would pay for itself, bring jobs to the community, and promote development from which everyone would profit. However, the only ones who have made any money at all are the owners. Now our city council and business leaders want to build a stadium to attract a

major-league baseball team. I have one question for them: Are you willing to put up your own money to underwrite this venture? Neither are we. (persuade)

3. "Canned hunts," that is what they are called, and what they are is an excuse for people who call themselves hunters to shoot exotic, often endangered, animals at as much as $3,500 a pop. Often the animals are drugged or chased out of cages into a fenced-in open area where they are trapped. Some sport that is. The real tragedy is that there is money in this grisly business, a lot of it. Exotic animal "preserves" are springing up in some states; these are the wildlife supermarkets where hunt organizers shop. Canned hunts are currently under investigation, but progress is slow because of weak and ambiguous laws. Legitimate hunters and sportsmen should deplore canned hunts and demand that their legislators become involved in this issue. (persuade)

4. When it comes to mate selection, do you believe in true love or propinquity? Those who believe in true love believe that love happens only once and that there is just one "right" person for everyone. Those who believe in propinquity believe that anyone can fall in love with any number of people, and that the "right" person may be the one who is the most available at the time. Propinquity means closeness or nearness in a physical sense. Two people sitting next to each other in a movie theater have propinquity. One reason so many people marry the girl or boy next door is propinquity. So when you are looking for a mate, chances are you will select someone from your own neighborhood, someone you went to school with, or someone you met at work. Other factors that play a role in mate selection are physical appearance, race, nationality, age, educational level, socioeconomic status, religion, personality characteristics, and shared interests. In other words, you are probably going to marry someone very much like yourself; most people do. (inform)

Exercise 2.8

Answers will vary, but, in general, the tones are appropriate for their purposes, and students' responses should approximate those below.

Zen and the Art of Motorcycle Maintenance: purpose is to inform; tone is that of a friendly teacher or parent giving advice.

"platypus": purpose is to inform; tone is scholarly but not academic, more like a popular science magazine than a textbook.

"baseball stadium": purpose is to persuade; tone expresses anger and indignation.

"canned hunts": purpose is to persuade; tone expresses anger, shock, and offense.

"mate selection": purpose is to inform; tone expressed is matter-of-fact or common sense.

Exercise 2.9

Answers will vary.

The Critical Thinker

1. The assignments require students to use both analysis (critical thinking) and invention (creative thinking). Writing about the Opera House by starting with one brick requires a student to think about the whole by examining one part. All three assignments (brick, thumb, and coin) require students to "see directly for themselves" and to see beyond the limits of what others have thought or said. The assignments ask students to use the tools of the creative thinker: careful observation, open-mindedness, and willingness to take risks, as explained in Chapter 1, pages 26–27.

2. The author's meaning of "The more you look the more you see" is stated in paragraph 12: "The narrowing down to one brick destroyed the blockage because it was so obvious that she had to do some original and direct seeing." In other words, the author believes that the more you look directly and on your own without the distraction of others' views, the more you see.

3. Students' lists will vary.

4. Students' answers will vary.

Chapter 3
Improving Your Paragraph Skills

The Critical Reader

1. Book smarts, art smarts, body smarts, street smarts, and people smarts are the Gilbert's ways of being smart.

2. Gilbert is probably writing for young people, high school to college age, as is evidenced by the many examples throughout the essay of how the different kinds of smarts affect performance in school.

3. Students' answers should summarize each kind of smarts, for example: book-smart people do well in school, score well on tests, are logical, are primarily interested in knowledge, but may be creative.

4. Gilbert's examples cover a broad range of activities. Everyone could identify their smarts in one or more of Gilbert's categories.

5. A person who says "I can't learn math" is probably not a book-smart person and probably does not realize that one can learn to develop this kind of smarts.

6. Intelligence tests measure only one kind of smarts: book smarts.
7. Gilbert's choice of language tells you that she is writing for ordinary people who may not know the terms *convergent, divergent, assimilating,* and *accommodating.* Her purpose is to clarify a complex subject, intelligence.

Exercise 3.1

Students' online searches and results will vary.

Exercise 3.2

In the answers below, the topic is underlined, and the focus is bracketed.
1. Fast-food junkies can break the habit [by following three simple steps.]
2. [Those who are against] the building of a new city hall [can think of better ways to spend the money it will cost.]
3. The macaw [has a number of features that make it a desirable pet.]
4. Cereal commercials [are aimed at two main groups: children and nutritious-conscious adults.]
5. The annual meeting of the EAA (Experimental Aircraft Association) in Oshkosh, Wisconsin, [provides activities that the whole family can enjoy.]

Exercise 3.3

Answers will vary, but students should limit the topic. Their topic sentences should be complete sentences in which topic and focus are clearly stated.

Exercise 3.4

Though students' answers will vary, they may approximate those below:
1. The "I" in the paragraph is a college student.
2. The student is going through registration.
3. The student feels frustrated.
4. The whole paragraph is about all the things that went wrong during this student's registration.
5. The one situation that the details add up to is college registration.

Topic sentence: The day I registered for classes, everything went wrong.

Exercise 3.5

Answers will vary, but students' facts should support their topic sentences.

Exercise 3.6

Answers will vary, but topic sentences should suggest that reasons will follow.

Exercise 3.7

Answers will vary.

Exercise 3.8

Level 1

Topic Sentence: Getting a college education has not been easy for me.

Level 2

I. <u>One thing</u> that makes it difficult is that I am a working mother.

Level 3

A. <u>I have two school-age children.</u>
B. <u>I have to make their breakfast and see them off.</u>
C. <u>I arrange my schedule to be at home when they arrive.</u>
D. <u>I have less time to do my own studying.</u>

Level 2

II. <u>My job is another thing that makes it hard for me to get an education.</u>

Level 3

A. I work as a receptionist from 8:30–11:30.
B. I have to postpone taking classes offered at these times.
C. It will take a long time to get my degree.

Level 2

III. Studying adds to these difficulties.

Level 3

   A. <u>I have been out of school for a while.</u>

   B. <u>My skills are rusty</u>.

Level 1

Concluding Sentence: Though getting a college education is difficult, it is worth it not only for me but for the good example I am setting for my children.

Exercise 3.9

The following sentences are off the topic and disrupt the unity of their paragraphs:

Paragraph #1:

Frankenstein is another character who appeals to filmgoers.
Lon Chaney plays the Wolfman as an ordinary fellow fallen on bad times.

Paragraph #2:

Barbara Jordan and Jesse Jackson, both Clinton supporters, addressed the convention.

Paragraph #3:

For a brief time, she had thought she wanted to be a court reporter.

Exercise 3.10

Students' paragraphs will vary, but they should be unified.

Exercise 3.11

Your students may find more or fewer words than these that signal how details are arranged:
1. it is important, most importantly (emphatic order)
2. first, next, before, once, then; time order (sequence)
3. halfway down the aisle, in the center, directly overhead, above, in front, on either side, from bottom to top, to the left, right, in back, to the end, in each direction, up the walls, on three levels (spatial order)

Exercise 3.12

Paragraphs will vary.

The Critical Thinker

1. Students' answers will vary.

2. Answers will vary but should match up the characteristics of the person chosen with one or more of Gilbert's categories.

3. Answers will vary, but Gilbert says in paragraph 2 that everyone possesses all of her types of intelligence to one degree or another. In other words, students who believe they are poor in math can develop math skills. The steps she refers to are stated at the end of paragraph 4: planning, perceiving, imaging, remembering, feeling, and acting.

4. Students' answers will vary. However, there are many theories of intelligence. Gardner's multiple intelligences include seven types, which bear some similarities to Gilbert's categories.

Chapter 4
Stating Your Thesis

The Critical Reader

1. The thesis is stated in the third sentence of paragraph 1. The word "these" in the third sentence refers to the topic (readers' questions), which is stated in the second sentence.

2. The "one-of-a-kind" questions are unique and often reflect the writer's field of interest. The "old standards" are those that always come up in interviews and are often boring. The "real weirdies" are odd questions that are difficult to understand and even more difficult to answer.

3. "Are you Morbid of razors?" is an example of a one-of-a-kind question, "Where do you get your ideas?" is an example of an old standard, and "Don't you wish you had a rubber stamp?" is an example of a real weirdie. Students' choices of examples from the essay may vary.

4. The first paragraph introduces King's topic (the questions readers ask) and central idea.

5. King suggests that making money is his inspiration for writing: "Royalty checks come in envelopes with windows for displaying the address."

6. At the end of the essay, King says that he doesn't mind the really interesting questions but he does mind those that have no real answers. Although his essay is designed to make readers laugh at the kinds of questions readers ask, he also has a serious message for his fans: think before you ask. Many word choices and examples throughout the essay make clear what King's attitude is. Your students' examples will vary.

Exercise 4.1

Students' search results will vary.

Exercise 4.2

1. I have been working as a teller at First Union Bank on Center Street for the last fifteen years.   SS
2. As a bank teller I have learned several effective ways to deal with difficult customers.   TS
3. It is not unusual to see women working as volunteer firefighters.   SS
4. I like my job as a firefighter because it is both personally rewarding and socially responsible.   TS
5. Armadillos should not be sold as pets because most people cannot provide the food, climate, and habitat these animals need.   TS

Exercise 4.3

Thesis statements will vary, but they should state a topic and comment like the following:

My dog is an expensive pet because he requires food, grooming, and medical care.

Exercise 4.4

Thesis statements will vary, but they should look like the one in Exercise 4.3 or those in the examples in Figure 4.1.

Exercise 4.5

Revised thesis statements will vary, but they should follow the guidelines below.

1. Teenage alcohol abuse is on the rise. (topic: teenage alcohol abuse; opinion: it is on the rise; no purpose, no parts)

2. People who run for office may have their private lives exposed in the press. (topic: people who run for office; opinion: may have private lives exposed in press; no opinion, no parts; also topic is too broad—needs narrowing to one candidate)

3. Many students are opting for careers in health care. (topic: students opting for health care careers; no opinion, purpose, or parts)

4. Even if I had the opportunity, I would not want to be sixteen years old again. (opinion: I would not want to be sixteen again; topic: not clear; no purpose, no parts)

5. To gain the approval of voters (topic), a new president of the United States must keep campaign promises, choose qualified people to serve in the cabinet, and act decisively in times of crisis. (opinion, purpose, and parts combined)

6. Right-to-work laws are in effect in several states. (topic: statement of fact, unclear; no opinion, purpose, or parts)

Exercise 4.6

Students should identify the following thesis statements and introductory strategies.

1. You can become a wise consumer by learning to spot the seven common tricks that advertisers use to make you want to buy their products. (facts and figures)

2. A school district in our area is considering abolishing athletic events as a way to cut costs in this year of budget cutbacks and an uncertain economy. (question)

3. If the future presidents of the United States want to capture the youth vote, they will have to do several things to gain young people's respect and support. (quotation and explanation)

4. From a dilapidated shed, described by one German chemist at the time as a "cross between a stable and a potato-cellar," came a discovery that would throw light on the structure of the atom, open new doors in medicine, and save lives in future generations. (background information)

Exercise 4.7

Students' paragraphs and introductory strategies may vary.

The Critical Thinker

1. The first paragraph introduces King's topic and central idea. The last paragraph concludes the essay by asking a revealing question: "Do I mind these questions?" The paragraphs between introduction and conclusion make up the

body of the essay. The headings state King's three types of questions and indicate what and where the major divisions of his essay are. This structure clearly leads readers from King's thesis, through its development, to his conclusion.

2. The questions King gets from readers probably are similar to those other celebrities get. For example, an "old standard" fans might ask of a film star is "What is your favorite movie?" However, students' examples will vary.

3. Students' choices of examples will vary.

4. Students' questions for King will vary.

Chapter 5
Supporting Your Thesis

The Critical Reader

1. Theroux's thesis is: "Shopping with children is exactly as awful as shopping with parents. But if the experience is to be survived there are certain rules all adults must follow."

2. Theroux introduces the thesis with an anecdote.

3. The major details that support the thesis are Theroux's eight rules for shopping with children.

4. Students should summarize the rules in their own words, so answers will vary.

5. Students' answers will vary.

6. Theroux wanted to dress like everyone else.

7. Theroux uses brand names that she thinks readers will identify as expensive. If readers do not know that *Pandora* is an expensive brand of sweater, then the example would be just as effective for them if this term were left out. For readers who know the name, the example might be less effective without it.

8. Students' answers may vary, but words and terms such as "flip," "awful," and "are you kidding?" give the essay its informal, conversational tone.

9. A *regalia* is a formal outfit associated with ritual, a special occasion, or high office. Examples of regalia include graduation or choir robes, wedding dresses, and officers' uniforms. The bishop's outfit denotes his office, so "regalia" is the best word to describe it.

Exercise 5.1

Students' subpoints will vary.

Exercise 5.2

Students' main ideas will vary.

Exercise 5.3

Students' major and minor details will vary.

Exercise 5.4

Students' answers will vary but should be similar to the following:

- Signal words to establish a relationship between paragraphs:
  Paragraph 5   "In the meantime"

- Repetition in the first sentence of a paragraph, a word, phrase, or idea mentioned in the previous paragraph:
  Paragraph 19   "Unfortunately, I remember that yellow Pandora sweater. . . ."

- Repetition of a key word or term throughout the essay:
  Rule, shopping, shop

Exercise 5.5

Students' essay revisions will vary.

Exercise 5.6

Students' Internet search results will vary.

Exercise 5.7

In the last paragraph of "Should My Tribal Past Shape Delia's Future," the author asks a revealing question that reinforces her thesis by expressing again her indecisiveness about the way she is bringing up her daughter.

The Critical Thinker

1. Theroux's tone is mock-serious. In other words, she copies the listing format of certain child-rearing books that are serious, but does so in a playful way. Her rules are meant to make readers laugh. The listing format helps readers to follow her ideas.

2. Answers will vary depending on students' experiences. However, Americans as a group do seem to place great value on appearances and the possession of material wealth.

3. How a person dresses has an effect on the first impression that person makes on others. The whole "dress for success" movement was based on this idea. Most students who grew up attending public schools would probably agree that kids were judged "cool" or "not cool" by what they wore. However, students' answers will vary.

4. Students' answers will vary, but one example of a generation gap between parents and children is their attitudes toward tattoos and piercing of body parts other than the earlobes. Most parents do not look favorably on such forms of body decoration whereas their children see nothing wrong with them.

Chapter 6
Revising Your Essays

The Critical Reader

1. The thesis is stated in the last sentence of paragraph 1.

2. The author's purpose is to express how he feels about storms. He makes this clear in the first paragraph when he tells readers how he used to feel about storms and that his feelings have changed.

3. He was unaware of the storm's approach because he and his girlfriend were watching movies they had rented, and they did not hear the weather report.

4. Answers may vary but should include details from paragraphs 4–6.

5. Answers may vary; there are numerous time markers throughout the essay.

6. Answers will vary.

7. These words suggest danger, and they create a mood of coming disaster. They help introduce the thesis by suggesting why the author's feelings about storms have changed.

Exercise 6.1

Students' responses will vary, but the example below is typical. Content that has been added to the original statement is underlined.

1. My college provides <u>financial aid</u> to students <u>who need money</u> by offering <u>grants, scholarships</u>, and <u>a work-study program</u>.

Exercise 6.2

Answers will vary.

Exercise 6.3

1. Paragraph 1 (introduction); paragraphs 2–4 (body); paragraph 5 (conclusion).
2. She uses facts and figures that help establish her tone, which is humorously serious.
3. Her purpose is primarily to entertain, and you can tell by the improbability of her subject. No one would seriously consider eating worms.
4. The thesis is the last sentence of the first paragraph.
5. The audience is a general one as indicated by the references to supermarkets and McDonald's, places most people are familiar with.
6. Topic sentences are the first sentences of paragraphs 2–4. Each topic sentence relates to the thesis by explaining one of its three parts: unappetizing, difficult to prepare, and unpopular.
7. Answers will vary but should include transitions such as "initially" and "most important."
8. Simmons stays on the topic and uses transitions.
9. Simmons concludes by summarizing her three main ideas. The choice is appropriate because the summary recalls the parts of the thesis and adds a note of finality.
10. Answers will vary.

Exercise 6.4

Students' essays will vary.

Exercise 6.5

Steve Hackney uses a foreboding tone, which fits his expressive purpose. Simmons's tone is both serious and funny, which fits her purpose to entertain. Students' choices of words and phrases that reveal the tone will vary.

Exercise 6.6

Students' Internet search topics and results will vary.

The Critical Thinker

1. Hackney introduces his topic by supplying background information that makes clear to readers what his thoughts and feelings about storms used to be. As a concluding device, he summarizes the difference between his feelings about storms then and now. Hackney's introduction and conclusion effectively frame his essay and leave readers with a clear understanding of what happened to the author and how it changed him.

2. Hackney uses time order effectively throughout the essay to show how quickly the storm progressed. He uses spatial order effectively in paragraph 4 to place himself in the scene and to describe what is happening on all sides. These details help readers to put themselves in his place and to experience the events from his point of view.

3. The essay, though well written and generally effective, is not perfect. Students' suggestions for improvement may vary.

4. Students' responses will vary.

Chapter 7
Editing Your Essays

The Critical Reader

1. By "clutter," Zinsser means the words, phrases, and expressions that get in the way of clear communication because they do not add information or ideas.

2. Answers will vary, but they should identify Zinsser's point: clutter comes in many forms, and it is difficult to get rid of it.

3. Zinsser wants writers to identify and eliminate clutter from their writing.

4. Zinsser's evidence consists mainly of examples.

5. The essay is coherent. Students' examples of transitional words and phrases will vary.

6. Zinsser carries out the weed metaphor in the sentence: "Clutter is the laborious phrase that has pushed out the short word that means the same thing." (Clutter pushes out words as weeds push out flowers.) He also says we should "prune" clutter, which is more of a gardening metaphor but which seems related to pulling weeds—both activities eliminate clutter.

7. Answers will vary.

Exercise 7.1

Recently, my husband and I took our kids to visit my father, who lives on a farm in Pennsylvania. He raises cattle and pigs, *and* he grows all his own vegetables. He sells most of them, but he saves enough to have all he wants to eat. He has an apple orchard, and he has a pretty good deal going with an Amish settlement near where he lives. He gives The Amish apples for making cider in exchange for the cider he can drink. We thought it would be good for our children to see what it is like living in the country, and it will not hurt them to participate in the chores. The trip was one of the best we have ever had. Much to our surprise, the kids loved helping their grandpa milk cows, feed the pigs, and tend the garden. Our sixteen-year-old sold vegetables from my father's produce stand at the entrance to his property and was thrilled that *he* let her keep some of the proceeds. Driving home, *we decided* to repeat the visit in the future.

Exercise 7.2

Students' Internet searches and results will vary.

Exercise 7.3

Students' responses will vary, but they should identify phrases such as the following as clutter: *Due to the fact that, today's society, There is,* and *Until such time as.*

Exercise 7.4

Students' responses will vary, but they should find and rewrite the following passive-voice constructions: trouble is caused by it; homework is done on a computer; everything on the screen is lost; has to be rewritten; have to be reset; letters of complaint have been written; phone calls have been made; nothing has been done.

Exercise 7.5

Students' lists will vary.

The Critical Thinker

1. Zinsser's use of the pronoun "you" suggests that he is addressing his audience directly. They may be students—he was a professor at Yale—but they could also be professional writers—he was a journalist. His audience seems limited to those who want to improve their writing.

2. Zinsser's types of clutter are unnecessary prepositions and adjectives (paragraphs 2 and 3), laborious phrases (paragraphs 4 and 5), euphemisms (paragraph 6), language of the interoffice memo (paragraph 7), language of the Pentagon (paragraphs 8 and 9), jargon from various fields (paragraphs 10 and 11), and little growths of ordinary words (paragraphs 12 and 13). Students' explanations and examples may vary but should be supported by the text.

3. Students' choices of articles and examples of clutter will vary.

4. Students' examples will vary.

Chapter 8
Using the Library, Doing Research

The Critical Reader

1. The thesis is stated in paragraph 1, second sentence.

2. Phrases such as "in the academic world" suggest that Murray is writing for college students.

3. The evidence includes what to do during prewriting and drafting and how and where to find information.

4. The evidence supports Murray's point by showing how thinking and writing require gathering information from many sources.

5. Answers will vary.

6. Answers will vary, but students should be able to relate fastwriting to freewriting as explained in Chapter 2.

7. Answers may vary, but the tone is more like that of a teacher lecturing to students.

Exercise 8.1

Answers will vary.

Exercise 8.2

Answers can be verified using a number of resources. Students' resources may vary.

Exercise 8.3

Students' Internet search results will vary.

Exercise 8.4

Answers will vary.

Exercise 8.5

Answers will vary.

Exercise 8.6

Answers will vary.

Exercise 8.7

Students' reports will vary.

Exercise 8.8

Students' lists will vary.

The Critical Thinker

1. The library's resources, organization, and helpful people make it a good starting point for finding any kind of information.
2. Students' topics will vary. For making good observations, Murray suggests taking notes for two reasons: This activity will make you see more clearly and will preserve what you observe. He also suggests using all your senses.
3. The author probably means that writing is a process of discovery. For example, you may choose a topic, start writing, and realize that you have nothing to say

about it. Or you may think you have nothing to say, but the process of thinking and writing about a topic jars your memory, making you realize that you know more than you thought you did. Either way, writing teaches what you know and do not know. However, students' answers may vary.

4. Students' responses will vary.

Chapter 9
Using Narration

The Critical Reader

1. Hughes's thesis is the first three sentences of the essay.

2. Some of the transitions that signal time order are then, still, and finally. Your students may find more.

3. Students' choices of examples will vary. Hughes's details throughout the essay clearly describe the church, the service, and the congregation.

4. The boy takes *see* literally. He thinks he will see Jesus in the flesh. The aunt means *see* figuratively.

5. The dialogue helps create the scene in readers' minds, as if they were there. The story might not be as effective without it because it might not seem as real.

Exercise 9.1

Students' lists will vary.

Exercise 9.2

Students should find and underline the following transitions and time markers in the breakfast cereal passage: "in the early 19th century"; "a century and a half later"; "as it was"; "most critically"; "in 1866; there, too."

Exercise 9.3

Comic strips chosen and students' responses will vary.

Exercise 9.4

Students' lists will vary.

Exercise 9.5

Hughes uses the first-person point of view because it enables him to tell the story as he sees it. Also, the story is about him. If he had used the third-person point of view, the story would not have seemed as personal. The writer of the breakfast cereal passage uses the third-person point of view because she is writing about events that happened in the past. She describes the events objectively, telling what each person thought but leaving her feelings out of it.

Exercise 9.6

Students should underline the first sentence as the main idea and number examples as follows: (1) subjects; (2) courses; (3) issues such as merit pay; (4) "those kids . . ."; (5) "that age . . ."; (6) their own kids; (7) ask questions.

Exercise 9.7

Students' incidents and examples will vary.

Exercise 9.8

Paragraphs 3, 6, 8, 9, and 10 contain dialogue. Students' choices of the one that makes the best use of dialogue may vary.

Exercise 9.9

Students' search results and essays will vary.

The Critical Thinker

1. Answers may vary, but essentially, Hughes is saying that he went through the motions of being saved. He did not really have a conversion experience. Hughes had expected to see Jesus (paragraph 2), but as he says in paragraph 15, "I hadn't seen Jesus" and "I didn't believe there was a Jesus any more."

2. Answers may vary, but the difference in character between the two boys is that Hughes is ashamed of having lied about being saved but Westley is not ashamed. Westley doesn't care about being saved; he just wants to go home. Hughes, however, wants to be saved and is disappointed. He is also afraid to tell his aunt the truth.

3. Hughes believes everything his aunt tells him. He expects to see Jesus, but when he does not, Hughes is disillusioned. His disillusionment is the result of having

taken his aunt's words literally. He is too young or too inexperienced to understand that being saved is a spiritual experience, not a physical one.

4. Students' interpretations of the poem will vary, but they should recognize that the speaker of the poem, a student, is responding to a writing assignment. He is also commenting on the student-teacher relationship and race relations in the America of his time.

Chapter 10
Using Description

The Critical Reader

1. Students' answers will vary but should generally reflect this central idea: *The bond between brothers can survive time and pain.* This thesis can be inferred from several of the author's details. For example, the home movie reminds him of something he had forgotten: his four-year-old brother's pinch that day at the pool (paragraph 9). What he does remember, and what is recorded in the photograph, is his arm around his brother and "the awkward and alien comfort of that touch" (paragraph 17). His question "Who's the other guy?" and the truth of his son's answer "I don't know" (paragraph 33) suggest that just as his son does not recognize his uncle in the photograph, the author, too, realizes that he doesn't really know his brother. More important, it doesn't matter. The author's assertion that his memories are "the proof of us two surfacing, alive but not unscathed" suggests that these brothers have survived their childhood fighting and hurt feelings—as brothers often do.

2. Paragraph 2 introduces the essay by providing background information about the author's family and their relationships as he remembers them.

3. In the movie, the brothers are children. In the photograph, they are adults. Other family members appear in the movie. The photograph shows only the two boys. Both the movie and the photo show the brothers in physical contact. The movie reveals the pain of childhood. The photo reveals adult forgetfulness and acceptance.

4. In paragraph 18, the author says that twenty years of memories lie between the movie and the photo. He acknowledges that his memories are selective—he remembers some things but not others. He also acknowledges that his memories are "no true picture" but only what he has made the truth. In other words, his memories may tell us more about him than about his brother. He sees his brother as a daredevil (the death drop from the jungle gym, the Chinese junk tattoo) and as a bully (fighting over a honeybun, watching while Lynn beats him

up). He seems to resent his brother while looking up to him at the same time. The relationship between the brothers suggested in this paragraph and in the rest of the essay is a complex mix of love and anger, closeness and detachment. Your students may make other inferences.

5. The essay is divided into several sections. The first section, paragraphs 1 through 12, introduces the topic and describes the home movie. The second section, paragraphs 13 through 16, describes the photograph. The third section, paragraphs 17 and 18, pulls together two essential facts about the brothers' relationship as revealed in the movie and photograph: the four-year-old's pinch, which the author had forgotten, and the feelings he had while holding his twenty-four-year-old brother, which he remembers. The fourth section, paragraphs 19 through 33, serves as a transition between the past and the present that helps the author make a connection between his own relationship with his brother and the relationship between his two children. "Zeb and Jake fight," states the author in paragraph 34, which begins the fifth section. The details in this section, paragraphs 34 through 53, describes the author's sons' relationship, which reminds him of his own relationship with his brother. The sixth section, paragraphs 54 through 57, conclude the essay with a brief summary of the movie and the photograph's essential details and what they mean. Students' inferences about the purpose of these sections and the effectiveness of the author's organization may vary.

6. Students' answers may vary, but like all brothers, these two fought in childhood. Although they may still retain some resentments ("He'd missed my wedding") and may not really know each other due to the passage of time and separation by distance, they share a bond.

7. Students' choices of examples and explanations may vary, but the color words in paragraphs 2 through 12 seem mainly descriptive (coal black hair, red lips, white skin, blue sky, green and white striped umbrella). The author says in paragraph 12 that the colors in the film, like his memories of that day, are fading. In paragraph 14, he refers again to these "sinking colors" and how they are a "prophecy" of the day on which the photograph was taken: The boys had become adults, one holding the other, their childhood differences forgotten. The photograph is in black and white. Therefore, the author describes the objects in the photo in shades of black and white except for the one color he does remember: the navy blue shawl collar of his cardigan. By including this seemingly unimportant detail, the author reminds us that he is reporting "facts" (paragraph 14) so that we will accept the accuracy of his memory concerning the more significant details—that his brother's smile and his smile in this photograph are both "real."

Exercise 10.1

Students' lists will vary.

Exercise 10.2

Students' charts will vary. The essay does contain sensory details for all five senses, so students should be able to find them.

Exercise 10.3

1. Subjective (She gives us her impressions.)
2. Objective (The author describes the plants exactly, not to express feelings about them or create a personal impression.)
3. Subjective (Lopez's purpose is to give us his impressions of the place.)

Exercise 10.4

Students' answers will vary, but they should agree that although some details are objectively reported, the author's overall purpose is subjective. The details that explain his feelings and impressions about the movie and photograph and the conclusions he draws about his own behavior and his sons' behavior are the clues.

Exercise 10.5

Because Lott's thesis is implied, students' statements of a controlling idea and the details that suggest it may vary. One example of a controlling idea is *the bond between brothers*.

Exercise 10.6

Students' lists and controlling ideas will vary.

Exercise 10.7

Students' search results and paragraphs will vary.

The Critical Thinker

1. Students' choices of paragraphs and details will vary, but here are some examples from paragraph 2: "Harmless children," "impossibly young," and

"dull and lifeless light green" convey the author's subjective impressions of himself and his brother, his mother, and the color of the bushes. Objective details such as "She sits next to me, on the right of the screen;" "Next to me, on the left of the screen, is Brad;" and "I am in the center" describe without emotion the exact location of people within one of the movie's scenes.

2. Answers may vary, but one explanation could be that Zeb and Jake fight for the same reason as the author and his brother fought: Fighting and competition between brothers are a natural part of growing up. Brothers usually outgrow these behaviors to become friends but the memories still remain. The author probably sees hope for Zeb and Jake. Just as their father and his brother successfully completed their journey from childhood to adulthood, so will Zeb and Jake.

3. The boys are on a journey from childhood to adulthood. The journey is universal and filled with the fighting, competition, and closeness that all brothers growing up share. The phrase "alive but unscathed" means that the boys have survived their childhood differences but some of the bad memories remain.

4. Students' responses will vary.

Chapter 11
Explaining a Process

The Critical Reader

1. Andy Rooney's thesis is implied: try my steps for putting off a job that you do not want to do.

2. Rooney assumes that most people in his audience try to put off doing difficult or unpleasant tasks.

3. Rooney describes the process of how to avoid work.

4. He has six steps: go to the store; tidy the work area; make phone calls; study the problem; take a coffee break; and think it over.

5. The steps do not have to be followed in order because the process is not one in which a sequence matters.

6. He is probably making fun of self-help books and experts who encourage us to avoid procrastination.

7. Rooney uses contractions, and conversational expressions and phrases such as "don't tell me" and "let's see now."

Exercise 11.1

Directional processes:
 how to build a fence
 how to document a research paper
 how to give CPR (cardio-pulmonary resuscitation)
 a method for reducing boredom
 how to prepare for the GRE (Graduate Record Examination)
 how to figure your income tax

Informational processes:
 the life cycle of a gypsy moth
 the making of a politician's image
 ways businesses have reduced energy consumption
 how a newspaper is printed
 how Congress spends your taxes

Exercise 11.2

1. The process is directional. Readers will be able to make the snack themselves by following the author's instructions.

2. As stated in paragraph 2, the ingredients needed to make the snack are nuts, raisins, sunflower seeds, and candy-coated chocolates.

3. The steps are as follows: Start with mixed nuts (paragraph 5); next, add raisins (paragraph 10); add candy-coated chocolates (paragraph 11); last, add sunflower seeds (paragraph 12); after mixing, place in jars (paragraph 13).

4. She mentions twice that she is a college student (paragraphs 1 and 3) so she probably is writing for other college students as well as anyone who is interested in making the snack that she describes.

5. The thesis is not directly stated but can be inferred from paragraph 1 and the author's list of directions in paragraphs 5 through 12: *You can follow a few simple steps to make a low-cost, quick-energy snack.* The author first suggests her controlling idea in paragraph 4, saying that she saw significance in the ingredients and how they pertained to life. She states the controlling idea clearly in paragraph 16: "Life is like a sample from the nut jar."

Exercise 11.3

Answers will vary.

Exercise 11.4

Answers will vary.

Exercise 11.5

Students' lists and details will vary.

Exercise 11.6

Transitions and topic sentences will vary.

Exercise 11.7

Students' paragraph choices and outlines will vary.

Exercise 11.8

Transitional words and phrases include "recipe begins" (paragraph 5), "next" (paragraph 10), "even though" and "add" (paragraph 11), "last" (paragraph 12), and "after" (paragraph 13).

Exercise 11.9

Students' Internet searches and results will vary.

The Critical Thinker

1. Rooney's purpose is to entertain readers with his steps for putting off a job. Most people who write about time management are seriously concerned with helping people overcome procrastination. In a good-natured way, Rooney is making fun of these self-help experts by telling people how to put off doing a job.
2. Rooney's tone is playful. Students can find many examples of words and phrases that reveal this tone. Their choices will vary.
3. Students' responses will vary.
4. Students' responses will vary.

Chapter 12
Choosing Classification or Division

The Critical Reader

1. The thesis is stated in the first paragraph, last sentence.
2. The categories based on how people wash dishes are Wash-and-Driers and Wash-and-Drippers.
3. The free spirits of the kitchen belong to the Wash-and-Drippers.
4. Wash-and-Drippers can be divided into two subgroups: right-brained stackers and left-brained stackers.
5. The categories based on when people wash dishes are the Casual Washers and the Clean-as-They Goers.
6. Answers will vary.
7. The thesis and categories are based on people's dishwashing behavior, or demeanor, and thus reflect the essay's title.

Exercise 12.1

Students should cross out the term in each list that does not belong. Headings and the terms to be crossed out (in parentheses) are listed below.

1. mythical creatures (witch)
2. desserts (bread)
3. eating utensils (spatula)
4. shoes (socks)
5. stinging insects (lady bug)
6. stringed instruments (trumpet)
7. board games (badminton)
8. flowers (fern)
9. animals of the cat family (hyena)
10. U.S. presidents (Gore)

Exercise 12.2

Answers will vary.

Exercise 12.3

Students' answers should follow the example given in the exercise.

    Topic: ways to exercise
    Purpose: to explain ways to exercise inexpensively

Exercise 12.4

Students should correctly identify the topics as calling for either a parts or categories classification. But their selections of topics from the list, their determination of purpose, and the categories they list will vary.

    ways to spend leisure time (categories)
    qualities to look for in a mate (parts)
    pressures college students face (categories)
    the components of a typical workday (parts)
    types of mathematical errors (categories)
    kinds of magazines (categories)
    sections of a newspaper (parts)

Exercise 12.5

    1. D
    2. D
    3. C
    4. D
    5. C
    6. D
    7. C
    8. D
    9. D
   10. C

Exercise 12.6

Students' topics and purposes will vary.

Exercise 12.7

Students' Internet searches and results will vary.

Exercise 12.8

Students' answers should approximate the following examples:

1. Topic: computer
   Purpose: to explain a computer's parts and their purpose
   Parts: Input Device, Processor, Output Device
2. Topic: oppression
   Purpose: to explain the ways people deal with oppression
   Categories: acquiescence, violence and hatred, nonviolent resistance
3. Topic: how we listen to music
   Purpose: to make the listening process clearer by breaking it down into parts
   Parts: the sensuous plane, the expressive plane, the musical plane

The Critical Thinker

1. The two main categories are *Wash-and-Driers* and *Wash-and-Drippers*. The *right-brained stackers* and *left-brained stackers* are subcategories of the Washers and Drippers. *Casual Washers* and *Clean-as-They-Goers* are additional subcategories of the two main categories. The wash-and-drying process is explained in paragraph 2; the wash-and-dripping process is explained in paragraphs 3 and 4. Because these processes are informational rather than directional, the order of the steps does not seem to be important.

2. Students' answers will vary. Here are two possible examples: the *Clean-Loaders* and the *Dirty Loaders*. These categories are based on whether the dishes are rinsed before loading or loaded without rinsing. Also, some people load dishes, silverware, and glasses in a certain order, but others do not. Encourage students to come up with descriptive names for their categories.

3. Bodett writes for a general audience. His assumptions are that everyone washes dishes, one way or another, and everyone has a characteristic way of doing this chore. He probably also assumes that many readers will see themselves, or people they know, in his categories. The second sentence of paragraph 1 and several phrases support these assumptions: "Everyone hates. . . ." (paragraph 2), "common practice" (paragraph 5), and "We've all been witness. . . ." (paragraph 6). Your students may find other examples.

4. Students' responses will vary.

Chapter 13
Comparing and Contrasting

The Critical Reader

1. The thesis is stated in paragraph 3, first sentence, beginning "Yet for all. . . ."

2. Both films involve women caught in tragic love triangles and both films depict a well-known historical event. Your students may cite other similarities.

3. Both films differ in their portrayal of comparable themes and in their views of men and women. Your students may cite other differences.

4. The films differ in their views of the ideal man or woman. Rhett Butler is mature and sophisticated, but Jack Dawson is young and immature. Although Scarlett and Rose and both vain and stubborn women, Scarlett is a grown-up and a businesswoman who makes sacrifices for her family. Rose is selfish and concerned only with fulfilling her desires, regardless of how her decisions affect her family. Your students may cite other differences.

5. The author's details in paragraphs 10 and 11 suggest that he favors the plot, performances, and artistic qualities of *Gone with the Wind*. However, he gives *Titanic* its due, calling it a "surprise hit." He says that each movie was more a reflection of its times than an accurate depiction of a historical event, and because of this each struck a chord with viewers. Although he says in paragraph 12 that he does not mean "to denigrate the director or his *Titanic*," it seems clear that he favors the older film.

6. Students' responses will vary.

Exercise 13.1

Answers will vary.

Exercise 13.2

Rewritten topics will vary but should include a judgment like the following:

To describe two neighborhoods and explain why you like one better than the other.

Exercise 13.3

Students' thesis statements will vary.

Exercise 13.4

Stark's essay is a point-by-point comparison. Students' outlines and explanations may vary.

Exercise 13.5

Students' Internet searches and results will vary.

The Critical Thinker

1. Students' answers may vary, but it seems clear that although Spark prefers *Gone with the Wind,* he is more interested in the ways both films reflect the eras in which they were made. As a result, his purpose is to explain how each film is a product of its times by analyzing their differences.

2. The author uses a point-by-point comparison. His transitional words and phrases both within and between paragraphs are numerous, so students' examples will vary.

3. The title suggests what the author sees as a basic difference between Scarlett and Rose: Scarlett would not have saved herself first because self-sacrifice is a part of her character. Rose, however, is more self-interested than self-sacrificing. Rose chose to follow her heart rather than ensure her family's financial welfare. The title also suggests that the author's primary focus is on the films' differences in dealing with characters and themes.

4. Students' responses will vary.

Chapter 14
Explaining Causes and Effects

The Critical Reader

1. The thesis is stated in the second sentence of paragraph 6: "I know that my brother. . . ."

2. In paragraphs 1 and 2, the author lists several examples of people close to him who died of alcohol-related causes. In the author's view, this evidence qualifies him as an expert on drunk driving.

3. According to the author, drinking among college students persists for the reasons stated in paragraph 8.

4. As stated in paragraph 6, one reason schools have been reluctant to address the problem of drunk driving is that they do not want to be held legally liable for what happens to students who drink. Your students may cite one of the author's other reasons.

5. The statistics suggest that the author has a factual basis for his claims. Therefore, his opinion is an informed one and more likely to impress readers.

6. The word choices in paragraphs 3 and 9 are designed to have an emotional effect on readers. The grisly details in paragraph 3 (blood and tissue being wiped off the car's broken windshield, the branch that had pierced Ryan's lips) are meant to shock readers with the violence of a drunk driving accident. The purpose of the details in paragraph 9 (the knock on your door, your brother or sister, your loved one) is to make readers identify with the victims' families.

Exercise 14.1

The author states questions and answers them in paragraphs 6, 8, 9, and 10. The purpose of the questions and answers in paragraph 6 is to explain why administrators are reluctant to take responsibility for students' drunk driving and to suggest what they could do. The purpose of the question and answer in paragraph 8 is to explain why drunk driving persists and, again, to suggest what administrators can do. The question in paragraph 9 and its answer in paragraph 10 are used as a concluding device. Waldron's purpose in these paragraphs is to move readers to action. He wants readers to insist that colleges do more to prevent drunk driving.

Exercise 14.2

Students' causes and effects will vary.

Exercise 14.3

An if . . . then statement appears near the middle of paragraph 6: "If administrators accepted this responsibility, they might ask themselves the following questions: Should we expel students who receive a D.U.I.?" The act is *taking responsibility for students' drunk driving,* and the consequence is *asking questions to find a solution to the problem.*

Exercise 14.4

Students' *if . . . then* statements and lists of evidence will vary.

Exercise 14.5

Students' statements will vary but should contain one of the words that signal probability: *if, probable, possible, likely, unlikely, may, might,* and *what if.*

Exercise 14.6

Students' Internet searches and results will vary.

The Critical Thinker

1. In the first paragraph, Waldron uses the device of building background to establish his qualifications as an expert on drunk driving. In the last two paragraphs, Waldron asks and answers a thought-provoking question to challenge readers.

2. In paragraph 6, Waldron acknowledges Ryan's responsibility for his own death. Similarly, readers can assume that Waldron believes anyone who drinks and then drives is responsible for what happens—this includes the students at Ryan's college. However, he also holds administrators responsible to some extent. He suggests several things they could do to discourage students from driving drunk and challenges readers as well to demand more of college administrators.

3. Students' responses will vary.

4. Students' responses will vary.

Chapter 15
Using Definition

The Critical Reader

1. The thesis is stated in paragraph 10, second sentence. In this sentence "It's" and "simple view" refer to the 1950s ideal of the perfect family.

2. Hoffman describes the typical 1950s family as consisting of a wage-earner father, a mother who does not work outside the home, and two or more children.

3. Hoffman grew up in a single-parent home as a child of divorced parents. Such families were not typical in the 1950s.

4. Hoffman suggests that there is no ideal family today. She says that only one in nineteen families match the 1950s ideal. However, she says that the values of caring for a child and providing for its welfare have not changed. From this we can infer that "family," in Hoffman's view, has a broad definition that includes

married parents with children, single parents with children, and other family members such as grandparents, aunts, or uncles who have assumed the role of parents. Foster families may also be included in this definition.

5. Answers may vary. However, Hoffman shows a disregard for traditional male and female roles within the family and toward people who make value judgments about others' family structures or who attempt to set standards of behavior (paragraphs 8 and 9). She seems to think that children who receive the love and care they need will do as well whether they have one parent or two.

6. The author's word choices reinforce her thesis and title. The "perfect" families of the 1950s were not perfect. Hoffman rejects the standards set by these families and the judgment of others according to these standards. She proposes a new definition of "family" that is less limiting than the old definition.

Exercise 15.1

Students' answers will vary but should resemble the following sample answer:

Term:	Self-control
Definition:	Self-control is a quality of people who are able to set standards for themselves and live by them.
Synonym:	Self-discipline
Example #1:	A student who refuses to sample drugs even though all the student's friends are doing it has self-control.
Example #2:	A person who is able to lose weight and keep it off has self-control.

Exercise 15.2

Answers will vary.

Exercise 15.3

Students should find and underline the following sentences:

What's behind such incidents? Some experts say the trend began in the 1960s when traditional values and manners came under fire.

Exercise 15.4

Students' paragraphs will vary.

Exercise 15.5

Students' examples may vary.

Exercise 15.6

Students' Internet searches and results will vary.

The Critical Thinker

1. The word "bargain" in this sentence refers to the bargain that is explained in paragraph 2: To exist in the comfortable world of 1950s "perfect" families, people had to forgo asking questions and ignore those who were different. In saying that her mother could not make this bargain, the author means that her mother was unable to ignore troubled families. By repeating the word "bargain" in this sentence, the author makes an effective transition between paragraphs.

2. Hoffman's friend could not visit her because Hoffman's parents were divorced. In the 1950s, divorce was unusual. Divorced people and children of divorce were looked down on. Therefore the author knew that her family was different, and she understood why her friend could not come over. This is what she means when she says that it "almost made sense."

3. Hoffman writes for a general audience that includes both people who favor traditional families and those who favor alternative families. She wants to convince the traditionalists that their views are unrealistic. Hoffman calls others "judgmental" and "self-righteous." Therefore, her tone is critical.

4. Students' responses will vary.

Chapter 16
Arguing Persuasively

The Critical Reader

1. Rodriguez's thesis is "It [minority student] is a term that should never have been foisted on me. One I was wrong to accept." He introduces the thesis by providing background information to show how and why he was placed in the category of minority student.

2. Rodriguez is a Hispanic-American, a Latino, a Mexican-American, a Chicano. (paragraph 7)

3. Rodriguez supports his thesis primarily with opinion, but he backs it up with facts. The statements of fact and opinion that students identify and their explanations will vary.

4. According to Rodriguez, one of the disadvantages is that you get rewarded for belonging to a racial group, not for what you have accomplished. (paragraphs 1 and 8) Your students may find others.

5. *Disadvantaged* means deprived in some way, such as economically, physically, or socially. A socially disadvantaged person is one who is treated differently because he is not a member of the dominant class. Black children might be socially disadvantaged in a predominantly white school, just as white children might be similarly disadvantaged in a predominantly black school. A *nonwhite* is a person of some race other than Caucasian. *Hispanic-American* and *Latino* are synonyms for Spanish-speaking people. *Chicanos* are Hispanic-Americans who come from Mexico.

Exercise 16.1

Students' lists will vary.

Exercise 16.2

Students' choices of issues will vary.

Exercise 16.3

Students' answers will vary, but the issue is affirmative action or minority student status. The claim is an assertion: Rodriguez says that, culturally speaking, he is not a minority and should never have been the beneficiary of affirmative action. He feels that people should be treated as individuals, not as members of groups.

Exercise 16.4

Students' statements of claims will vary.

Exercise 16.5

Students' examples will vary.

Exercise 16.6

Students' lists of hard and soft evidence will vary.

Exercise 16.7

Students' answers will vary. One opposing claim is that Rodriguez has no racial pride. Another is that minority status is only an issue of race.

Exercise 16.8

Students' lists of opposing claims will vary.

Exercise 16.9

Students' Internet searches and results will vary.

Exercise 16.10

1. The fallacy is begging the question. You can get drunk on only one drink if the alcohol content is high enough. To say that "everybody knows" does not make a statement a fact.
2. Calling someone a redneck is argument to the person. It ignores the issue of whether to buy the dress.
3. The fallacy is hasty generalization. One experience is not enough evidence to make a judgment.
4. The fallacy is either-or. You can dislike certain things that are going on in America without having to leave it.
5. The fallacy is cause and effect. Other results are possible.
6. The fallacy is false analogy. A shirt that looks nice on one person may not look nice on another.
7. The fallacy is a non sequitur. Ray's changed hours at work may have nothing to do with his academic probation.
8. The fallacy is bandwagon. You should go to a movie because you want to, not because everyone else is going.
9. The fallacy is red herring. The issue is "Where was I?" The person ignores the issue by changing the subject to "I sure am glad to see you."
10. The fallacy is circular reasoning. Part of the claim that programs are violent is restated in different words as evidence: The programs are forceful and extreme.
11. The fallacy is faulty cause and effect. The instructor's choice of questions did not depend on whether you studied.

Exercise 16.11

Students' paragraphs will vary. The claim in the first sentence is invalid because it implies a faulty analogy. What is true of one decade (the 1960s) may not be true of the decades that follow. The claim in the second sentence is invalid because of faulty cause and effect. The Electoral College's benefit to small states might not be enough to keep senators from voting to abolish it if they had other good reasons. For example, most senators vote according to what opinion polls show. The claim in the third sentence is invalid because it contains the either-or fallacy. Parents might have alternatives other than those the author presents.

The Critical Thinker

1. Rodriguez says that he was neither disadvantaged nor lacking in good early schooling. For these reasons, he says, he was not a minority in a cultural sense.

2. The fallacy is faulty cause and effect. Rodriguez's ability to communicate effectively with nonwhites could be the result of many factors other than his race.

3. Rodriguez's professors assumed that all minority students were in need of some kind of aid (paragraph 8), were socially and economically disadvantaged (paragraphs 9 and 10), and lacked good early schooling (paragraph 12).

4. Students' responses will vary.

The Selective Writer

Section A   Basic Choices   The Parts of Speech

Exercise 1

Answers will vary, but here are some examples.

1. club
2. generosity
3. Maine
4. paper, pens, books
5. turkey, dressing
6. team

Exercise 2

Answers will vary.

A.2 Pronouns

Exercise 3

1. Ellen, she, her
2. What
3. Ellen told her
4. Demonstrative; rides, animals, food, souvenirs
5. "She" refers to Soo Yin; "they" refers to Soo Yin and Ellen; "them" refers to some friends
6. whatever
7. her, mine
8. everyone
9. reflexive
10. you, sentence 9

A.3 Verbs

Exercise 4

1. will take
2. molded
3. is arriving
4. has been showing
5. had produced
6. had been typing
7. lay, yesterday
8. was developing
9. will go
10. will be choosing

A.4   Adjectives and Adverbs

Exercise 5

1. dusty, musty
2. quiet
3. scariest
4. narrow
5. bright
6. unfortunate
7. youngest
8. healthiest
9. small
10. sharper
11. whiter
12. palest
13. darkest

Exercise 6

1. usually
2. lately
3. regularly
4. more efficiently
5. more easily
6. slowly
7. carefully
8. carelessly
9. extremely
10. really
11. harder

Exercise 7

Answers will vary.

Exercise 8

Students should find the incorrect comparative adjectives and make corrections as shown in parentheses:

more easier (easier); most (more) beneficial; more farther (farther); more harder (harder) work; most importantest (most important) reason; newest (new) saying

A.5   Prepositions

Exercise 9

These sentences contain many prepositions and prepositional phrases. You will probably not expect your students to find all of them. Therefore, students' identification of phrases and explanations may vary, but they should correctly identify the prepositions and objects in the phrases they do identify.

1. prep.: by; obj.: characteristics
   The prepositional phrase explains the condition that would repel her.
2. prep.: on; obj.: plate (space)
3. prep.: on; obj.: outside (space)
   prep.: in; obj.: mouth (space)
4. prep.: on; obj.: inside (space)
   prep.: from; obj.: dirt (condition)
   prep.: in; obj.: digestive tract (space)
5. prep.: of; obj.: gum (condition)
   prep.: to; obj.: undersides (direction)
   prep.: of; obj.: desks (direction)
6. prep.: of; obj.: Winn-Dixie (direction)
   prep.: between; obj.: chicken legs and cube steaks (space)
7. prep.: at; obj.: deli (space)
8. prep.: with; obj.: eggs (condition)
   prep.: for; obj.: breakfast (condition)
   prep.: over; obj.: ice cream (space)
   prep.: as; obj.: appetizer (condition)
   prep.: on; obj.: Hi-Ho crackers (space)
   prep.: on; obj.: sandwiches (space)
9. prep.: by; obj.: coworkers (condition)
10. prep.: until; obj.: McDonald's creates a McWorm item (time)
    prep.: for; obj.: menu (condition)
    prep.: for; obj.: birds (condition)

A.6 Conjunctions,   A.7 Interjections

Exercise 10

1. along, preposition
2. you, pronoun
3. handcrafted, adjective
4. try, verb
5. out, preposition
6. slowly, adverb
7. passion, noun
8. historic, adjective
9. oh, interjection
10. and, conjunction

Section B   Sentence Effectiveness Choices

B.1 Sentence Parts, Purposes, and Types

Exercise 11

1. Diana Ross and the Supremes (S), performed (P)
2. fans (S), celebrate (P)
3. generation (S), has (P)
4. music (S), brings and gives (P)
5. generations (S), can be torn (P)
6. courses (S), explore and teach (P)
7. children (S), do not respond (P)
8. country music (S), has enjoyed (P)
9. parents (S), cannot understand (P)
10. who (S), knows (P)

Exercise 12

Students' answers may vary, but here are some examples.

1. The forecast is for warm weather, so I think I will go to the beach.

2. Terry sings in the church choir, and she plays a clarinet in the university band.

3. My car is in perfect shape even though it has 50,000 miles on it.

4. Chris fought learning to use a computer, but he couldn't get along without it now.

5. Because the concert was cancelled, hundreds of angry fans protested.

6. I am definitely not a morning person; therefore, eight o'clock classes are not for me.

B.2   Eliminating Sentence Fragments

Exercise 13

All the sentences are fragments except sentence 2. Students' corrected sentences will vary.

Exercise 14

Students should identify the following groups of words as fragments. Their rewritten sentences will vary.

1. Because there were no stores where they were going. A helicopter to drop off supplies at certain points along the way.

2. Once when Luis was walking across a frozen river.

3. Wrapped him in sleeping bags until his clothes could dry, and then they resumed their journey.

4. Rested before the long trip back down.

B.3   Eliminating Fused Sentences and Comma Splices

Exercise 15

Students' sentences will vary.

Exercise 16

Answers will vary.

B.4 Sentence Combining: Coordination

Exercise 17

Answers may vary, but the following example is typical:

> Robert B. Parker is a popular writer of detective novels, and most of his books are about Spenser, a private eye.

Exercise 18

Answers will vary.

Exercise 19

Students' paragraphs will vary.

B.5 Sentence Combining: Subordination

Exercise 20

Answers will vary, but the following example is typical:

> Since mid-May through mid-November is hurricane season in Florida, residents prepare for it.

Exercise 21

Answers will vary, but the following example is typical:

> Nancy wants an unusual pet, so she is going to buy a parrot called a macaw.

Exercise 22

Answers will vary, but the following examples are typical:
1. Mary McCarthy is an author who wrote The Group.
2. The Group is about several young women who go to the same college.

Exercise 23

Students' paragraphs will vary.

B.6   Expanding Your Sentences

Exercise 24

Answers will vary, but students should complete each sentence with a phrase of the type called for, and their completed sentences should be error-free.

Exercise 25

Answers will vary, but students should complete or rewrite each sentence with a clause of the type called for, and their new sentences should be error-free.

Exercise 26

Students' answers may vary, but they should be able to identify the types of phrases and clauses explained in Section B.6, for example: *in the ocean, at the beach* (prepositional phrases), and *that she was in trouble* (dependent clause).

B.7   Varying Your Sentences

Exercise 27

Students' sentences will vary.

Exercise 28

Students' sentences will vary.

Exercise 29

Students' sentences will vary.

Exercise 30

Students' essays will vary.

Exercise 31

Students' revisions will vary.

Exercise 32

Students' revisions will vary.

Exercise 33

Students should revise their paragraphs completely. Because their paragraphs will vary, evaluate their writing for its overall effectiveness and the degree of sentence variety they are able to achieve.

Section C   Punctuation Choices

C.1–C.5   End Punctuation, Colon, Dash, Hyphen, Semicolon

Exercise 34

1. The fight-or-flight response . . .
2. . . . he will do the only thing left to him—fight back.
3. Grizzly bears have a reputation for aggressiveness—they actually prefer to avoid confrontation—but they will often flee . . .
4. Most people try to avoid physical conflict—unless . . .
5. Even the most mild-mannered people . . .

Exercise 35

Students' corrections will vary.

Exercise 36

Students should punctuate the paragraph as follows:

deeper meaning.
Mouthwashes . . . consumers' minds:
no one . . . product.
According . . . projects.
A . . . no-nonsense germ-fighting image.
Product B . . . sexual image:
clean . . . sexy breath.
Product B's . . . mouthwash.
Product A's . . . people—more concerned . . . kissable—

however . . . love.
Which . . . more people buy?

C.6   The Comma

Exercise 37

1. Marta, I . . . (comma after words of direct address)
2. First, turn on the monitor. (comma after a transitional word and before a coordinating conjunction)
3. When a list of icons appears, (comma after a dependent clause that begins a sentence)
4. Wait for a blank screen, a little flashing line in the upper left corner, and . . . (commas to separate items in a series)
5. Now you are ready to use the keyboard, which works just like a typewriter, to . . . (commas before and after interrupting nonrestrictive clause)
6. There are more things you will need to know, but . . . (comma before a coordinating conjunction)
7. I will be out of the office until Tuesday, April 21. (comma between day and month)
8. A list of these instructions, which I have typed out for you, should . . . (commas before and after interrupting nonrestrictive clause)
9. Also, you can request a free manual from the downtown office at 1600 West Central Street, Clarksville, Oklahoma 32102. (comma after transition, between street and city, and between city and state)
10. I hope you have an interesting, rewarding . . . (comma between coordinate adjectives)

Exercise 38

Students should place commas as follows: office, you; spare room, you can; computer, a printer, and a fax; office, you might; sturdy, comfortable; closet space, hang; desk, you can; light fixture, or; for books, supplies, or; closet, simply install; small, stackable, and affordable.

C.7   The Apostrophe,   C.8   Quotation Marks

Exercise 39

1. "Loveliest of Trees"
2. Who's
3. Don't, wouldn't
4. "This . . . mileage,"; "I . . . one."
5. "Matadors Secure Another Win,"
6. boys', girls'
7. '57
8. "Love Me Do."
9. "Ouch!"
10. "May . . . volunteer?"

Section D   Choices for Special Problems

D.1   Pronoun Case, Reference, and Agreement

Exercise 40

1. she, one
2. She, She
3. her
4. she, her, they, her
5. he, her, she, she

Exercise 41

Answers may vary but should approximate the following:

1. Nga's
2. the store
3. the clerk
4. the blouse
5. Nga

Exercise 42

1. who
2. whomever
3. whom
4. who
5. whoever
6. whom
7. who
8. whom, who

Exercise 43

1. Students, (their)
2. José, (he)
3. test (it)
4. me
5. I
6. she
7. she
8. a student (his or her)
9. anyone (his or her)
10. Answers will vary.

Exercise 44

1. his
2. their
3. their
4. their
5. his or her

Exercise 45

Students' paragraphs will vary, but the pronouns should be consistent and correct. Depending on how your students revise the paragraph, they may have to make changes in verb agreement as well.

D.2   Verb Tense Consistency and Agreement

Exercise 46

Students should circle the following verb tenses:

1. takes
2. likes, does not
3. felt
4. thinks, likes
5. is looking
6. attends
7. wants, knows
8. has talked
9. worries
10. is

Exercise 47

Students should underline the following subjects and verbs:

1. Margaret and Steve, arrive
2. They, decide
3. Margaret, rides
4. She, spots
5. they, look
6. horns, curl
7. the person, operates
8. Steve, spends
9. each, likes
10. the wolves, pay; warthog, snorts

Exercise 48

1. likes
2. prefer
3. sells

4. serve

5. likes

Exercise 49

Students should make the following corrections:

thing, <u>happened</u>; MasterCard, <u>work</u>; people, <u>were</u>; wallets, <u>were not</u>; mystery, <u>was</u>;
   you, <u>lay</u>

D.3   Misplaced and Dangling Modifiers

Exercise 50

Students' corrected sentences will vary. Listed below are the misplaced modifiers
they should underline.

1. only

2. wearing a tuxedo that was too small

3. on television

4. after being mixed up in a blender three times a day

5. driving home in a pickup truck

6. with his stationary bike

7. nearly

8. for a refund

9. after throwing it in the trash can

10. wearing a tuxedo that fit just right

Exercise 51

Students' corrected sentences will vary. Listed below are the dangling modifiers they
should underline.

1. studying for the algebra exam

2. finding another chair

3. after adjusting the temperature

4. feeling hungry after all this work

5. trying once more to study

6. to do well on the test

7. ringing on the table beside her bed

8. telling her friend she had to study

9. sitting down once more

10. deciding she needed a better study place

Exercise 52

Students' corrected paragraphs will vary, but they should find and correct the following misplaced or dangling modifiers.

1. with his Christmas bonus

2. hoping for a healthful summer of swimming laps every morning

3. doing their homework

4. in their bathing suits

5. in their camper

6. wearing an innertube around his waist

7. during breakfast

8. only are young once

9. bobbing with children

D.4   Articles

Exercise 53

1. a

2. a

3. The

4. the

5. the

6. the

7. a

8. the

9. The

10. an

11. the

12. a

Section E   Word Choice

E.1   Denotation and Connotation

Exercise 54

Students should identify the terms as follows:
  a. obese (negative), large (neutral), plump (positive)
  b. persistent (positive), stubborn (negative), unyielding (neutral)
  c. synthetic (positive), fake (negative), artificial (neutral)
  d. act (neutral), stunt (positive), trick (negative)
  e. stroll (positive), swagger (negative), walk (neutral)
  f. to boss (negative), to control (neutral), to manage (positive)
  g. disrobe (positive), strip (negative), undress (neutral)
  h. cheap (negative), bargain-priced (positive), inexpensive (neutral)
  i. crippled (negative), differently abled (positive), handicapped (negative)
  j. show (neutral), expose (negative), display (positive)

Exercise 55

Students' explanations and choices of replacement words will vary.

E.2   Making Sense of Confusing Words

Exercise 56

Corrections students should make are in parentheses: you're (your); their (there); its (it's); passed (past); to (too); there (they're); you're (your).

E.3   Spelling Tips

Exercise 57

Students' lists of spelling errors will vary.

CLASP and TASP Reading and Writing Competency Tests and The Confident Writer, Third Edition

Competency tests in reading and writing evaluate students' mastery of basic reading and writing skills. Several states, notably Florida and Texas, require students to take competency tests in reading and writing. Correlation Charts 1.1 and 1.2 list the reading and writing competencies and where they are covered in *The Confident Writer,* Third Edition.

Chart 1.1 Florida College-Level Academic Skills Project (CLASP)

Essay Competencies	Pages
Select a subject which lends itself to development.	38–39, 188–190, 220–221, 235–236, 260–263, 276–278, 283, 297–298, 348, 353
Determine a purpose and audience for writing.	13–15, 48–55, 190–191, 245–247, 259, 263, 278–280, 298–299, 322–323, 342
Limit subject to reflect purpose and audience.	53–55, 66–71, 101–106, 190–191, 220–221, 260–263, 278–280, 298–299, 323–324, 343–346
Formulate a thesis or main idea statement that reflects purpose and focus.	11–13, 53–55, 66–71, 92–118, 192–193, 267–268, 286–287, 300–301, 323–324, 343
Provide support that distinguishes between general and specific evidence.	16–17, 71–78, 119–140, 145–147, 202–205, 228–230, 243–244, 263–267, 288–289, 301–306, 322–323, 335–341
Arrange ideas and details in a pattern appropriate to topic and focus.	17–20, 78–86, 148–150, 231, 265–267, 306–307, 322–323, 335–341
Write unified and coherent prose.	78–86, 128–133, 247–251, 265–267, 364–365
Use transitional devices.	78–86, 221–222, 266, 289, 326

Writing competencies:

Demonstrate effective word choice

Use denotative and connotative meanings	506–508
Eliminate slang, jargon, clichés, wordiness	(wordiness) 171, (slang, etc.) 171–174

Employ conventional sentence structure

Place modifiers correctly	498–502
Use correct coordination and subordination of sentence elements	(coord.) 446–450, (subord.) 450–457
Use parallel expressions	464–465
Avoid fragments, comma splices, and fused sentence elements	(frags) 440–443, (C-S and fused) 443–446

Employ effective sentence structure

Maintain sentence variety	462–469
Avoid overuse of passive voice	171–173

Observe conventions of standard American-English grammar

Use standard verb forms	421–425
Maintain subject-verb agreement	495–498
Maintain pronoun-antecedent agreement	485–494
Use proper pronoun case forms	419–421
Maintain consistent point of view	224–227
Use adjectives and adverbs	425–428
Avoid tense shifts	494–495
Make logical comparisons	428–429

Use standard practices for spelling and punctuation

Observe common spelling rules	514–517
Observe comma rules	475–480
Observe other punctuation rules	470–485

| Revise, edit, and proofread | 23–26, 141–158, 159–178 |

Reading Competencies	**Pages**
Literal reading skills	
Recognize main ideas	11–12, 66–71, 101–106
Identify supporting details	16–17, 71–78
Determine meanings of words in context	506–508 (Note: These are the pages that cover denotation and connotation; however, a discussion of meanings of words in context and the last section exercise addresses this skill.)
Critical reading skills	
Determine author's purpose	14–15, 53–55
Recognize overall organizational pattern	17–20 and Chapters 9–16
Distinguish between facts and opinions	71–72
Recognize author's tone	55–57
Determine relationships within sentences	446–457
Determine relationships between sentences	467–469
Recognize valid arguments	Chapter 16 (The whole chapter is about arguing validly and logically.)
Make inferences and draw conclusions	66, also "Implications" in The Critical Reader and The Critical Thinker sections in every chapter ask students to make inferences

Chart 1.2   Texas Academic Skills Program (TASP)

Essay Competencies	**Pages**
Recognize purpose and audience	
Determine purpose for writing	14–15, 53–55, 190–191, 245–249, 260–263, 278–280, 288–299, 322–323

The Writing Sample Characteristics

Appropriateness

Use of language	171–174, 506–508, 509–516
Audience and purpose	13–15, 48–55, 190–191, 245–247, 269–273, 278–279, 283, 298–299, 323–324, 342–346

Unity and focus

Main idea	11–12, 53–55, 66–71, 92–118, 192–193, 265–266, 286–287, 298–300, 324, 342
Point of view	224–227, 485–494

Development

Amount, depth, and specificity of detail	6–7, 71–78, 119–140, 145–147, 202–205, 228–230, 243–244, 260–263, 288–289, 301–306, 322–326, 335–341, 364–365

Organization

Clarity and logical sequence of ideas	17–20, 78–86, 148–150, 232, 265–267, 306–307, 322–323

Sentence structure

Effective sentences	434–469

Usage

Word choice	171–174, 506–508, 509–516

Mechanical conventions

Spelling	514–517
Punctuation	470–485